ADAPTIVE 2020

The Twelfth International Conference on Adaptive and Self-Adaptive Systems and Applications

October 25 - 29, 2020

ADAPTIVE 2020 Editors

Marc Kurz, University of Applied Sciences Upper Austria, Faculty for Informatics, Communications and Media, Austria
Erik Sonnleitner, University of Applied Sciences Upper Austria, Faculty for Informatics, Communications and Media, Austria
Cosmin Dini, IARIA, EU/USA
Boris Düdder, Assistant Professor, University of Copenhagen, Department of Computer Science, Denmark
Sebastian Lawrenz, Technische Universität Clausthal, Department of Software and Systems Engineering, Clausthal-Zellerfeld, Germany
Priyanka Sharma, Technische Universität Clausthal, Department of Software and Systems Engineering, Clausthal-Zellerfeld, Germany

Printed from e-media with permission by:

Curran Associates, Inc.
57 Morehouse Lane
Red Hook, NY 12571

Printed with permission by Curran Associates, Inc. (2020)

International Academy, Research, and Industry Association (IARIA)
412 Derby Way
Wilmington, DE 19810

Phone: (408) 893-6407
Fax: (408) 527-6351

petre@iaria.org

Additional copies of this publication are available from:

Curran Associates, Inc.
57 Morehouse Lane
Red Hook, NY 12571 USA
Phone: 845-758-0400
Fax: 845-758-2633
Email: curran@proceedings.com
Web: www.proceedings.com

Table of Contents

ADAPTIVE 2020

Forward

The Twelfth International Conference on Adaptive and Self-Adaptive Systems and Applications (ADAPTIVE 2020), held on October 25 - 29, 2020, continued a series of events targeting advanced system and application design paradigms driven by adaptiveness and self-adaptiveness. With the current tendencies in developing and deploying complex systems, and under the continuous changes of system and application requirements, adaptation is a key feature. Speed and scalability of changes require self-adaptation for special cases. How to build systems to be easily adaptive and self-adaptive, what constraints and what mechanisms must be used, and how to evaluate a stable state in such systems are challenging duties. Context-aware and user-aware are major situations where environment and user feedback is considered for further adaptation.

The conference had the following tracks:

- Self-adaptation
- Adaptive applications
- Adaptivity in robot systems
- Fundamentals and design of adaptive systems

Similar to the previous edition, this event attracted excellent contributions and active participation from all over the world. We were very pleased to receive top quality contributions.

We take here the opportunity to warmly thank all the members of the ADAPTIVE 2020 technical program committee, as well as the numerous reviewers. The creation of such a high quality conference program would not have been possible without their involvement. We also kindly thank all the authors that dedicated much of their time and effort to contribute to ADAPTIVE 2020. We truly believe that, thanks to all these efforts, the final conference program consisted of top quality contributions.

Also, this event could not have been a reality without the support of many individuals, organizations and sponsors. We also gratefully thank the members of the ADAPTIVE 2020 organizing committee for their help in handling the logistics and for their work that made this professional meeting a success.

We hope ADAPTIVE 2020 was a successful international forum for the exchange of ideas and results between academia and industry and to promote further progress in the area of adaptive and self-adaptive systems and applications.

ADAPTIVE 2020 General Chair

Jaime Lloret Mauri, Universitat Politecnica de Valencia, Spain

ADAPTIVE 2020 Steering Committee

Constantin Paleologu, University Politehnica of Bucharest, Romania

Claudia Raibulet, University of Milano-Bicocca, Italy
Sebastian Herold, Karlstad University, Department for Mathematics & Computer Science, Sweden
Andreas Rausch, TU Clausthal, Clausthal-Zellerfeld, Germany
Marc Kurz, University of Applied Sciences Upper Austria, Faculty for Informatics, Communications and Media, Austria
Valerie Camps, Paul Sabatier University - IRIT, Toulouse, France

ADAPTIVE 2020 Publicity Chair

Javier Rocher, Universitat Politecnica de Valencia, Spain

ADAPTIVE 2020 Industry/Research Advisory Committee

Habtamu Abie, Norwegian Computing Center/Norsk Regnesentral-Blindern, Norway
Marc-Philippe Huget, Polytech Annecy-Chambery-LISTIC | University of Savoie, France

ADAPTIVE 2020

Committee

ADAPTIVE 2020 General Chair

Jaime Lloret Mauri, Universitat Politecnica de Valencia, Spain

ADAPTIVE 2020 Steering Committee

Constantin Paleologu, University Politehnica of Bucharest, Romania
Claudia Raibulet, University of Milano-Bicocca, Italy
Sebastian Herold, Karlstad University, Department for Mathematics & Computer Science, Sweden
Andreas Rausch, TU Clausthal, Clausthal-Zellerfeld, Germany
Marc Kurz, University of Applied Sciences Upper Austria, Faculty for Informatics, Communications and Media, Austria
Valerie Camps, Paul Sabatier University - IRIT, Toulouse, France

ADAPTIVE 2020 Publicity Chair

Javier Rocher, Universitat Politecnica de Valencia, Spain

ADAPTIVE 2020 Industry/Research Advisory Committee

Habtamu Abie, Norwegian Computing Center/Norsk Regnesentral-Blindern, Norway
Marc-Philippe Huget, Polytech Annecy-Chambery-LISTIC | University of Savoie, France

ADAPTIVE 2020 Technical Program Committee

Ibrahim Abdallah Abbas Atwa Elgendy, School of Computer Science and Technology | Harbin Institute of Technology, China
Habtamu Abie, Norwegian Computing Center/Norsk Regnesentral-Blindern, Norway
Harvey Alférez, Universidad de Montemorelos, Mexico
Raid Al-Nima, Northern Technical University, Iraq
Nik Bessis, Edge Hill University, UK
Antonio Brogi, University of Pisa, Italy
Valerie Camps, Paul Sabatier University - IRIT, Toulouse, France
Enrique Chirivella Perez, University West of Scotland, UK
Angel P. del Pobil, Jaume I University, Spain
Ioanna Dionysiou, University of Nicosia, Cyprus
Holger Eichelberger, University of Hildesheim, Germany
Fairouz Fakhfakh, University of Sfax, Tunisia
Hongsheng He, Wichita State University, USA
Sebastian Herold, Karlstad University, Department for Mathematics & Computer Science, Sweden

Copyright Information

What Are You Doing? Real-Time Activity Recognition using Mobile Phone Sensors

Bernhard Hiesl, Marc Kurz, Erik Sonnleitner

University of Applied Sciences Upper Austria
Faculty for Informatics, Communications and Media
Department of Mobility and Energy
4232 Hagenberg, Austria
email: {firstname.lastname}@fh-hagenberg.at

Abstract—**This paper focuses on recognizing different activities of people by utilizing the smart-phone as sensor delivering unit. For the sake of simplicity, five different activities (i.e., modes of locomotion) are considered: (i) standing, (ii) walking, (iii) running, (iv) walking upstairs and (v) downstairs. The research challenge is the fact that the phone is placed on the body of the subjects dynamically and orientation independent – thus the system has to adapt autonomously to these characteristics. The sensor data was collected from the built-in accelerometer, gravity and gyroscope sensors of a common smartphone (i.e., Google Pixel XL). The data collection procedure is part of the dynamic placement of this paper addressing position and orientation independent recording and recognizing of activities. Additionally, to acquire full orientation independence, data transformation (horizontal and vertical movement) is applied on the gathered data. Within the framework of this study, five different phone positions are taken into account and are therefore considered in the classification process. To achieve the best approach concerning performance and recognition, different classifiers are evaluated (i.e., (i) k-nearest neighbours (KNN), (ii) Naive Bayes, (iii) Decision Trees and (iv) Random Forest).**

Keywords–Activity recognition; Mobile sensing; Self-adaptation; Adaptive application; Adaptive real-time strategies.

I. INTRODUCTION

This paper is a follow-up of the work-in-progress paper published in 2019 [1]. There, the idea of utilizing smart phones for activity recognition (i.e., gait recognition) in real-time with varying positions of the smart phone has been introduced. Conceptual ideas have been presented – subsequently, this paper focuses on the solution to the problem and the evaluation and results.

The problem statement can be summarized as follows. The major challenge behind this work is the correct detection of people's activities regardless of the mobile phone's position and orientation. In other words, the system should be able to recognize the actual activity of the user by gathering sensor data from the built-in mobile phone sensors only. This should be performed independently of the device's position and orientation - thus being adaptive to contextual details. The changing position and orientation of the mobile phone is also referred to as "dynamic placement" within this paper. To actively detect the activity of a user, an application using a real-time system is required. Therefore, sensor data from the built-in mobile phone sensors need to be collected, processed and classified in real-time. To put it in other words, only a few seconds should be sufficient to detect the activity performed by the user. In detail, the research question can be formulated as follows [1]: *How can highly accurate real-time activity recognition be realized utilizing a dynamically (i.e., rotation, position and orientation independent) on-body placed commercial smartphone?* For the sake of simplicity, five modes of locomotion are specifically considered: (i) standing, (ii) walking, (iii) running, (iv) walking upstairs and (v) downstairs. Generally – as stated in the previous WiP paper [1] – the idea of recognizing activities utilizing commercial smartphones is not new and has been subject to research in numerous publications [2]–[10]. The challenging aspects are the facts that the recognition should be executed at real-time and rotation-, orientation- and position-independent –not forcing the user to conduct an initial calibration.

The WiP paper [1] presented the data collection progress and the accompanying smartphone application allowing for instant labelling of activities upon recording. Additionally, feature extraction methodologies and machine learning models have been evaluated. As related work shows, low level features (e.g., mean, max, min, std deviation, variance, energy, entropy, etc.) are significant enough for activity classification [3][4][10]. To classify the activities correctly and user independently, the system was trained with the help of 15 subjects (10 males and 5 females) and a total sensor data amount of 4 hours and 50 minutes per sensor unit. The focus of this paper is the technical implementation of the autonomous adaptation to the current phone position for the recognition task, as well as the aspect that the recognition should be executed instantly at real-time.

The rest of the paper is structured as follows. Section II (*Methodology & Implementation*) explains the methodological approach to realize the dynamic and orientation independent placement of the phone on the subjects body. Section III (*Results*) summarizes the results achieved during the evaluation. Section IV (*Summary & Outlook*) closes with a summary and an outlook to future work.

II. METHODOLOGY & IMPLEMENTATION

In order to implement the mobile sensing real-time dynamic gait recognition approach, the following steps have to be done: (i) Data Acquisition, (ii) Data Preprocessing, (iii) Feature Extraction, (iv) Model Training. Within the process of the Data Acquisition, subjects are asked to collect sensor data from the built-in mobile phone sensors including the accelerometer, gyroscope and gravity sensor. In the next step, the Data Preprocessing, the gathered data is transformed using a horizontal and vertical movement calculation which is done by utilizing the accelerometer and gravity sensor (orientation and position independent = dynamic placement). Additionally, the transferred data is "smoothed" by applying a Savitzky-Golay filter and is then split into smaller data segments using a sliding window approach [11] with an overlap of 50%. The Feature Extraction routine is then used to extract time and frequency domain features. In the last step, a machine learning approach is realized. In total, four different machine learning models are trained offline. These machine learning models are then integrated into the smartphone application for realizing the recognition task. In order to provide a dynamic real-time recognition system using a mobile phone the three steps including (i) Data Acquisition, (ii) Data Preprocessing and (iii) Feature extraction need to be developed within the smartphone application (see WiP paper for further details [1]).

A. Real-Time

Burns and Welling [12] describe the term real-time as the actual response time that a system takes to generate an output from several input values. In other words, it is the actual time it takes to get a result of a system after applying an input. In general, real-time systems can be distinguished between hard and soft real-time systems. In hard real-time systems, a delay of a response can lead to an entire system failure. In soft real-time systems, a delay only degrades the performance of the system. Depending on the place of use, real-time systems can have response times from milliseconds to minutes. By utilizing a technique called sliding window [11] (see Figure 1), the approach in this paper targets a soft real-time activity recognition system with a response time of 2.56 seconds for the first recognition and 1.28 seconds for the following ones. Subsequently, each recognition iteration of the developed real-time approach includes the following steps: (i) gathering 2.56 seconds (time) activity data of a user utilizing mobile phone sensors, (ii) passing the data to the recognition process (input), (iii) performing different calculations on the sensor data and provide the actual gait of the user while performing it (output). Figure 2 shows an example of horizontal and vertical movement within one single window.

Figure 1. Illustration of the sliding window approach.

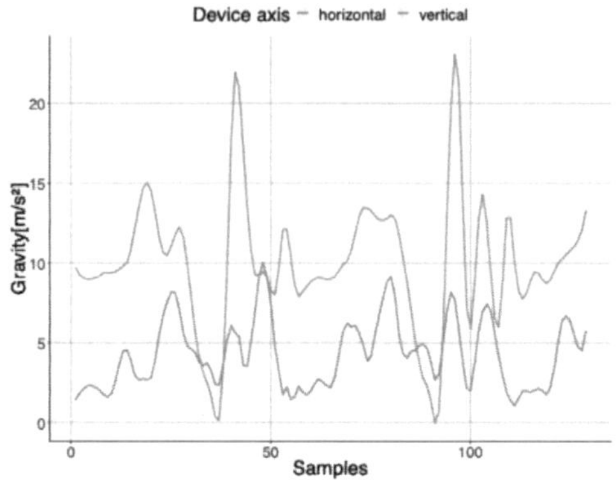

Figure 2. Time series data of a single window showing horizontal and vertical movement.

B. Dynamic Placement

In order to realize the dynamic placement recognition system (position and orientation independent system), the following steps were implemented:

- Sensor recording of activities within several body positions to get position independent data
- Sensor data transformation (horizontal and vertical transformation) to become orientation independent
- Usage of entire recorded and transformed data to train different machine learning models

To be more precise, the first step to achieve a dynamic recognition system was to record sensor data in different pocket locations on the body. In total, five pocket positions are covered in the current version of the system and it was done during the Data Acquisition process (see Figure 3). Within the second step, the sensor data was transformed into a different coordinate system representing the data in horizontal and vertical accelerations. By applying this transformation, the data becomes independent regarding the orientation of the sensing device. The actual transformation is performed using data from the accelerometer and gravity sensor.

After the second step the preprocessed data (transformed, smoothed and segmented data) from different pocked positions was then used to train four different machine learning models. Therefore, the models are "generalized" concerning pocket positions, because each pocket position is within the "trained" machine learning model. In other words, the models "trained" within the training process are all using the same data and therefore do not distinguish between the front right or back left trouser pocket to detect the gait type of a user.

III. Results

Three different testing scenarios were applied to the developed system including environment changes, varying performing speeds and changing positions. Each test scenario is evaluated using gallery dependent (subject within the training set) and independent (subject not inside the training set) sensor data. The goal of the evaluation was to prove that the system is able to classify the activity correctly even despite changing performing parameters. These changing parameters consider a position change of the mobile phone as well as changing speed.

A. Scenarios

1) Environment: The first testing scenario covers the changing of the environment. It is assumed, that the environment during the recognition process can change during or for each execution. In other words, this means that the ideal outcome was to create an environmental independent recognition system. Therefore, the developed recognition system was evaluated using different environments including, different stairs, different floor surfaces and indoor (house) or outdoor environments. The main reason why there is a distinction between an indoor and outdoor environment is that users usually put off their shoes indoors.

The recorded data was only collected from subjects moving forward and straight on a flat surface. The environment testing routine was also performed moving forward and straight only. This environment evaluation is marked as S1 in the system results Section III-C. This environment test was only performed while the phone was in the front right trouser pocket (i) walking on street / grass / indoor, (ii) running on street / grass, (iii) ascending stairs indoor / outdoor, and (iv) descending stairs indoor / outdoor.

2) Speed: Within the second testing scenario covering speed, varying execution speeds are performed and evaluated on the activity recognition system. However, the freedom of the actual execution speed within this evaluation is limited in terms of direction. In other words, the subjects participating in the evaluation of the system are only able to change the speed, not altering the motion process of walking itself in an abnormal or directional way. This is because the data within the training set only provides motion data in that recognizes forward direction limiting the evaluation itself in terms of direction. To be more precise, the speed test investigates the correct classification if there are changes regarding the walking speed. This is possible, because subjects within the training set have already personal speed interpretations performing the activities. For example, participant P1 walks with a speed of 3 km/h, whereas participant P2 walks with a speed of 3.6 km/h. Both participants perform the gait "walking", but at individual pace. Therefore, the system should still recognize the gait correctly with varying speeds. Another example, could be running or climbing stairs where each participant executes the activity at a different pace. Within the result overview Section III-C, this execution evaluation scenario is marked as S2. The speed adjustment evaluation consists of the following test cases where the phone was placed in the front right trouser pocket: (i) walking slow / normal / fast, (ii) running slow / normal / fast, (iii) ascending stairs slow / normal / fast, and (iv) descending stairs slow / normal / fast.

3) Position: In order to fulfil the main focus of this paper – the dynamic placement of the mobile phone – the third evaluation scenario addresses the position evaluation. It is used to evaluate the correct recognition performance of the system regardless of the device's orientation. Nevertheless, there are limitations concerning the mobile phone placement during the evaluation. The current version of the system only supports gait recognition within five mobile phone positions including the two front trouser pockets, the two back trouser pockets and the chest pocket of a shirt or the inner jacket pocket (see Figure 3). In Section III-C the position evaluation scenario is marked as S3.

Figure 3. Relevant pocket positions within the position evaluation.

B. Participants

Within the entire evaluation process, two subjects were asked to participate in the process of testing the system. This was one of the most important parts of the evaluation, because the system should either work with participants which are inside the training set (i.e., gallery dependent) or participants not enrolled within the training process (i.e., gallery independent). In other words, gallery dependent participants are testing subjects, which are known by the machine learning model. In contrast, participants which are gallery independent are test subjects which are not known by the trained machine learning model beforehand. The gallery dependent tests are annotated as *S1D* (environment), *S2D* (speed) and *S3D* (position) depending on the test scenario. Accordingly, the tests for the gallery independent cases are marked with *S1I* (different environments), *S2I* (different execution speeds) and *S3I* (the varying position evaluation).

C. Result Overview

The system is evaluated applying two cases: (i) offline (by using newly recorded data and performing recognition offline) and (ii) online (at real-time) using sensor data processed in real-time on the smart-phone. Therefore, the results for the offline and online cases are presented in the following two Sections III-C1 and III-C2.

1) Offline Evaluation: The offline evaluation process uses a computer to recognizing the actual gait of newly provided sensor data from a subject performing different activities. It is done by creating sensor data which is not covered by the training data applied during the machine learning model creation. Therefore, a subject gallery dependent and a subject gallery independent were asked to record new sensor data with changing environments, speeds and mobile phone positions. In the next step, the data is transferred to a computer to evaluate the different machine learning models. The following Tables I to III summarize the accuracies for the cases *S1D*, *S2D* and *S3D* (gallery dependent case).

TABLE I. RECOGNITION ACCURACIES FOR *S1D* (ENVIRONMENT).

Model	Grass	Street	Outdoor	Indoor	Combined
KNN	91.6%	100%	100%	93.75%	96.1%
Naive Bayes	97.2%	100%	88.8%	93.75%	94.8%
Decision Tree	94.4%	100%	100%	91.6%	96.1%
Random Forest	94.4%	100%	100%	95.8%	97.4%

TABLE II. RECOGNITION ACCURACIES FOR *S2D* (SPEED).

Model	Slow	Normal	Fast	Combined
KNN	80.0%	98.3%	91.6%	90.0%
Naive Bayes	83.3%	100%	55.0%	79.4%
Decision Tree	88.3%	91.6%	75.0%	85.0%
Random Forest	96.6%	100%	86.6%	94.4%

The abbreviations used in Table III have the following meaning: (i) FC = front chest, (ii) FR = front right trouser pocket, (iii) FL = front left trouser pocket, (iv) BR = back right trouser pocket and (v) BL = back left trouser pocket (see also Figure 3).

TABLE III. RECOGNITION ACCURACIES FOR *S3D* (POSITION).

Model	FC	FR	FL	BR	BL	Combined
KNN	86.6%	100%	100%	100%	100%	97.6%
Naive Bayes	80.0%	98.3%	100%	96.6%	100%	95.0%
Decision Tree	88.3%	88.3%	100%	90.0%	95.0%	92.3%
Random Forest	86.6%	100%	100%	93.3%	100%	96.0%

The gallery independent case (the system is evaluated with data of a person that is not included in the training set) is more meaningful. It proves that the system is also capable of recognizing activities from any person at an acceptable accuracy. The following Tables IV to VI summarize the accuracies for the cases *S1I*, *S2I* and *S3I* (gallery independent case).

TABLE IV. RECOGNITION ACCURACIES FOR *S1I* (ENVIRONMENT).

Model	Grass	Street	Outdoor	Indoor	Combined
KNN	83.3%	100%	100%	100%	97.4%
Naive Bayes	100%	100%	86.1%	81.2%	91.0%
Decision Tree	77.7%	94.4%	91.6%	91.6%	89.1%
Random Forest	94.4%	100%	100%	100%	98.7%

TABLE V. RECOGNITION ACCURACIES FOR *S2I* (SPEED).

Model	Slow	Normal	Fast	Combined
KNN	93.3%	100%	96.6%	96.6%
Naive Bayes	81.6%	91.6%	61.6%	78.3%
Decision Tree	75.0%	91.6%	100%	88.8%
Random Forest	96.6%	100%	91.6%	96.1%

The following Figure 4 shows the results of the gallery dependent test scenarios whereas Figure 5 displays gallery independent results of each test scenario. As shown in Figure 4, the Random Forest algorithm performs best regarding environment changes (97.4%) and speed adjustments (94.4%), whereas the KNN algorithm achieves the highest accuracy of 97.6% in the last position evaluation. Figure 5 displays the recognition accuracy rates of a subject which is not considered in the training set. Even though the activity data provided by the subject was not used to train the model, the accuracy rates are very similar to the accuracy rates shown in the gallery dependent evaluation test. The highest precision of 98.7% was achieved by applying the environment evaluation on the Random Forest classifier followed by the KNN model evaluating the speed adjustment by reaching an accuracy of 96.6%. In the last evaluation scenario (position), the KNN and Random Forest algorithm achieved a recognition rate of 94%.

TABLE VI. RECOGNITION ACCURACIES FOR *S3I* (POSITION).

Model	FC	FR	FL	BR	BL	Combined
KNN	91.6%	100%	96.6%	83.3%	98.3%	94.0%
Naive Bayes	71.6%	91.6%	88.3%	83.3%	90.0%	85.0%
Decision Tree	71.0%	91.6%	93.3%	93.3%	91.6%	88.0%
Random Forest	71.6%	100%	98.3%	100%	100%	94.0%

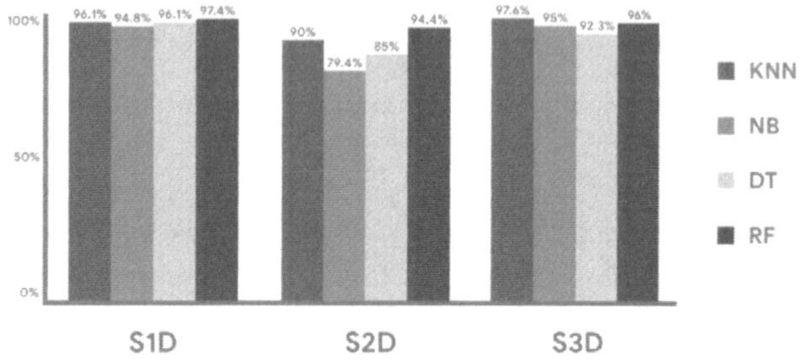

Figure 4. Recognition accuracies of each machine learning model (K-nearest Neighbour, Naive Bayes, Decision Tree and Random Forest) applying the offline gallery dependent scenarios evaluation including environment, speed and position changes.

2) Online Evaluation: In contrast to the offline evaluation, a real-time/online evaluation was carried out within this paper. The real-time evaluation is supported by the developed smart phone application. Instead of labelling and transferring sensor data to a computer, the application collects sensor data of the subject performing an activity, preprocesses it, extracts time and frequency domain features and classifies the actual activity/gait in real-time utilizing machine learning models which were integrated into the application beforehand. In order to decrease the effort of the evaluation process including testing different machine learning models, the application was extended to provide a "ground truth". In other words, the resulting feature vector provided by the smart phone application was extended with the actual gait type the subject was performing. The feature vector containing the ground truth was then used to evaluate the machine learning models on the computer. However, all evaluation scenarios were performed by using the machine learning models on the mobile device itself. The following Tables VII to IX summarize the accuracies for the cases *S1D*, *S2D* and *S3D* (gallery dependent case), whereas For the real-time (online) environment evaluation a gallery dependent subject performed the exact same testing routine, which was executed during the offline environment evaluation.

TABLE VII. RECOGNITION ACCURACIES BASED ON ENVIRONMENT CHANGES (*S1D*) OF A PERSON INSIDE THE TRAINING DATA FOR THE ONLINE CASE.

Model	Grass	Street	Outdoor	Indoor	Combined
KNN	97.2%	100%	100%	95.8%	98.0%
Naive Bayes	100%	100%	83.3%	83.3%	91.0%
Decision Tree	100%	97.2%	100%	89.5%	96.1%
Random Forest	100%	100%	100%	100%	100%

The next evaluation step were the gallery independent evaluation scenarios, which means that a subject, whose data was not taken into account within the training, provided the real-time sensor data for the online evaluation of the

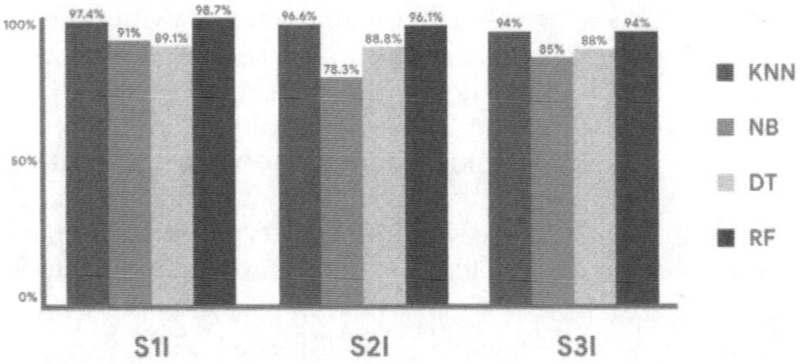

Figure 5. Recognition accuracies of each machine learning model (K-nearest Neighbour, Naive Bayes, Decision Tree and Random Forest) applying the offline gallery independent scenarios evaluation including environment, speed and position changes.

TABLE VIII. RECOGNITION ACCURACIES BASED ON SPEED CHANGES (*S2D*) OF A PERSON INSIDE THE TRAINING DATA FOR THE ONLINE CASE.

Model	Slow	Normal	Fast	Combined
KNN	96.6%	100%	73.3%	89.4%
Naive Bayes	80.0%	90.0%	48.3%	72.7%
Decision Tree	80.0%	98.3%	68.3%	82.2%
Random Forest	96.6%	100%	83.3%	93.3%

recognition system. The smartphone application was used to record, preprocess and classify sensor data in real-time. The following Tables X to XII summarize the accuracies for the cases *S1I*, *S2I* and *S3I* (gallery independent case) for the online scenario.

Figure 6 shows the accuracies of the different gallery dependent evaluation scenarios including environment (S1D), speed (S2D) and position (S3D) for each machine learning model whereas Figure 7 shows the accuracies of the gallery independent evaluation scenarios (environment, speed and position). As shown in Figure 6, the Random Forest algorithm achieved an accuracy of 100% using gallery dependent sensor data on the evaluation test scenario, whereas utilizing activity motion data from a subject, whose data is not in the training set, the accuracy reaches 97.4% (Figure 7). Due to fact of high accuracies in both evaluations (gallery dependent and independent), it can be said that the real-time recognition system is independent of environment changes and users. The second evaluation scenario is the the speed adjustment evaluation (S2D and S2I). In other words, the correct detection of the gait regarding pace changes utilizing different machine learning models. As shown in the bar charts of Figure 6 and Figure 7 the overall accuracies decrease. This is because slower and faster motions can lead to incorrect classifications. For example, if a user is walking faster than usual the classification process can lead to incorrect results. Nevertheless, the highest accuracy of 97.2% concerning execution speed changes was achieved by the Random Forest algorithm during the real-time speed gallery independent evaluation. The last position evaluation scenario that was compared is shown as well (S3D and S3I). Even though the position of the phone changes between the front chest, front right, front left, back right and back left pocket, the KNN algorithm of the gallery dependent or the Random Forest of the gallery independent test evaluation achieved high recognition rates (KNN= 94.6% and RF = 95.3%). The other algorithms including the Naive Bayes and Decision Tree detect the gait types between an accuracy rate of 85% and 90.3%. All in all it can be said, that the developed recognition system is able to detect the actual gait of a user dynamically. It is capable of detecting the activity regardless the phone position and orientation, is user independent and recognizes gait types in real- time (within 2.56 seconds for the first recognition) with a satisfying result.

TABLE IX. RECOGNITION ACCURACIES BASED ON DIFFERENT BODY POSITIONS (*S3D*) OF A PERSON INSIDE THE TRAINING DATA FOR THE ONLINE CASE.

Model	FC	FR	FL	BR	BL	Combined
KNN	85.0%	100%	100%	96.6%	95.0%	94.6%
Naive Bayes	80.0%	90.0%	95.0%	90.0%	96.6%	90.3%
Decision Tree	86.6%	98.3%	86.6%	83.3%	96.6%	90.3%
Random Forest	88.3%	100%	100%	90.0%	93.3%	94.3%

TABLE X. RECOGNITION ACCURACIES BASED ON ENVIRONMENT CHANGES (*S1I*) OF A SUBJECT NOT CONSIDERED IN THE TRAINING DATA FOR THE ONLINE CASE.

Model	Grass	Street	Outdoor	Indoor	Combined
KNN	97.2%	97.2%	97.2%	97.9%	97.4%
Naive Bayes	97.2%	100%	77.7%	54.1%	80.1%
Decision Tree	91.6%	80.5%	94.4%	83.3%	87.1%
Random Forest	97.2%	97.2%	100%	95.8%	97.4%

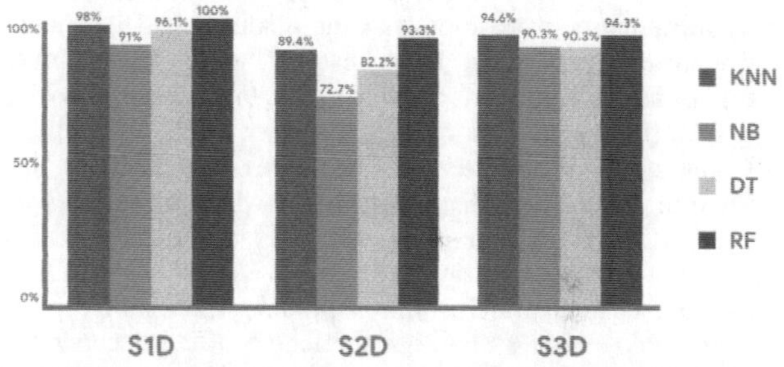

Figure 6. Recognition accuracies of each machine learning model (K-nearest Neighbour, Naive Bayes, Decision Tree and Random Forest) applying the online gallery dependent scenarios evaluation including environment (S1D), speed (S2D) and position (S3D) changes.

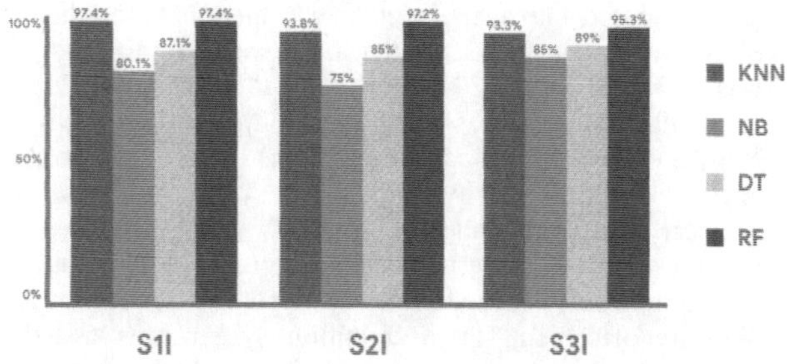

Figure 7. Recognition accuracies of each machine learning model (K-nearest Neighbour, Naive Bayes, Decision Tree and Random Forest) applying the online gallery in- dependent scenarios evaluation including environment (S1D), speed (S2D) and position (S3D) changes.

TABLE XI. RECOGNITION ACCURACIES FOR *S21* (SPEED).

Model	Slow	Normal	Fast	Combined
KNN	93.3%	98.3%	90.0%	93.8%
Naive Bayes	88.3%	85.0%	51.6%	75.0%
Decision Tree	80.0%	91.6%	83.3%	85.0%
Random Forest	98.3%	98.3%	95.0%	97.2%

TABLE XII. RECOGNITION ACCURACIES FOR *S31* (POSITION).

Model	FC	FR	FL	BR	BL	Combined
KNN	90.0%	98.3%	98.3%	93.3%	86.6%	93.3%
Naive Bayes	80.0%	85.0%	98.3%	78.3%	83.3%	85.0%
Decision Tree	91.6%	91.6%	88.3%	86.6%	86.6%	89.0%
Random Forest	88.3%	98.3%	96.6%	93.3%	100%	95.3%

IV. CONCLUSION

To summarize, the aim to create a system, which is able to adaptively recognize activities regardless the position and orientation of the recording device (i.e., commercial smartphone) with built-in motion sensors was achieved with a recognition accuracy of 96.1%. Activity recognition systems apply supervised classification machine learning approaches in order to "classify" (detect) an actual activity on new data provided by users. In total, 15 subjects were asked to participate in the data acquisition process where motion data from the accelerometer, gravity, linear accelerometer and gyroscope sensor was collected. Each subject provided sensor data from five different body positions (position independence) as well as five different activities. To achieve orientation independence, the gathered data was transformed into another coordinate system (horizontal and vertical movements). Additionally, the second preprocessing step was the usage of the Savitzky-Golay filter in order to "smooth" the data while preserving high and low signal peaks. Furthermore, data segmentation (sliding window) was applied on the transformed and smoothed data in order to realize a real-time approach. The sliding window of the recognition system has the length of 2.56 seconds and an overlap of 50%. In the next step, the segmented data was then passed to the feature extraction routine in order to derive time and frequency domain features. The last step was the machine learning model creation. In order to find the best machine learning model concerning performance and accuracy, four different algorithms (i.e., k-nearest Neighbour, Naive Bayes, Decision Tree and Random Forest) were compared and integrated into the implemented smartphone application. Subsequently, the real-time dynamic gait recognition system was evaluated using 12 different evaluation scenarios. Half of the evaluation scenarios were taken offline on the computer and the other half was performed online using the smartphone application. The activity recognition system was tested on subjects which are gallery dependent (data included in the training set) and gallery independent (data not included in the training set). To underline the hypothesis concerning the dynamic placement, the recognition system was tested on recognizing the actual gait in five different body positions. The best overall recognition accuracy (offline and online evaluation combined) of 96.1% was achieved by the Random Forest algorithm, which turns out to be the most suitable algorithm for the developed system. Overall, it can be said that the developed real-time dynamic gait recognition system running on a smartphone is able to detect the actual activities (i.e., the gait) of a user regardless the position and orientation of the device with an recognition accuracy of up to 96.1%. Having proven the feasibility of developing a gait recognition system which is position and orientation independent it is legitimate to state that the system could be hugely beneficial to tracking and analysing human activity in different commercial use-cases (e.g., physiotherapy, elderly care, industrial manufacturing, etc.).

The Feature Extraction process applied within this paper uses standard mathematical features and includes among other things maximal, minimal, mean, standard deviation values from time and frequency domains. Although standard mathematical features are applied, the current version of the real-time dynamic recognition system achieves a satisfyingly result. However, the feature extraction process could be further improved by using more "complex" features (e.g., signal peaks in time domain) or utilizing different feature selection approaches (e.g., grid search or relief). For example, by applying a grid search on the current feature vector (177 features), the number of significant features for the classification process could be improved and therefore most likely increase the performance.

ACKNOWLEDGMENT

This paper and all corresponding results, developments and achievements are a result of the Research Group for Secure and Intelligent Mobile Systems (SIMS).

REFERENCES

[1] M. Kurz, B. Hiesl, and E. Sonnleitner, "Real-time activity recognition utilizing dynamically on-body placed smartphones," in The Eleventh International Conference on Adaptive and Self-Adaptive Systems and Applications (ADAPTIVE 2019), 2019, pp. 84–87.

[2] A. Anjum and M. U. Ilyas, "Activity recognition using smartphone sensors," 2013 IEEE 10th Consumer Communications and Networking Conference (CCNC), 2013, pp. 914–919.

[3] X. Su, H. Tong, and P. Ji, "Activity recognition with smartphone sensors," Tsinghua science and technology, vol. 19, no. 3, 2014, pp. 235–249.

[4] L. Bao and S. S. Intille, "Activity recognition from user-annotated acceleration data," in International Conference on Pervasive Computing. Springer, 2004, pp. 1–17.

[5] G. Bieber, J. Voskamp, and B. Urban, "Activity recognition for everyday life on mobile phones," in International Conference on Universal Access in Human-Computer Interaction. Springer, 2009, pp. 289–296.

[6] M. Derawi and P. Bours, "Gait and activity recognition using commercial phones," computers & security, vol. 39, 2013, pp. 137–144.

[7] Y. He and Y. Li, "Physical activity recognition utilizing the built-in kinematic sensors of a smartphone," International Journal of Distributed Sensor Networks, vol. 9, no. 4, 2013, p. 481580.

[8] A. Henpraserttae, S. Thiemjarus, and S. Marukatat, "Accurate activity recognition using a mobile phone regardless of device orientation and location," in Body Sensor Networks (BSN), 2011 International Conference on. IEEE, 2011, pp. 41–46.

[9] M. Kurz, "Opportunistic activity recognition methodologies," Ph.D. dissertation, Johannes Kepler University Linz, Jun. 2013.

[10] J. R. Kwapisz, G. M. Weiss, and S. A. Moore, "Activity recognition using cell phone accelerometers," ACM SigKDD Explorations Newsletter, vol. 12, no. 2, 2011, pp. 74–82.

[11] L. Sun, D. Zhang, B. Li, B. Guo, and S. Li, "Activity recognition on an accelerometer embedded mobile phone with varying positions and orientations," in International conference on ubiquitous intelligence and computing. Springer, 2010, pp. 548–562.

[12] A. Burns and A. J. Wellings, Real-time systems and programming languages: Ada 95, real-time Java, and real-time POSIX. Pearson Education, 2001.

A Visible Light Vehicle-to-Vehicle Communication System Using Modulated Taillights

Michael Plattner

Department Mobility and Energy
University of Applied Sciences Upper Austria
Hagenberg im Mühlkreis, Austria
Email: Michael.Plattner@fh-hagenberg.at

Gerald Ostermayer

Research Group Networks and Mobility
University of Applied Sciences Upper Austria
Hagenberg im Mühlkreis, Austria
Email: Gerald.Ostermayer@fh-hagenberg.at

Abstract—**In this paper, we propose a visible light vehicle-to-vehicle communication system by modulating the taillights of a car and receiving the signal with a camera. Safety critical communication in applications like platooning requires a fast and secure wireless connection. Such a connection can be established by using our optical communication as an out-of-band channel to transmit a public key to another car following on the road. We are able to transmit 60 bit/s via the optical channel with an average BER (Bit Error Rate) of 3.46% and it takes about 5 seconds on average to receive the transmitted code word containing a 128-bit key in a non-synchronized system. Such an optical channel is very hard to manipulate for a third party and hence the transmitted public key can be used to verify the identity of the communication partner and man-in-the-middle attacks are made more difficult.**

Keywords–Automotive applications; Connected vehicles; Vehicle safety; Visible light communication; Differential phase shift keying

I. INTRODUCTION

Advanced Driver Assistance Systems (ADAS) and semi-autonomous driving technologies are already built into the newest luxury class cars. However, some future functionalities require cars to communicate with each other, e.g., platooning. Platooning means to group vehicles on the road into platoons and decrease the distance between these vehicles. An electronic coupling of the participating cars allows to accelerate and decelerate simultaneously. This enables the cars inside the platoon to drive in the slipstream of the cars ahead. Due to the smaller amount of drag, fuel can be saved and emissions are reduced. Additionally, this is a method of increasing the capacity of the roads and hence traffic jams can be prevented.

In a platoon, the car ahead needs to control the car following it remotely [1]. Thus, it is crucial to establish a secure connection between the participants. In this paper, we propose a method to transmit a public key via an optical out-of-band channel using the taillights of a car. The following car receives the message using a camera pointing in direction of driving. The public key can then be used to establish a secure encrypted communication via, e.g., 802.11p representing the main channel between two vehicles, where the identity of the car in front is verified via the out-of-band channel. For an attacker, it would be very difficult to fake such a transmission, as the true identity of the sender can be verified using the camera image.

Due to various environmental conditions on the road, caused by daytime, weather, shadows, car model, other light sources, etc., the system needs to adapt to those conditions to ensure a low transmission error rate. Therefore, the system uses convolutional neural networks (CNN) for detecting a transmitting car and for classifying the states of its taillights. By using a broad spectrum of training data in different environments, the resulting system is able to adapt to various lighting conditions and transmitting car models.

In section II, we give an overview of other projects working on VLC using cameras, especially for vehicle-to-vehicle communication. Section III describes our concrete approach for vehicular VLC using modulated taillights. The results of our proof-of-concept are then evaluated in section IV. In section V, we then conclude our findings and give an outlook into future work.

II. RELATED WORK

Visible Light Communication (VLC) refers to an optical wireless communication system that uses the modulation of light in the visible spectrum (400–700 nm) that is principally used for illumination [2]. The information is encoded on top of the illumination light. A precondition for most cases of VLC is that the modulation of the visible light is not perceived by the human eye. Low modulation frequencies lead to noticeable flickering. Therefore, the base frequency of the illumination light must be higher than the Critical Flicker Frequency (CFF). The CFF is defined as the frequency at which an intermittent light stimulus appears to be completely steady to a human observer [3]. It depends on various factors, e.g., the age of a person, but on average the human eye is able to notice flickering of visible light if the frequency is below 35-50Hz [4].

Viriyasitavat et al. [5] used an off-the-shelf scooter taillight and a photo diode for a VLC system and developed a channel model for vehicle-to-vehicle (V2V) visible light communication. They limited the maximum distance between scooter taillight and photo diode to 10m, for higher distances highly directed light sources would be needed, e.g., lasers (VCSEL) like used by Lu et al. [6]. In contrast to these works, we used a camera instead of a photo diode for receiving the signal. This way we can distinguish between multiple transmitters by analyzing the image using computer vision algorithms, but of course the modulation frequency is limited in comparison to the cut-off frequency of a photo diode.

Using a camera on the receiving side also enables computer vision algorithms to crop the regions of interest of the image that show the modulated taillights of a preceding car. However, assuming the system is able to recognize the correct information of the transmitter in each frame, we are still limited by Shannon's sampling theorem. Luo et al. [7] suggest a modulation variant called Undersampled Phase Shift On-Off Keying (UPSOOK), which overcomes this problem by utilizing the rolling shutter effect of CMOS cameras. This method chooses a modulation frequency between the critical flicker frequency and the cut-off frequency of a camera, which depends on the exposure time. This way the information encoded onto the modulated light source can be recognized by a camera with a very short exposure time, but the human eye does not perceive flickering. Other works from Liu et al. [8] or Lee et al. [9] also propose multiple variations of the utilization of the rolling shutter effect. Liu et al. [8] extend the modulation method by encoding the message into phase shifts between frames and use two modulated light sources to detect errors caused by slight synchronization offsets. Lee et al. [9] propose a variation where the modulated light is visible in the whole camera image and hence are able to encode information into the width of every single pulse of the modulation signal. However, information encoded into pulses that are not visible in the camera image is lost. For this reason, this is not applicable for our system, as the taillights of a car only cover a very small portion of the image.

III. Approach

This paper proposes an out-of-band channel for vehicle-to-vehicle communication using the taillights of a car. A 128-bit public key is transmitted from a car to its follower on the road. This key can then be used to establish a wireless, secure and encrypted connection in the main communication channel over, e.g., the 802.11p standard. The taillights are modulated using Undersampled Differential Phase Shift On-Off Keying (UDPSOOK) [8]. This enables a CMOS camera with a very short exposure time to receive the signal utilizing the rolling shutter effect, while there is no flickering perceivable for the human eye.

A. Rolling shutter effect

CMOS cameras, which are widely used in digital cameras, Digital Single-Lens Reflex (DSLR) cameras and smartphones use a rolling shutter. This means the image is sampled line by line and hence, e.g., the top of the image is sampled earlier than the bottom of the image. If the object in front of the camera is moving or changing while the image is captured, weird patterns occur like shown in Figure 1. In contrast, a global shutter camera captures all the pixels of the image at once, and hence quick changes or movements while capturing an image with short exposure time have no effect.

B. Modulation of taillights

The taillights used in the system are state-of-the-art LED taillights, which means they have very low latency when turning on or off (single-digit nanoseconds) compared to conventional halogen taillight bulbs. The chosen modulation frequency must be higher than the critical flickering frequency of approx. 50 Hz. In order to modulate information onto the signal, we need a consistent state throughout the communication. This is achieved by setting the modulation frequency to an exact multiple of the receiving camera's frame rate, which is 30 FPS in our system. However, the modulation frequency should be chosen as low as possible, to detect the states of the taillights easier in the camera images, but high enough

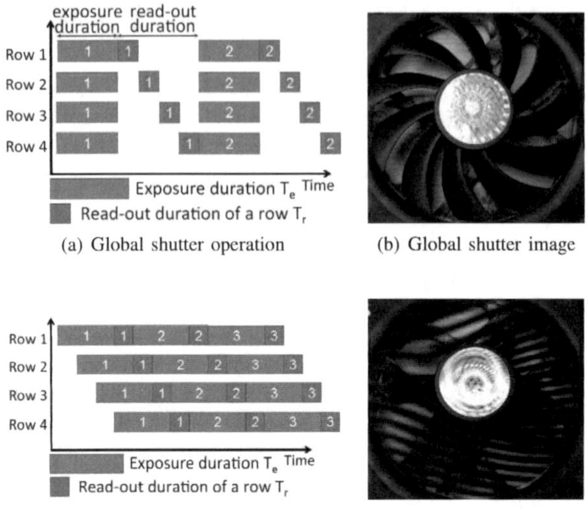

(a) Global shutter operation (b) Global shutter image

(c) Rolling shutter operation (d) Rolling shutter image

Figure 1. Comparison between global shutter and rolling shutter [9]

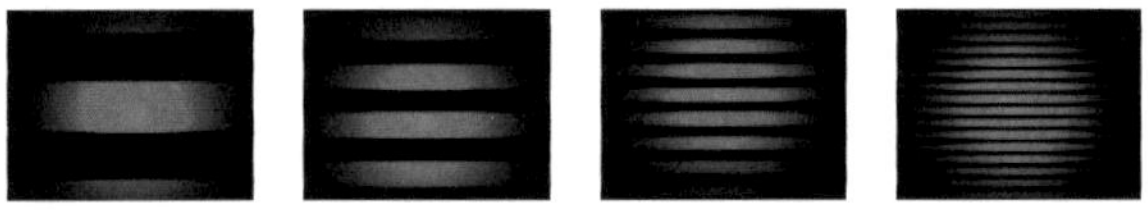

(a) 60 Hz (b) 120 Hz (c) 240 Hz (d) 480 Hz

Figure 2. Close-up pictures of a modulated LED with different frequencies

to not cause perceivable flickering. Figure 2 compares close-up images of a modulated LED with different modulation frequencies. The stripe pattern occurs due to the rolling shutter effect, the width of the stripes depends on the modulation frequency.

As depicted in Figure 3, if the camera is farther away from the light source, the area covered by it gets smaller. However, the stripe pattern remains the same, therefore, the state of the taillights in a specific frame depends on the position of the car. Thus, the taillight's state in a single frame is not sufficient to transmit information. The UDPSOOK [8] modulation method hence uses two consecutive frames to encode the information in the phase shift between them. For this reason, the modulation frequency must be an exact multiple of the camera's frame rate. Thus, the strip pattern and the state of the taillights respectively, stay the same in two successive frames if there was no phase shift between them. If there was a phase shift, the stripe pattern changes and the state of the light source changes, which can be detected by the receiver. Figure 4 depicts the idea how this modulation method encodes the information and the receiver samples the signal at a lower frequency, independent of the offset. Precondition for this method is that the modulation frequency of the light source is an exact multiple of the camera's frame rate and that there are no striking movements of the transmitting LED between two frames.

With this modulation method, the information is encoded into the phase shifts between frames. The phase switches between 0 and π, which is just an inversion of the signal.

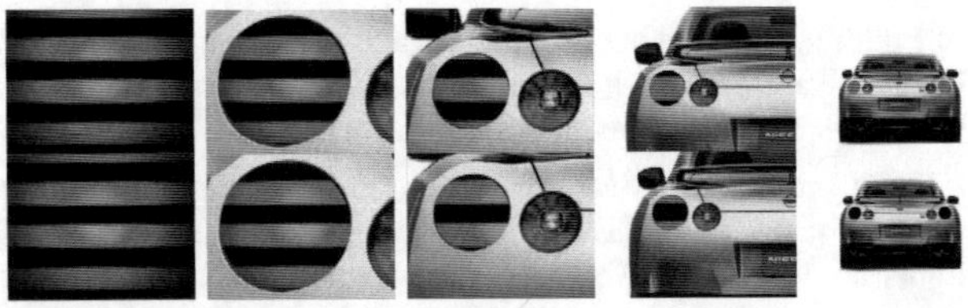

Figure 3. Modulated taillights in different distances from close-up to farther away

Figure 5. Modulated taillights showing transitions between ON and OFF, depending on the vertical position in the image

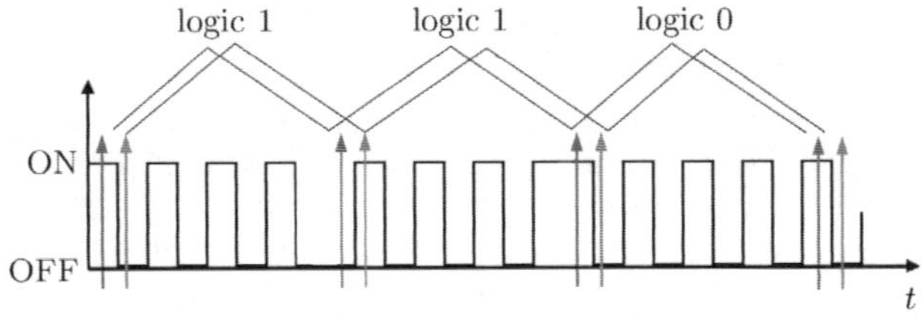

Figure 4. Different sampling timing for UDPSOOK [8]

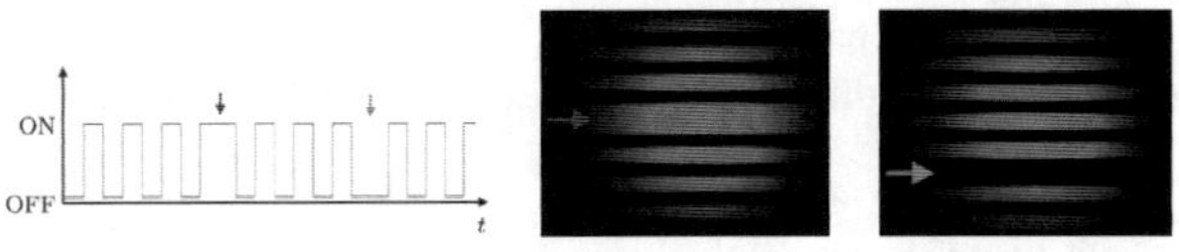

(a) Phase shifts in signal (b) Two consecutive ON states (c) Two consecutive OFF states

Figure 6. Phase shifts shown in signal and resulting stripe pattern

If the signal is sampled by the receiving camera and the phase changed in comparison to the previous frame, a logical 1 was transmitted. Otherwise, if the phase is the same, a logical 0 was transmitted. Thus, we can transmit one bit per frame and per modulated light source. In our system, we utilize two taillights, that can be modulated separately. So, we can transmit two bits per frame, which results in a transmission rate of 60 bit/s when having a 30 FPS camera at the receiving car. The center high mount stop light (CHMSEL) of cars is not suitable to transmit information by modulation, because a modulated light source is perceived as half-on by the human eye. A stop light must only be turned on, if the car is braking, otherwise it must be turned off. So, in our system, we can transmit data while the car is driving and the modulated taillights are perceived as normal taillights by other drivers. When braking, the transmission is stopped and the taillights are continuously on. For other drivers this looks like the light is brighter and the modulated taillights can additionally be used as brake lights. An alternative for this limitation of the data transmission would be to only adjust the brightness of the LED to differentiate between normal brightness and braking brightness of the taillights. Thus, the transmission would not be interrupted, however this was not in the scope of this work.

This modulation method is prone to errors in some special cases, where the light source does not show one distinct state of the stripe pattern, but the transition between the ON and OFF state. An example for this is shown in Figure 5. In this case, it is hard to detect the correct state and changes of the phase between frames. So, the only way here is to reduce the probability of such a situation to occur by using a stripe pattern, where the stripes are as wide as possible, which means to use a very small modulation frequency. However, we need to make sure to never cause perceivable flickering, even if a phase shift is applied, like shown in Figure 6, and therefore, the frequency is halved for one single pulse. For these reasons we chose a modulation frequency of 120Hz, with a 30 FPS camera at the receiving side in our system.

C. Demodulation of the signal

This system will be used to establish a secure wireless connection between two cars driving in succession on the motorway to enable platooning. This means our system needs to transmit a public key from one car to another car behind, before the platooning process is started. Thus, the two cars are still driving with a safety distance of usually between 30 m and 50 m. This is the main operating range of the optical out-of-band communication channel.

For receiving the signal, we use a common CMOS camera with a rolling shutter and a fixed exposure time of 1 ms. Additionally, the ISO value and gain of the camera is set to its maximum, to still have a bright enough image and to be able to detect the car inside the frame of the camera. The receiving process of a single bit consists of the three following steps:

1) Vehicle Detection: The first step of the receiving process is to detect the bounding box of the vehicle in front. We decided to use the YOLO framework proposed by Redmon et al. [10], [11], [12] for detecting the car, Junsheng Fu [13] created a vehicle detection pipeline using the YOLO framework in Python. This framework is able to detect different types of cars and car models and is even able to detect miniature cars printed onto cardboard like used in our first prototype without the context of a real road. However, the detection process is not fast enough to detect the car in real-time in every frame of the camera stream. So, we only detect the car in every 20th frame of a video. This might result in errors if the transmitting car is moving too much inside the camera frame while using a deprecated position of the car for receiving the data. Concrete consequences are covered in the evaluation section. However, faster vehicle detection using a better detection algorithm or ASICs (application-specific integrated circuits) would prevent errors caused by movements of transmitter or receiver.

2) Taillights ROI Estimation: When the position of the car in the image is detected, we estimate the regions of interest (ROI) for the taillights using a static calculation depending on the bounding box of the detected car. This is a rather simple

(a) Mercedes-Benz B-Class (b) VW Beetle

Figure 7. Taillight detection on example images of cars on a road

approach, but is sufficient when the rear end of the car was detected accordingly. For this calculation the positions of the car C and the taillights TL and TR are defined by l, r, t and b representing the left, right, top and bottom border of the bounding box, respectively.

$$l_{TL} = l_C + \frac{r_C - l_C}{16} \quad (1)$$

$$r_{TL} = l_C + \frac{5 \cdot (r_C - l_C)}{16} \quad (2)$$

$$l_{TR} = r_C - \frac{5 \cdot (r_C - l_C)}{16} \quad (3)$$

$$r_{TR} = r_C - \frac{r_C - l_C}{16} \quad (4)$$

$$t_{TL} = t_{TR} = t_C + \frac{b_C - t_C}{4} \quad (5)$$

$$b_{TL} = b_{TR} = t_C + \frac{7 \cdot (b_C - t_C)}{12} \quad (6)$$

Figure 7 shows two examples of cars on a road where we detected the car using the YOLO framework and based on that estimated the positions of the taillights. The cars are marked with a blue rectangle and the positions of their taillights are highlighted red for the right and green for the left one. As we are using a rather big ROI for the taillights, it fits for the majority of car models. Additionally, we do not need the whole taillight inside the ROI, as the transmitted data can be reconstructed using just a fraction of the light source. However, it might be helpful for future works to use a more sophisticated detection approach, as the static calculation relies on an accurate detection of the car's rear.

3) Taillight State Recognition: The detected ROI containing the taillights of the car, are reshaped to match the size of 28x28 RGB pixels and then passed into a simple convolutional neural network to classify the current state of the taillight. The network is using two convolutional layers with 16 and 64 channels with two max-pooling layers and a single hidden dense layer with 64 neurons. All three layers use the ReLu activation function. For the two neurons for the states "on" and "off" in the output layer the softmax activation function is used.

This network was implemented using Keras with the TensorFlow backend. For training the network, a dataset of approx. 4450 labeled images was used. The training images show the taillights of sending prototypes in different environment and lighting conditions, to get an adaptive network, performing well in different scenarios with different car models. In order to prevent overfitting on the training data, a dropout probability of 50% was implemented during the training. After only 6 epochs of training, the network reached an accuracy of more than 98% in cross-validation. The final network scored an accuracy of 99.4% on an unseen evaluation dataset.

The proposed network design might be changed in future work, if it is not capable of classifying states of real car taillights appropriately. However, the performance of the network is sufficient for the current use case.

The recognized taillight state is then compared with the previous state of the taillight to demodulate the sent message. If the recognized state is the same as in the last frame, a logical 0 was received, otherwise a logical 1.

D. Channel Coding

Wireless communication, especially visible light communication with cameras, is fragile. As already mentioned, some potential error causes cannot be prevented. To get a stable connection, even if errors occur, we used Reed-Solomon [14] channel coding. In our system we want to transmit a 128 bit public key, using the optical out-of-band channel built by the taillights of a car. The transmitted message effectively is always the same, the transmitter just waits until somebody receives the message and starts connecting via the main wireless channel using the transmitted key. We use a RS(24,16) channel coding with 8-bit or 1-byte symbols. This means we use code words with a length of 24 symbols, where 16 symbols carry the message and the remaining 8 symbols are used for error detection and error correction. With 8 error correction symbols we are able to detect and correct 4 erroneous symbols in a code word.

Due to the lack of a synchronization signal, we need a starting sequence of 8 bits to indicate the start of a new code word. Including the starting sequence, the code word to send has a length of 200 bits. After sending 200 bits, the transmitter restarts to send the message again. With two modulated taillights we need 100 frames to transmit 200 bits. As we use a 30 FPS camera, it takes 3.33 seconds to transmit a 128 bit public key via the optical out-of-band channel.

Figure 8 shows a block diagram of the previously explained parts of our system. As depicted, we use two modulated light sources to send a message, where both of them are captured by a single camera.

IV. EVALUATION

For the evaluation we used various videos recorded with the Canon EOS 1100D DSLR camera. We used different cardboard car models in scale 1:24 for the transmitter in different settings. The distance between the transmitter and the camera was approx. 1.5 m, which represents a distance of 36 m in the real world. We recorded test videos in dark indoor and bright outdoor environments, with and without movement of the sending model inside the video frame.

Figure 9 shows the BER for the optical data transmission for different subsets of test videos. In total, the average BER for the evaluated videos is 6.81% with a standard deviation 5.18%. If we divide the videos into two subsets with videos where the transmitter is and is not moving inside the video frame, we see that movement of the transmitter causes many bit errors. This obviously is due to the fact that we only detect the transmitter every 20th frame to be able to receive the message in almost real-time. Without movement of the

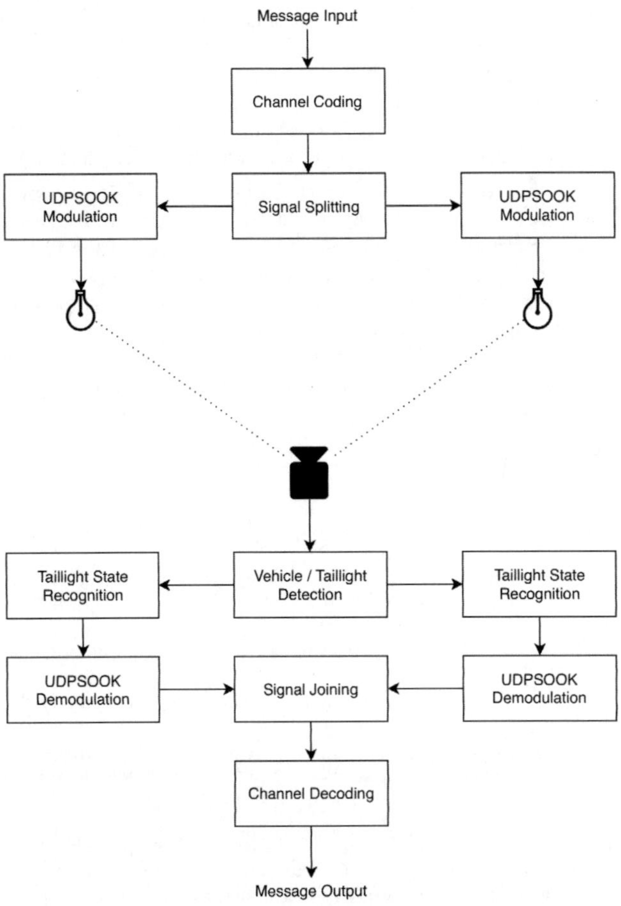

Figure 8. Optical data transmission block diagram

transmitter the BER is at 3.46% on average with a standard deviation of 1.94%, with a moving transmitter it is significantly worse in our setup. Splitting the set of videos with not moving transmitters further down to videos with bright and dark environments we see something interesting. The mean BER of both sets is pretty much the same with 3.6% for dark and 3.2% for bright videos, but the standard deviation of 2.44% is much bigger for dark environments compared to 0.84% for bright ones. This is caused by two different factors. In bright environments, the vehicle detection works very well, but the taillight state recognition is much harder compared to videos with dark light settings. In dark videos, the hard part is to

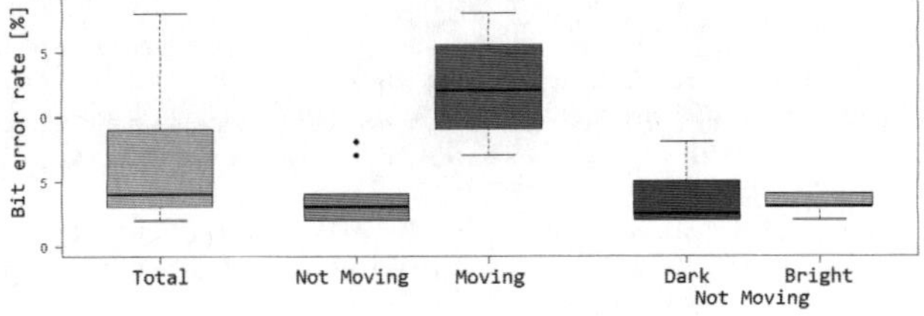

Figure 9. Boxplots of BER for different settings

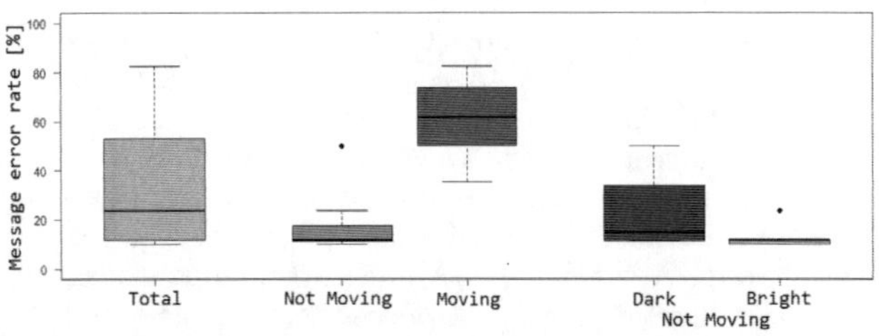

Figure 10. Boxplots of Message Error Rates for different settings

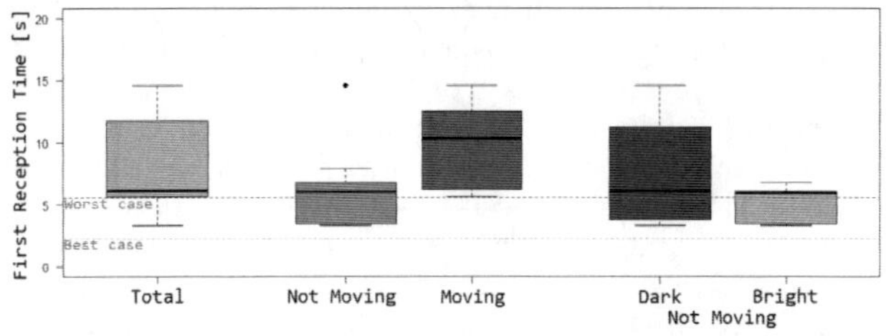

Figure 11. Boxplots of First Reception Time for different settings

detect the transmitter. However, if the detection was successful, it is pretty easy to recognize the state of the taillight because of the good contrast in the dark background. In some of the dark videos, the vehicle detection works fine, so the BER is very low, but if the car is not detected properly, a burst of bit errors occurs and increases the BER massively. On the other hand, in bright light setting the detection of the transmitter is easier, but there are more single bit errors caused by the taillight state recognition. The difference between dark and bright lighting in the message error rates depicted in Figure 10 encourages this assumption. Error bursts in the received bit strings cause corrupted messages that cannot be corrected. Single bit errors can be corrected using the error correction code of the channel coding, and hence the message error rate of 13.41% on average for bright videos is better compared to dark videos with a mean message error rate of 22.63%.

What we can also see in this chart is that the message error rate is never below 10% in our experimental setup. These errors are caused by the offset in synchronization between transmitter and receiving camera. Approximately every 20th message the stripe pattern that appears due to the UDPSOOK modulation of the taillights is moving over the area of the taillight inside the camera frame and causes ambiguous taillight states that cannot be decoded properly. Those transitions of stripes were already mentioned as know error causes. They cause error bursts that usually affect two consecutive messages and hence about 10% of the sent messages get corrupted. In our setup, we want to send the messages as quick as possible, therefore, we decided to not use interleaving approaches in our channel coding. Interleaving might correct messages that got corrupted by error bursts, but the time until a single message is transmitted would be significantly higher.

Another interesting metric to evaluate is the first reception time of the sent message in the test videos. Boxplots for this are shown in Figure 11. In our test scenario, we send code words with a length of 200 bits, this means we need at least 100 frames with 2 bits per frame to transmit the whole code word. With a frame rate of 30 FPS, this takes 3.33 seconds. On average, it takes 5.244 seconds until the message was successfully transmitted for the first time, however, the minimum reception time in our test videos is 3.30 seconds and hence lower than the theoretically possible time to send the whole code word. This is possible because of the channel coding in our system. Assuming we have an error free transmission of the code word, we are able to decode the message even before the whole code word was sent. In our case, if we received the starting sequence and the first 20 bytes of the 24-byte code word correctly, we can set the last 4 symbols of the code word to any value and the channel coding enables us to decode the message correctly. This can be done because we can detect and correct 4 erroneous symbols in the code word, using the 8 error correction symbols. In the case of an error free transmission, those 4 errors are the 4 symbols that were not transmitted yet. This means we just need the 8-bit starting sequence and 20 bytes of the code word for a correct reception. These are 136 bits, where we need 68 frames to transmit them, which takes 2.267 seconds. This means if the test video starts exactly when the first bit of the starting sequence is sent, the first reception of the message is possible after 2.267 seconds. The worst case with error free transmission would be that the video starts after the first bits of the starting sequence were sent. In this case, we would not be able to detect that the first message is sent and therefore, the first reception would be possible after 5.567 seconds. Those two times for the best and the worst case with error free connection are also shown as dashed horizontal lines in Figure 11.

V. Conclusion

We can conclude that our proof-of-concept experiment of an optical out-of-band channel for vehicle-to-vehicle communication using modulated taillights was successful. We managed to build prototypes of different car models in a scale of 1:24 with LEDs representing the taillights. Those LEDs where modulated using the UDPSOOK modulation method, where a camera with a very short exposure time of 1 ms is able to capture distinct states of the light source, but the human eye is not able to perceive any flickering. On the receiving side we used a Canon EOS 1100D DLSR camera to receive the signal and record evaluation videos, but actually any other CMOS camera with rolling shutter can be used. The only precondition is that videos can be recorded while the shutter speed is set manually.

The results showed that we were able to transmit messages with an average BER of 3.46% with a standard deviation of 1.94% in videos where no striking movements of the transmitter inside the camera frame occur. As our system is designed for vehicle-to-vehicle communication on the highway with two cars driving in succession, we can assume that the relative position of the car in front is quite stable and only changes slowly. Of course, the total BER is improved by the Reed-Solomon channel coding. However, only 90% of the sent 200-bit code words can be decoded correctly, due to error bursts when the transitions of UDPSOOK modulation pulses are aligned with the taillights of the sending car. Such error bursts can only be corrected with interleaving methods in the channel coding, which would make the time until a code word is received for the first time significantly longer. In our evaluation, it took 5.244 seconds on average to receive the correct code word, in a platooning application, this would mean that after just a few seconds we can establish a secure and encrypted connection between two cars in the main wireless communication channel, e.g., using 802.11p. This connection then might be running for dozens of minutes or even multiple hours, if the two cars have a similar path to their destination.

A future goal for this work is to port this proof-of-concept system using a 1:24 prototype into a full-sized car and testing the performance of the communication system on the road. In the real world, there will be much more interfering factors like other cars that are not sending any information using their taillights or other light sources like traffic lights, lamp posts or the sun, which might interfere. Another idea is to not just use a single camera for receiving the signal, but to have two or multiple cameras that add redundancy and therefore, a better BER, or they could be used to filter specular reflections from other light sources by merging the camera images like suggested by Plattner and Ostermayer [15].

References

[1] D. Swaroop, "String stability of interconnected systems: An application to platooning in automated highway systems," Ph. D. Dissertation, University of California, 1997.

[2] S. Arnon, Visible light communication. Cambridge University Press, 2015.

[3] H. Luczak, Arbeitswissenschaft. 2, vollständig bearbeitete Auflage. Springer-Verlag Berlin und Heidelberg, 1998.

[4] G. Kircheis, M. Wettstein, L. Timmermann, A. Schnitzler, and D. Häussinger, "Critical flicker frequency for quantification of low-grade hepatic encephalopathy," Hepatology, vol. 35, no. 2, 2002, pp. 357–366.

[5] W. Viriyasitavat, S.-H. Yu, and H.-M. Tsai, "Short paper: Channel model for visible light communications using off-the-shelf scooter taillight," in Vehicular Networking Conference (VNC), 2013 IEEE. IEEE, 2013, pp. 170–173.

[6] H.-H. Lu, Y.-P. Lin, P.-Y. Wu, C.-Y. Chen, M.-C. Chen, and T.-W. Jhang, "A multiple-input-multiple-output visible light communication system based on vcsels and spatial light modulators," Optics Express, vol. 22, no. 3, 2014, pp. 3468–3474.

[7] P. Luo, Z. Ghassemlooy, H. Le Minh, X. Tang, and H.-M. Tsai, "Undersampled phase shift on-off keying for camera communication," in Wireless Communications and Signal Processing (WCSP), 2014 Sixth International Conference on. IEEE, 2014, pp. 1–6.

[8] N. Liu, J. Cheng, and J. F. Holzman, "Undersampled differential phase shift on-off keying for optical camera communications," Journal of Communications and Information Networks, vol. 2, no. 4, 2017, pp. 47–56.

[9] H.-Y. Lee, H.-M. Lin, Y.-L. Wei, H.-I. Wu, H.-M. Tsai, and K. C.-J. Lin, "Rollinglight: Enabling line-of-sight light-to-camera communications," in Proceedings of the 13th Annual International Conference on Mobile Systems, Applications, and Services. ACM, 2015, pp. 167–180.

[10] J. Redmon, S. Divvala, R. Girshick, and A. Farhadi, "You only look once: Unified, real-time object detection," arXiv, 2015.

[11] J. Redmon and A. Farhadi, "Yolo9000: Better, faster, stronger," arXiv preprint arXiv:1612.08242, 2016.

[12] ——, "Yolov3: An incremental improvement," arXiv, 2018.

[13] J. Fu. Vehicle detection for autonomous driving. Visited on 2020-06-02. [Online]. Available: https://github.com/JunshengFu/vehicle-detection

[14] I. S. Reed and G. Solomon, "Polynomial codes over certain finite fields," Journal of the society for industrial and applied mathematics, vol. 8, no. 2, 1960, pp. 300–304.

[15] M. Plattner and G. Ostermayer, "Filtering specular reflections by merging stereo images," in Scandinavian Conference on Image Analysis. Springer, 2019, pp. 164–172.

A Context-enhanced Sector-based Indoor Positioning Library

Alexander Stelzhammer and Jens Krösche

University of Applied Sciences Upper Austria
Faculty for Informatics, Communications and Media
Department of Mobility and Energy
Softwarepark 11
4232 Hagenberg im Mühlkreis, Austria
Email: firstname.lastname@fh-hagenberg.at

***Abstract*—The position context is still one of the key features when it comes to building context-aware mobile applications. In the outdoors, today's GNSS provide the necessary information without much problem to all interested users but indoors reliable data and systems are still a big problem. The presented approach provides a novel approach to evaluate the position of an entity in such an indoor environment. It trades accuracy for robustness and environmental flexibility by neglecting concrete position coordinates and concentrating on sector-based positioning.**

***Keywords*–sector-based position; context-aware; indoor position**

I. INTRODUCTION

With the global proliferation of smartphones, the chances to disseminate context-aware applications and initiate the ubiquitous computing era envisioned by Weiser [1] on a large scale are higher than ever. In the wake of this development, the knowledge of one's own position has become one of the most crucial factors. Even as pioneers of the context-aware computing domain like Abowd and Dey [2] or Schmidt et al. [3] discussed its significance, the position information was and still is one of the most used key features when it comes to building adaptable and mobile context-aware systems. Whereas context-aware systems should be considered as systems that not only take into account the direct input of its users, but also consider environmental and situational parameters to provide suitable services, matching information or adaptive behaviour. The provision of the needed position information in today's world is strictly separated between the outdoor and the indoor domain. In the outdoor domain, modern Global Navigation Satellite Systems (GNSS) like GPS, Galileo, GLONASS or Baidou provide a reliable positioning service. However, in the indoor domain, no industrial standard has been established even after decades of research and technological advances.

Approaches used by today's indoor positioning systems usually rely strongly on highly complex algorithms trying to deduce the users' positions facilitating intensive pre-measuring, modelling, training and/or computing power. Based on the assumption that a very accurate position information is not needed in many indoor scenarios the presented system tries to approach the problem domain from a different angle. It is assumed that a general information in which part of the building an entity resides in is a good enough position information. Therefore, a robust and adaptable (regarding the used indoor environment) library for mobile applications that provides a sector-based position information is presented in this paper.

Based on a simple descriptive file containing the positions and provided networks of a building's WiFi infrastructure, a building is divided into sectors. These sectors are later used to reference the position of an entity. The main input to the system are regular scans of the current WiFi environment (particularly BSSID and RSSI values). The decision which sector is the "target" sector is calculated based on a pipes and filters pattern [4] approach. The measured access point values together with historical measurements are filtered and prioritized by a set of parameterizable filters (s. Section III) until one or more sectors are identified as "target" sectors reflecting the position sector(s) of the entity. The filters themselves can be rather simple or sometimes more complex. They range from simple white list or threshold ones over plausibility checking graph filters to context regarding filters. Taking into account the positioning taxonomy of Küpper [5], the presented approach uses proximity sensing to deduce the position. Our library tries to address the problem of multiple signals being received simultaneously, and the strongest signal not always reflecting the best matching signal respectively position, by applying a set of filters and plausibility checks. Even if the provided system is not adaptable on its own, it uses context to improve its calculation results and provides the foundation for mobile adaptable systems targeting the indoor domain by providing a novel, robust, and reliable indoor positioning system.

The rest of the paper is structured as follows. We start with a short overview of the current developments in indoor positioning in Section II which we use to motivate our own novel approach in Section III. In order to test and evaluate the presented approach we developed a simulation environment which is presented in Section IV. Section V shows the first promising results of our positioning library in four different scenarios and we close with a short conclusion and an outlook on the next steps to improve our approach.

II. RELATED WORK

As indoor positioning is still an ongoing topic for context-aware systems even after decades of research, many different approaches have been tried to address the problem. What started with the Active Badge system from Want et al. [6] and the PARKTAB system by Schilit et al. [7] only slowly gained momentum in the beginning. In today's world where nearly everyone is using mobile applications on smartphones and the Internet of Things (IoT) is reality, the big companies like Google and Apple try their best to support indoor positioning but current solutions are still unsatisfying.

A rather recent indoor localization system based on WLAN fingerprinting was Sectjunction presented by He and Chan [8].

The special aim of the project was to reduce measurement uncertainty by dividing the coverage area into sectors. Each sector corresponded to a distinct access point and had its size modelled according to its access point's signal strength. The location of a target could then be constrained to the overlap of those sectors with the strongest RSS value, thus tightening the search space without leading to a dispersed set of reference points. Another project was Redpin from Bollinger [9], which was also a fingerprint-based indoor localization system based on WiFi, GSM and Bluetooth. One of the key factors of Redpin was that the system tried to omit the time-consuming offline/training-phase by training and improving itself during usage time by the operators. The LoCo framework from Biehl et al. [10] used a supervised classification scheme to provide a highly accurate room-level localization. The classification was based on the relative ordering of access points regarding their RSSI. Kumar et al. [11] aimed at a low "cost" (regarding training) implementation of an indoor localization method. They facilitated an angular approach by emulating a large antenna array using a new kind of Synthetic Aperture Radar (SAR) to orientate and localize the device in 3-D space. In order to gain a good overview on indoor positioning systems Zafari et al. [12] together with Jang and Kim [13] conducted some surveys.

What can be seen in recent projects is that one common aspect is the attempt to omit time consuming training and measuring phases. One of the main problems here is the lifespan of the collected data which typically is only valid as long as the environment isn't changed. It is also striking that many indoor systems do not specify concrete coordinates as a location reference. These developments are reflected by the proposed system by working without a training phase, being applicable to any building and facilitating the use of location sectors.

III. POSITIONING LIBRARY

In order to estimate the most probable position sector, the data collected from scanning the environment has to be processed. Because of this, the main part of the positioning library is structured as a filter pipeline (depicted in Figure 1) that analyses, processes and refines the provided raw data step by step.

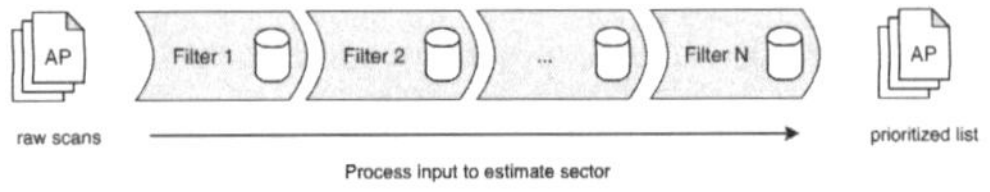

Figure 1. Structure of filter pipeline

A. Structure

The filter pipeline consists of a set of filters, each applying transformations to the original input data. Each filter in the pipeline has a single streamlined responsibility. With each step in the pipeline, the input data is further processed, taking the input from the previous filter and producing output for the next. Each filter can be applied an arbitrary number of times and is configurable on its own using a set of internal parameters. Each occurrence of a filter in the pipeline may therefore use a different configuration. Additionally, filters are able to hold a state (its memory) to keep track of previously analyzed scans. This way, the form of movement can be derived based on the changes in sensor values over time. In the following, we will present two example filters namely the Pressure Filter and the Graph Filter.

1) Pressure Filter

As buildings typically contain multiple floors it is important to know on which floor an entity is. The Pressure Filter, which keeps track of the contextual value ambient air pressure, is used to recognize possible floor changes. Looking at the temporal progression of the measured air pressure, the elevation changes of the target can be derived. The filter stores the most recent air pressure measurements, provided by the smartphone's barometer, ordered from least to most recent measurement. The number of measurements stored is determined by its configurable parameter capacity defining the internal window size. For these measurements, the change in pressure from one measurement to the next is calculated. In case of a significant increase or decrease a possible change of the floor level was deduced.

2) Graph Filter

Another important aspect of buildings is that floor changes cannot be carried out at any given location and that one can only move within a building on defined paths namely the hallways. Jumping from one building wing to another is considered not realistic. The Graph Filter restructures this topological information based on the installed access points forming a so called Access Point Graph as seen in Figure 2 where each node represents an access point and therefore a possible positioning sector. Nodes are only connected if they are directly reachable through, i.e., a hallway or a stair case if a floor change is depicted. The graph can therefore be used to establish a plausibility check to recognize impossible access point respectively sector jumps. It prioritizes the possible sectors in its calculation set based on a certain distance from the previously estimated sector. This prevents the algorithm from jumping from one sector to the other without passing through the connected sectors between them and therefore jumping floors or building wings. The maximum jump distance is defined using the parameter n and describes the smallest number of hops it accepts to reach one sector from the other. If $n = 0$, then the estimation prioritizes only sectors that have been part of the previous estimation. If $n = 1$ only sectors of the previous estimation and those adjacent to them are considered to be relevant estimates. The graph representation of the access points installed in the building is passed as another part of the filter input.

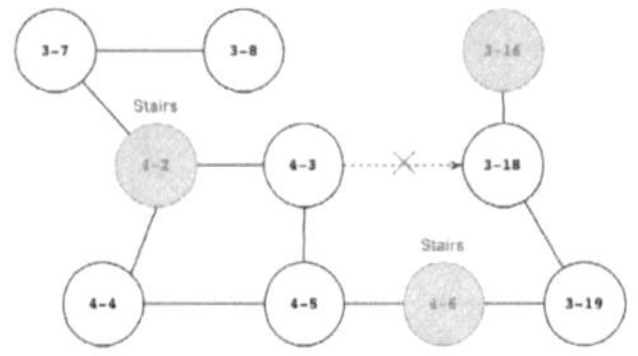

Figure 2. An Access Point Graph representing the topology of a building

B. Input

The input received by a filter contains on the one hand the scanned access points (namely RSSI and BSSID) and on the other hand additional parameters and contextual data that aid in filtering the access point scans. The contextual data, which is passed into the filter pipeline, is based on an Android smartphone's sensors and the additionally needed data like the building's access point structure is integrated as an additional parameter file and will be described in more detail in Section IV.

C. Output

The last filter in the pipeline provides the final set of access points. This set then serves as the prioritized list of sectors with the target's most likely position at the top and the least likely at the bottom. Only this final result set is then considered for the position estimation, providing the ID of the most probable access point-based positioning sector.

IV. Testing Environment

To test different configurations of the filter pipeline and the integrated filters in different scenarios (buildings and routes) a simulation system has been constructed. This system consists of two applications: a simulator and a smartphone application to record the necessary data. Both provide the means to simulate and evaluate pre-recorded walks through different buildings.

A. Labeled WiFi/Context Recording

The required data to simulate walks is collected by an Android application. The application initiates a number of scans of the environment along so-called recording route. These recording routes are defined using a set of arbitrary way points, which are defined in special JSON files. Each way point serves as a calibration point and is, in turn, being defined by its location using X and Y coordinates regarding the blueprint of the building as well as the floor it resides on. Any arbitrary location can be used as a way point. Connecting these way points form the describted recording routes.

During a recording process, the users move in a steady pace on the recording route. When passing a way point, the users signal (by pressing a corresponding application button) that a way point has been reached and the application will automatically start scanning the environment. These scans are referred to as way point scans. Way point scans are automatically associated with the respective way point's location and reflect the internal calibration points. While moving from one way point to the next, additional scans are applied automatically in the background at a fixed interval. These scans are referred to as intermediate scans. Unlike way point scans, these are not explicitly labelled with a location but their location will later be interpolated.

With each scan, information on the installed access points in the near proximity are collected. Next to RSS values and frequency, physical measurements taken by the sensors installed in the user's smartphone are recorded as well. For example, barometers, photometers, and thermometers are environmental sensors used to capture air pressure, illumination, and temperature respectively. Each scan is tagged with a timestamp, representing the time of recording the data and is later exported as a JSON file to be used in the simulator.

B. Simulator

The simulator provides the means to evaluate and adapt the indoor positioning library. Pre-recorded walks in form of JSON files can be simulated while the results of the indoor positioning library are visualized on a map of the building. A screenshot of the user interface can be seen in Figure 3.

The main view of the application displays a map of the current floor. The sectors of the installed access points are calculated based on a Voronoi algorithm and provided as an overlay of the simulator's map. Using the recorded scans, the simulator reconstructs different walks through the building. These recorded walks are visualized by blue dots on the map indicating the way points of the recording route. When a recording is playing, the actual position of the target is represented by a bright green dot on the map. If a way point scan is processed, the position of the way point is used to paint the indicator on the map. If an intermediate scan is processed, the position to draw on the map is interpolated based on its surrounding way point scans. During playback, the recorded scans are fed to the filter pipeline in sequence. With each scan, the current position is calculated based on the scan that is currently being processed. The sector that is estimated to most likely contain the target is highlighted in light-green, but the simulator can be configured to extend the highlighting to multiple sectors if necessary taking into account the calculated prioritization.

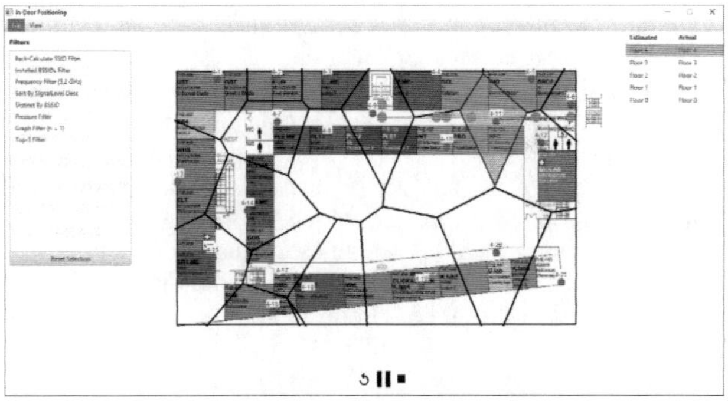

Figure 3. Screenshot of simulator

In addition, the currently configured filter pipeline is displayed left of the map. The filters in the pipeline are displayed from top to bottom, with the top most filter being applied first, and the lower most filter being applied last as part of a position estimation iteration. Via the context menu of the application, a dialogue can be accessed that enables the adaptation of the configured pipeline. Furthermore, the settings dialogue can be opened with which the simulation properties can be adapted and filters added or moved. When adding a filter to the pipeline, however, a dialogue window pops up where the parameters of the added filter can be adapted.

V. Evaluation

A. Scenarios

In order to evaluate the performance of the system, different tests at the campus Hagenberg of the University of Applied Sciences Upper Austria with different filter combinations in different pipelines have been conducted. In total, four scenarios have been defined to collect the test data and five different pipelines (three of them presented here) have been used to prioritize the access points. Each of the scenarios' focused on a different type of movement.

Scenario A focused on the change of direction. At a certain point on the route, the target turned around, followed the route back to where it came from, and finished the route in a different direction. This route covered the case that sectors were passed through multiple times.

Scenario B aimed at the changing of floors. Two different flight of steps were used on this route to change from a higher to a lower floor and back to the higher floor again.

Scenario C concentrated on the target standing still for an arbitrary amount of time at a certain point on the recording route. The target started walking the predefined route, paused for several seconds before walking again.

Scenario D consisted of a regular round trip, starting from a distinct location and arriving at the same location again. The route was finished without a change of floors.

B. Metrics

In order to determine and compare the accuracy of different iterations and therefore filter combinations and configurations of the positioning library, two metrics have been defined and used. In this paper, we reference the results of the Number of Correctly Estimated Sectors (NCES) metric.

As the proposed system tries to estimate in which sector the target resides in at the current point in time, an estimation can either be correct or incorrect. The evaluated target's position is considered to be correct when the target's actual position is inside the estimated sector. So, the NCES metric determines how many of the overall performed estimations have been correct. The metric can be configured using the *toleratedDistance* parameter, which, by default, is set to 0. If a distance larger than 0 is set, an estimated sector is considered to be correct, when it is within the specified distance from the actual sector in the Access Point Graph.

C. Results

The results presented in this paper reflect the results for the four scenarios with regards to the NCES metric. For each iteration of the pipeline, the NCES metric has been calculated once with a tolerated distance of 0 (only the sector with the highest priority is regarded valid) and once with a tolerance value of 1 (the sector with the highest priority and its direct neighbours are regarded valid). The Table I displays the results of three pipeline configurations: Pressure, Graph ($n = 1$), and Graph ($n = 2$).

TABLE I. MATRIX DISPLAYING THE PERFORMANCE OF EACH ITERATION OF THE PIPELINES

		Pressure	*Graph* ($n = 1$)	*Graph* ($n = 2$)
Scenario A:	NCES (td = 0)	0.640	0.680	0.640
Change of Direction	NCES (td = 1)	0.980	1.000	0.980
Scenario B:	NCES (td = 0)	0.479	0.352	0.479
Change of Floors	NCES (td = 1)	0.930	0.634	0.986
Scenario C:	NCES (td = 0)	0.718	0.205	0.744
Standing Still	NCES (td = 1)	0.974	0.359	1.000
Scenario D:	NCES (td = 0)	0.580	0.420	0.470
Roundtrip	NCES (td = 1)	0.960	0.710	0.950

The worst result was achieved by the Graph ($n = 1$) pipeline. Even with a tolerated distance of 1, the pipeline only estimated 67.57 % of the sectors correctly on average. This can be traced back to the limited range of potential candidates considered to be the target's position. The pipeline tended to get stuck within its previous estimation after a while because the newly scanned AP at this point were too far off from the previous estimations to be considered realistic.

Overall, the best results were achieved using the Graph ($n = 2$) pipeline, with an average accuracy of 0.611 using a tolerated distance of 0 and an average accuracy of 0.979 using a tolerated distance of 1. With a tolerated distance of 1, almost perfect results were achieved. This variation ($n = 1$ vs. $n = 2$) indicates that the cell approximation of each sector is not accurate enough and more sophisticated approaches, such as signal propagation models for a better approximation of a sector's true coverage area, would be very promising extensions to improve the estimation for the Graph ($n = 1$) pipeline.

VI. CONCLUSION

In this paper, we presented the first results of our novel indoor localization library together with its evaluation system. Our first results are very promising but some challenges are still visible. One of the main error sources could be traced back to the unrealistic sectorization of the building based on its access point infrastructure by using Voronoi-based cells. Another promising improvement will be the integration of additional context sources. This should provide the system with more calibration points and help to further deduce realistic movement trajectories throughout a building. Therefore, the integration of movement trajectory and context-based calibration filters will be our next steps to improve the system.

REFERENCES

[1] M. Weiser, "The Computer for the 21st Century," Scientific American, vol. 265, no. 3, 1991, pp. 94–104.

[2] G. D. Abowd et al., "Towards a Better Understanding of Context and Context-Awareness," in Proceeding 1st International Symposium on Handheld and Ubiquitous Computing (HUC '99), June 1999, pp. 304–307.

[3] A. Schmidt, M. Beigl, and H.-W. Gellersen, "There is more to Context than Location," Computers and Graphics, vol. 23, 1998, pp. 893–901.

[4] F. Buschmann, R. Meunier, P. Sommerlad, and M. Stal, Pattern-Oriented Software Architecture, Volume 1, A System of Patterns. Wiley, Chichester, England, 1996.

[5] A. Küpper, Location-Based Services: Fundamentals and Operation. Wiley, Chichester, England, 2005.

[6] R. Want, A. Hopper, V. Falcao, and J. Gibbons, "The Active Badge Location System," ACM Transactions on Information Systems, vol. 10, no. 1, 1992, pp. 91–102.

[7] B. Schilit, N. Adams, R. Gold, M. Tso, and R. Want, "The PARCTAB mobile computing system," in Proceedings of the Fourth Workshop on Workstation Operating Systems, 1993, pp. 34–39.

[8] S. He and S. . G. Chan, "Sectjunction: Wi-Fi indoor localization based on junction of signal sectors," in Proceedings of the IEEE International Conference on Communications (ICC), 2014, pp. 2605–2610.

[9] P. Bolliger, "Redpin – Adaptive, zero-configuration indoor localization through user collaboration," in Proceedings of the ACM International Workshop on Mobile Entity Localization and Tracking in GPS-less Environments, MELT 2008, 2008, pp. 55–60.

[10] J. Biehl, M. Cooper, G. Filby, and S. Kratz, "LoCo: A ready-to-deploy framework for efficient room localization using Wi-Fi," in Proceedings of the 2014 ACM International Joint Conference on Pervasive and Ubiquitous Computing – UbiComp 2014, 2014, pp. 183–187.

[11] S. Kumar, S. Gil, D. Katabi, and D. Rus, "Accurate indoor localization with zero start-up cost," in Proceedings of the Annual Intern. Conf. on Mobile Computing and Networking, MOBICOM, 2014, p. 483–494.

[12] F. Zafari, A. Gkelias, and K. K. Leung, "A Survey of Indoor Localization Systems and Technologies," IEEE Communications Surveys Tutorials, vol. 21, no. 3, 2019, pp. 2568–2599.

[13] B. Jang and H. Kim, "Indoor Positioning Technologies Without Offline Fingerprinting Map: A Survey," IEEE Communications Surveys Tutorials, vol. 21, no. 1, 2019, pp. 508–525.

Estimating Internal Power in Walking and Running with a Smart Sock

Dicle Yilmaz

University of Applied Sciences Upper Austria
School of Informatics, Communications and Media
Hagenberg, Austria
Email: S1810455025@students.fh-hagenberg.at

Stephan Selinger

University of Applied Sciences Upper Austria
School of Informatics, Communications and Media
Hagenberg, Austria
Email: stephan.selinger@fh-hagenberg.at

Florian Eibensteiner

University of Applied Sciences Upper Austria
School of Informatics, Communications and Media
Hagenberg, Austria
Email: florian.eibensteiner@fh-hagenberg.at

***Abstract*—The aim of this study is to investigate whether it is possible to estimate internal power in walking and running with a smart sock which is equipped with textile pressure sensors. Since commercially available smart socks are already used by runners to classify injury-prone running styles, such as running with low cadence and heel-striking, incorporating power measurement into the socks would make the usage of a separate power meter obsolete. While walking and running with different velocities and gradients on a treadmill, four subjects wore a pair of smart socks as well as a Stryd power meter as a reference system. The measurements from the pressure sensors were used to train regression algorithms, such as linear regression, trees of linear regressions (M5P), random forest, and k-nearest neighbors (KNN) to predict power. Preliminary results after a total of 42 runs show that depending on the actually used regression algorithm correlation coefficients between 0.75 and 0.99 and a mean absolute error between 1.5 and 21.8 Watts could be achieved. Although these results appear promising, the number of participants and test runs must be increased significantly in order to arrive at valid conclusions.**

Keywords–Smart textile; Smart socks; Running; Internal power.

I. INTRODUCTION

Together with measuring training volume, determining intensity is one of the most important measures to quantify physical stress or training load on athletes [1] which can subsequently be used to prescribe and adapt training [2] as well as make predictions [3]. While in the past heart rate or velocity have been mainly used to gauge intensity, we can nowadays observe an increased use of power meters in distance running [4]. They are superior to heart-rate measurements since they react instantly and are not prone to cardiac drift, and they are better than deriving the intensity from the velocity because changing external conditions such as wind and hills can be taken into account [5].

Commercially available power meters, such as Stryd [6] or RunScribe [7] are based on inertial measurements units and designed as small footpods, which are mounted directly on the shoe. With the increasing popularity of smart textiles in sports, such as Sensoria's smart socks [8] or Hexoskin's smart garments [9], it seems promising to investigate whether it is basically possible to estimate power in walking and running with a smart sock equipped with textile pressure sensors [10]. Incorporating power measurement into the socks would make the usage of a separate power meter obsolete.

The remainder of this paper is structured as follows. In Section 2 we review the related work, in Section 3 we describe the study design, then we continue with a discussion of the results in Section 4, and conclude with Section 5, in which we briefly summarize our findings and discuss possible future work.

II. RELATED WORK

Because power is defined as the derivative of work, it is sufficient for our discussion to first deal with the determination of work while walking or running. Cavagna [11] measures the external work by means of a force plate to record the horizontal and vertical components of the resultant force applied by the body to the ground and air. Forward and vertical velocities are then calculated by integrating the force signals, which allows determining the kinetic energy in forward and upward directions, as well as the potential energy caused by the vertical displacement of the center of mass. However, as this only gives external work, i.e., it does not take into account the energy needed to swing the legs and arms, internal energy is determined by means of a cinematographic analysis [12] which calculates the kinetic and potential energy of the body segments relative to the center of mass.

Since this is difficult to perform outside a controlled laboratory environment, van Dijk and van Megen [5] assume the energy expenditure of running (Cr) which is based on indirect calorimetry with 0.98 J/kg/m and add the energy to overcome the air resistance, as well as the influence of uphill and downhill running. Of course, assuming a fixed Cr value does not allow for different running surfaces [13] or running economy, nor does it consider walking where the energy cost varies as a function of velocity. Contemporary power meters for running therefore combine both approaches: they estimate external power with accelerometers mounted on the subject and then assume a gross metabolic efficiency of around 25% to map mechanical energy to metabolic energy [14].

Oks et al. [15] show that ground contact time can be adequately measured with a smart sock system with piezo-resistive knitted structures. One sock has six pressure sensors to gather the data. Validation was performed for walking, race-walking and running with an optical system as well as a force plate. Petz et al. [10] show that a smart sock system with three piezo-resistive pressure sensors can be used to detect steps and to make reasonable statements about the subject's activity. Smart sock systems are also used for gait analysis and foot pressure control for human locomotion and to detect excessive pronation and supination [16][17]. Again, the system consists of piezo-resistive sensors and conductive lines knitted in. Foot strike patterns are important characteristics in human locomotion. The strike types – heel strike, mid foot and fore foot strike [18][19] – can be classified with a smart socks system [20].

Since smart socks with pressure sensors have been previously successfully used to detect various gait-related parameters and to the best of our knowledge there are no studies trying to predict internal power with smart socks, the aim of this study is to investigate, whether it is possible to estimate internal power with a smart textile.

III. METHODS

In this section we describe how we gathered the training data from numerous runs on a treadmill and show how we processed the data so that it could be fed into the machine learning suite to derive regression algorithms.

A. *Participants*

Four recreational runners (two male, two female) took part in our study. The runners' age is between 18 and 28 (average age: 26.5, SD=0.5) and their weekly running volume is between 10 and 20 kilometers. All of them are heel-strikers. In total, 42 test runs have been gathered so far. The study is still work in progress and therefore the number of participants and test runs is quite small.

B. *Study design*

Participants had to wear a pair of smart socks [10] (Figure 1), as well as a Stryd sensor together with a Garmin Fenix 3 sports watch to record the power data from the Stryd power meter (Figure 2). They were then instructed to walk or run 100 meters on a treadmill with velocities of 4 km/h, 6 km/h, 8 km/h, and 10 km/h, each velocity with different gradients (0, 4, 6, and 8 percent).

For each run, we measured and recorded the power output with a Stryd sensor, as well as the sensor data from the smart sock system, which in addition to the pressure measurements also contains rotation and acceleration, which, however, are not yet used in the analysis. Using various regression algorithms, we then predicted the power measurement given by Stryd with sensor data gathered with the smart sock. We used the Stryd sensor instead of a test setup with a force plate such as in [11][12], or a metabolic cart because our aim is simply to find out whether a correlation between pressure measurements from the socks and internal power can be found and according

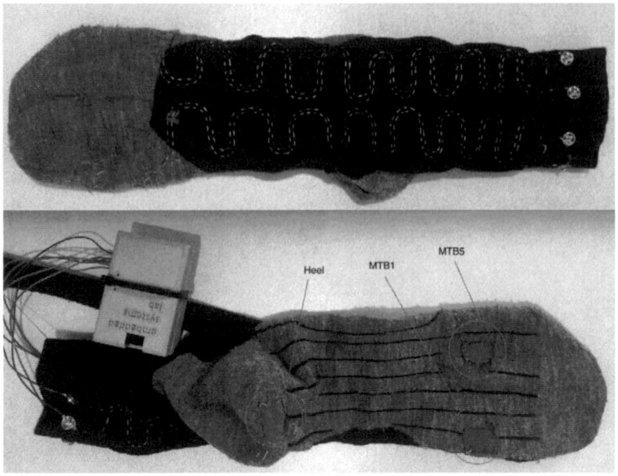

Figure 1. Smart socks with sensors and data acquisition unit provide the independent variables for the analysis.

to Cerezuela-Espejo et al. [4] there is a close relation between power output and VO2.

Figure 2. The dependent variable power output is measured with the Stryd sensor and recorded on a Garmin watch.

C. *Devices*

Measurements were performed on a Technogym MYRUN treadmill. Our smart socks developed by Petz et al. [10] (see Figure 1) have three piezo-resistive sensors placed according to the foot strike pattern, six conductive lines and a data acquisition unit. One sensor (referred to as MTB1) is placed in the left front, one sensor (MTB5) is in the right front and the third sensor (Heel) is located in the heel part of the sock. The sensors are sampled at a rate of 160 Hz and the recorded data is transferred to an Android smartphone and stored as a CSV file.

The Stryd power meter (firmware version 2.0.2) is connected to a Garmin Fenix 3 sports watch (firmware version 5.40) that stores power data and cadence. The Garmin watch stores data in the .fit file format and uploads the recordings to the Garmin Connect website. We use the FIT File Explorer [21], version 2.3, to retrieve the data from the .fit file.

D. Data Processing

After collecting the smart sock data from the smartphone and power data as well as cadence from the .fit file, we calculate an arithmetic mean over the measured sensor values to generate features for the regression analyses (Figure 3).

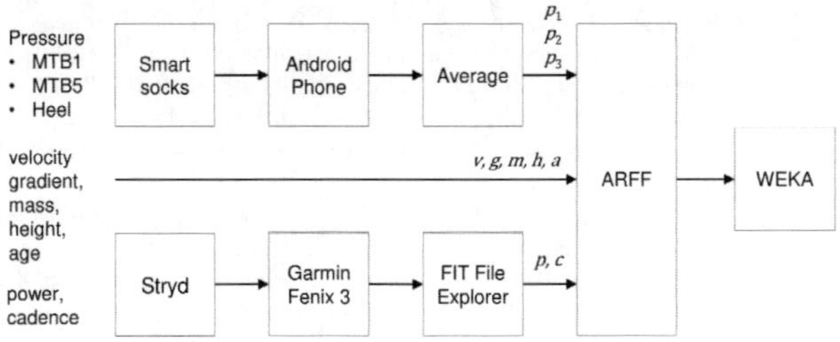

Figure 3. Devices and data processing.

Since we use the WEKA machine learning suite [22], the features are stored in the Attribute Relation File Format (ARFF). To process the data, ten input variables have been considered from the smart socks, and two input variables from the Garmin watch along with the output from Stryd. These are averages of the three sensor pressure sensors (MTB1 (p_1), MTB5 (p_2), heel (p_3), cadence (c) and power (p). Additionally, velocity (v) of the run, gradient (g), and related user information such as age (a), height (h), and mass (m) are also recorded. The units of measurements are shown in the ARFF file which looks as follows:

```
@relation smartsocks
@attribute velocity numeric % v  km/h
@attribute mass numeric     % m  kg
@attribute height numeric   % h  cm
@attribute age numeric      % a  years
@attribute aveMTB1 numeric  % p1 mV
@attribute aveMTB5 numeric  % p2 mV
@attribute aveHeel numeric  % p3 mV
@attribute cadence numeric  % c  steps/min
@attribute gradient numeric % g  %%
@attribute watts numeric    % p  Watt

@data
4 80 1.75 27 2379 2369 2438 44 0 61
6 53 1.63 27 2980 2365 3006 63 0 105
% ...
```

We then tried different combinations of independent variables and different regression algorithms to find out which combination performed best. Since the number of instances in our data set is yet quite small and we want models that are computationally inexpensive, we go for simple algorithms such as linear regression, decision trees with regressions (M5P), random forest and K-nearest neighbours. In WEKA, we used the default settings for each regression algorithm, as well as tenfold cross-validation.

IV. Results and Discussion

Since most runners nowadays routinely wear a GPS-enabled device such as a smart phone or sports watch, we first try to define a baseline by determining how well we can estimate power based on velocity, gradient, and mass. Hence, we can find out whether estimating power with the smart sock offers any added value at all. Even a simple linear regression with v, g, and m as independent variables ($p = 23.220v - 0.0568m - 0.3489g - 24.2518$) is able to approximate the Stryd data quite well (see Tables I and II for correlation coefficients and mean absolute errors).

Next, we want to predict the power output based solely on the signals coming from the pressure sensors. The linear regression model $p = -0.0418p_1 - 0.0385p_2 + 0.0915p_3 + 35.819$ ($r = 0.74$) can be minimally improved by additionally considering mass which gives $p = 1.8752m - 0.0468p_1 - 0.0356p_2 + 0.1679p_3 - 290.0082$ ($r = 0.75$).

Since the cost of locomotion and therefore power is quite different for walking and running [23], with a U-shaped curve and a distinct minimum at the preferred walking speed of approx. 1.3 $\mathrm{m\,s^{-1}}$, while it remains constant across running speeds, non-linear regression-algorithms perform better. Weka's M5P approximates a continuous function by building a decision tree where each leaf has a linear regression model; with p_1, p_2, p_3 as independent variables, the regression coefficient r is 0.88.

Random forest and KNN achieve even better results (see Tables I and II). However, both methods are not able to extrapolate and therefore – with our limited data set – will perform poorly for power data outside of 61 to 206 Watts.

TABLE I. Correlation coefficients.

Independent variables	*Linear regression*	*M5P*	*Random forest*	*KNN*
v, g, m	0.98	0.99	0.99	0.99
p_1, p_2, p_3	0.74	0.88	0.95	0.98
p_1, p_2, p_3, m	0.75	0.88	0.95	0.98
c	0.98	0.99	0.99	0.99
p_1, p_2, p_3, m, c	0.98	0.99	0.99	0.99

Since steps can be easily detected and derived from either acceleration or pressure signals which is done in [10], we could determine cadence c and estimate the power output with $p = 0.0323m + 2.9232c$ ($r = 0.98$). Currently, we use cadence data from Stryd. Combining c with the pressure readings does not improve the result ($p = -0.6921m + 0.0143p_2 - 0.0437p_3 + 3.2741c + 38.0002$, $r = 0.98$), which means that we can predict Stryd's power data with cadence and mass alone quite well.

TABLE II. Mean absolute errors.

Independent variables	*Linear regression*	*M5P*	*Random forest*	*KNN*
v, g, m	7.32	3.93	2.13	3.86
p_1, p_2, p_3	22.76	15.91	10.43	5.31
p_1, p_2, p_3, m	23.79	16.84	10.94	5.31
c	7.90	4.25	2.16	1.53
p_1, p_2, p_3, m, c	10.30	5.81	4.15	3.07

However, this is certainly only possible when running on a treadmill without external influences, such as headwind or tailwind and the uniform nature of the running surface. Deriving VO2 and hence power from step-rate alone is well known and, e.g., used in pedometers [24].

V. Conclusion and Future Work

In this paper, we described how to estimate internal power using smart socks equipped with three piezo-resistive pressure sensors.

Under ideal conditions on a treadmill without any headwind or tailwind and on a uniform running surface, using the pressure sensors alone does not perform better than basing the estimation on velocity and gradient or cadence. However, given the right regression algorithm, the estimation is also not much worse which means that it can provide power data without GPS, which would be the case under dense foliage or indoors.

Basing the estimation on cadence, which can be derived from the pressure sensors, gives – at least under ideal conditions – a better result than using the average pressure data. However, when running on sand or grass or with headwind, the assumption of approx. 0.98 J/kg/m is not valid anymore and using pressure data might be applicable.

Since the preliminary results seem promising, we plan to increase the number of participants, and perform more runs at different velocities and gradients as well as take different running surfaces such as sand or grass into account.

References

[1] L. K. Wallace, K. M. Slattery, and A. J. Coutts, "A comparison of methods for quantifying training load: relationships between modelled and actual training responses," *European journal of applied physiology*, vol. 114, pp. 11–20, 2014.

[2] M. F. Stephen Mcgregor, Ed., *The Runner's Edge: High-tech Training for Peak Performance*. Human Kinetics Publishers, Oct. 2009, ISBN: 0736081151.

[3] R. Morton, J. Fitz-Clarke, and E. Banister, "Modeling human performance in running," *Journal of applied physiology (Bethesda, Md. : 1985)*, vol. 69, pp. 1171–1177, 10 1990.

[4] V. Cerezuela Espejo, A. Belmonte, J. Courel Ibáñez, E. Conesa-Ros, R. Mora-Rodriguez, and J. Pallarés, "Are we ready to measure running power? repeatability and concurrent validity of five commercial technologies," *European Journal of Sport Science*, pp. 1–22, 03 2020.

[5] H. Van Dijk and R. Van Megen, Eds., *The Secret of Running : Maximum Performance Gains Through Effective Power Metering and Training*. Meyer Meyer Sport (UK) Ltd, May 2017, ISBN: 1782551093.

[6] "Stryd," 2020, URL: https://www.stryd.com/ [accessed: 2020-09-01].

[7] "RunScribe," 2020, URL: https://runscribe.com/ [accessed: 2020-09-01].

[8] "Sensoria," 2020, URL: https://www.sensoriafitness.com/ [accessed: 2020-09-01].

[9] "Hexoskin," 2020, URL: https://www.hexoskin.com/ [accessed: 2020-09-01].

[10] P. Petz, F. Eibensteiner, and J. Langer, "Performance evaluation of conductive textiles for movement pattern recognition in smart socks," in *2019 International Conference on Information and Digital Technologies (IDT)*, 2019, pp. 370–375.

[11] G. A. Cavagna, "Force platforms as ergometers," *Journal of Applied Physiology*, vol. 39, pp. 174–179, July 1975.

[12] P. Willems, G. Cavagna, and N. Heglund, "External, internal and total work in human locomotion," *The Journal of experimental biology*, vol. 198, pp. 379–393, 03 1995.

[13] H. C. Pinnington and B. Dawson, "The energy cost of running on grass compared to soft dry beach sand," *Journal of Science and Medicine in Sport*, vol. 4, no. 4, pp. 416 – 430, 2001.

[14] "How to Lead the Pack: Running Power Meters & Quality Data," 2017, URL: https://blog.stryd.com/2017/12/07/how-to-lead-the-pack-running-power-meters-quality-data/ [accessed: 2020-09-01].

[15] A. Oks, A. Katashev, E. Bernans, and V. Abolins, "A Comparison of the Accuracy of the Smart sock System to Force Platform and Optical System for Measurement of Temporal Parameters of Locomotion," *IOP Conference Series: Materials Science and Engineering*, vol. 254, pp. 1 – 6, 2017.

[16] A. Oks, A. Katashev, M. Zadinans, M. Rancans, and J. Litvak, "Development of Smart Sock System for Gate Analysis and Foot Pressure Control," in *XIV Mediterranean Conference on Medical and Biological Engineering and Computing 2016*. Springer International Publishing, 2013, pp. 472–475.

[17] P. Eizentals, A. Katashev, A. Okss, Z. Pavare, and D. Balcuna, "Detection of excessive pronation and supination for walking and running gait with smart socks," in *World Congress on Medical Physics and Biomedical Engineering 2018*, L. Lhotska, L. Sukupova, I. Lacković, and G. S. Ibbott, Eds. Singapore: Springer Singapore, 2019, pp. 603–607.

[18] P. R. Cavanagh and M. A. Lafortune, "Ground reaction forces in distance running," *Journal of biomechanics*, vol. 13, no. 5, p. 397—406, 1980. [Online]. Available: https://doi.org/10.1016/0021-9290(80)90033-0

[19] A. Ogueta-Alday, J. Rodriguez-Marroyo, and J. Garcia-Lopez, "Rearfoot striking runners are more economical than midfoot strikers," *Medicine & Science in Sports & Exercise*, vol. 46, pp. 580–585, 03 2014.

[20] A. Oks, A. Katashev, E. Bernans, and V. Abolins, "Smart socks system as an equipment to analyze temporal parameters of human gait and running," *Environment. Technologies. Resources. Proceedings of the International Scientific and Practical Conference*, vol. 3, no. 0, pp. 238–241, 2017.

[21] "FIT File Explorer," 2020, URL: https://apps.apple.com/us/app/fit-file-explorer/id1244431640?mt=12 [accessed: 2020-09-01].

[22] I. H. Witten, E. Frank, M. A. Hall, and C. J. Pal, *Data Mining, Fourth Edition: Practical Machine Learning Tools and Techniques*, 4th ed. San Francisco, CA, USA: Morgan Kaufmann Publishers Inc., 2016.

[23] D. Farris and G. Sawicki, "The mechanics and energetics of human walking and running: A joint level perspective," *Journal of the Royal Society, Interface / the Royal Society*, vol. 9, pp. 110–118, 05 2011.

[24] A. Kuo, "The six determinants of gait and the inverted pendulum analogy: A dynamic walking perspective," *Human movement science*, vol. 26, pp. 617–656, 09 2007.

Robot Cognition in Disassembly

Advanced Information Processing for an Adaptive Dismantling Ecosystem

Hendrik Poschmann
Institute of Production Technology
Ostfalia University of Applied Sciences
Wolfenbuettel, Germany
email: he.poschmann@ostfalia.de

Holger Brüggemann
Institute of Production Technology
Ostfalia University of Applied Sciences
Wolfenbuettel, Germany
email: holger.brueggemann@ostfalia.de

Daniel Goldmann
Institute of Mineral and Waste Processing, Waste Disposal and Geomechanics
Clausthal University of Technology
Clausthal-Zellerfeld, Germany
email: daniel.goldmann@tu-clausthal.de

***Abstract*—Disassembly is an elementary process step for efficient recycling. In order to improve disassembly operations, the implementation of digitalization technologies and advanced robotic systems is investigated in this paper. The authors propose an agent-based robotic system which is capable of classifying components in a hierarchical structure for an optimized determination of an ecologically and economically feasible level of disassembly. By utilizing a machine-learning classifier, an adaptive system is facilitated being able to react to the dynamic change of conditions in the reverse supply chain. Holistic information management processes are the foundation of the advanced disassembly system. It is shown that the application of cognitive robotics fosters the progression towards an advanced circular economy by being able to reliably classify End-of-Life options autonomously.**

Keywords—disassembly; recycling 4.0; robotics; decision making; machine-learning.

I. INTRODUCTION

Resource scarcity and the necessity of limiting emissions in order to tackle the climate change issue are hard constraints in today's manufacturing industries. Following the Sustainable Development Goals (SDGs) set by the United Nations, responsible dealing with rare materials and elaborate products becomes a strategically important objective for every enterprise [1]. Reuse, remanufacturing and recycling as End-of-Life (EoL) options seem to be mandatory consequences of this development.

However, the current situation with EoL products often shows the inability to deal with them appropriately in terms of economic efficiency and technical dexterity. A key point in all possible EoL treatment paths is the process of disassembly. Disassembly can be understood as the entirety of actions required to separate manufactured products to their modules, components or resource constituents [2]. Advanced robotic systems can provide an automation solution so that high quality component output for reuse, remanufacturing or high grade material recycling can be achieved while reducing the planning complexity for the companies and saving costs due to decreasing process time. Admittedly, the implementation of a robotic system often requires a great effort in programming for each variant which needs to be dismantled. In order to overcome this impetus, advanced cognitive robotic systems are capable of perceiving their environment through camera and sensor technologies and make decisions based on available data autonomously. The field of cognitive robotics embodies the study of knowledge representation and reasoning problems in dynamic and incompletely known environments by a robotic agent [3]. In the *Recycling 4.0* project, the authors develop an informationally integrated disassembly system by employing the characteristics of cognitive robotics to fulfil highly complex tasks, such as the disassembly of different (and partly unknown) products by the example of electric vehicle battery systems in varying product conditions.

This paper proposes an adaptive system-approach for robotic disassembly in dynamic environments. Through connecting the disassembly system to a superordinate, cloud-based information system [4], the robot is able to stream real-time information for each process step, taking different requirements of individual supply chain actors into account while constantly updating available data. A machine-learning empowered decision making process is established and presented to assist in making improved decisions for the disassembly grade in respect to economic, ecologic and social dimensions of the available EoL-options. In contrast to existing disassembly systems, such as those of Jungbluth et al. [5] and Vongbunyong et al. [6], the system actively contributes to the cloud information system and receives live data updates from various sources and system participants, making it an ecosystem adaptable to changes in the general market situation of the targeted product. Furthermore, the system is able to generalize knowledge from existing product structures so that it is able to work on previously unknown products. By scanning the product with its vision system, the robot is also able to rate the visual condition of the product as first-time hands-on experience in the recycling process-chain.

The paper is structured as follows: In Section 2, the initial problem of robotic disassembly automation is described and the research question is formulated. Section 3 introduces the concept of the agent based system and explains the methods proposed to answer the question based on a standardized product structure model and a feature based machine learning classifier. An evaluation of this classifier using generic product data is described in Section 4. A conclusion on the results and its contribution to disassembly as well as an outlook to future research within this project is given in Section 5.

II. Problem Statement

Disassembly operations usually include the largest number of employees and the highest complexity regarding the amount of possible variants in all EoL-treatments, making automation approaches difficult to establish in most of the contemplable use-cases. Advantages of human workforce, such as accurate perception, craftsmanship and intelligent behaviour are needed in disassembly scenarios, whereby time effort, cost and volatile quality of manual processes have to be overcome. In order to keep the required investment for disassembly automation feasible in terms of an overall benefit in cost compared to the fully-manual process, a hybrid disassembly scenario with Human Robot Collaboration (HRC) should be realized. Another benefit of HRC is the capability of implementing a correction functionality for the robotic agent in favour of enabling learning behaviour as a fail-safe strategy for the robot cognition processing.

The general requirements of a cognitive robotic disassembly system are [7]:

- Disassembly sequence planning and optimization
- Determination of the level of disassembly (technical possibility vs. economic feasibility)
- Capability of dealing with high numbers of product and product state variants
- Including market information regarding cores, resource data and component reselling
- Including life-cycle information and product data

The problem of profitability and optimal decisions exists mostly due to a lack of information spanning various participants in the EoL-value-chain. These optimal decisions cannot be made due to missing conspectus of all relevant data.

In order to locate this work within the canon of disassembly planning research, the focus lies more on disassembly decision making (in respect to multiple criteria) than the actual sequence planning depending on the product model. Feng et al. [8] presented a stage-wise decision making process on each hierarchy level, determining the EoL-option at the last stage of the process, whereas this decision marks the initial input of the proposed system in this work. Focusing directly on a robotic disassembly, Li et al. [9] presented a multi-criteria assessment with a score-system which is difficult to maintain in the dynamic environment of a circular economy with many different value-streams and stakeholders. The consideration of varying component quality and operational cost is introduced by Tian et al. [10], taking the randomness and fuzziness of real processes into account. However, such a quantified, designated assessment is often not possible due to a lack of information. Furthermore, quality level ratings would be different for various purposes depending on the market rather than technical process experience.

At this point, the *Recycling 4.0* model introduces a superordinate information marketplace which is connected to the disassembly system. All relevant data for optimized decision making can then be obtained from the information marketplace and from the robotic system's vision unit. However, anticipation from existing rules is not possible, because market principles of a full-scale reverse supply chain cannot yet be foreseen. Therefore, dynamic models which take various types of data from different sources into account need to be utilized. These forms of disassembly grade decision systems have not been implemented before. To gain a wider conspectus of the topic, the authors already conducted an analysis of a vast number of robotic disassembly automation examples which can be found in [11].

The proposed system must be able to constantly respond to changes and also show evolutionary behaviour in terms of how the adaption is performed (second-order adaption). An important foundation for the depicted approach is the information exchangeability and cross-system interoperability within the *Recycling 4.0* ecosystem. Summarized, the challenges of automated disassembly can be seen as a problem of information management along the EoL process-chain. The addressed research question of this paper therefore aims at this very point:

How can the available supply chain information, lifecycle-knowledge and sensory information be used in the disassembly process in order to benefit the overall recycling efficiency?

III. Concept and Methods

The developed concept of the robotic disassembly system consists of three different agents, each fulfilling specific requirements of the proposed tasks (Fig. 1). As an external junction, an information marketplace is established, serving as a central information node for all participants of the reverse supply chain. A presumption of the developed concept of this paper is that semantic and structural information required for the robot cognition process can be obtained from this marketplace [4].

The main module of the system is the *Robot Cognition Processor* (RCP), responsible for information synthesis and decision making regarding the step-wise decision of disassembling the product structure up to the optimized grade by economic, ecological and social considerations at the time of disassembly. The required sensory information is gathered by the *System Perception Unit* (SPU). The module captures the target object with a specially designed 3D-camera in order to identify, detect (localize) and rate the part pertained. This agent's contribution to the RCP process is an optical condition diagnosis factor which is used in addition to the product's internally assigned health factor. Finally, the *Disassembly Execution Unit* (DEU) is formed by the operative robotic system (robot arm and tooling), as well as an affiliated execution monitoring system. Based on the disassembly command of the RCP, the DEU is responsible for path planning, tooling and actual disassembly action execution. An HRC pairing of the robot and a human worker enables the

DEU to accomplish complex tasks and take instructional input of the human worker, in the case of the autonomous path planner failing to achieve its objective.

The core process of the RCP is the handling and processing of relevant information in order to make a decision compliant to economic, ecological and social objectives. After an initial decision about the general feasibility of core disassembly, the disassembly request for the target part is forwarded to the RCP. Available product data and technical documentation as well as a standardized set of relevant information are gathered from the superordinate information system. Product states from the optical assessment via the SPU are merged with the gathered information into a single attributed dataframe per object, forming a set of all available data for the target product or component. This augmented information set is transferred back to the cloud information system to make predictions about future batches of related products possible.

The next step in the RCP process is a machine-learning sub-process of step-by-step decision making along the hierarchical structure of the product. By the time of individual disassembly decision for each component, three possible classifications are taken into account (Fig. 2). Reuse and remanufacturing are clustered in one category, as they both strive for functional integrity and component resale. The

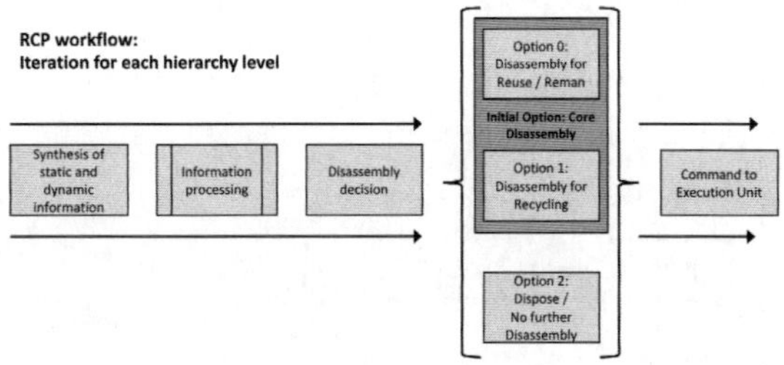

Figure 1. RCP workflow process

second option is disassembly for improved material recycling. The third option is not to disassemble any further, thereby determining the final grade of disassembly. If at any point, the system is not able to make an acceptable or technically feasible decision, human decision making and manual teaching in a possible interaction phase may give the missing input to the system, which is then learned for future appliance and adaption, improving the possible system autonomy with an increasing number of iterations and variants. The desired disassembly sequence is thereby automatically determined by the order of parts and components eligible for profitable disassembly. Physical disassembly commands are then forwarded to the DEU for path planning and execution.

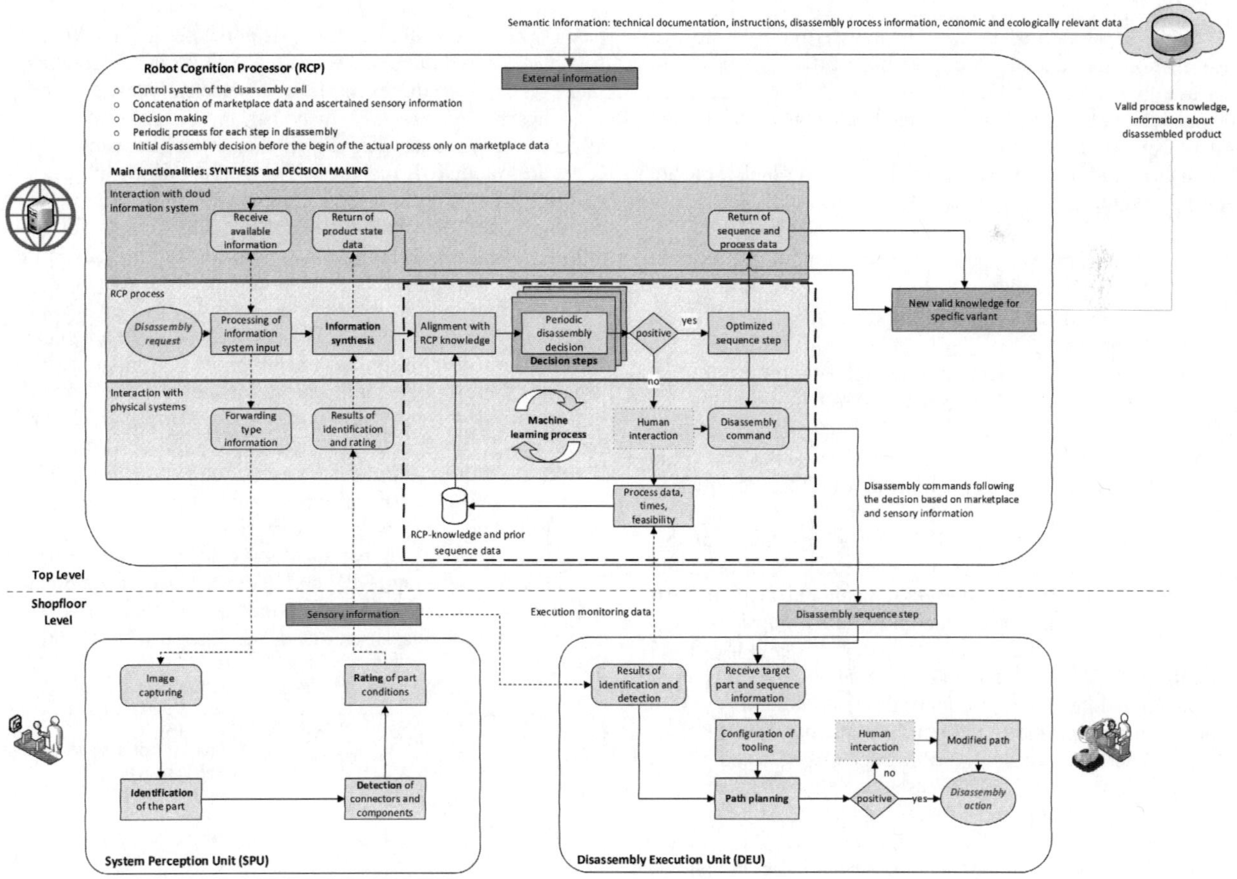

Figure 2. System concept of the agent-based disassembly system

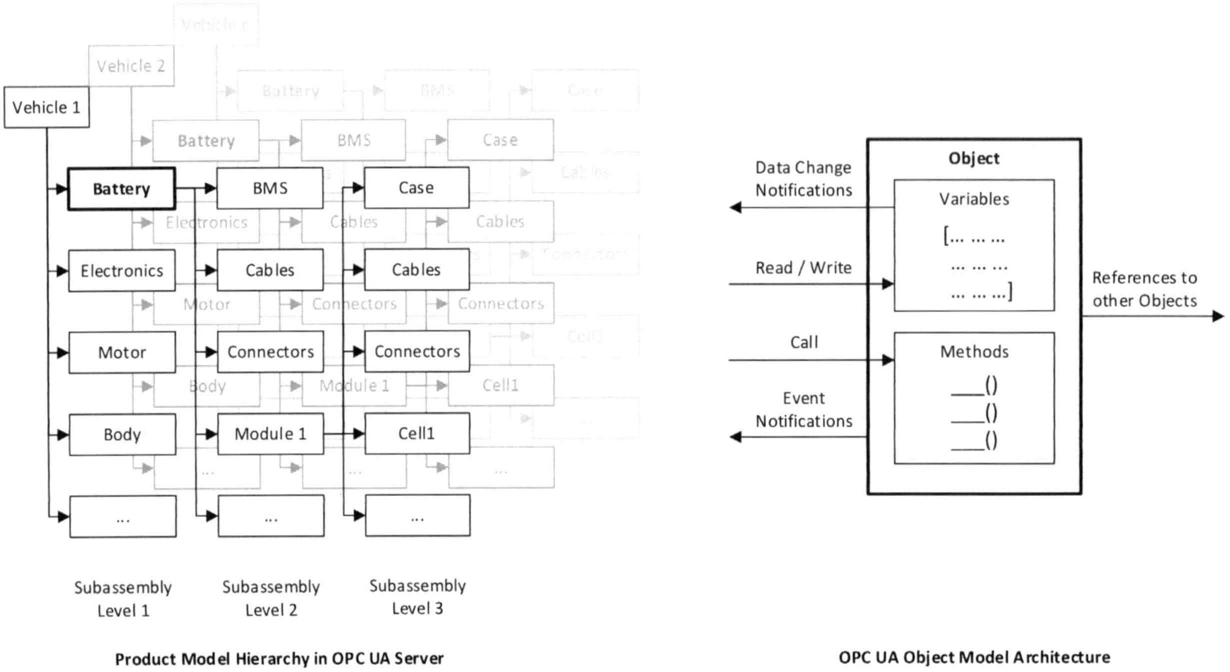

Figure 3. OPC UA product model hierarchy and object architecture

Sequence and process data is transferred back to the information marketplace for possible utilization in future disassembly targets of the same type or in other locations respectively other disassembly facilities connected to the *Recycling 4.0* framework.

In order to achieve the functionality as described, there are several preliminaries which have to be met:

- Accessible data structure for each hierarchy level of the target product
- Standardized data format to ensure cross-system interoperability
- Sufficient amount of training data based on real decisions of current processes for initial training

One elementary idea of the system is to use data processing capacities most efficiently at the information sources and sinks (edge computing principle). Bottlenecks in data transfer can be avoided that way and the available capacity is solely used for useful and requested information transfer. All agents in this configuration are independent parts of the system which can act inherently autonomously.

In order to align the dynamic data of the SPU to the model data from the information marketplace, a common framework of the digital model is required for interoperability. As a solution to this problem, the platform-independent interface OPC Unified Architecture (OPC UA) was selected in the project *Recycling 4.0*. The communication between the stakeholders can either take place as publisher/subscriber or client/server model [12]. The structure of the OPC UA model allows the alignment of external and sensory data in a single attributed dataframe per object node of each hierarchy level (see Fig. 3). Communication and data transfer in the OPC UA framework rely on the quality of the digital model deposited. In *Recycling 4.0*, the example of an electric vehicle battery was chosen. The structure of the car, the battery system and all relevant sub-assemblies, components and connectors are therefore modelled on the OPC server. Each object is represented by a node in the hierarchy tree.

The cognition module uses the available data for AI-enforced decision making. Decisions considering advanced circular economy models are too complex and dynamic for standard classification algorithms (such as decision trees or linear regression models). Up to the present, such connected information systems as described above do not exist in practice, therefore research cannot deliver the mechanisms and rules those systems would follow. However, Neural Networks (NN) as universal function approximators [13] deliver valuable output in dynamic and highly complex systems, being able to deal with manifold relations in wide, non-linear feature-maps. The approach presented in this paper is based on generic battery data of three different battery types (small BEV, mid-range BEV and PHEV). The composition of material rates and weight was defined according to [14]. The features used for classification in the RCP can be found in Table 1.

TABLE I. TABLE OF INPUT FEATURES

Feature	Symbol	Description
Type	Pr_V	Component type assigned to node (0=functional part, 1=connector, 2=case part, 3=wire, 4=board)
Hazmat	Pr_{Hz}	Containing hazardous materials, Boolean
ProductionDate	T_{Prod}	Date of Production

functionalIntegrity	Pr_{FI}	Potential operability / direct reuse possible, Boolean
PriceCore	C_{Core}	Purchasing price of the target core
CondDiagSOH	Pr_{SOH}	Diagnosed condition by state-of-health (SoH)
CondOpt	Pr_{Opt}	Optical diagnosis value after first step of disassembly
NodeIDASSEMBLY	Pr_{ID}	Individual node ID of the digital model
TDISASSEMBLY	T_{Diss}	Time for disassembly to next hierarchy level
PDISASSEMBLY	C_{Diss}	Specific cost of disassembly (hourly rates plus overhead surcharge)
ExpCompResale	I_{ComRes}	Expected profit from component resale
Demand	D_{Cmp}	Market demand indicator measured by time between last two orders of component
GradientPrice	∇_{Price}	Gradient of core price development from historical data
SocialAssessment	A_{Soc}	Social assessment factor of disassembly operation
EnvironmentalAssessment	A_{Env}	Environmental assessment factor of disassembly operation
WeightTHEORETICAL	Pr_{Wt}	Product weight according to technical documentation
WeightACTUAL	Pr_{Wa}	Actual product weight
MassConstituent (multiple)	$M_{Constituent}$	Material constituent shares
PriceConstituent (multiple)	$C_{Constituent}$	Material prices on a daily basis (given for each constituent)

In order to process the data for decision making in a NN, vectorization of the relevant datasets is required as input format. In pursuance of a highly concentrated information-set, a multistage pre-processing of the obtained node-data is performed in advance. In a first step, the material concentration and material price information can be condensed into a single value (I_{MatRec}), as both feature sets are only of relevance to a decision towards material recycling.

$$I_{MatRec}=\sum_{i=0}^{n_{Constituent}} Pr_{Wa} * M_{Constituent_i} * C_{Constituent_i} \quad (1)$$

The expected value of material-focused recycling is higher for a more advanced level of disassembly (L_{Diss}), as the achievable standard of purity can be increased by the removal of less important fractions, such as case components made of plastics or aluminium. Therefore, a factor is assigned to the expected material value considered to be recoverable, dependent on the disassembly grade.

$$I_{MatRec}(L_{Diss})=I_{MatRec} * \frac{e^{\frac{L_{Diss}}{L_{max}}}}{e} \quad (2)$$

The disassembly grade is determined by the initial node of the target object's structure at the point of disassembly request in respect to the maximum achievable level of disassembly (L_{max}). The factor delivers values between 36.7% and 100% of I_{MatRec} as an approximation to a realistic expectable return. Technologically achievable recycling rates of downstream processes are not taken into account at this point.

In the case of a decision for option 2, no further disassembly, the remaining components can be transferred to an established recycling process, such as the *JX* [15], *Umicore* or *LithoRec* battery recycling processes [16] for battery modules or other established material recovery processes for the remaining parts, such as case components, fasteners or electronics.

This first stage of pre-processing has reduced the number of input features per battery from 43 to 17.

The second stage of pre-processing reduces the number of input features by all features which are steady for all variants of the considered hierarchy level, such as hazmat factor and type in the case of the entire battery level. The node ID as structural model information is also removed, as it has no direct contribution to the disassembly decision. Moreover, features containing only redundant information are also excluded (e.g., T_{Diss}, as its information is already contained in the specific C_{Diss}). This step further simplifies the final processing by extracting irrelevant noise from the data affected. Finally, 13 features will be the input for the classification task.

A third and last step of pre-processing is the normalization of data.

$$\text{Feature}_{\text{Normalized}} = \frac{Feature\text{-}Feature_{min}}{Feature_{max}\text{-}Feature_{min}} \quad (3)$$

By normalization, the feature data is concentrated in a value range between 0 and 1, making the assessment of weights to each feature more balanced, as strong differences between value domains can be avoided.

On core disassembly level (entire battery), the decision has to be made before the actual disassembly process begins in order to avoid economic loss due to counterfactual process intake. Two modifications have to be made to apply the generalized cognition processor in this first step:

- The optical diagnosis factor cannot be applied as it has not yet been assessed for the target core concerned.
- The output category options zero and one both determine the target to be disassembled. The process is therefore pseudo-binary, as there is no difference to the first step in the process between the two categories. This modification is important for assessment of a validation data set as described in the final evaluation section.

For the evaluation of the first decision making approach of the RCP in this paper, the entire car is defined as the intake core eligible for a feasible disassembly. The decision making step in focus of this work is the disassembly decision on the level of the integral battery, which is investigated as a compliant three-class-classification problem. For the processing of the classification task, we consider a NN composed as a deep multilayer-perceptron. The network consists of six hidden layers, including two dropout-layers after the first and the second hidden layer (Fig. 4).

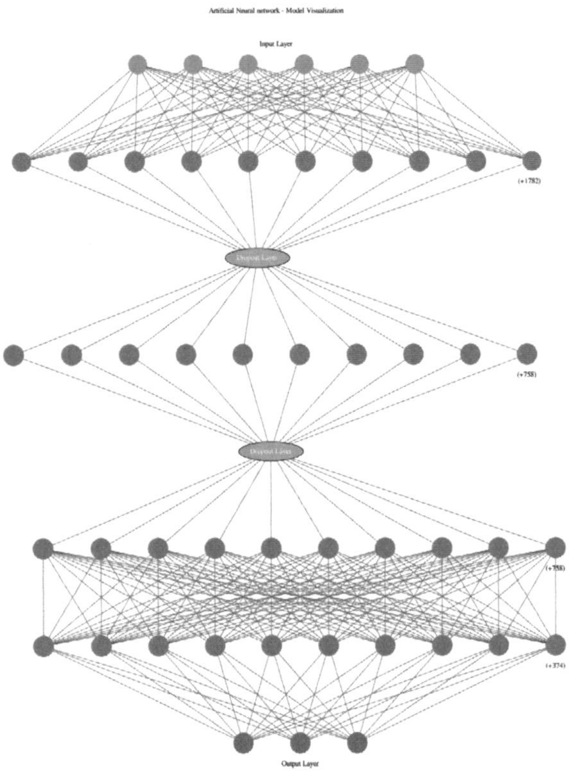

Figure 4. Schematic architecture of the Neural Network

The type of layers is "dense", as the network is fully connected. Apart from the output layer, whose activation function is "softmax" for classification purposes, the activation of the other layers is a rectified linear unit for better training behaviour [17]. The dropout rates are 0.2 for the first and 0.1 for the second dropout layer. As the Keras-API [18] is used for realization, the kernel initializer for initial weights is set to a randomized Gaussian with a standard deviation of 1.5. The model is compiled with Stochastic Gradient Descent (SGD) optimizer and categorical cross entropy as loss-function. The SGD optimizer is parameterized with a learning rate of 0.00015, a momentum of 0.3 and Nesterov accelerated in order to prevent early overfitting. All the hyperparameters were optimized following the general principles as described in [18] and [19] and fine-tuning the values manually in a narrow range around the given recommendations.

The model described is adaptable to new data, as the training of the model can be continued with each new sample available in the database for each level of disassembly hierarchy. Furthermore, each part that passes the process will deliver new aspects for improved training results even with constant architecture and hyper-parameters. In this way, the RCP is able to evolve in dynamic and constantly changing conditions of a global advanced circular economy.

IV. Evaluation

Based on the generic battery data from literature [14], 600 individual generic battery cores with random values in given ranges for each of the relevant features according to Table 1 were generated for training and validation. The supervised training on pre-classified data is performed with weighted categories according to the amount and deviation of the regarded classes in the available samplings. As displayed in Fig. 5, the correlation magnitude between the features apart from correlation in price related features is relatively low. The strongest impact on the pre-classified training set has the battery's state of health (SoH) and the expected component resale value. The fact of a widely minor to none correlation in a linear model assures the proposal of a non-linearly activated multilayer-perceptron for the classification task. However, the analysed pre-classified training set only provides the starting input for the NN, as the main adaption phase would begin with the implementation in real processes.

The training process itself is performed as a k-fold cross validation (k=9) [20] after an initial holdout of 10% of the samples for a final double-check. Each training cycle runs over 120 epochs with 490 samples for training and 60 samples for validation. To prevent bias, the two datasets were separated in advance randomly by the time of loading the dataframes. The batch size is 8 and the samples are shuffled each time in advance. For each of the k-fold iterations, the output for training loss and accuracy as well as for validation loss and accuracy are documented (Fig. 6). In most cases, the validation accuracy reaches its best value after approximately 60 epochs, albeit in a few runs, the validation accuracy starts converging to its maximum value only at the end of the training. Furthermore, considering also the loss functions, it is shown that a gradual overfitting only intensifies after a high number of epochs, especially if the general level of convergence was notably higher than in other runs. As a result, an accuracy of **77.96%** with a standard deviation of 3.91% could be achieved for a correct classification in the validation data. A prediction for the isolated holdout dataset could confirm this result with an accuracy of 76.67%. The baseline of the classifier's accuracy considered is 33.34% (3 options).

A closer look at the prediction matrices shows that most failures in classification occur due to a wrong decision between option 0, disassembly for part recovery, and option 1, disassembly for improved recycling. Considering that, the physical output of the disassembly process regarding the level

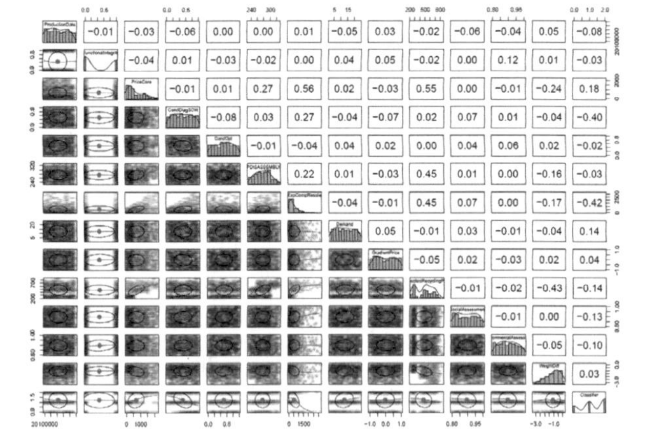

Figure 5. Correlation matrix of input features in training data

of disassembly determined by the decision processor would clearly have a higher success rate, as this physical process only has a binary option (whether to disassemble or not).

In conclusion, the evaluation of the training and validation sets shows that the network considered is capable of contributing to the determination of the product's disassembly grade with multiple EoL options by its ability to classify. The amount of data provided in this work can only be an initial input for the advanced disassembly system. In order to improve its decision quality in future operation phases, more data from real applications is required for the system to adapt to the dynamic and highly complex structure of the disassembly task. In operation, human decision should always be able to override the output of the system. These particular corrections are of great importance as they add valuable process knowledge to the future abilities of the RCP.

V. CONCLUSION

Disassembly is a key element of every complex products' recycling process. However, market principles of the reverse supply chain cannot be estimated holistically in advance, therefore a high level of adaptability is needed. Digitalization tools and advanced robotic systems can augment these processes as long as the necessary amount of information is provided. The integration of a cloud information system and a robot cognition processor enables the herein presented system to adaptively react to dynamic changes of the process environment by generalizing knowledge, both regarding the product as well as the process itself. Furthermore, the system actively contributes to the product knowledge by visual assessment and rating of individual parts.

Interoperability is also a key feature in the depicted structure, as the exchange of knowledge and information demands specific requirements for systems containing several, diverse types of agents. The use of an OPC UA framework for semantic interoperability also enables the transfer of concrete commands and sequence data of the robot in a standardized model back to the OPC server, enabling different stakeholders to exercise the acquired process knowledge on individual hardware. The authors developed an agent-based system, which is capable of integrating the disassembly operation into a holistic information flow management system. The available information can be utilized to predict and decide feasible levels of disassembly reliably and thereby increase the overall recycling process's efficiency. In-line, feature-based decision making by a machine-learning approach facilitates an adaptive EoL ecosystem at a critical point of the entire reverse supply chain.

The actual disassembly sequence is determined by the product's structure in the OPC model as well as the step-wise decision process of the RCP. Moreover, the classification of an assembly group or component strongly correlates with its position within the OPC structure, therefore these relational sequences have to be included in future approaches. Integrating sequential forecasting for individual features in order to predict future values can be considered by using recurrent networks, although the general economic system dynamics has to be taken into account. However, sequences and possible connections can become extraordinarily wide,

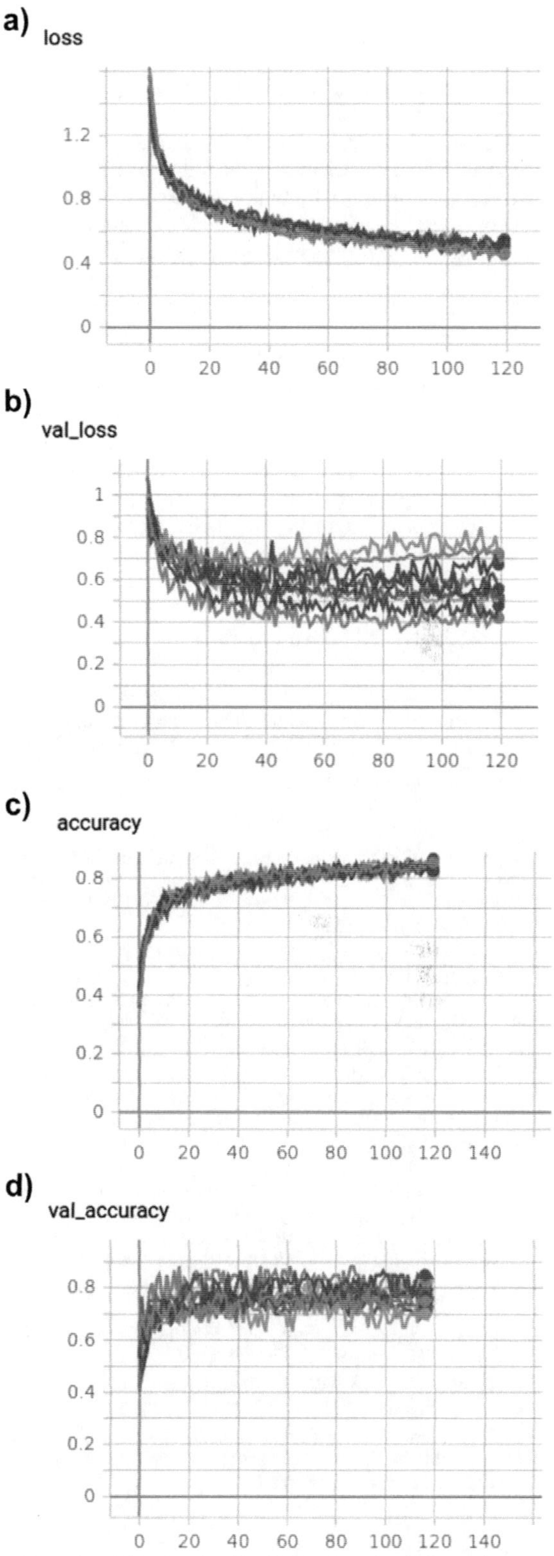

Figure 5. a) loss-function b) validation loss-function c) accuracy d) validation accuracy, all for k=9 on 120 training epochs

depending on the level of detail of the product and relevant data per component included. The integration and communication between the control architecture and the perception agent, especially regarding its rating capabilities as a system-immanent source of relevant information for the classification process as well as an optimization of the feature intake based on the experiences in the full-scale reverse supply chain model are subject to future research of this project. Moreover, the case of false-positive classification would in this concept lead to a disassembly at a potential loss for the disassembler. To overcome this, an optimization of the classification rate is necessary as a future improvement to the proposed architecture.

The benefits of the presented system for disassembly and therefore the circular economy process lie in the faster and more exact decisions based on predicted features available through the marketplace infrastructure. This enables the *Recycling 4.0* ecosystem to contribute to EoL processing feasibility no matter what the final option, as all system participants profit from the available information being processed into actual knowledge.

ACKNOWLEDGMENT

This paper evolved from the research project *Recycling 4.0* (Digitalization as the Key to the advanced circular economy using the Example of Innovative Vehicle Systems) which is funded by the European Regional Development Fund (EFRE | ZW 6- 85017703) and managed by the Project Management Agency NBank, Germany.

REFERENCES

[1] Resolution adopted by the General Assembly on 25 September 2015: A/RES/70/1, 2015. Accessed: Apr. 15 2019. [Online]. Available from: https://www.un.org/ga/search/view doc.asp?symbol=A/RES/70/1&Lang=E

[2] G. Seliger, "Assembly and Disassembly," in Handbook of Mechanical Engineering, H. Dubbel, K.-H. Grote, and J. Feldhusen, Eds., 23rd ed., Berlin, Heidelberg: Springer-Verlag Berlin Heidelberg, pp. 97-103, 2011.

[3] H. Levesque and G. Lakemeyer, "Chapter 23 Cognitive Robotics," in Foundations of Artificial Intelligence, Handbook of knowledge representation, F. van Harmelen, V. Lifschitz, and B. Porter, Eds., 1st ed., Amsterdam, Boston: Elsevier, pp. 869–886, 2008.

[4] C. Knieke, S. Lawrenz, M. Fröhling, D. Goldmann, and A. Rausch, "Predictive and Flexible Circular Economy Approaches for Highly Integrated Products and their Materials as Given in E-Mobility and ICT," MSF, vol. 959, pp. 22–31, 2019, doi: 10.4028/www.scientific.net/MSF.959.22.

[5] J. Jungbluth, W. Gerke, and P. Plapper, "An Intelligent Agent-Controlled and Robot-Based Disassembly Assistant," IOP Conf. Ser.: Mater. Sci. Eng., vol. 235, no. 1, p. 12005, 2017, doi: 10.1088/1757-899X/235/1/012005.

[6] S. Vongbunyong and W. H. Chen, Disassembly Automation. Cham: Springer International Publishing, 2015.

[7] H. Poschmann, H. Brüggemann, and D. Goldmann, "Robotized Disassembly as an Essential Driver for Digitalization in Future Recycling Processes," in Recycling und Rohstoffe, vol. 13, E. Thomé-Kozmiensky, O. Holm, B. Friedrich, and D. Goldmann, Eds., Nietwerder: Thomé-Kozmiensky Verlag GmbH, pp. 570–587, 2020.

[8] Y. Feng, Y. Gao, G. Tian, Z. Li, H. Hu, H. Zheng, "Flexible Process Planning and End-of-Life Decision-Making for Product Recovery Optimization Based on Hybrid Disassembly", IEEE Trans. Automat. Sci. Eng., vol. 16, no. 1, pp. 311-326, 2019, doi: 10.1109/TASE.2018.2840348.

[9] J. Li, M. Barwood, S. Rahimifard, "A multi-criteria assessment of robotic disassembly to support recycling and recovery", Resources, Conservation and Recycling (Elsevier), no. 140, pp. 158-165, 2019, doi: 10.1016/j.resconrec.2018.09.019.

[10] G. Tian, M. Zhou, P. Li, "Disassembly Sequence Planning Considering Fuzzy Component Quality and Varying Operational Cost", IEEE Trans. Automat. Sci. Eng., vol. 15, no. 2, pp. 748-760, 2018, doi: 10.1109/TASE.2017.2690802.

[11] H. Poschmann, H. Brüggemann, and D. Goldmann, "Disassembly 4.0: A Review on Using Robotics in Disassembly Tasks as a Way of Automation," Chemie Ingenieur Technik, vol. 92, no. 4, 2020, doi: 10.1002/cite.201900107.

[12] OPC Foundation, "OPC Unified Architecture. Part 1 : Overview and Concepts: Release 1.04," Accessed: Feb. 09 2020. [Online]. Available from: https://opcfoundation.org/ developer-tools/specifications-unified-architecture/part-1-overview-and-concepts/

[13] K. Hornik, M. Stinchcombe, and H. White, "Multilayer feedforward networks are universal approximators," Neural Networks, vol. 2, no. 5, pp. 359–366, 1989, doi: 10.1016/0893-6080(89)90020-8.

[14] J. Diekmann et al., "Ecological Recycling of Lithium-Ion Batteries from Electric Vehicles with Focus on Mechanical Processes," J. Electrochem. Soc., vol. 164, no. 1, A6184-A6191, 2017, doi: 10.1149/2.0271701jes.

[15] Y. Haga, K. Saito, and K. Hatano, "Waste Lithium-Ion Battery Recycling in JX Nippon Mining & Metals Corporation," in The Minerals, Metals & Materials Series, Materials Processing Fundamentals 2018, G. Lambotte, J. Lee, A. Allanore, and S. Wagstaff, Eds., Cham: Springer International Publishing, pp. 143–147, 2018.

[16] T. Elwert et al., "Current Developments and Challenges in the Recycling of Key Components of (Hybrid) Electric Vehicles," Recycling, vol. 1, no. 1, pp. 25–60, 2016, doi: 10.3390/recycling1010025.

[17] X. Glorot, A. Bordes, and Y. Bengio, "Deep Sparse Rectifier Neural Networks," Proceedings of the Fourteenth International Conference on Artificial Intelligence and Statistics, no. 15, pp. 315–323, 2011. Accessed: Apr. 2 2020. [Online]. Available from:http://proceedings.mlr.press/v15/glorot11a/glorot11a.pdf

[18] F. Chollet, Deep learning with Python. Shelter Island, NY: Manning Publications Co, 2018.

[19] A. V. Joshi, Machine Learning and Artificial Intelligence. Cham: Springer International Publishing, 2020.

[20] R. Kohavi, "A study of cross-validation and bootstrap for accuracy estimation and model selection," IJCAI'95: Proceedings of the 14th International Joint Conference on Artificial intelligence, no. 2, pp. 1137–1143, 1995. Accessed: Feb. 3 2019. [Online]. Available from: https://dl.acm.org/doi/10.5555/1643031.1643047

A Catalog-based Platform for Integrated Development of Simulation Models

Arthur Strasser[1], Peter Engel[2] and Mirco Schindler[3]
Institute for Software and Systems Engineering
Clausthal University of Technology
Clausthal, Germany
[1] Email: arthur.strasser@tu-clausthal.de
[2] Email: peter.engel@tu-clausthal.de
[3] Email: mirco.schindler@tu-clausthal.de

Wilhelm Tegethoff[4], Sebastian Lempp[5]
TLK-Thermo GmbH
Brunswick, Germany
[4] Email: w.tegethoff@tlk-thermo.com
[5] Email: s.lempp@tlk-thermo.com

Abstract—**In the automotive domain, it is common practice to develop a vehicle system with reusable components in order to reduce development time and costs. Several suppliers are responsible for the development of the components on behalf of one leading manufacturer, who ensures the integration of the components into the system. Thereby, models are used for simulation and test of components in advance. The manufacturers integrate these models of different suppliers into their system under development using its own simulation environment. However, in order to optimize the system in a simulation, manufacturers often rely on the supplier's expert knowledge regarding components property values. But often the models must also be modified to allow their execution in a target simulation environment. Thus, manufacturers have to cope with manual steps and a decreasing re-usability of models. To overcome these difficulties, significant additional effort and costs in every development iteration is involved. A platform for automating the optimization and version management of models is a promising approach, to reduce this development effort as a common basis of the development teams. Hence, we propose a component simulation-software catalog platform for a cooperatively organized development environment. It provides a domain specific language as a meta model for modeling catalogs consisting of model variants and versions. Furthermore, the platform provides automation services for model import and export, refactoring and simulation.**

Keywords–Metamodeling; Software Ecosystem; Software Platform; Architecture Description; Simulation.

I. INTRODUCTION

In the development of electrical vehicles, manufacturers apply model-based system simulations to a great extent. In general, a simulation can be used to approximate the behavior of a system before its construction in a real world environment. In the field of Heating, Ventilation and Air Conditioning (HVAC) system development, for example, the energy saving potential of different topologies can be estimated within a simulation before starting the construction in a further development step. The development of such a system simulation is cooperatively organized. The models are usually developed by suppliers using model-based simulation tools. Then, a system manufacturer integrates these models into his own simulation environment, such as, for example, as a so-called co-simulation. Thereby, these models are coupled in an execution environment, which is different than initially planned by the design of the models. Thus, each model must be configured in such a way that it can be executed in conjunction with all other models within a third party simulation environment. As a result, manufacturers have additional expenses for software licenses and training of software developers. In addition, the interfaces of models are often modified to enable their integration into the simulation environment. But this approach hampers the reuse of models in different system simulations.

The following scenario illustrates the cooperative development of a system simulation: In order to fulfill the requirements of a future electric vehicle generation, existing subsystems of a car are further developed. For example, a manufacturer must identify the potentials for energetic savings of the next generation HVAC system. The manufacturer selects suitable components from the supplier's component catalog to develop a HVAC system simulation. However, the interfaces of the selected models can be either in a standardized format (e.g., Functional Mock-up Unit [1]) or other third party formats as Matlab or Dymola. As depicted in Figure 1, a catalog consists of hierarchies of models, which are differentiated as series and variants. For example, there are mechanically or electrically driven air conditioning compressor series. A variant from a series represents a model of a specific compressor with its specific properties (e.g., refrigerant type, discharge volume, etc.). All models are managed in version managed repositories: The further development of a model is then represented as a model version. For example, the modification of the model interface or the fix of a model error can be stored in the repository. The description of the properties of series, variants and versions is hereafter referred to as metadata. Those metadata are managed in-house by the supplier. As a consequence, the models must be selected on the basis of their metadata and configured to be compatible with each other in order to achieve energy savings. Hence, the manufacturers have to cope with the following additional effort.

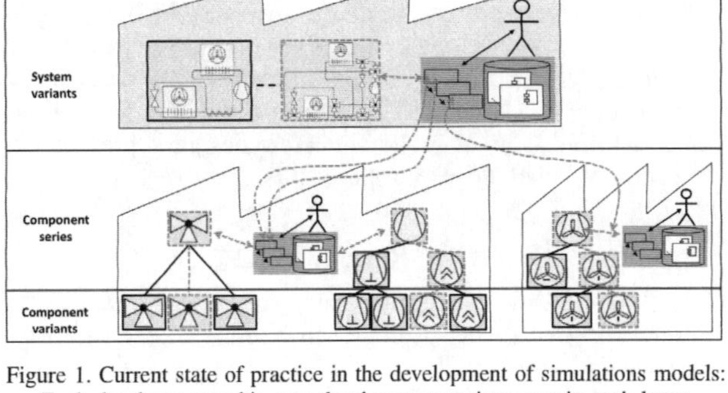

Figure 1. Current state of practice in the development of simulations models: Each developer uses his own development environment in each layer.

- Selection and configuration of a suitable model with regard to the individual requirements with the support of the supplier.
- To carry out the optimization and commissioning of FMUs, the manufacturer must implement ad hoc solutions that cannot be reused for the development of next-generation systems.
- Using ad hoc solutions to implement the model in the own simulation environment, which hampers the reuse of models.

In order to complete the development in a time and cost efficient manner and to ensure the reuse of models in a cooperative organized development, we propose a catalog based platform, which is described in greater detail in the following.

According to German Association of Engineers (VDI) guideline 2206 [2], a seamless tool support is necessary for a systematic system development. However, the current development practice is often not seamless, as seen for example in the development of customer-specific solutions used in the supplier's tool chain. Thus, the contribution of this paper is a proposal for a software-driven catalog platform that provides components for developers and users to support integrated development of simulation models in a systematic, cost and time-efficient way. To achieve these goals, the platform must fulfill the following targets:

- The platform must enable developers to describe metadata on the basis of a model's description language.
- The platform must enable developers to describe catalogs as compositions of components and systems.
- The platform must provide a versioning and refactoring services to increase the reusability of simulation models.
- The platform must provide model inversion techniques to ensure a maximum of usability for different development and simulation environments.
- The platform must provide services to facilitate model search, model commissioning and model changes on the basis of the catalog.

In the following, it is assumed that the exemplary models are based on the FMU format as one exemplary format for the catalog.

In Section II, the current research topics are discussed. To tackle the issues in the cooperative development, such as the HVAC systems, the concepts for the development of the catalog platform are proposed as infrastructure and as services in Section III. Afterwards, in Section IV the realization of the concepts as an overall architecture design is presented and Section V concludes from the results.

II. Related Work

In the following, we introduce the related work that addresses some aspects of our contribution. To the best of our knowledge, no overall infrastructure, and services - platform for seamless development and integration of catalog models in the field of HVAC system simulation modeling exists.

A. Frameworks for Modeling Compositions from FMUs

The creation and adaptation of simulations are development steps that belong to the composition. There are some frameworks from research approaches for the composition of FMUs.

In [3], the MOKA framework for object-oriented modeling of FMU-based CoSimulations is presented. The framework provides a language for modeling the structure of integrated FMUs based on the classes FMUBlock, FMUPort. The FMU-Master takes over the execution and instantiate the FMU blocks. An algorithm for the master-slave based execution of composed FMUs is also presented in [4]. The OMSimulatior is another FMU based modeling and simulation tool presented in [5], which provides Transmission Line Modeling connectors to enable the composition of TLM based buses using connectors. Furthermore, there are approaches to adapt the communication behavior of an FMU through wrappers. [6] presents a FMU wrapper descriptions framework for the implementation of a client-server interface. DACCOSIM [7], FMIGo [8] and FMU-Proxy [9] are further approaches for the distributed execution of an FMU based simulation. Another work deals with semantic adaptation to adapt the interaction for the communication of FMUs [10].

B. Merge of Simulation Models

In collaborative development processes, system variants are developed in parallel by different teams. In order to automate the integration step, an approach for the integration of ASCET-based simulation models with the Team.Mode tool is presented in [11]. The tool provides a mechanism to import ASCET models in AXL format and automatically integrates them into one ASCET model in a subsequent step.

C. Integrated Development Environment

In the automotive sector, seamless integration is known as the integration of tools using a common development environment. In [12] Broy et al. present requirements which a seamless development environment has to meet. A fundamental property of the concept is a one main repository for storing and maintaining information common to all development teams. Reichmann et al. present approaches for the implementation of this concept [13] [14].

III. Catalog Platform Infrastructure and Services

We define the catalog platform as a platform for the administration, development and versioning of the catalogs and their components. This includes the description of catalogs and modeling metadata using the catalog description language as well as services for the configuration on the basis of metadata from the catalogs. These concepts are then used for the integration of the platform into an overall architecture design for simulation development environments in Section IV.

Infrastructure. In Section III-A, we present the description language and their modeling rules. We call it infrastructure of the platform, since it is the basis for the description of catalogs and metadata as well as their composition to complex systems.

Services. The services of the platform provide additional user interfaces in order to automate the development steps

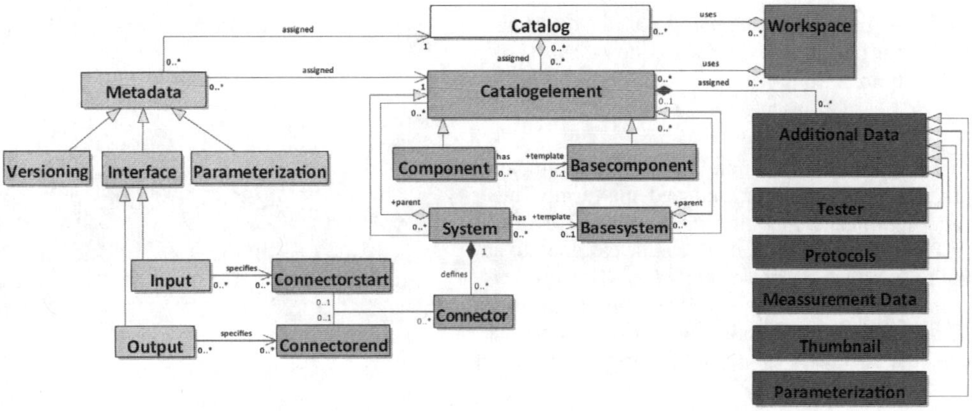

Figure 2. The Platform Meta Model for the description of workspaces and catalogs.

when reusing models from the catalog. All services are described in more detail in Sections III-B, III-C, III-D, III-E.

A. Description Technique

Catalog The catalog is the shared resource between manufacturers and suppliers in the economic market for simulation models of physical components. Using the platform, the manufacturer is able to import the catalogs of various suppliers into his development environment and is then able to create a simulation model, for example, a HVAC system. Therefore, these sections present the description language as the meta model of the platform to describe catalogs. The meta model defines the syntax and the semantics of the language, which is depicted in Figure 2. In the following paragraphs, all class names are written in italic lower case letters - clarifies the textual notation - for the explanation of the meta model from Figure 2.

Workspace The *workspace* is the working area integrated into the development environment. It can contain *catalogs*, where areas a *catalog* can contain systems and components. The language syntax defines a *workspace* that can contain any number of *catalogs*. *Catalogs* for components and for systems can then be created using the simulation environment in the *workspace*. Therefore, the meta model defines the classes *component*, *system* as subclasses of the superclass *catalogelement*.

Component A component from the catalog represents a model that can be executed in a simulation environment of a simulation tool. It declares interfaces for the communication to other *components*. Hence, for example, an FMU or a composition of FMUs can be described by a *component*. A *catalog* that contains only *systems* and can be used as the manufacturers in-house *catalog*, which is not offered on the market to other competitors. As depicted in Figure 2, the *system* can contain any number of *components* and *connectors*.

Connector A *connector* describes a directed point-to-point connection for the communication from one *component* to another *component* by using *connectorstart* and *connectorend*. Therefore, a *connector* must have a reference to a *connectorstart* and to a *connectorend*.

Metadata The *metadata* is defined as the superclass of different *metadata* subclasses that can be assigned to a particular *catalogelement*. The *versioning* subclass describes a unique node in a version graph for the description of further developments of *catalogelements* and variants of *catalogelements* (see Section III-B). An *interface* class describes the declaration of a variable with a data type from the platform. The component is the origin of a variable declaration description and hence is part of a particular *component* that uses it to define its communication to other *components*. The *parameterization* subclass describes differential states and initial values that are required to calculate the initial conditions of a *component* that is a prerequisite to execute it in a simulation (see Section III-E).

Basecomponent To ease development of a *catalogelement* from reused *components*, we introduce the *basecomponent*. The *basecomponent* is a *catalogelement*, that is defined only by the *interfaces* from its *metadata* record. It is an abstract *catalogelement*, as it does not implement its *interface*. But, it describes a template for the development of a *component* that is expected to implement that *interface* from the *basecomponent*. For example, a new *component variant*, in addition to an existing *component variant*, can be introduced as part of a commonly shared *basecomponent*.

Basesystem A *basecomponent* can also be used to develop new composition *variants* from existing *catalogelements*. For that purpose, the *basesystem* is used to describe a composition from *basecomponents*. To develop a new *system variant* from a *basesystem*, *components* must be selected by developers that are compatible to the *basecomponents* from a particular *basesystem*.

Constraints for valid descriptions. Developers can create correct and not correct descriptions using the description language. A description is in the set of all correct **catalog** descriptions, if it holds the following constraints:

- A *connector* must reference a *connectorstart* and a *connectorend*.
- The *interface* of a *connectorstart* and of the *connectorend* must be compatible.
- A *catalog* contains only a *basecomponent* set and a *model* set. Each *component* depends on a *basecomponent*.
- A *basesystem* must only contain a set of *basecomponents*.

- The *metadata* of a *basecomponent* has an *interface* description but has no *versioning* and no *parameterization* descriptions.

B. Version and Variant Management

This section describes the version and variant management, which is a central service of the introduced platform. This is of fundamental significance, as all *catalogelements* evolve over time. Therefore, each *catalogelement* can be assigned to a version information via the concept of *metadata*. The *version* is defined as a successor relationship: If n_i is a *catalogelement*, then $i \in$ INDEX is the version number of a given index set INDEX and n_{i+1} the successor of n_i and represented by the following relation:

$$\texttt{successorOf} := \{(x, y) \mid y \text{ is successor of } x \text{ with } x, y \in \text{CATALOGELEMENT}\} \quad (1)$$

As described in the meta model (see Figure 2) a *component* as well as a *system* can be derived from a *basecomponent* or *basesystem*. In the following, all relations are specified regarding a *component*, for *systems* the same relations are defined accordingly. This allows the implementation of variants, whereby the base element is the smallest feature shared by all variants. The variant concept is defined by the following relation:

$$\texttt{basedOn}_{\text{COMPONENT}} := \{(x, y) \mid y \text{ is derived from } x \text{ with } x \in \text{BASECOMPONENT and } y \in \text{COMPONENT}\} \quad (2)$$

If n and m without loss of generality are two *components* and x is a *basecomponent* from which both *components* are derived, then n and m are variants of the same *basecomponent*. Like the *components* themselves, a *basecomponent* can of course also be versioned, generally, the `basedOn` relation can exist between concrete versions of *catalogelements*. Each *catalogelement* can be assigned to one or more *catalogs*. There are no restrictions regarding the version or variant, e.g., a *component* can be contained in different versions or a derived *component* without its *basecomponent* in one *catalog*. The `assignedTo` relation between a *catalog* C and a *catalogelement* n is defined as follows:

$$\texttt{assignedTo} := \{(n, C) \mid n \in C \text{ with } n \in \text{CATALOGELEMENT and } C \in \text{CATALOG}\} \quad (3)$$

A successor relationship, known as a version, can also be defined between two *catalogs*. The introduction of a *catalog* as a group for versioning, distinguishes this approach from existing ones such as CVS (concurrent versions system), SVN (subversion) or git. Another special feature of common versioning systems is shown in Figure 3 by the `replacedWith` relation. This relation describes a successor relation but not in the sense of a new version, because it does not have to be a further development of the previous *component*. In practice, the most common case for this relationship is when a product is no longer supported and, as a consequence, another product has to be used instead. This is also a relation, as the `succesorOf` relation, which can be defined between two *components* as follows:

$$\texttt{replacedWith}_{\text{COMPONENT}} := \{(x, y) \mid x \text{ is replaced with } y \text{ whereby } x,\ y \in \text{COMPONENT}\} \quad (4)$$

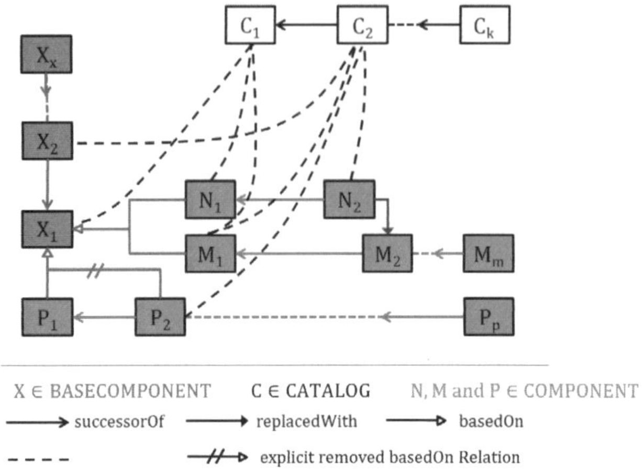

Figure 3. The versioning graph notation for the representation of the version snapshot provided by the versioning service.

As an exemplary, in Figure 3, the five specified relations between the different *catalogelements* and the *catalog* itself are illustrated. For the purpose of simplicity not all existing or possible connections and elements have been drawn up. Another notation constituted in Figure 3 allows to illustrate a remove, as a development step, of a `basedOn` relation. This is another typical case from real practice, which is the customer-specific or prototypical development, result in the fact that a *component* is no longer part of a series.

In addition to the new types of relations described above, the challenges of version and variant management include the storage of this information and the construction of the customer-specific version graph. This is determined by the architecture of the platform, but it also offers mechanisms for a solution. Due to the fact that a customer does not have to purchase every *catalog*, it might be that the customer does not own all versions of a *catalog*, e.g., the version and variant graph has to be constructed for every platform instance. From this, the requirement for a *catalog* instance is derived. The new instance has to keep all necessary information available. This can be automated by another central service: The service provides additional or up-to-date information for the *catalog* owned by the producer. This mechanism allows that not every *version* and variant must necessarily be assigned to a *catalog*. This is also consistent with practical experience, because only certain releases of a *component* are offered to customers of *catalogs*.

C. Thumbnail Search

The common use cases with regard to data intensive or file-based systems are searching and comparing, so this is also the case with the platform introduced here. Finding and accessing of *catalogelements* is not only, as described in this section, an important tool for human interaction. But also important as a base for the automated discovery of *components*. For example, this automation is mandatory for the refactoring service.

To improve the search and also the comparability between components, an own variant of the so-called tag cloud [15] was developed. In general, the information stored in the *metadata* is used as a basis for the search.

The *metadata* are also used to generate the thumbnail shown in Figure 4, which shows two tag clouds, each visualizing series of fans. This view constitutes an overview of the stored properties and their distribution within the series at a glance. In most cases the properties are technical ones. Hence, the illustration is based on the triplet consisting of identifier, value and unit. Furthermore, the following rules are used for the generation step:

1) Elements that have the same identifier are grouped together.
2) Elements that have the same unit are grouped together.
3) The font size per group is determined as follows:
    a) The font size of an identifier is the larger the more variants exist for this identifier.
    b) The font size of a value is the larger the more elements have this value.

These rules can be adapted or extended as required. For example, the added value can be further increased. Also, semantic approaches are applicable as described in [16].

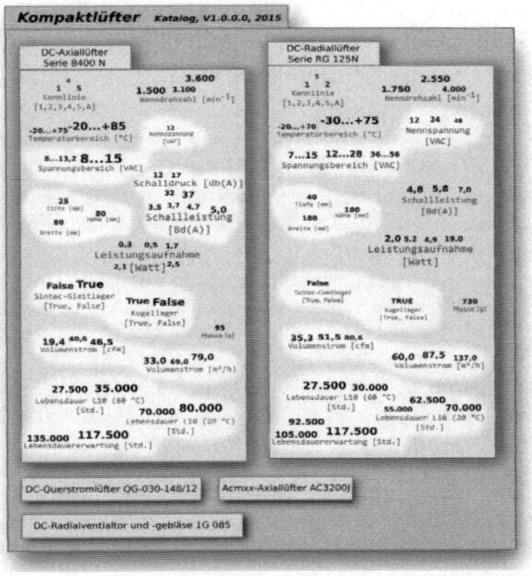

Figure 4. Thumbnail Example: Visualization of Variants

The thumbnail based search allows to create an overview even of a large number of different variants. To reduce the storage space, the thumbnails themselves are generated exclusively from the *metadata*.

D. Refactoring

The versioning of a *catalog* was introduced in Section III-B. A new *version* in the version graph describes a change to a *component* as a relation to its predecessor *version*. Customers of *components* from that version graph must be aware of these changes, in particular critical bug fixing updates should be made available in their *catalog*s and *catalogelement* compositions, e.g., *systems*. In the following, we introduce a platform service that provides automation in the following distinct cases:

1 To replace a *component*, because it has a bug.

2 To improve an existing *component*.

3 To replace a *component* by another different *component* (The behavior of the new *component* and the original *component* need not be identical).

Using the service in the last case, can make changes to the bahavior of a simulation. Hence, notwithstanding with the general definition [17], we define *Refactoring* as a service for the automatic propagation of changes of a *component* to all *catalog*s and *systems* which use this *component*.

If a new *version* of a *component* exist, in the first case, the service replaces the *component* with the new *component version*. If no new *component version* exist, then the service informs the user to treat the error in that particular *component* manually. In the second case, the service automatically replaces the *component* by the improved *component*, if the *interface* of the improved *component* is identical to the *interface* of the predecessor *component*. In the third case, it is often necessary to replace an outdated and no longer supported *component* by a another *component*. The outdated *component* is then automatically replaced, if one of the conditions from case one or two can be applied.

E. Modelinversion

As stated in Section I, HVAC simulation *component*s can influence their performed control tasks to achieve a certain system behavior, e.g., to control the temperature of a vehicle cabin. To control the temperature to a certain operating range, an appropriate state of the simulation behavior must be reachable. Therefore, the overall simulation behavior must consider error signals of the control environment to reach the necessary state of operation called steady-state. Moreover, the control operations of the *component* must be performed in such a way that the system consumes as less energy as possible. In the first case, initialization conditions must be found for a *component*. In the second case - in addition to correct initialization conditions - a certain optimization and solution method must be applied to find an optimized solution. We introduce Modelinversion as a platform service that allows the robust and accurate as well as fast solving of algebra-differential equation systems to calculate steady-state simulation results. The calculation of simulation results for different stationary operating points is the core application of the Modelinversion.

The service forms the basis for the following applications: (1) for stationary model fitting, (2) for calculating optimal experimental designs (DoE) and (3), it offers "numerical inversion". Thereby, differential states, which are otherwise calculated by integration, can be specified externally using the *metadata* from the *catalog*s. The robustness, accuracy and speed of solution finding is achieved by a combination of DAE solvers and algebraic solution methods. Depending on the model, the appropriate solution method or a combination is selected: DAE solvers integrate a simulation model over time and can simulate robustly down to the steady state by methods such as flexible step size and event handling. Algebraic solvers based on a zero-point search of the state derivatives provide accurate results and are very fast in calculating many similar operating points, e.g., for different measurement points.

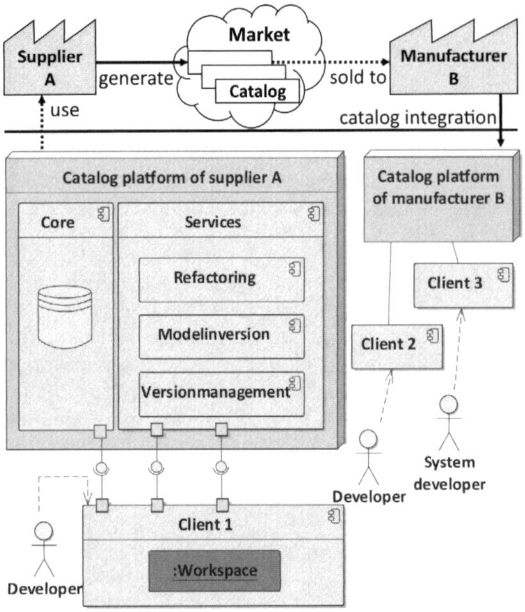

Figure 5. The overall design of the platform

IV. The Overall Context and Design of the Platform

The design and the usage context of the platform are depicted in Figure 5. The platform enables suppliers and manufacturers to exchange *catalogs* on a common market to develop simulation models based on *components* and *systems*. The *catalog* description language from the platform defines a standardized format for the automation of the exchange tasks and simulation model commissioning tasks using platform services. This eliminates the time-consuming manual effort required to implement ad hoc solutions in the cooperatively organized development of simulation *models*. Manufacturers can obtain the *catalogs* from the market and reuse them for the development of different *system* simulations. The *metadata* from the descriptions of the *catalogs* is used for the purchase process via a web service of a certain supplier or via a market place organized centrally by all suppliers. This enables suppliers to provide customer information about the *components* of *catalogs* in advance without having to provide the *catalogs* themselves. From the technical point of view, the client-server architecture was selected as the architecture style for the platform: several developers can access the *catalogs* of a centrally managed repository bidirectionally and independently of each other, regardless of the development environment they use, and carry out their development locally on their client *workspace*. The clients use the graphical user-interface for developing the *catalogs* and for using the services. The platform, as the server, then manages clients access to the repository and to the platform services.

V. Conclusion

The current state of practice in the development of the HVAC *system* domain requires great expertise from *components* suppliers and additional manual handling from suppliers and *system* manufacturers to exchange and to commission simulation models in the cooperatively organized development of process *system* simulations. We proposed a *catalog* platform particularly for *components* that are exchanged to enable seamless and integrated simulation based development process. Therefore, an infrastructure for modeling and for the exchange of *catalogs* was introduced. *Catalogs* contain *components* and compositions from *components* called *systems*. Both are generalized as *catalogelements* and differentiated by *metadata* assigned to them. Thereby, the *metadata* of *catalogelements* is used for platform services and is used to support marketplace technologies, e.g., purchase procedures. Besides the infrastructure, we proposed also a set of services provided by the platform to automate several development tasks. This proposal is part of an ongoing research, where we study upcoming use cases for the application of our platform as a future research work.

Acknowledgment

The results of this contribution are based on the work of the project "Kataloggestützte interdisziplinäre Entwurfsplattform für Elektrofahrzeuge (KISEL)". KISEL is supported by a funding from the Federal Ministry of Education and Research of Germany in the framework of "KMU-innovativ: Informations- und Kommunikationstechnologien".

References

[1] Modelica Association. Fmi standard.

[2] "Design methodology for mechatronic systems," Verein Deutscher Ingenieure, Beuth Verlag GmbH, 10772 Berlin, Standard, Jun. 2004.

[3] M. Aslan, H. Oundefineduztüzün, U. Durak, and K. Taylan, "Moka: An object-oriented framework for fmi co-simulation," in Proceedings of the Conference on Summer Computer Simulation, ser. SummerSim '15. San Diego, CA, USA: Society for Computer Simulation International, 2015.

[4] M. U. Awais, W. Gawlik, G. De-Cillia, and P. Palensky, "Hybrid simulation using sahisim framework: a hybrid distributed simulation framework using waveform relaxation method implemented over the hla and the functional mock-up interface," in SimuTools, 2015, pp. 273—-278.

[5] L. Ochel and et al., "Omsimulator–integrated fmi and tlm-based co-simulation with composite model editing and ssp," in Proceedings of the 13th International Modelica Conference, Regensburg, Germany, March 4–6, 2019, no. 157. Linköping University Electronic Press, 2019, pp. 69–78.

[6] L. I. Hatledal, A. Styve, G. Hovland, and H. Zhang, "A language and platform independent co-simulation framework based on the functional mock-up interface," IEEE Access, vol. 7, 2019, pp. 109 328–109 339.

[7] V. Galtier and et al., "Fmi-based distributed multi-simulation with daccosim," in Proceedings of the Symposium on Theory of Modeling & Simulation: DEVS Integrative M&S Symposium, ser. DEVS '15. San Diego, CA, USA: Society for Computer Simulation International, 2015, pp. 39—46.

[8] C. Lacoursière, "FMI Go! A simulation runtime environment with a client server architecture over multiple protocols," in Linköping Electronic Conference Proceedings. LiU E-press, 2018, pp. 653–662.

[9] L. I. Hatledal, H. Zhang, A. Styve, and G. Hovland, "Fmu-proxy: A framework for distributed access to functional mock-up units," in Proceedings of the 13th International Modelica Conference. Linköping University Electronic Press, 2019.

[10] C. Gomes and et al., "Semantic adaptation for FMI co-simulation with hierarchical simulators," Simulation, vol. 95, no. 3, 2019.

[11] M. Janßen, C. Bartelt, and A. Rausch, "Tool-support in cooperative modeling and variantmanagment of electronic control unit software," in INFORMATIK 2012, U. Goltz, M. Magnor, H.-J. Appelrath, H. K. Matthies, W.-T. Balke, and L. Wolf, Eds. Bonn: Gesellschaft für Informatik e.V., 2012, pp. 843–852.

[12] M. Broy, M. Feilkas, M. Herrmannsdoerfer, S. Merenda, and D. Ratiu, "Seamless model-based development: From isolated tools to integrated model engineering environments," Proceedings of the IEEE, vol. 98, no. 4, 2010, pp. 526–545.

[13] C. Reichmann, M. Kiihl, P. Graf, and K. Müller-Glaser, "Generalstore - a case-tool integration platform enabling model level coupling of heterogeneous designs for embedded electronic systems." 06 2004, pp. 225 – 232.

[14] C. Reichmann, D. Gebauer, and K. D. Müller-Glaser, "Model level coupling of heterogeneous embedded systems," in 2nd RTAS Workshop on Model-Driven Embedded Systems, 2004.

[15] B. Y.-L. Kuo, T. Hentrich, B. M. . Good, and M. D. Wilkinson, "Tag clouds for summarizing web search results," in Proceedings of the 16th international conference on World Wide Web, C. Williamson, Ed. New York, NY: ACM, 2007, p. 1203.

[16] M. Schindler, A. Rausch, and O. Fox, "Clustering source code elements by semantic similarity using wikipedia," in Proceedings of 4th International Workshop on Realizing Artificial Intelligence Synergies in Software Engineering (RAISE), 2015, pp. 13–18.

[17] M. Fowler, Refactoring: Improving the Design of Existing Code. Addison Wesley, 1999.

Towards Improving Software Architecture Degradation Mitigation by Machine Learning

Sebastian Herold
Karlstad University
Karlstad, Sweden
Email: sebastian.herold@kau.se

Christoph Knieke, Mirco Schindler, Andreas Rausch
Clausthal University of Technology
Clausthal-Zellerfeld, Germany
Email: firstname.surname@tu-clausthal.de

***Abstract*—Mitigating software architecture degradation is a task in evolving large and complex software-intensive systems that is as important as it is challenging. One aspect adding to the complexity of the task is the amount of information in the implementations of most real-world systems to be digested in order to detect, analyse, and remedy degradation. In domains with similar challenges, machine learning techniques have been applied in recent years and partially delivered exciting results. Hence the question arises whether, and to which degree, machine learning can be successfully applied to tackle software architecture degradation. In this paper, we propose a novel combination of existing techniques for different phases of the task of mitigating software architecture degradation from detecting it to repairing it. We outline how these techniques could be complemented by machine learning to increase their accuracy and efficiency over time.**

Keywords–Software Evolution; Software Architecture Degradation; Machine Learning.

I. INTRODUCTION

Mitigating Software Architecture Degradation (SAD) plays an important role for the longevity of evolving software-intensive systems. Today SAD is a big challenge in modern architectures like the architecture of software ecosystems and services and leads to a deteriorates of the quality of such systems. Architecture degrades/erodes when the implemented architecture of a software system diverges from its intended architecture [1]. This usually happens during software evolution when the software undergoes changes as a result of bug fixes and further development, but may also happen during initial implementation of the system. Architecture erosion hinders the further development of systems and leads to less reusability, maintainability, understandability and decrease in performance.

There has been a lot of research on how to mitigate SAD [1]. However, studies show that in practice it is still difficult to remedy SAD [2]. The study in [1] concludes that none of the available methods singly provides an effective and comprehensive solution for controlling architecture erosion.

There are many reasons why the reduction of SAD causes so many difficulties. One is the inherent complexity of the task. Modern software systems are highly complex and have a long lifespan. The system experts have to filter and find the information relevant to SAD in the huge amount of data contained in large (and potentially old) repositories of source code and other relevant artefacts. Current approaches to SAD seem not to scale well with this complexity [1].

In other domains with similar challenges Machine Learning (ML) techniques are already used to support maintenance and evolution tasks ("predictive maintenance"). Generally, ML is taken to encompass automatic computing procedures based on logical or binary operations that learn a task from a series of examples, i.e., ML provides systems the ability to automatically learn and improve from experience without being explicitly programmed to so [3]. ML is divided into three subdomains supervised, unsupervised, and reinforcement learning [4].

Over the past decade, ML techniques have been widely adopted in a number of massive and complex data-intensive fields such as medicine, biology, and astronomy, for these techniques provide possible solutions to mine the information hidden in the data [4]. The question motivating this article is whether and how such techniques can be applied to mitigate SAD more effectively and efficiently. In this paper we look at the state of the art in mitigating SAD and propose a combination of existing techniques and how to add ML to them in order to increase the techniques' accuracy and efficiency over time.

The paper is structured as follows: Section II gives an overview on the related work. Our idea towards a learning environment for mitigating SAD is presented in Section III. Finally, Section IV concludes.

II. STATE OF THE ART IN MACHINE LEARNING FOR DEALING WITH SAD

In order to characterize the state of the art in using ML, or related techniques, to mitigate SAD, we conducted a systematic literature review of 26 eventually relevant papers. This review is currently being finalized, however, a few important characteristics can already be noted.

We were particularly interested in which activities of SAD mitigation are covered by research. In an earlier mapping study on SAD in general, activities were distinguished into detection, analysis, repairing, and prevention of degradation [5]. We added architecture recovery as an important subsequent step that is intertwined with detection in many techniques and categorized the relevant papers according to the five resulting activities (multiple categories per paper were possible). The results show that a majority of papers fall into the activities of recovery (7 papers) and detection (9 papers). These can be considered the "early" phases of SAD mitigation as one has to have the intended architecture and to know the present inconsistencies before actions against SAD can be taken. Seven papers were considered to cover the analysis of degradation and only three look at the usage of ML for repairing degradation. Preventing erosion was the motivation for four papers.

The use of ML for architecture recovery appears quite natural as clustering is one of the commonly used techniques used in this activity and also a main application of many unsupervised learning techniques. Hence, these techniques are used relatively frequently in this context [6] [7] [8].

The usage of such techniques as a part of detecting and analysing SAD is very diverse. It covers very distinct activities like automating the creation of architecture-implementation mappings required in most consistency checking techniques [9], the detection of design defects [10], or the analysis of the use of architectural tactics [11]. To our best knowledge, no approach applies ML to help software engineers understand potential causes of instances of SAD to better mitigate it as proposed in literature [12]. In preventing SAD, the identified studies were mainly about preventing architecture smells which are often considered to be an important factor leading to degradation (e.g., Fontana et al. [13]).

Most of the studies report positive results regarding the performance of the applied ML techniques as measured by precision, accuracy, or recall. It can thus be concluded that the use of ML techniques in the context of SAD seems beneficial even though a potential publication bias in favour of positive results cannot be completely excluded. However, a few studies outline that there is space for improvement. Khomh et al., for example, apply Bayesian Belief Networks for code and design smell detection with comparably low precision [14]. Lenhard et al. describe a study in which they investigate whether "smelly" code can be used as an indicator for architectural inconsistencies [15]. They tried to train a classifier for this task and describe the results as unsatisfying as they show low precision and recall.

We can conclude from these preliminary findings that an holistic approach making use of ML techniques, supporting the software engineering coherently from the detection of degradation to counteracting it, is missing. Moreover, ML is less frequently applied directly to the phenomenon of degradation, i.e., the divergence between intended architecture and implementation of a system but with aspects indirectly connected to it, such as code/design/architecture smells, design defects, architecture tactics, etc. A stronger research focus on the analysis activity in general with the goal of providing insights to degradation causes might also provide a better ground for applying ML techniques in the activities of repairing and preventing degradation.

III. The Envisaged Approach

In this section, we present our idea towards a learning environment for mitigating SAD.

A. Overview

The suggested approach follows conceptually the ideas of repairing architecture degradation presented by Mair et al. and extends them [12]. The authors follow the analogy of medical doctors that, for treating a disease, first assess symptoms to exclude and diagnose possible diseases or conditions to eventually suggesting and executing a suitable therapy. According to that metaphor, we propose an approach consisting of three main activities as depicted in Figure 1: *Architecture Recovery and Consistency Checking (ARC)*, *Degradation Cause Analysis (DCA)*, and *Recommending Repair Actions (RRA)*.

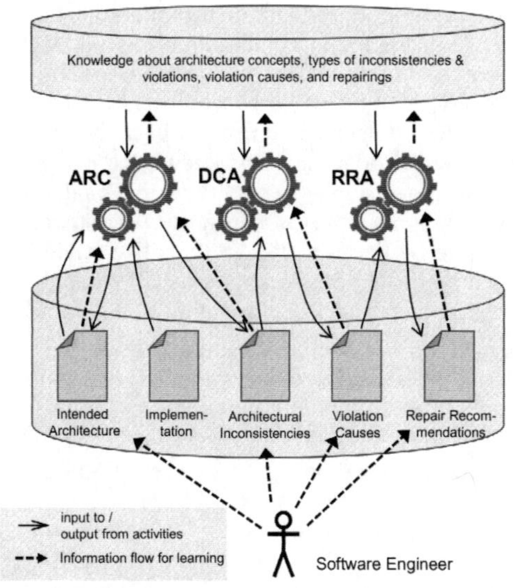

Figure 1. Conceptual Overview of the Proposed Approach

Comparable to assessing medical symptoms, the ARC step aims at assessing the status quo of software architecture degradation in the software system at hand. This means it consists of inspecting its intended software architecture and the implementation of a system and detecting inconsistencies between them. It might also involve recovering (parts of) the intended architecture as its specification might not exist or be outdated. The result of this activity is—beside a potentially updated intended architecture—primarily a set of architectural inconsistencies each of which might either be considered tolerable or to represent an actual, potentially harmful violation of the intended architecture.

Similar to how the presence or absence of several different symptoms might point to a certain medical condition, combinations of several architectural inconsistencies and properties of the implementation fragments connected to them might indicate a deeper problem behind those inconsistencies. The activity DCA is hence about aggregating information about single instances of architectural inconsistencies to form an overall picture of the underlying causes of the degradation which potentially helps to remedy it more efficiently.

Recommending Repair Actions (RRA): In analogy to deciding on the appropriate therapy based on the diagnosed medical condition, decisions on whether and how to repair the present architecture degradation based on the identified causes have to be made. The activity RRA targets at recommending repairing of the implementation and the intended architecture based on the identified degradation causes in the system under investigation.

One essential aspect of the proposed approach is to complement existing techniques for each of these activities by a "learning component" with the aim of making the use of those techniques more accurate and efficient. ML shall be applied to interpret feedback from and interaction with the user, a software engineer, to increase accuracy and efficiency of those techniques over the lifetime of a system and for application in other systems. For example, a classifier could learn over time to distinguish architectural violations from inconsistencies that are considered allowed architectural divergences based on a software architect's manual classification of such exceptions in the set of identified inconsistencies in the past. We postulate the hypothesis that such a classifier could improve the accuracy of an architecture consistency technique.

Most techniques for any of these three activities rely on explicitly specified conceptual knowledge as depicted in the upper part of Figure 1. This knowledge is system-independent and comprises architectural concepts and the constraints they imply in the implementation, types of architectural inconsistencies and violations, etc. This knowledge is either embodied in the technique applied (e.g., reflexion modelling as ARC technique with its fix set of dependency constraints [16]) or to be specified by the user (like in tools like ArCh [17]). In the proposed approach, ML techniques shall be applied to extend such conceptual knowledge over time semi-automatically.

In the following sections, we look at these activities in more detail and the potential and envisaged usage of ML techniques.

B. Architecture Recovery and Consistency Checking

The techniques proposed to be used in this step are those suggested by Schindler and Rausch for architecture recovery [18] and by Herold for architecture consistency checking [17]. In the first approach, architectural concepts (e.g., patterns, conventions, communication paradigms, or architectural tactics) are described as set of properties that source code elements implementing these concepts have to fulfil. Based on these formally specified properties, instances of known architectural concepts can be recovered from a system's implementation. The difficulty lies in the exact definition of the relevant properties for such a concept. The authors instead suggest to make use of ML techniques to classify elements as instances of a particular architectural concept based on the already existing instances and their properties. This classifier could be refined over time and lead to more accurate recovery results.

This approach can be easily connected to the aforementioned approach to architecture consistency checking [17]. In this approach, architectural rules are attached to architecture concepts as first-order logic statements expressing constraints that a consistent implementation needs to fulfil. These rules are very similar to the properties used by Schindler and Rausch [18]. An interesting area for the application of ML techniques is the detection of exceptions from those architectural rules. Often, identified violations of consistency rules are considered acceptable exceptions from the rules (see also Buckley et al. [19]). ML techniques could help to identify common properties among such exceptions to reduce the number of such false positives in future consistency checks.

Moreover, almost all checking techniques and architectural concepts require some form of mapping between architecture elements and implementation elements. This is often considered a cumbersome and time-consuming task [19]. While there exist techniques to semi-automate this task [20] [21], the use of ML techniques has been investigated only for reflexion modelling with promising results [8] [9].

C. Degradation Cause Analysis

For the step of analysing degradation causes, we propose to further extend an approach proposed by Herold et al. [22]. This approach originally complemented reflexion modelling as ARC technique of choice but can be easily adapted to the technique suggested here. Violation causes are expressed as a combination of (1) structural patterns over architectural models, source code, and architectural inconsistencies between them and (2) quantitative properties formulated as metrics and target values to express likely properties of architecture or implementation elements if a specific degradation cause seems to be the reason for an identified architecture violation. The closer the actual metric values are in the context of a specific violation, the more likely the degradation cause is considered to be the actual reason. A recommendation system integrated into a reflexion modelling tool proposes the potential causes in descending order according to their computed probabilities to the user.

We assume that ML techniques can improve these recommendations based on previous user feedback that confirmed or declined suggested recommendations. In particular in cases of competing degradation causes (with similar probabilities), supervised techniques could utilize other features of the relevant architecture and implementation fragments to prioritise certain causes over others based on previous experiences. In a similar way, a system could learn weightings of the "symptoms" expressed in the quantitative properties of a degradation cause, to adapt to system-specific characteristics. If, for example, degradation causes refer to textual similarity metrics (among other metrics) to measure conformance with naming conventions, but users very often decline such causes despite high scores computed by the recommendation system (because the naming convention does not apply in the system at hand), a lower weight decreasing the naming convention's influence might be beneficial. Furthermore, unsupervised techniques could help to identify new types of degradation causes based on existing but yet unclassified inconsistencies and relevant features of the implementation elements related to them.

D. Recommending Repair Actions

For the step of recommending repair actions, we envisage to adapt the approach proposed by Terra et al. who describe a recommendation system that suggests refactorings for violations of dependencies as modelled in an architectural model of a system [23]. Instead of producing recommendations per single violations as in the original approach, the degradation causes identified during DCA will be the units for which recommendations will be made such that they do not look at violations in isolation but consider their semantic context.

ML techniques can help to overcome one of the main limitations of the technique so far which is the fix and predefined priorities of refactorings. If two or more refactorings are applicable to resolve an architecture inconsistency, the one with the higher priority will be recommended. Again, the technique could be improved in this regard through learning from previous actions of the user, having accepted and rejected recommended refactorings, and looking at which recommendation alternatives were chosen in different contexts. Moreover, we envisage to also observe how these recommendations are actually turned into actions. If the recommended (series of) refactorings are frequently extended by additional actions, for example, the recommended refactoring could be adapted, or a new recommendation could be added to the recommendation system. Similarly, unsupervised learning techniques could identify recommendations from repair actions that the user performs without following any of the suggestions of the system at all.

IV. Conclusion and Future Work

In this paper, we sketched a novel holistic approach to counteracting software architecture degradation in software-intensive systems through extending existing techniques by machine learning. Based on the preliminary results of a systematic literature review, we conclude that an holistic approach making use of machine learning techniques is missing. We assume that this new direction leads to improved accuracy and efficiency in mitigating SAD and, hence, to a higher acceptance of the corresponding techniques in practice.

In the immediate future work, we intend to adapt and extend the tools for the three activities identified. This includes extending them by the means to retrieve feedback on suggested architecture violations, degradation causes, etc. from the user and to feed this information into appropriate learning mechanisms.

In addition, this involves gathering and formalising some of the conceptual knowledge as outlined in Section III and Figure 1. This would serve as baseline knowledge in the evaluation of the approach based on which the learning mechanisms would adapt to project or system-specific settings over time. This data can partially come from literature, such as the formalization of patterns as architectural constraints. Given the lack of studies in analysing degradation causes, however, empirical observations from case studies with real-world software projects and potentially from experiments with students or practitioners will be performed. Based on this, we will thoroughly evaluate our approach to identify the strengths, and possible weaknesses.

REFERENCES

[1] L. De Silva and D. Balasubramaniam, "Controlling software architecture erosion: A survey," *Journal of Systems and Software*, vol. 85, no. 1, pp. 132–151, 2012.

[2] N. Ali, S. Baker, R. O'Crowley, S. Herold, and J. Buckley, "Architecture consistency: State of the practice, challenges and requirements," *Empirical Software Engineering*, vol. 23, no. 1, pp. 224–258, 2018.

[3] Y. Zhang, *New Advances in Machine Learning*. BoD–Books on Demand, 2010.

[4] J. Qiu, Q. Wu, G. Ding, Y. Xu, and S. Feng, "A survey of machine learning for big data processing," *EURASIP Journal on Advances in Signal Processing*, vol. 2016, no. 1, p. 67, 2016.

[5] S. Herold, M. Blom, and J. Buckley, "Evidence in architecture degradation and consistency checking research: Preliminary results from a literature review," in *Proceedings of the 10th European Conference on Software Architecture Workshops*, ser. ECSAW '16. ACM, 2016, pp. 1–7.

[6] A. Grewe, C. Knieke, M. Körner, A. Rausch, M. Schindler, A. Strasser, M. Vogel, and (Keine Angabe), "Automotive software product line architecture evolution: Extracting, designing and managing architectural concepts," in *International Journal on Advances in Intelligent Systems*, Hans-Werner Sehring, Ed. IARIA, 2017, pp. 203–222.

[7] A. Corazza, S. Di Martino, V. Maggio, A. Moschitti, A. Passerini, G. Scanniello, and F. Silvestri, "Using machine learning and information retrieval techniques to improve software maintainability," in *Trustworthy Eternal Systems via Evolving Software, Data and Knowledge*, A. Moschitti and B. Plank, Eds. Springer, 2013, pp. 117–134.

[8] S. M. Naim, K. Damevski, and M. S. Hossain, "Reconstructing and evolving software architectures using a coordinated clustering framework," *Automated Software Engineering*, vol. 24, no. 3, pp. 543–572, Sep 2017.

[9] T. Olsson, M. Ericsson, and A. Wingkvist, "Semi-automatic mapping of source code using naive bayes," in *Proceedings of the 13th European Conference on Software Architecture - Volume 2*, ser. ECSA '19. ACM, 2019, p. 209–216.

[10] A. Ghannem, G. El Boussaidi, and M. Kessentini, "On the use of design defect examples to detect model refactoring opportunities," *Software Quality Journal*, vol. 24, no. 4, p. 947–965, Dec. 2016.

[11] M. Mirakhorli, J. Carvalho, J. Cleland-Huang, and P. Mäder, "A domain-centric approach for recommending architectural tactics to satisfy quality concerns," in *2013 3rd International Workshop on the Twin Peaks of Requirements and Architecture (TwinPeaks)*, July 2013, pp. 1–8.

[12] M. Mair, S. Herold, and A. Rausch, "Towards flexible automated software architecture erosion diagnosis and treatment," in *Proceedings of the WICSA 2014 Companion Volume*, ser. WICSA '14 Companion. ACM, 2014, pp. 1–6.

[13] F. Arcelli Fontana, P. Avgeriou, I. Pigazzini, and R. Roveda, "A study on architectural smells prediction," in *2019 45th Euromicro Conference on Softw. Eng.and Advanced Applications (SEAA)*, Aug 2019, pp. 333–337.

[14] F. Khomh, S. Vaucher, Y. Guéhéneuc, and H. Sahraoui, "A bayesian approach for the detection of code and design smells," in *2009 Ninth International Conference on Quality Software*, Aug 2009, pp. 305–314.

[15] J. Lenhard, M. M. Hassan, M. Blom, and S. Herold, "Are code smell detection tools suitable for detecting architecture degradation?" in *Proceedings of the 11th European Conference on Software Architecture: Companion Proceedings*, ser. ECSA '17. ACM, 2017, p. 138–144.

[16] G. C. Murphy, D. Notkin, and K. Sullivan, "Software reflexion models: Bridging the gap between source and high-level models," *SIGSOFT Softw. Eng. Notes*, vol. 20, no. 4, p. 18–28, Oct. 1995.

[17] S. Herold and A. Rausch, "Complementing model-driven development for the detection of software architecture erosion," in *2013 5th Int. Workshop on Modeling in Software Engineering (MiSE)*, May 2013, pp. 24–30.

[18] M. Schindler and A. Rausch, "Architectural concepts and their evolution made explicit by examples," in *Proceedings of The Eleventh International Conference on Adaptive and Self-Adaptive Systems and Applications, ADAPTIVE 2019*. IARIA, 2019, pp. 38–43.

[19] J. Buckley, N. Ali, M. English, J. Rosik, and S. Herold, "Real-time reflexion modelling in architecture reconciliation: A multi case study," *Information and Software Technology*, vol. 61, pp. 107 – 123, 2015.

[20] A. Christl, R. Koschke, and M.-A. Storey, "Automated clustering to support the reflexion method," *Information and Software Technology*, vol. 49, no. 3, pp. 255 – 274, 2007, 12th Working Conference on Reverse Engineering.

[21] R. A. Bittencourt, G. J. d. Santos, D. D. S. Guerrero, and G. C. Murphy, "Improving automated mapping in reflexion models using information retrieval techniques," in *2010 17th Working Conference on Reverse Engineering*, Oct 2010, pp. 163–172.

[22] S. Herold, M. English, J. Buckley, S. Counsell, and M. Ó Cinnéide, "Detection of violation causes in reflexion models," in *2015 IEEE 22nd International Conference on Software Analysis, Evolution, and Reengineering (SANER)*, March 2015, pp. 565–569.

[23] R. Terra, M. T. Valente, K. Czarnecki, and R. S. Bigonha, "A recommendation system for repairing violations detected by static architecture conformance checking," *Software: Practice and Experience*, vol. 45, no. 3, pp. 315–342, 2015.

Automated Configuration in Adaptive IoT Software Ecosystems to Reduce Manual Device Integration Effort: Application and Evaluation of a Novel Engineering Method

Fabian Burzlaff
Institute for Enterprise Systems (InES)
University of Mannheim
Email: burzlaff@es.uni-mannheim.de

Steffen Jacobs
Institute for Enterprise Systems (InES)
University of Mannheim
Email: steffen.jacobs@hotmail.de

Christian Bartelt
Institute for Software and Systems Engineering (ISSE)
Clausthal University of Technology
Email: christian.bartelt@tu-clausthal.de

***Abstract*—Existing scientific approaches that integrate non-standardized software components automatically are seldom used in practice. Consequently, practitioners currently rely on standardization initiatives or they implement software adapters manually. However, standards quickly lose their claim for correctness as fast innovation cycles prohibit timeliness of machine-understandable domain standards for open and dynamically evolving software ecosystems. Although scientifically driven approaches can be applied in order to automatically generate software adapters reliably, they require a formal mapping specification for all possible integrations between a provided and a required interface at system design-time. In contrast, imprecise matching approaches based on service specifications can be applied at run-time but cannot produce reliable interface mappings. In this paper, we provide our first evaluation for a novel integration method that can integrate components automatically based on incomplete mapping knowledge. Although this method explicitly embraces manual integration efforts, we aim at achieving automatic adapter generation by making additionally formalized integration knowledge reusable. By storing integration knowledge only when a concrete use case is present, generated software adapters remain reliable. Using an empirical within-subject evaluation design, we quantify how reusing formal interface mappings can speed up integration tasks in an agile development setting. We expect the proposed method to be applied in adaptive software ecosystems that evolve in short innovation cycles such as the Internet-of-Things.**

Keywords*–*Semantic Interoperability; Knowledge Reuse; Software Component Compatibility; Engineering Methods

I. Introduction

Manual integration effort for open dependable software systems currently increases exponentially [1]. Although there exist standardization initiatives, semantic service interoperability is still a challenge [2] [3]. Software innovation cycles iterate faster each year and top-down standardization initiatives are too slow to keep up with the increasing rate of change. Furthermore, most standards pre-define a machine-readable (can be parsed) or machine-understandable (can be reasoned about) domain-specific vocabulary by relying on the assumption that syntactically identical words also expose the same meaning. Despite the fact that formalized and executable model checkers to ensure software component interoperability exist (e.g., AUTOSAR [4] for the automotive industry), standards describing a domain completely and unambiguously are currently not applied by other industries. Hence, independent software engineers implement point-to-point adapters without having the ability to reuse existing integration knowledge across software ecosystems. Standards quickly lose their claim for correctness as fast innovation cycles prohibit timeliness of domain knowledge for open and dynamically evolving software systems [5].

Formal approaches can couple heterogeneous software components in an automated way [6] [7]. Although selected semantic interface mappings can be deduced by exploiting reasoning, the applicability of such logic-based approaches is limited in practice. One key challenge such approaches face is the high specification effort needed upfront for open software ecosystems [6] [8]. Describing all interfaces for use cases based on fixed requirements and an increasing number of Internet-of-Things (IoT) devices is not practical for most open software systems [9]. From a platform owner viewpoint, it is not guaranteed that formalized integration knowledge derived from requirements is used during run time by the available components. This is mainly due to the circumstance that end-users express their requirements and use cases during run-time (e.g., by using *If-this-then-that* statements) and IoT device manufacturers cannot be forced to adhere to one service specification syntax and one domain-specific model. Formal mapping approaches can automatically generate highly reliable software adapters for closed and well-defined application contexts. They assume that integration knowledge is specified in an almost complete manner.

Service Matching Solutions, such as semantic interface matching approaches [10] [11] or fuzzy matching approaches [12] for comprehensive service specifications (e.g., MatchBox [2] [13]) allow for matching required against provided services based on their interfaces and/or behavioural description. Although these approaches can be applied in an open system context, they produce only probabilistic results. If no perfect match is found, then these approaches only serve as an assistant for manually selecting relevant interfaces. Furthermore, they may outsource knowledge engineering for a domain to an ontology which, like industrial standards, are prone to be outdated and/or contain inconsistencies [5]. Consequently, their matching result cannot be processed automatically and cannot be used reliably for adapter synthesis. Matching approaches abstract away from concrete use cases and device interfaces and are therefore widely applicable in open systems. Nonetheless, they do not produce reliable results as they mainly work on concrete syntax and only approximate service meanings in a given context. Practitioners require a method that maximizes interface mapping formalization effort in open software systems. Otherwise, similar software adapters are implemented all over again.

In this paper, we apply a novel integration method that formalizes interface mappings incrementally in the context of a home automation system. We evaluate the applicability of the method onto this system class by performing an empirical experiment to demonstrate how integration knowledge is formalized, stored and reused by 15 students. In Section 2, we define all the required terms. Next, in Section 3 the novel integration method is introduced within the smart home context and in Section 4 we outline the experiment and its results. Finally, in Section 5 we conclude our work.

II. Context and Definitions

In order to explain the concepts of the novel integration method within an open IoT software ecosystem, the following definitions are used:

Software Component: A software component is a software element that conforms to a component model that can be independently deployed and that can be composed without modification according to a composition model [14]. Software component's actions can be accessed by a well-defined interface. An action contains a function name, a list of parameters that are inputs, and an output.

Interface Description Language: An Interface Description Language defines a set of actions in a programming-language independent way. Depending on the expressiveness of the language, the syntactic level (e.g., data types and representation), the semantic level (e.g., range of parameters or pre- and postconditions), and the behavioural level (e.g., constraints on the ordering of interactions sequence) can be described.

Component Integration: An interface description can be either used to express actions a component requires from its environment or to express actions that are provided to the environment. Hence, software components are compatible if there exists a contract between their interfaces that maps all necessary interface description elements (i.e., they can be integrated). In distributed systems (e.g., based on web services), this is similar to the concept of interoperability - or integration in a more colloquial style.

Semantic Interoperability: Semantic Interoperability ensures that services and data exchanged between a provided and a required interface makes sense - that the requester and provider have a common understanding of the "meaning" of services and data [15]. Semantic interoperability in distributed systems is mainly achieved by establishing semantic correspondences (i.e., mappings) between vocabularies of different (data) sources [16].

Software Ecosystems: A Software Ecosystem is a socio-technical system (e.g., it contains organizations, people, digital systems, and partnerships). Independent participants collaborate together to generate mutual benefits.

Adaptive Software Ecosystems : Adaptability in Software Ecosystems can be achieved by engineering principles (e.g., explicitly planned component configurations), emergent properties (e.g., implicitly derived from cooperation patterns of the participants) or evolutionary mechanisms (e.g., replacing components) [17]. The higher the degree of adaptability, the more the human is involved.

Open- vs. Closed-world models : A closed-world model of a system directly represents the system under study. This means that there is a functional relation between language expressions and the modelled world. Even when modelling is used to create a conceptual model of a domain, the represented knowledge is implicitly viewed as being complete. As software ecosystems have to be aware of constraints for ensuring adaptability and controllability, an open-world assumption is being assumed for this system class [17].

Top-Down vs. Bottom-Up System Engineering Approaches: In the context of web services, service compositions can be either performed from top-down or bottom-up [18]. Bottom-up refers to whether pre-existing service interfaces are composed and thus adapters may be required due to mismatches. Top-down refers to given a pre-existing composition model, which suitable interfaces need to be discovered and possibly adapted to fit into the composition.

Semantic Integration happens in a software ecosystem within the digital software system. This task is mostly performed by a System Integrator. Now, based on the assumption that Software Ecosystems are based on open-world models (see Definition II), bottom-up integration approaches for software adapter creation are required. Hence, a system integrator has to take the inter-dependencies between the models of all involved systems (e.g., IoT components and the platform models) into account. Consequently, integrating software components from bottom-up may be a valuable engineering approach, in contrast, to designing a machine-readable domain-model from top-down. Nevertheless, a formal underpinning is still required as it facilitates meaningful integration and transformation among models, which is needed for automation through tools.

A. Example

Assume that there exist multiple software component interfaces that were developed by independent software vendors. A semantic integration effort between provided and required software component interface exists when domain models are used by heterogeneous parties. This is mainly due to the circumstance that the device developer determines the concrete syntax based on a self-created semantic domain S for each interface element at component design-time. The semantic domain S is imagined (e.g., *Open door in the living room*) and the respective mappings from the concrete syntax to a semantic domain element is identified. At component integration time, a mapping can be identified by a system integrator to semantically map two syntaxes each from one distinct vocabulary by providing e.g., a function "map(close,close)" (see Figure 1).

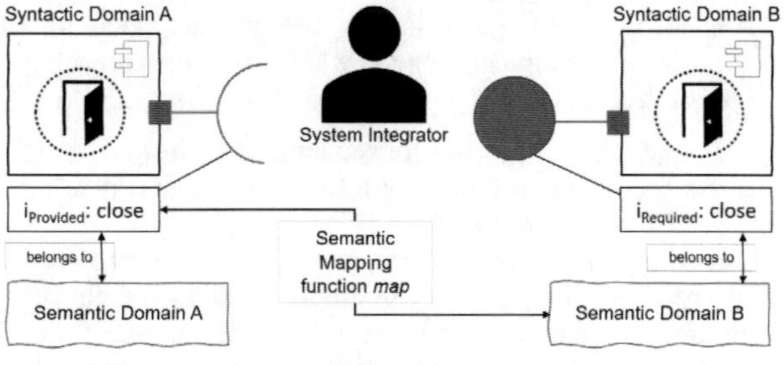

Figure 1. Semantic Interoperability Example for a Home Automation Platform

This mapping does not only take place on the syntactic but also on the semantic interface level. Depending on the use case (i.e., context), close can mean to *undo open* or *close in proximity*. This semantic integration knowledge is codified into the respective software adapter. Please note that this example is more related to being able to execute a corresponding automation process on various IoT devices (i.e., vertical integration). Another integration case is to connect home automation process elements in a horizontal way. For instance, a wall switch defines a required interface to close a door.

III. Knowledge-driven Architecture Composition applied to House Automation Rules

In this section, we briefly introduce the novel integration method [19]. This method is one answer to the underlying research question *How can software components be semantically coupled in an automated way based on partially incomplete integration knowledge*? Then, we will mainly focus on how this method has been applied to integration tasks within a home automation platform.

A. Principles of Knowledge-driven Architecture Composition

As most IoT-related communication, the messages being sent within a smart home environment are predomenantliy data-driven (i.e., following the HATEOS principle) for REST (Representational State Transfer) services. Similar to most engineering approaches that aim at achieving semantic interoperability, this method also abstracts away from networking protocols (e.g., HTTP) and syntactic characteristics (e.g., JSON). Overall, the method aims at 1) storing mappings between two devices based on their interface definition using a declarative language and 2) to logically reason about these mappings. Finally, platform-specific software adapters can be automatically generated by reusing stored mappings or based on derived mappings. The method aims at finding all necessary mappings between a provided and required interface based on the following four principles:

- We do not require all component interface specifications and mappings to be present at system design-time but formalize them incrementally when a concrete use case is available
- If all mappings for one use case are present, then a software adapter can be generated in an automated way
- Manual implementation effort (e.g., software adapter) is explicitly allowed
- By storing and evaluating interface mappings for each use case, integration knowledge becomes reusable and decreases manual implementation effort

The set of all principles for semantic component integration can be subordinated under the term Knowledge-driven Architecture Composition (KDAC).

During the component design phase at time t=0, component provider, as well as requester can design their service interfaces without using a machine-readable interface description language that contains semantic data annotations based on a machine-understandable domain model (see Figure 2). Furthermore, a home automation process is created which uses software component B.

Assume at time t=1, an integration is necessary as a new device is present and the home automation process should not be changed. In addition to writing an individual software adapter to connect component model A (see Syntactic Domain A in Figure 1) to the component model of B (see Syntactic Domain B in Figure 1), the system integrator adds declarative mappings between both data vocabularies. This is illustrated in the rectangles above the KB in Figure 2 where a node represents a word from a vocabulary and an edge represents a mapping. These mappings are stored in a knowledge base KB (e.g., specifying *map* functions from the running example).

Over time, various other components are integrated as well (i.e., indicated by frames in Figure 3) and new mappings are added. For example, software component A* (i.e., another door from another manufacturer in Figure 1) uses the same domain model as software component A. Hence, the stored mappings for component A can be reused automatically. Now assume that there exists no common domain model between component A and A*. However, there exist mappings between components A and C (not shown in Figure 2) and from component C to A*. Due to the transitive relationship $A \leftrightarrow C \leftrightarrow A*$, the mappings from component $A \leftrightarrow A*$ can be calculated by logical reasoning.

At time t=n, only a few new mappings are required which could ultimately result in fully automated component integration at run-time by generating the required software adapter.

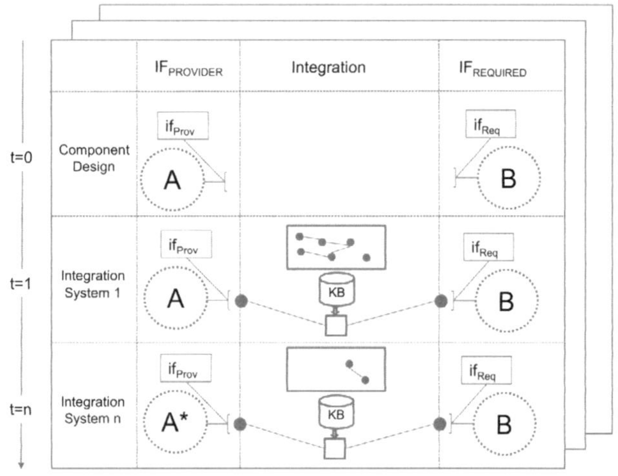

Figure 2. Knowledge-driven Architecture Composition Method

The novelty of this approach is the evolutionary process of formalizing integration knowledge without requiring a closed domain model from requirements. Rather, the focus lies on the incremental formalization of semantic mappings per use case. More details about the proposed method itself can be found in [19] [20].

B. Related Work

In general, there are two movements for solving syntax/semantic interoperability problems for independently developed components: 1) Interface Mapping Solutions [6] [7] as well as 2) Interface Matching Solutions [13].

Bennaceur et al. [6] [21] present MICS, a mapping approach that can infer interface mappings between operations and data of software components based on a formal component composition model. Their main motivation lies within the fact that other adapter synthesis approaches assume that all interface mappings are provided for all components at hand. Assuming that each application domain has its machine-understandable vocabulary, they use description logic properties (i.e., SHOIN(D) to identify implicit interface mappings (e.g., using subsumption). For modelling the behaviour of a software component interface, they used labelled transition systems, which implement concepts of finite-state processes. In contrast to KDAC, this approach can deal with more complex interfaces (i.e., stateful services) but relies on the assumption that sub-models used in the service descriptions for each IoT component are fixed at component design-time.

When the semantic domain of an application domain is not formally specified, then matching solutions can be applied. For example, in the component-based software engineering community, configurable matching approaches such as MatchBox [13] are currently regarded as the state-of-the-art. Matchbox automates the re-configuration of individualized matching scenarios in service discovery scenarios. In this approach ontological signature matcher, condition matcher, privacy matcher and others can be combined automatically. The difference to KDAC lies within the automation property. Here, the matching approach always provides a probabilistic value for unseen automation rules. In contrast, mappings formalized within KDAC can be automated as a use-case with tested automation rule and device properties must be present (i.e., it can be applied in dependable systems such the presented home automation scenario). Other matching approaches for service-based components emerged in the web service community [10] [11]. For example, semantic web service descriptions such as SAWSDL and corresponding matching approaches such as SAWSDL-MX2 [10] can be applied similarly as code-based component matchers like MatchBox [13].

In practice, there is a tendency to solve interoperability problems by creating informal, machine-readable or machine-understandable standards. Such standards are created by multiple companies (e.g., OPC UA [22] or ZigBee [23]) or are dictated by a dominating market player (e.g., Apple Smart Home [24]). Some standardization such as IoT-Lite [25] also provide a machine-understandable domain models for device description. If one standardized vocabulary was used and interpreted by all device developers identically, then there would not be interoperability problems at the syntax/semantic interface. However, standards cannot cope with the increasing rate of change with software innovation cycles iterate faster each year in most application domains. If no single standard exists, then the system integrator must interpret the software component interface in the context of the automation rule. This currently means implementing similar imperative software adapters manually all over again (no domain model or multiple machine-readable domain models) or automated re-configuration is not feasible in a dependable way (no machine-understandable domain model). The latter problem is primarily tackled by KDAC.

C. Applying KDAC within Home Automation Platforms

To enable a system integrator to apply the KDAC method, the following infrastructure assumptions must hold for an IoT software ecosystem (see Figure 4)

- All software components must be already integrated at the technical and the syntactical level. This means, that the platforms must support all required communication protocols (e.g., MQTT or HTTP) as well as the syntactic payload definition (e.g., JSON or XML)
- The platform handles all calls/requests and the serialization/deserialization to/from the components
- A Formalization Editor must be able to retrieve all syntactically available device attributes provided by the connected software components. Furthermore, there must be a declarative language that can be used to formalize interface mappings
- The Formalization Editor must be connected to a knowledge base that is used to store, retrieve and evaluate available interface mappings

The main architectural components are the following:

Formalization Editor: For specifying interface mappings in a declarative style, we use JOLT [26]. JOLT is a JSON to JSON transformation library where the specification for the transformation itself is a JSON document. An example of a declarative JOLT specification can be seen in Figure 3. *Platform A*: We used openHAB [27] as a home automation platform. OpenHAB can syntactically integrate various IoT components out-of-the-box by providing over 200 adapters from heterogeneous device manufacturers. In addition, openHAB can be accessed using a REST-like interface to manipulate home automation rules, data channels that are offered by the IoT devices, a rule execution environment and a user interface to monitor the state of all devices.

Knowledge Base: The Knowledge Base stores formalized mappings in JOLT. Here, a graph-based structure is implemented where each node represents a data-channel and each edge represents a mapping specification. This allows for calculating new mappings (e.g., traversing the graph from a required to a provided interface to identify transitive relationships).

Component: A component is an IoT-device, which is connected to the platform by its interface. The required software adapter, that makes all data channels syntactically available within the platform, is provided by the platform.

User Interface for Formalization Editor: Automation Rules within the IoT context often follow the IFTTT (*If-This-Then-That*) structure. This structure also holds for openHAB. For example, the automation rule *Turn on Heating* contains a trigger, a condition and an action (*RuleBuilder* panel in Figure 3). Each rule part contains a drop-down menu where all available data channels provided by the connected devices are listed. A data-channel is called *Item* in openHAB and has a unique name, a description label and a type. For instance, the data-channel $Living\_Heating$ offered by a software component A has been used within the automation rule *Turn on heating*. Now, the rule should be executed in another environment where only the data-channel $Heating\_GF\_Living$ exists. Hence, the required interface $Living\_Heating$ by the automation rule must be integrated with the provided data-channel $Heating\_GF\_Living$. Now, the system integrator can map the data-channels $Heating\_GF\_Living$ provided by software component B to $Living\_Heating$. All currently provided data-channels are displayed in the *Integration-Items* perspective and all required items for one rule are displayed in the *Remote-Items* panel.

If no mapping for a data-channel exists, it must be created by the system integrator in addition to re-configuring the automation rule (i.e., adapting the software adapter over a user interface). The operation *shift* displayed in the *Mapping-Specification* panel is part of the JOLT specification language and is the application of the *map* function as seen in the running example. This mapping is stored to the knowledge base.

If a mapping specification for a data-channel within the rule is available, then it is retrieved from the knowledge base,

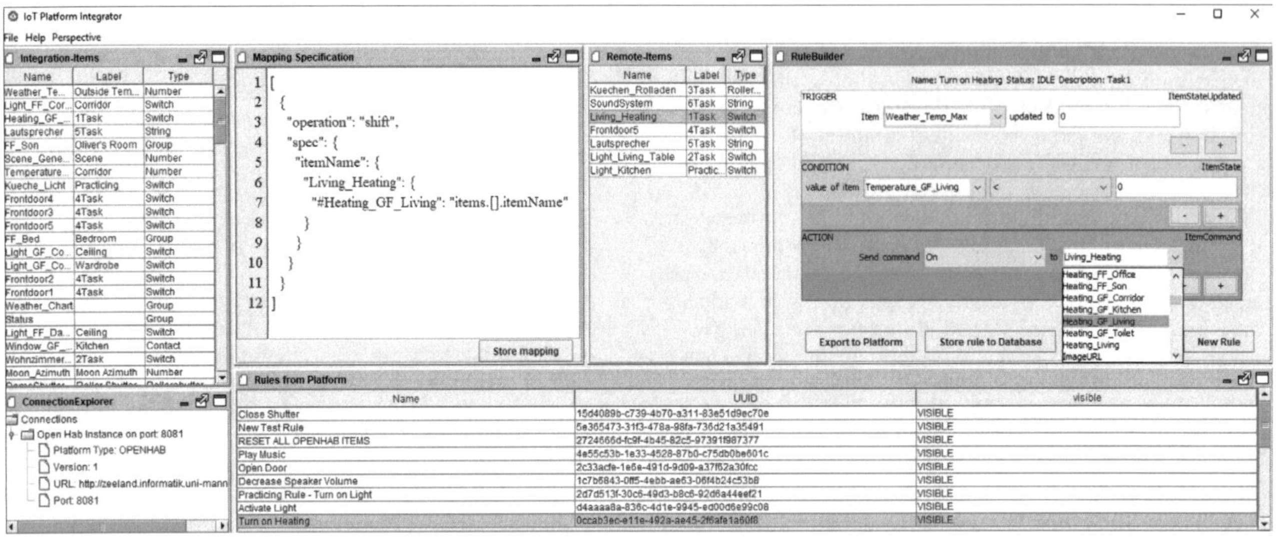

Figure 3. User Interface Formalization Editor

displayed (see *Mapping Specification* and selected *Remote-Items*). The availability of an interface mapping is indicated to the system integrator by a green background. If no specification or not all required specifications for an automation rule are found, then the system integrator has to create new mapping specifications and configure the system accordingly.

If all required mappings are available, the required configuration calls (cf. software adapter from the method) are generated and issued automatically to the connected platform. Finally, the system integrator can test the adapted rule by executing it and supervising the device status changes within the dashboard provided by openHAB (not displayed).

The main effect of applying the proposed method is helping to achieve automated adaptability in software ecosystems. Based on the provided definition II in the section Context and Definitions, this method focuses on *engineered adaptability* and *evolutionary adaptability*. Engineered Adaptability as the platform is now able to re-configure itself during run-time and execute context-sensitive automation rules. Evolutionary adaptability as new components can be integrated manually by the system integrator. Furthermore, human involvement is minimized over time as mapping specifications can be reused and/or generated by reasoning principles without having to rely on a predefined machine-understandable domain from requirements. As this method always requires a concrete use case, the formal specification effort gets controllable without losing the ability to automatically integrate new devices on-the-fly.

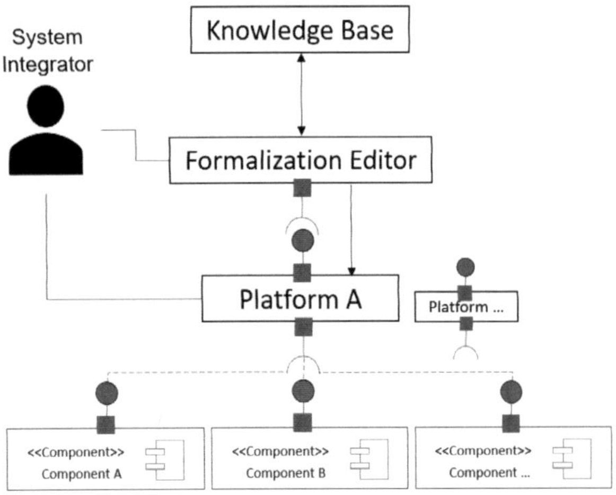

Figure 4. Logical System Architecture

IV. EVALUATION

We designed a controlled experiment based on a within-subject evaluation design to validate our claim. Therefore, we used well-known design principles for empirical studies in software engineering [28] [29]. Our goal is to provide evidence that, over time, reusing interface mappings formalized based on concrete use-cases speeds up integration tasks. Hence, additional specification effort should pay off regarding system re-configuration. Therefore, we measure the time in seconds per home automation rule until the correct data-channels are found. Furthermore, we measure the time for additional specification creation and the time for specification reuse. Thus, in our study, the independent variable is determined by either using the conventional approach (i.e., re-configuring the platform each time a new IoT device enters the environment) or by using KDAC. The dependent variable is the required time for solving integration tasks [28].

Participants: We conducted the experiment within a project cooperation between a German and a Romanian university. All students studied within an Informatics-related profession and can either speak English, German or Romanian. Overall 15 students participated in the evaluation.

- 7 students are currently pursuing their master studies and 8 students their bachelor studies
- 4 out of 15 students own IoT devices and 2 out 15 have been already involved in IoT software development projects

- 4 out of 15 students have read about home automation platforms like openHAB [27] and 3 have already worked with IFTTT rules
- 5 out 15 students knew the IoT-related protocol MQTT [30]

Student Setup: Two groups of students were formed and competed against each other [31]. By assigning students to one group, it was made sure that they were balanced in terms of experience and knowledge. The control group could not reuse interface mappings, but the experimental group could. This means that the control group had to manually re-configure the automation rule. The experimental group could reuse already specified mappings. However, if no mapping was found they had to re-configure the system (i.e., perform the task of the control group) and specify a mapping using JOLT in addition.

Evaluation Execution: The story line that was presented to the students is:
A new automation rule has been downloaded to your home automation platform. However, the rule is not working as other devices have been initially used. Your task is to replace all data-channels until the graphical state visualization provided by the home automation platform of each device is acting accordingly to the meaning conveyed by the displayed automation rule.

Overall, all participants had to work on six automation rules. As an example for the experimental group, one automation rule was:
Task 1: Find the correct item for the rule *Turn on Heating* based on the data-channels

1) $Living\_Heating$
2) $Heating\_Living$
3) $Heating\_GF\_Living$

at the ground floor.
If the correct item is found, select (1) $Living\_Heating$ from the Remote Item Panel and create the mapping specification.

Hence, the automation rule was initially configured with the data-channel $Living\_Heating$, but the device that provided this data-channel was not available anymore. The other automation rules exposed a similar structure.
The participants were instructed that they had to follow the given order of data-channels replacements and then performed the following loop:

- *Configuration Time*: Configure next data-channel from the task and export it to the connected home automation platform by using the tool (see Figure 3).
    - The experimental group could also directly select a correct data-channel if a mapping has been retrieved from the knowledge-base (i.e., indicated by a green background). Hence, existing mappings are automatically evaluated and the necessary re-configuration calls to the platform are generated, but the students had to manually trigger their invocation. Otherwise, they had to stick to the data-channel order from the task.
- *Testing Time*: Next, the participant switched to the home automation platform user interface and executed the adapted rule. Then, the respective device state icon was inspected if the desired action had been executed (e.g., the heating icon label switched its status from OFF to ON). If the item changed its status according to the rule, then the task is solved. If not, the next item had to be tested.
    - *Specification Time*: As soon as the correct item is found, then a mapping specification had to be created based on a template (experimental group only).

All created mapping specifications are stored in the knowledge base and are available to other students that have been assigned to the experimental group.

A. Results

The main reason for carrying out an empirical evaluation was the trade off between the cost of having additional formalization effort for automated data-channel replacement and the benefits of reusing interface mappings for configuring the home automation platform (i.e., software adapter generation). Each task involved different amounts of item replacements and only task 1, 3 and 5 were equipped with mapping specifications for the experimental group. Overall, the following total times for all reuse rules have been measured (see Figure 5).

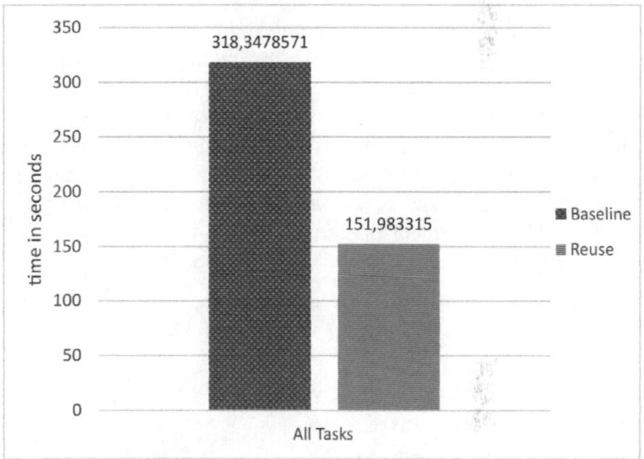

Figure 5. Reuse Tasks - Time Comparison for both groups

Therefore, we first calculate the total time in seconds for the rule using 3 for the control group and 4 for the experimental group. Here, *Y* returns the average time in seconds and *X* is an integer. Then, the sum of each rule result per group is calculated.

$$X = AmountOfReplacementOperationsPerRule \quad (1)$$

$$Y = \frac{TotalAmountOfReplacementOperations}{TotalTimeForAllRules} \quad (2)$$

$$TimeControlGroup = X * Y \quad (3)$$

$$TimeReuseGroup = \frac{(X-1) * Y + ReuseTime}{X} \quad (4)$$

Table I displays the averages and variances per rule in more details for both groups. Here, *Baseline* refers to the sum of *Configuration Time* and *Testing Time* for the control group. *Specification Time* means the time to create a mapping specification in JOLT (experimental group only). *Reuse* (also *Configuration* and *Testing Time* translates to a task (i.e., one of 1,3 or 5) where a mapping specification was found and evaluated so that one correct data-channels is available (experimental group only). Overall, *Specification Time* occurred only once to a student of the experimental group. This specification then influenced the *Configuration Time* for the next student in the experimental group as it was automatically evaluated. *Testing Time* was almost identical for all students and groups.

TABLE I. INTEGRATION TIME IN SECONDS PER DATA-CHANNEL (AVERAGE : VARIANC)

	Baseline	Specification	Reuse
Rule 1	42 : 12	57 : 30	38 : 22
Rule 2	38 : 10	59 : 26	0 : 0
Rule 3	32 : 9	54 : 29	25 : 13
Rule 4	31 : 10	43 : 18	0 : 0
Rule 5	31 : 10	40 : 20	30 : 16
Rule 6	34 : 16	51 : 19	0 : 0

If a green data-channel (i.e., indicated by a green background as depicted in Figure 3) was present, measured *Reuse* times also refer to the sum of *Configuration Time* and *Testing Time* for the experimental group. However, the difference between the control group is the number of replacement operations. For instance, assume that 5 data channels must be tested in the given order. Furthermore, data channel 4 is the correct one and there exist a mapping from data channel 1 to 4. Then, the control group must perform 3 replacement operations (i.e., 1-2, 2-3, 3-4) and the experimental group must perform 1 replacement operation (i.e., 1-4).

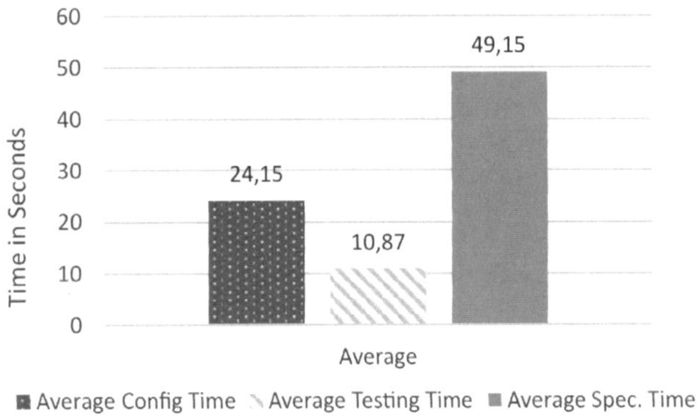

Figure 6. Average Participant Performance

Overall, 211 item replacement operations have been measured (i.e., Average Config Time) and have been tested within the home automation environment (i.e., Average Testing Time). For specification tasks, we measured 54 runs. On average, configuration time lasted 24 s, testing time lasted 11 s and specification time 49 s (see Figure 6).

Figure 5 suggests that the experimental group (i.e., reuse) is faster than the control group (i.e., baseline). Hence, our initial claim to outline the applicability of KDAC within an IoT software ecosystem is fulfilled. However, the point in time where specification effort pays off can only be estimated (e.g., based on the metrics in Table I).

B. Threats to Validity

There are several threats to internal and external validity. *Internal Validity*: Our evaluation targets the causal relationship between either re-configuring the home automation platform each time a new IoT device enters the system or by using KDAC (independent variable) and time (dependent variable). However, the presented results provide one result for one concrete implementation that may be subject to change in another run. This is mainly due to confounding factors (e.g., User Interface Design). Furthermore, the evaluation design ensured an early applicability of data-channels mappings. In large-scale engineering projects, it is unclear when and how often such mappings can be actually reused.

External Validity: The population size is too small to be generalized from. Hence, we cannot say whether the presented results are statistically significant. The respective variances strengthen this circumstance. However, the empirical evaluation, the presented architecture and the technical implementation illustrate how the novel engineering method KDAC can be applied in a home automation system.

V. Conclusion and Future Work

Interoperability without modifying software component interfaces is needed in today's open and adaptive IoT software ecosystems. In this paper, we applied and evaluated a novel integration method called Knowledge-driven Architecture Composition that explicitly allows for manual integration effort without sacrificing reliability. First, we propose an adapted architecture for a home automation platform. Second, we provide a tool and six use-cases that allow for specifying interface mappings for data-driven IoT devices and automation rules from bottom-up. By using the tool, created mappings can be stored in a knowledge base and are made reusable for future integration scenarios. By doing so, we do not lose the ability to re-configure adaptive home automation platforms in an automated way. Formalization effort becomes controllable as a concrete use case must be present. There is no need to specify all possible interface mappings completely at design-time. Third and last, we evaluate the novel incremental, bottom-up integration method with 15 students. We could show that the data-channel mapping specifications created by the proposed method do speed up the overall reconfiguration of the home automation platform.

In the future, we plan to transfer our approach to other system classes such as HTTP-based micro-services in an enterprise setting. This will require more complex transformation functions and will enable a practical comparison to existing mapping approaches. Furthermore, we are currently working on incorporating reasoning services that can transitively infer extended mapping specifications by a sequential execution of mappings. By doing so, we expect to decrease the manual specification effort for the presented approach even further.

Acknowledgment

This work has been developed in the project BIoTope (Research Grant Number 01IS18079C) and is funded by the German Ministry of Education and Research (BMBF).

References

[1] L. Baresi, E. Di Nitto, and C. Ghezzi, "Toward open-world software: Issues and challenges," Computer, vol. 39, no. 10, Oct. 2006, pp. 36–43.

[2] A. Broring et al., "The BIG IoT API - Semantically Enabling IoT Interoperability," IEEE Pervasive Computing, vol. 17, no. 4, Oct. 2018, pp. 41–51.

[3] F. Burzlaff, N. Wilken, C. Bartelt, and H. Stuckenschmidt, "Semantic Interoperability Methods for Smart Service Systems: A Survey," IEEE Transactions on Engineering Management, 2019, pp. 1–15.

[4] S. Bunzel, "AUTOSAR – the Standardized Software Architecture," Informatik-Spektrum, vol. 34, no. 1, Feb. 2011, pp. 79–83. [Online]. Available: http://link.springer.com/10.1007/s00287-010-0506-7 [retrieved: 2020.09.04]

[5] P. Barnaghi, W. Wang, C. Henson, and K. Taylor, "Semantics for the internet of things: early progress and back to the future," International Journal on Semantic Web and Information Systems (IJSWIS), vol. 8, no. 1, 2012, pp. 1–21.

[6] A. Bennaceur, "Dynamic Synthesis of Mediators in Ubiquitous Environments," phdthesis, Université Pierre et Marie Curie - Paris VI, Jul. 2013. [Online]. Available: https://tel.archives-ouvertes.fr/tel-00849402 [retrieved: 2020.09.04]

[7] P. Inverardi and M. Tivoli, "Automatic Synthesis of Modular Connectors via Composition of Protocol Mediation Patterns," in Proceedings of the 2013 International Conference on Software Engineering, ser. ICSE '13. Piscataway, NJ, USA: IEEE Press, 2013, pp. 3–12. [Online]. Available: http://dl.acm.org/citation.cfm?id=2486788.2486790 [retrieved: 2020.09.04]

[8] R. Spalazzese, "A Theory of Mediating Connectors to achieve Interoperability," Apr. 2011. [Online]. Available: https://tel.archives-ouvertes.fr/tel-00660816 [retrieved: 2020.09.04]

[9] L. Cavallaro, E. Di Nitto, and M. Pradella, "An automatic approach to enable replacement of conversational services," in Service-Oriented Computing. Springer, 2009, pp. 159–174.

[10] M. Klusch, P. Kapahnke, and I. Zinnikus, "SAWSDL-MX2: A Machine-Learning Approach for Integrating Semantic Web Service Matchmaking Variants," in 2009 IEEE International Conference on Web Services, Jul. 2009, pp. 335–342.

[11] H. Dong, F. K. Hussain, and E. Chang, "Semantic Web Service matchmakers: state of the art and challenges," Concurrency and Computation: Practice and Experience, vol. 25, no. 7, 2013, pp. 961–988.

[12] M. C. Platenius, M. von Detten, S. Becker, W. Schäfer, and G. Engels, "A Survey of Fuzzy Service Matching Approaches in the Context of On-the-fly Computing," in Proceedings of the 16th International ACM Sigsoft Symposium on Component-based Software Engineering, ser. CBSE '13. New York, NY, USA: ACM, 2013, pp. 143–152. [Online]. Available: http://doi.acm.org/10.1145/2465449.2465454 [retrieved: 2020.09.04]

[13] M. C. Platenius, W. Schaefer, and S. Arifulina, "MatchBox: A Framework for Dynamic Configuration of Service Matching Processes," in Proceedings of the 18th International ACM SIGSOFT Symposium on Component-Based Software Engineering, ser. CBSE '15. New York, NY, USA: ACM, 2015, pp. 75–84, event-place: Montreal, QC, Canada. [Online]. Available: http://doi.acm.org/10.1145/2737166.2737174 [retrieved: 2020.09.04]

[14] I. Crnkovic, S. Sentilles, A. Vulgarakis, and M. R. Chaudron, "A classification framework for software component models," IEEE Transactions on Software Engineering, vol. 37, no. 5, 2010, pp. 593–615.

[15] S. Heiler, "Semantic interoperability," ACM Computing Surveys (CSUR), vol. 27, no. 2, 1995, pp. 271–273.

[16] N. F. Noy, A. Doan, and A. Y. Halevy, "Semantic integration," AI magazine, vol. 26, no. 1, 2005, pp. 7–7.

[17] A. Rausch, C. Bartelt, S. Herold, H. Klus, and D. Niebuhr, "From software systems to complex software ecosystems: model-and constraint-based engineering of ecosystems," in Perspectives on the Future of Software Engineering. Springer, 2013, pp. 61–80.

[18] G. Alonso, F. Casati, H. Kuno, and V. Machiraju, "Web services," in Web services. Springer, 2004, pp. 123–149.

[19] F. Burzlaff and C. Bartelt, "Knowledge-driven architecture composition: Case-based formalization of integration knowledge to enable automated component coupling," in 2017 IEEE International Conference on Software Architecture Workshops (ICSAW). IEEE, 2017, pp. 108–111.

[20] F. Burzlaff, L. Adler, and C. Bartelt, "Towards automating service matching for manufacturing systems: Exemplifying knowledge-driven architecture composition," Procedia CIRP, vol. 72, 2018, pp. 707–713.

[21] A. Bennaceur and V. Issarny, "Automated Synthesis of Mediators to Support Component Interoperability," IEEE Transactions on Software Engineering, vol. 41, no. 3, Mar. 2015, pp. 221–240.

[22] M. Schleipen, S.-S. Gilani, T. Bischoff, and J. Pfrommer, "OPC UA & Industrie 4.0 - Enabling Technology with High Diversity and Variability," Procedia CIRP, vol. 57, Jan. 2016, pp. 315–320. [Online]. Available: http://www.sciencedirect.com/science/article/pii/S2212827116312094 [retrieved: 2020.09.04]

[23] ZigBee Alliance, "ZigBee Specification," Sep. 2012. [Online]. Available: https://zigbee.org/zigbee-for-developers/network-specifications/ [retrieved: 2020.09.04]

[24] Apple Inc., "HomePod," 2019. [Online]. Available: https://www.apple.com/homepod/ [retrieved: 2020.09.04]

[25] "IoT-Lite Ontology." [Online]. Available: https://www.w3.org/Submission/2015/SUBM-iot-lite-20151126/ [retrieved: 2020.09.04]

[26] Jolt JSON to JSON transformation library written in Java, 2019. [Online]. Available: https://github.com/bazaarvoice/jolt [retrieved: 2020.09.04]

[27] openHAB Foundation e.V., "openHAB," 2019. [Online]. Available: https://www.openhab.org [retrieved: 2020.09.04]

[28] G. Leroy, Designing User Studies in Informatics. Springer Science & Business Media, Aug. 2011, google-Books-ID: IqR7M1h1yDQC.

[29] A. J. Ko, T. D. LaToza, and M. M. Burnett, "A practical guide to controlled experiments of software engineering tools with human participants," Empirical Software Engineering, vol. 20, no. 1, Feb. 2015, pp. 110–141. [Online]. Available: https://doi.org/10.1007/s10664-013-9279-3 [retrieved: 2020.09.04]

[30] U. Hunkeler, H. L. Truong, and A. Stanford-Clark, "MQTT-S—A publish/subscribe protocol for Wireless Sensor Networks," in Communication systems software and middleware and workshops, 2008. comsware 2008. 3rd international conference on. IEEE, 2008, pp. 791–798. [Online]. Available: http://ieeexplore.ieee.org/xpls/abs_all.jsp?arnumber=4554519 [retrieved: 2020.09.04]

[31] D. Falessi et al., "Empirical software engineering experts on the use of students and professionals in experiments," Empirical Software Engineering, vol. 23, no. 1, Feb. 2018, pp. 452–489. [Online]. Available: https://doi.org/10.1007/s10664-017-9523-3 [retrieved: 2020.09.04]

Dynamic Adaptive System Composition Driven By Emergence in an IoT Based Environment: Architecture and Challenges

Nils Wilken*[1] Mohamed Toufik Ailane†[2] Christian Bartelt†[3] Fabian Burzlaff*[4] Christoph Knieke†[5]
Sebastian Lawrenz†[6] Andreas Rausch†[7] Arthur Strasser†[8]
*Institute for Enterprise Systems (InES), University of Mannheim
Schloss, 68131 Mannheim, Germany
†Institute for Software and Systems Engineering (ISSE), Clausthal University of Technology
Arnold-Sommerfeld-Straße 1, 38678 Clausthal-Zellerfeld, Germany
Email: [1]wilken@es.uni-mannheim.de [2]mohamed.toufik.ailane@tu-clausthal.de
[3]christian.bartelt@tu-clausthal.de [4]burzlaff@es.uni-mannheim.de
[5]christoph.knieke@tu-clausthal.de [6]sebastian.lawrenz@tu-clausthal.de
[7]andreas.rausch@tu-clausthal.de [8]arthur.strasser@tu-clausthal.de

Abstract— **Applications provided by software intensive systems in an Internet of Things environment offer new business opportunities from the industry. An application describes the expected behavior of the software system. Thereby, the steps of a business process (e.g., event booking) are determined using objects from the Internet of Things environment at run-time. The system behavior is determined at run-time and described as a composition of software components based on service descriptions. These software systems can be developed as so-called dynamic adaptive systems. Therefore, developers define a structure based on software components of the system for an application from the system context at design-time. Then, the selection of software components instances by the system takes place at run-time. However, an Internet of Things environment changes its state constantly over life time and thus, the required structure of a software system can not be defined at design-time. Hence, applications of a dynamic adaptive system must be determined at run-time. In this paper, we introduce our vision of an emergent platform as an architecture for the development of a dynamic adaptive system. Such a system is capable of determining an application and compose a service based process that fulfills this application at run-time. Furthermore, we provide two Internet of Things scenarios and describe challenges on the basis of the scenarios which need to be tackled to enable the implementation of our architecture.**

Keywords–Internet of Things; Dynamic Adaptive System; Service Interoperability; Emergence.

I. INTRODUCTION

The environment of today's software systems (e.g embedded systems and information systems) can consist of complex and powerful objects connected. Each object is running software and providing applications for customers over the internet. This environment is well-defined as the *Internet Of Things (IoT)* [1]. For example, the software running on these devices can be provided as software components from the domain of social events, the domain of transportation or the domain of home automation. Such an environment offers new business opportunities to component providers and to providers of business applications from the industry. From the technological point of view, a software system is then needed to enable providers to offer applications and enable customers to make use of these applications: We refer to such a software system as a *Platform Ecosystem* [2].

In the field of business to customer applications, IoT objects from an environment are used to provide business related applications. All necessary objects for an application are represented in a structure as *user requirements*. This structure can be described as steps of a business process, which are expected by customers and thus must be fulfilled by an application provided by the system. In this context, we refer to *formal user requirements* as an appropriate machine readable representation of user requirements. Hence, an *application* can be defined as a structure that describes a set of component-based software interfaces, which must fulfill the formal user requirements.

Consequently, the application and all required IoT components can not be predefined at design-time because an IoT environment changes its state continuously over life time [3]. Hence, a software system providing applications must automatically and dynamically conduct a composition in response to a state change. We refer to this as an *emergent property* of a software system in an IoT environment. The resulting behavior of the system is not predefined at design-time and not anticipated by individual components. As a consequence, a composition containing executable software components and their bindings for interfaces of a software system is neither known at development time, nor at deployment time. Its composition is changing over time considering changes of its environment.

Hence, each time its IoT environment changes, the software system must be maintained. However, in each maintenance phase additional costly steps must be conducted to find a suitable application from available services. To avoid these problems, a dynamic adaptive software system must be developed, such that it is capable to determine an application from available service at run-time using the state of the IoT environment at run-time.

Thus, we introduce our vision of an software architecture for the development of a dynamic adaptive system, which can fulfill the emergent property required for its applicability in an IoT based environment. The goal of this paper is to investigate if our proposed software architecture can be used by software engineers to develop the appropriate system in practise.

The remainder of this paper is structured as follows: In Section II, the vision architecture of the Emergent Platform and its building blocks are introduced. The activity booking and home automation examples are then used to describe how our Emergent Platform can be applied in the IoT environment in Section III. In Section IV an investigation of challenges follows on the feasibility of approaches from research to discuss how a possible development path of our Emergent Platform can be realized.

II. Our Vision of an Architecture for an Emergent Platform Design

Dynamic adaptive software systems in an IoT based environment can be designed from reusable software components [1], e.g., as proposed in the DAiSI component model [4], which describes the structure and the behavior of the system. Therefore, software components and interfaces are used to describe the building blocks of the architecture. The behavior is described on the basis of a contract based approach. The contracts are used by the system to check required and provided interfaces of software components for semantic compatibility at run-time.

As introduced in Section I, the software components used in our scenario are service software components. A *service software component* is similar to the definition of a software component in component-based software development [5][6]. Here, a software component is a deployable and executable software entity. It defines required and provided interfaces. A software component is executed by calling functions from its implemented provided interfaces, whereas a *service instance* is defined as a software component which has been already deployed for execution by en execution environment.

An *interface* defines a set of actions, which is understood by the provider and the user of an interface [7]. An *action* contains a function name, a list of parameters that are inputs and an output. Thereby, the interpretation of a parameter from a service description is called *semantic* and thus are used to test semantic compatibility of software components. Furthermore, an interface can exist independently of a component which makes it possible to specify and test the system behavior without its concrete implementation. Hence, the syntax of an interface can be described by a service description language (e.g., WSDL defined by W3C).

In order to check the compatibility of a provided and required interface, the term contract is used [7]. A *contract* can be hierarchically classified on the syntactic, semantic, behavioral and non-functional level. A contract is instantiated by defining all necessary mappings between required and provided interfaces.

As already explained in Section I, the process of a dynamic adaptive system must fulfill the expected system behavior. The latter is described as a sequence of business process related steps. A *process* is a composition of service descriptions from many service software components to describe the developed system behavior, which can be executed by an execution engine.

After introducing the basic terms, we now show our vision of a software architecture for the development of a dynamic adaptive system. Figure 1 illustrates the architecture of our emergent platform. The architecture consists of six major parts (see letters A-E in Figure 1) and will be briefly explained in the following:

Run-Time. At first, the system determines formal user requirements from interactions with the end user of an IoT environment in (A). Next, an appropriate application needs to be identified for identified user requirements. Therefore, a set of implementation independent component based interfaces is calculated. In principle this calculation checks if a subset of service descriptions, which are useful to fulfill the formal user requirements from (A), can be found. In a next step, the software system must determine available and executable software components for an application by evaluating registered software components from (D) of the software system and by compositing them to a process (B). (B) then provides a set of software components for execution to (C). The expected system behavior is then fulfilled by the system behavior as an ongoing interaction (E) between user and system invoking software components (C).

Design-Time. In (D), all those service descriptions and software components are developed and maintained by a service integrator which could not be identified by (C) at run-time.

In the following subsections, we explain how the interplay between the blocks (A) to (E) of a dynamic adaptive system in an IoT based environment is achieved in detail. The numbering of the subsections refers to the letters A-E as used in Figure 1.

A. User Goal and Requirements Handling

The user requirements handler (A) (see Figure 1) is responsible for automatic elicitation and formalization of emerging user requirements. Basically, user requirements of a software system express *what* a user wants to achieve and partially also *how* this should be achieved by the help of the software system [8]. Thus, more formally, user requirements specify parts of the process (i.e., how) that should be executed to achieve one or several user goals (i.e., what). Where we consider a user goal to be defined by a distinct state of the operating environment of a software system. A software system is then considered to fulfill the user requirements when the execution of its underlying process eventually leads to an environmental state that corresponds to a set of specified user goals.

Usually, such user requirements are elicitated and formalized manually by requirements engineers during requirement-analysis-time and design-time of software systems. However, as already mentioned in Section I, a key aspect of IoT based execution environments is that user requirements do emerge during the run-time of software systems. As a consequence, the software system has to handle the challenges of eliciation and formalization of emerging user requirements automatically at run-time. In our proposed architecture, the user requirements might be communicated in two different ways: As an *explicit request* or as an *implicit request*. The difference between explicit and implicit user requests is characterized by different interaction patterns between user and platform. An explicit user request is actively formulated (e.g., in Natural Language (NL)) and forwarded to the platform by a user. Further, the user requirements handler might actively interact with the user (e.g., via a chatbot) to clarify possible ambigiouties in the request. In contrast, an implicit request is not actively provided by a user, but rather triggered implicitly by conclusions drawn from inference over constant monitoring of a user. Besides a request, the user requirements handler (A) takes a user profile as a second type of artifact as input. Such a user profile can capture any kind of additional information about a user like for example information about a personal profile, preferences, or interests. Therefore, in the case of an explicit user request, the user requirements handler (A) takes an actively formulated request and a user profile that captures additional information about the user as input. Based on this input, it tries to

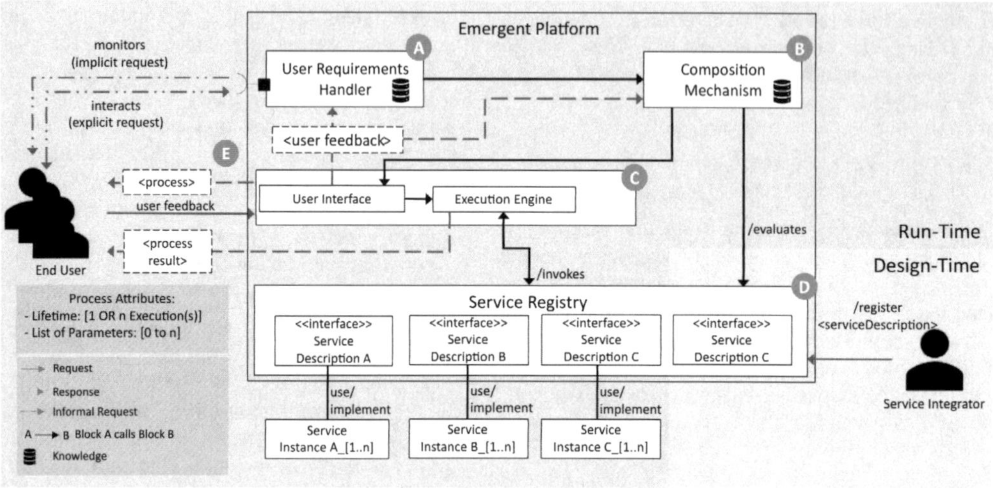

Figure 1. Our architecture to enable composition of software services based on emergence

automatically elicitate and formalize the formulated user goals and requirements. In this context, "formalized" means that the determined user requirements are encoded in a structured, machine-readable format (e.g., JSON). In contrast, in the case of an implicit user request, the user requirements handler (A) takes unstructured observational data of the end user and a user profile that captures additional information about the user as input. Then it tries to extract and formalize meaningful user requirements through continuous analysis of the data stream from user monitoring and creation of an implicit request when it is recognized that the user currently plans to achieve a supported user goal. In both cases, a formal domain model of the environment is needed that models important aspects of the operating environment of the software system (e.g., user goals, objects, possible user actions, etc.). As a next step, the service registry (D) component is checked to determine available and executable software components that are relevant for an application. Here, the main challenge is to match the identified user requirements from the domain model of the environment with service descriptions. As the composition mechanism should support an emergent property, the matching is performed by an algorithm at run-time. After determining an application for the identified user requirements, the user requirements handler forwards the service descriptions to the composition mechanism (B).

B. Composition Mechanism

The composition mechanism (B) is responsible on determining a process of a set of service instances that reflects the order by which services are supposed to be called, to fulfill an application which is provided by the user requirements handler (A). An evaluated service instance in (D) can represent one among many implementations for one service description.
Consequently, different compositions can be identified by the mechanism to fulfill the same application. The decision of choosing the right composition is influenced by many factors. In our architecture we consider the user feedback (see Section II-E) and quality attributes (e.g., economic costs).
In this regard, we aim to enable new composition patterns that can emerge dynamically at run-time as illustrated in Figure 2. A pattern describes the structure of a process considering the factors mentioned above. The most optimal pattern is the pattern that achieves a high score meeting the factors after evaluation. As an example, Figure 2-B shows a chain pattern consisting of different providers and consumers as service instances. Yet, a different pattern (e.g., a tree pattern as shown in Figure 2-B) might be more optimal. For this, an evaluation mechanism that reasons over the factors is needed (as also mentioned in [9]). For these patterns to emerge, we review the description languages and discovery mechanism that can contribute not only to a pre-designed dynamic solution, but also enable these patterns to emerge and offer the possibility for the system to adopt one pattern. Hence, in order to define a robust composition mechanism, a unified formal description for both: (i) the service description of the interfaces (achieved by (B) in Figure 1), and (ii): the available software and component services (which will be invoked by (D) in Figure 1) are necessary.

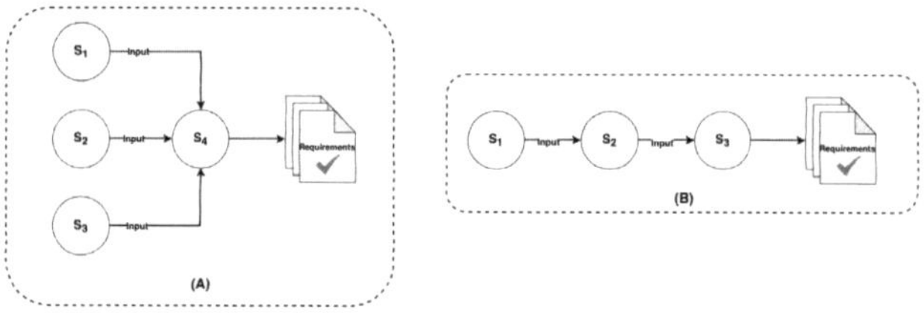

Figure 2. Service Composition Patterns: (A): Tree pattern, (B): Chain pattern

Fulfilling an application and ensuring a positive feedback of the end user can be seen as a problem of navigation in a three dimensional space as shown in Figure 3. The first axis consists of the *availability of services*, that are the available service instances or descriptions at a given point in time: The more services are available, the more flexible is the composition mechanism towards different end user feedback. The second axis consists of the *environments*, each environment can be related to different applications that require a variety of available services, which has to be handled by the composition mechanism. This cross-environments composition is a key element in the emergent composition of services. Thirdly, the *application axis* consists of a set of applications that are present in one or more environments, they may share the same service instances or reuse the same process. Hence, an emerging composition pattern is the result of a en efficient navigation through this space and thus, can not be provided at design-time, but rather emerges from the continuous interaction of the system with its environment (e.g., end user and IoT environment) at run-time. To evaluate a pattern composed from service instances for given subset of service descriptions, the results from three different evaluation mechanisms must be considered: The service registry block must evaluate the interface compatibility of the service instances. As shown in Figure 3, new applications can be identified after the execution of an emergent composition. Thus, the service descriptions used by service instances of the new application must be evaluated. If the interfaces are compatible (see in Subsection II-D) and the new application from the emergent composition can be semantically matched to formal user requirements, then a pattern can be considered for evaluation in the three dimensional space.

C. Execution Engine and User Interface

The execution engine (D) is responsible for executing the process generated by the composition mechanism (B). The user interface (E) is a front-end component that is accessed by the end user to execute the generated process. As user interface design and process execution are not part of our main research focus, we rely on state-of-the-art technologies. In general, the following steps are performed:
An ordered set of service descriptions (i.e., a process) which has been identified by the composition mechanism (B) is displayed to the user. All services contained within the set of services descriptions are available or compatible to available service instances.
Next, the user interface collects feedback from the user and forwards this feedback to the user requirements handler (A) and the composition mechanism (B). Components (A) and (B) use the feedback to improve their performance for future requests and compositions. Afterwards, when positive user feedback is received, the execution engine invokes the respective service instances by using the needed interaction style.
Finally, values and messages as returned by the provided service instances are passed from the service registry (D) to the execution engine (C).

D. Service Integration in the Service Registry

The service registry (D) answers the questions which service instances and descriptions are available and which service instances fulfill a request. Hence, the service registry stores a set of service descriptions and manages the location as well

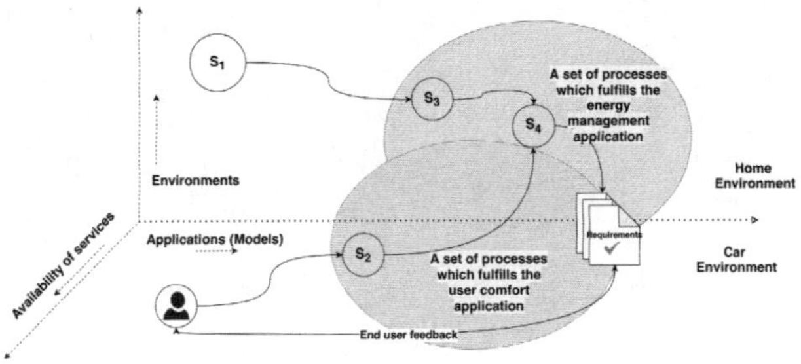

Figure 3. Composition space as a Cartesian plane,

as the interaction style with the service instances. Here, the execution engine (C) invokes available services during process execution. Now, the question becomes how service descriptions and service instances are managed within the platform and by whom.
Service descriptions may or may not conform to standards, common vocabularies or namespaces. Hence, the semantic level is unrestricted. However, the composition mechanisms is based on a service description language which specifies the syntactical level so that the composition mechanism (B) is able to process available service descriptions. A service integrator is responsible to describe service instances with a service description language. Service descriptions contain domain-specific parameters that are mapped to other service descriptions. The service integrator has a technical role within the platform team (e.g., no third parties). One service description can be fulfilled by multiple service instances (see "[1..n]" in Figure 1). The following steps are performed during system design-time (i.e., every time the system is maintained):
The input to the service registry are service descriptions that should be registered.
Next, the service integrator must decide whether to create a new service description or provide a compatibility contract from a provided (e.g., new service instance) to a required Service Description (e.g., already available in the platform). These mappings are called vertical mappings. Furthermore, service descriptions can be mapped to existing service descriptions for establishing a relationship between outputs of a service that may serve as an input to another service. These mappings are called horizontal mappings.
Finally, the service registry contains all service descriptions and associated service instances which potentially can be accessed by the platform. Furthermore, all possible mappings found by the service integrator to translate similar service descriptions into each other are specified. This can be done based on services or on a process produced by the composition mechanism (B).

E. Process Result and Feedback

A given process is only accepted based on the feedback of the end user. In addition to the evaluation of processes, the end user feedback is necessary to determine if the process can be accepted for execution by the execution engine. For example, the user can not afford the quoted price for booking an event and consequently decline a step of a process. Hence, a user feedback mechanism has to be defined and deployed and a validation process is required. Hence, a service instance, service description or the whole composed process can be declined by the end user. Based on the end user feedback, new composition patterns are pushed to emerge by the composition mechanism (see Section II-B). Once, a composition pattern is accepted, the execution engine can then execute the chosen process. In addition, the user requirements handler can use the feedback to evaluate whether the recognized requirements matched the real requirements of the user.

III. Application Scenario

In order to get a better understanding of emergence, this section will present two use cases and discuss their emergent behavior. The use cases are related to different application environments.

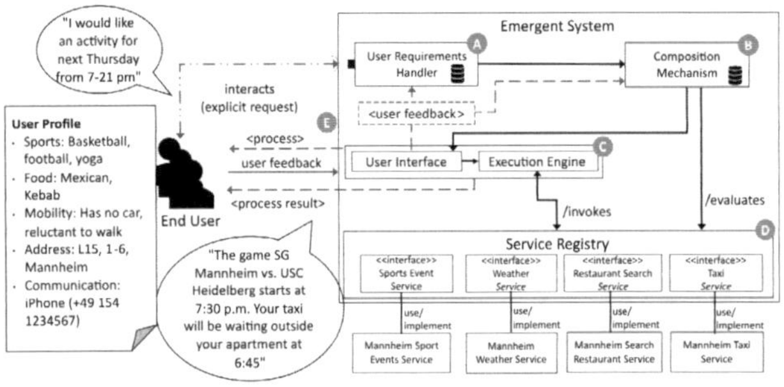

Figure 4. This scenario illustrates how the taxi service is provided in addition to the the booking service.

A. Automated Event Booking

The automated event booking can support the end user to manage his spare time. Therefore, an end user provides a profile to the software system: For example, favorite sports, food and public transport (e.g., because he does not own a car). Figure 4 illustrates the interaction between the end user and our proposed emergent platform.
The user requirements handler (A) starts to identify possible formal user requirements from the profile and from the message explicitly provided by the end user: These can be basketball, football and yoga as sport activities. Moreover, it identifies the time schedule and the location of the end users spare time. As a next step, applications in form of a set of service descriptions from the service registry (D) are determined which are semantically equivalent to the identified formal user requirements.
In this scenario, a set of possible applications can be identified: One can consist of the service descriptions Sports Event Service and Taxi Service. Another application can consist of Restaurant Search Service in addition to, the same service descriptions as in the first application.
The Sports Event Service can provide different sport events in a specific area, such as football and basketball games. The Weather Service provides the current temperature and the weather forecast. The Restaurant Search Service provides different restaurants, including the type of kitchen (Spanish fast food, etc.) in a specific area. And the Taxi Services enables booking a taxi from taxi companies such as Uber.
The set of applications is then provided to the composition mechanism (B). Based on the available service instances, the composition mechanism evaluates possible composition patterns in order to determine a process. Since the end users residence is Mannheim, the mechanism determines a set of services instances regarding their availability: Figure 4 constitutes the service instances used in the service registry (D), which can be used by (B) to compose a process. The process is then provided to the front-end software component (C) and is executed by the execution engine (C). As a result, the software system provides process steps to the end user which enable the user to book a football event and a taxi for transportation to the event-location (E). If the end user accepts this event, the platform will book the tickets and the taxi for him, if not it will try to evaluate another activity as an emerged composition: For example, a dinner in a Mexican restaurant. The emergence is represented by the behavior of the software system driven by the feedback from the end user and the IoT environment.

B. Home Automation

The smart home automation is responsible for managing energy flows of a house. Its goal is to manage the temperature and controlling the alarm system as economic efficient as possible for the end user. Unlike the first use case the user request is implicit, thus the smart home automation is observing the end user. The alarm should be turned off and the room temperature adjusted to a comfortable level, when the end user arrives at home: The user requirements handler (A) observes the actions and preferences of the end user and, based on the available services (see Figure 5), evaluates the best subset of service instance for composition to meet the user preferences and goals (B). The execution engine starts to execute the process provided by (B), after the end user acknowledge the process with the user interface (C) by providing his feedback (E). The process is executed as follows: It uses the actual GPS position from the user. When the end user getting closer to the house, then the home automation starts the climate control and turns off the alarm. Furthermore, the automation manages the energy flow in the house. For example, if the weather conditions are good, then the climate control can be powered by energy from the solar system of the home. This can be achieved by a balanced energy consumption strategy in cooperation urban energy suppliers.

IV. Challenges

A. Regarding User Goal and Requirements Handling

Specifying accurate and correct user requirements is crucial to ensure that a software system, which is developed from these user requirements, will be useful to the end users. As already highlighted in Section II, currently these tasks are handled manually by requirements engineers that specify the user requirements at design-time of a software system in cooperation with the end users. Over the past decades several different frameworks for requirements engineering were proposed and researched [8]. One popular framework is the KAOS framework [10], which is a multi-paradigm goal oriented modelling framework. Another example is the agent-oriented modelling framework i* [11], which is built around concepts such as goals, abilities, beliefs and commitments, and is the base of the Tropos methodology [12] which allows for validation by model-checking. However, all these frameworks include much manual work of requirements engineers during design-time of a software system. This contradicts to an important envisioned ability of the proposed platform, which is the automatic eliciation and formalization of user requirements

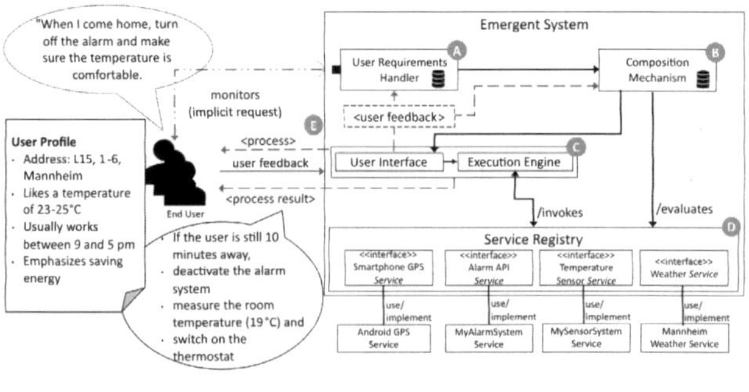

Figure 5. This scenario illustrates how the different services are provided in addition to the the alarm service.

that emerge during run-time of a software system. Hence, the following two challenges are relevant in the context of the user requirements handler (A):

How can user requirements be elicitated automatically from unstructured data? Along the lines of the distinction between explicit- and implicit user requirements, this challenge can be further subdivided into two sub-challenges. Both cases represent significant challenges that require different methods to be solved. In the case of an explicit request (like the example described in Section III-A) untrained end users are usually not able to express their requirements in a structured, machine-readable format, but rather describe their goals in NL. This is a major challenge, as descriptions in NL are commonly incomplete and ambiguous [13]. The same holds for an implicit request, where user goals are not even explicitly described, but are rather hidden in unstructured observational data that is generated through continuous monitoring of the end users. In the context of the example scenario described in Section III-B, an implicit request could be created when the system recognizes that the end user currently has the goal to go home from the past observed changes of the environment (e.g., change of user location). Hence, to achieve automatic elicitation of user requirements, the proposed platform has to be able to extract the relevant user goals and requirements from an unstructured input data format (e.g., NL or observational data), in order to use them for the composition of a useful software service.

Over the past decade first efforts towards automatic extraction of user requirements from explicit user interaction appeared. For example, van Rooijen et al. [14] try to automatically generate user requirements from sets of input examples that are created by the end users in the form of sequence diagrams. As an extension to this approach, van Rooijen et al. [15] try to learn such sequence diagrams directly from NL descriptions. Recently another approach uses a chatbot to refine user requirements that were extracted from NL input in a feedback communication cycle with the end users [16]. Some of these approaches might also be applicable in the context of the platform architecture proposed in this paper. In contrast, there has not been done much work yet towards the direction of automatically recognizing user requirements from unstructured observational data in the field of software systems engineering. However, the topic of automatically recognizing user goals and plans from observational data is a long standing research area in the Artificial Intelligence (AI) community. First works in this area appeared in the mid 80s and early 90s [17][18]. Several prominent recent approaches formulate the goal recognition problem as a planning problem which can be solved by the use of classical AI planners [19][20]. Another approach that adopts machine learning techniques, was proposed by Zeng et al. [21]. They use inverse reinforcement learning to model human behaviour to recognize goals in a dynamic local network interdiction environment. We envision that some of these approaches might be useful for automatic requirement elicitation in the context of implicit user interaction.

How can user requirements be formalized? Once the relevant user goals and requirements were extracted, they have to be transformed to a formal, machine-readable format so that the composition mechanism (B) can handle them. In literature there exist several approaches to formalize user requirements like for example state machines, activity diagrams, or sequence-diagrams [14][22]. Another possibility would be to use a Domain Specific Language (DSL) to formally encode the elicitated user requirements. Besides these formats that focus on behavioral aspects, there are also some approaches that focus on the structural aspects of software systems, like class diagrams or entity relationship models [22]. However, as the structure of the composed software component process is considered to be an emergent property, which emerges during composition, of the proposed platform, these kinds of models might be to restrictive regarding the structure of composed services. Hence, it is not clear which kind of formalization format is suited best for the application in the context of the proposed emergent platform architecture.

In addition, also the transformation which is required to translate the elicitated requirements to such a format is challenging, because it requires a mechanism that is able to interpret the semantic meaning of them. To achieve this some kind of domain model (e.g., a domain ontology) that encodes relevant semantic information about the environment is required. Overall, the formalization format and transformation mechanism that are used have to provide a level of semantic, behavioral, and structural information that on the one hand is sufficient to compose meaningful software component processes from it, but on the other hand does not restrict the degrees of freedom of the composition mechanism (B) in a way that its emergent behaviour is harmed or prohibited.

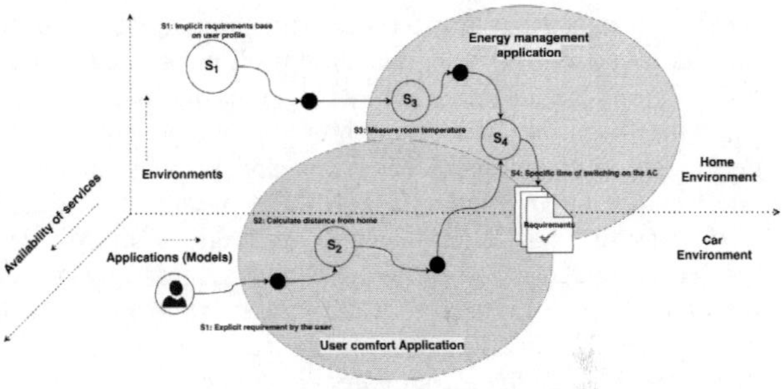

Figure 6. Composition space navigated using Markov Decision Process (MDP)

B. Regarding Composition Mechanism

As introduced in Section III, several application types can be identified in the home automation use case. Two examples are, energy management and user comfort applications (see Figure 6). The composition is governed by certain quality attributes of available service instances to fulfill the two possible concrete applications described in Section III and navigate through the three dimensional space (as introduced in Subsection II-B). Similar research has been made in this regard such as multi-agent solutions [23] and genetic algorithms [24]. The two challenges are to construct a suitable structure for the three dimensional problem space and and to evaluate emerged composition patterns. In order to enable a composition pattern to emerge, two main questions need to be answered:

How to compose? One fundamental question that rises when speaking of service composition is how the composition component is able to compose the relevant service instances.

As the composition mechanism is responsible to compose a process that fulfills an application, discovering the instances in the service registry (D) is a main challenge. In our suggested solution, which is provided later in this section, we consider all possible compositions and evaluate each composition if it fulfills a given application or not. This leads us to the second question:

How to evaluate a given composition? After composing a set of service instances, the validity and optimality of the obtained process has to be evaluated. We also consider this in our suggested solution later in this section by speaking of an optimal policy (the formal term for the evaluation function). To answer the questions, we suggest to formulate the composition problem as a markovian problem [25]. A Markov Decision Process (MDP) is a mathematical tool that is used to solve decision problems, it consists of a 4-tuple *M = (S, A, P, R)*, such that:

- *S*: Is a set of the system states (State space)
- *A*: Is a set of actions that the system can act on based on the current state (Action space).
- *P*: Is the probability function that indicates the probability of transitioning to state s' when taking action a at state s (Pr($s'|s, a$).
- *R*: The expected immediate reward for taking action a at state s and transiting to state s' (r = R($s'|s, a$).

Similar to [9], a dynamic composition is realized using a reinforcement learning method, the main challenge of such an approach is the definition of the sets of states and actions. Furthermore, engineering a reward function for the expected reward based on an emergent composition is a challenging task. Once, the challenge of designing the problem as a MDP, the solution challenge is how to obtain a policy π that helps detect all emergent behaviors and provide an optimal one. As shown in Figure 6, a MDP will emerge based on navigating different environments, applications and available service instances and descriptions. The compatibility of composed services is referred to as *Semantic Interoperability* and explained in the Section IV-C). Finally, the emergent process that is found to be the most optimal is then provided to the end user. If the feedback of the end user shows that the emergent process is accepted, the process is executed by the execution engine. Otherwise, it is not executed.

C. Regarding Service Integration in the Service Registry

Semantic Interoperability and Semantic Integration is a research topic since the 90s [26][27]. The interoperability of a required and a provided service is ensured when their syntactic level (e.g., data types and representation), semantic level (e.g., range of parameters or pre- and postconditions) and behavioural level (e.g., constraints on the ordering of interactions sequence) can be mapped [7]. In the context of distributed systems such as the presented platform, interactions styles implemented by the communication protocols (e.g., client-server) and non-functional properties are added. In most systems, syntactic incompatibility cannot happen as IoT components support standard communication protocols like HTTP over JSON. Consequently, the compatibility challenge shifts to the semantic level. In a distributed system, this is commonly referred to as Semantic Interoperability [26].
Semantic Interoperability ensures that services and data exchanges between a provided and a required interface makes sense - that the requester and provider have a common understanding of the "meaning" of services and data [26]. Semantic interoperability in distributed systems is mainly achieved by establishing semantic correspondences (i.e., mappings) between vocabularies of different sources [27]. The question how to achieve semantic interoperability in dynamic and adaptive systems is still actively researched. For instance, formal domain standards such as ontologies or Linked Open Data vocabularies quickly lose their claim for correctness. Linked Open Data sources are prone to errors and inconsistencies (due to a lack of quality control) and ontologies must be constantly monitored and updated due to the pervasiveness and volatility of the underlying IoT environments [28]. In the scope of the presented architecture, the following challenges are relevant:

How are service components integrated? IoT services can be combined with other applications and services to create complex, context-aware business services. Therefore, service integration can either be performed from top-down or bottom-up [29]. Bottom-up refers to whether pre-existing service interfaces are glued together and thus adapter may be required due to mismatches. Top-down refers to, given a pre-existing composition model, which suitable interfaces need to be discovered and possibly adapted to fit into the composition.
From the viewpoint of distributed systems (i.e., semantic interoperability), flow-based composition tools are commonly used to model an automation process by plugging in service instances. A common modelling pattern for such tools is *If this then that but only if.* This pattern may be visualized by using graphical elements (e.g., IFTTT [30]) or textual templates (e.g., TASKER [31]). When a process is modelled, all of these platforms integrate the available service instances by implementing a software adapter that manages the communication between the service description used in the process and the services instance. Here, no service registry is used as all software adapters must be manually implemented by software engineers. Hence, the end user himself must choose 1) which of the available services satisfies his requirements (c.f. service registry (D)) and 2) how services may be composed (c.f. composition mechanism (B)). A modification of just passing data and services offered by the service instance to the user interface of a platform is to define a domain-specific model. For example, the smart home platform openHAB [32] defines its data properties in a device vendor-independent way. In fact, the top-down defined domain model must be used to map device specific characteristic during software adapter implementation. Hence, the service integrator interprets both, the provided device interfaces and the required domain-specific model. However, this integration knowledge is not stored in a searchable format. Furthermore, this kind of integration knowledge is hard to reuse as every platform designs its own domain model.
On the one hand, the proposed platform in this paper should rely on heterogeneous and dynamically moving software components to provide emergent behaviour (i.e., vertical mappings between service instance and service description). On the other hand, the composition mechanism (B) requires a uniform representation of semantically interoperable service instances (i.e., horizontal mappings between service descriptions). Now, the question is whether the service integrator maps available service instances based on a top-down defined domain model or if a domain model of services is built up from the available service descriptions. In both ways, mappings are required. Hence, engineering approaches that can adapt and compensate

efficiently for a reconfiguration of service provisioning when context changes are necessary [28].

How can semantic interoperability between service components be achieved automatically? If mappings are required anyways when dealing with heterogeneous software components, the service integrator should be supported to create them. Current approaches such as INTER-IoT [33] heavily rely on the usage of domain ontologies. Therefore, a wide body of ontologies for different application domains can be used (see the website [34] for an overview). For example, Lov4Iot defines a subset of linked data vocabularies that are relevant within several domains that are affected by IoT (e.g., Home Automation or Wearables). When all service descriptions do refer to the same ontology concepts for a certain domain, then the ontologies can be queried for available mappings for needed vocabularies. As a consequence, generating a software adapter automatically is reduced to a technical challenge. However, most service instances do not provide semantic annotations and/or a machine-readable service description. Furthermore, it must be ensured that the domain ontology does contain all needed concepts so that the service integrator can map them based on a service instance. Hence, semantic annotations are critical for engineering integration knowledge in IoT.

From the viewpoint of artificial intelligence (i.e., semantic integration), ontologies are the state-of-the-art for storing the meaning of data. As IoT systems themselves offer data-driven service interfaces (i.e., mostly RESTful with no state or special behaviour), ontologies are often used in platform-based systems [33][35]. Naturally, the usage of an ontology is also possible within the proposed architecture.

However, what makes semantic data handling in IoT more challenging and fraught with technical difficulties is the scale of data generated by its corresponding resources, continuous changes in the state (and consequently description) of the resources and volatility of the IoT environments [28]. Hence, creating engineering tools that allow to cope with the increasing amount of IoT devices, their services and, most importantly, their combination by providing automation, reasoning and intelligence need to be designed. Furthermore, the question which service description language (e.g., OpenAPI or SA-WSDL) [36] and which mapping language is applicable by the service integrator and, more importantly, how semantic correspondences are captured during the lifecycle of the proposed platform must be answered.

To tackle these two challenges, a novel integration method called Knowledge-driven Architecture Composition that relies on an incremental formalization process for semantics can be used [37]. This method explicitly allows for incompleteness of integration knowledge and supports an evolutionary instead of an revolutionary definition of domain models (i.e., not based on fixed domain ontologies at system design-time). The novelty of this approach is formalizing semantic integration knowledge per use-case in a bottom-up manner. By focusing on integration knowledge instead of conforming to technological-oriented interface descriptions and standards, the method maximizes the impact for formalizing the semantic mappings as a concrete use-case must be present. Hence, formalization does only take place if it is specifically needed. The additional formalization effort in addition to implementing software adapters pays off as adapters for future devices can be generated (semi-) automatically through the usage of reasoning principles.

V. Conclusion and Future Work

We proposed a vision of an architecture as a so-called Emergent Platform. Using the architecture, a software engineer is able to develop a dynamic adaptive system which fulfills the emergent properties of an IoT based environment. The main building blocks of the architecture are separated into run-time and design-time. At run-time, the building blocks are capable to determine an application for user requirements, which emerge from the IoT environment based on available services. In a next step, the composition mechanism of the system provides the system behavior as a process which fulfills the expected behavior of an application. Thus, the mechanism to determine a process for an required application that emerged at run-time may minimize manual system maintenance. The feasibility of the architecture is exemplified with two use-cases from the home automation and event booking domain. In the future, we plan to evaluate the feasibility of identified techniques. Thus, our next step is a prototypical implementation including the technical basis for the composition mechanism.

Acknowledgment

This work has been developed in the project BIoTope (Research Grant Number 01IS18079C) and is funded by the German Ministry of Education and Research (BMBF). The following partners were involved in this project: Universität Mannheim, Technische Universität Clausthal, Wolfsburg AG, StoneOne AG. Special thanks go to Mohamad Ibrahim, Abram Lawendy and Michael Pernpeintner for their valuable contribution to the project.

References

[1] A. Al-Fuqaha, M. Guizani, M. Mohammadi, M. Aledhari, and M. Ayyash, "Internet of things: A survey on enabling technologies, protocols, and applications," IEEE Communications Surveys Tutorials, vol. 17, no. 4, 2015, pp. 2347–2376.

[2] M. G. Jacobides, C. Cennamo, and A. Gawer, "Towards a theory of ecosystems," Strategic Management Journal, vol. 39, no. 8, 2018, pp. 2255–2276. [Online]. Available: https://onlinelibrary.wiley.com/doi/abs/10.1002/smj.2904 [retrieved: 2020.09.04]

[3] A. Bröring, S. K. Datta, and C. Bonnet, "A categorization of discovery technologies for the internet of things," in Proceedings of the 6th International Conference on the Internet of Things, ser. IoT'16. New York, NY, USA: Association for Computing Machinery, 2016, pp. 131–139. [Online]. Available: https://doi.org/10.1145/2991561.2991570 [retrieved: 2020.09.04]

[4] K. Rehfeldt, M. Schindler, B. Fischer, and A. Rausch, "A component model for limited resource handling in adaptive systems," in ADAPTIVE 2017: The Ninth International Conference on Adaptive and Self-Adaptive Systems and Applications. IARIA, 2017, pp. 37–42.

[5] T. Vale et al., "Twenty-eight years of component-based software engineering," Journal of Systems and Software, vol. 111, 2016, pp. 128–148.

[6] C. Szyperski, Component Software: Beyond Object-Oriented Programming, 2nd ed. USA: Addison-Wesley Longman Publishing Co., Inc., 2002.

[7] I. Crnkovic, S. Sentilles, A. Vulgarakis, and M. R. Chaudron, "A classification framework for software component models," IEEE Transactions on Software Engineering, vol. 37, no. 5, 2010, pp. 593–615.

[8] A. van Lamsweerde, "Requirements engineering in the year 00: a research perspective," in Proceedings of the 22nd international conference on Software engineering, ser. ICSE '00. Limerick, Ireland: Association for Computing Machinery, Jun. 2000, pp. 5–19. [Online]. Available: https://doi.org/10.1145/337180.337184 [retrieved: 2020.09.04]

[9] H. Wang et al., "Adaptive service composition based on reinforcement learning," in International conference on service-oriented computing. Springer, 2010, pp. 92–107.

[10] A. Dardenne, A. van Lamsweerde, and S. Fickas, "Goal-directed requirements acquisition," Sci. Comput. Program., vol. 20, no. 1–2, Apr. 1993, pp. 3—50. [Online]. Available: https://doi.org/10.1016/0167-6423(93)90021-G [retrieved: 2020.09.04]

[11] E. Yu, "Towards modelling and reasoning support for early-phase requirements engineering," in Proceedings of ISRE '97: 3rd IEEE International Symposium on Requirements Engineering. IEEE, Jan. 1997, pp. 226–235.

[12] J. Castro, M. Kolp, and J. Mylopoulos, "Towards requirements-driven information systems engineering: the Tropos project," Information Systems, vol. 27, no. 6, Sep. 2002, pp. 365–389. [Online]. Available: https://linkinghub.elsevier.com/retrieve/pii/S0306437902000121 [retrieved: 2020.09.04]

[13] F. S. Bäumer and M. Geierhos, "How to deal with inaccurate service descriptions in on-the-fly computing: Open challenges," in Natural Language Processing and Information Systems, M. Silberztein, F. Atigui, E. Kornyshova, E. Métais, and F. Meziane, Eds. Cham: Springer International Publishing, 2018, pp. 509–513.

[14] L. Van Rooijen and H. Hamann, "Requirements specification-by-example using a multi-objective evolutionary algorithm," in 2016 IEEE 24th International Requirements Engineering Conference Workshops (REW). IEEE, 2016, pp. 3–9.

[15] L. van Rooijen et al., "From user demand to software service: Using machine learning to automate the requirements specification process," in 2017 IEEE 25th International Requirements Engineering Conference Workshops (REW). IEEE, 2017, pp. 379–385.

[16] E. Friesen, F. S. Bäumer, and M. Geierhos, "Cordula: Software requirements extraction utilizing chatbot as communication interface," in Joint Proceedings of REFSQ-2018 Workshops, Doctoral Symposium, Live Studies Track, and Poster Track co-located with the 23rd International Conference on Requirements Engineering: Foundation for Software Quality (REFSQ 2018), vol. 2075. CEUR-WS.org, 2018.

[17] H. A. Kautz and J. F. Allen, "Generalized plan recognition," in Proceedings of the Fifth AAAI National Conference on Artificial Intelligence, ser. AAAI'86. AAAI Press, 1986, pp. 32—37.

[18] E. Charniak and R. P. Goldman, "A bayesian model of plan recognition," Artif. Intell., vol. 64, no. 1, Nov. 1993, pp. 53—79. [Online]. Available: https://doi.org/10.1016/0004-3702(93)90060-O [retrieved: 2020.09.04]

[19] M. Ramírez and H. Geffner, "Plan recognition as planning," in Proceedings of the 21st International Jont Conference on Artifical Intelligence, ser. IJCAI'09. San Francisco, CA, USA: Morgan Kaufmann Publishers Inc., 2009, pp. 1778—1783.

[20] ——, "Probabilistic plan recognition using off-the-shelf classical planners," in Proceedings of the Twenty-Fourth AAAI Conference on Artificial Intelligence, ser. AAAI'10. AAAI Press, 2010, pp. 1121–-1126.

[21] Y. Zeng et al., "Inverse reinforcement learning based human behavior modeling for goal recognition in dynamic local network interdiction," 2018. [Online]. Available: https://aaai.org/ocs/index.php/WS/AAAIW18/paper/view/16162 [retrieved: 2020.09.04]

[22] T. Yue, L. C. Briand, and Y. Labiche, "A systematic review of transformation approaches between user requirements and analysis models," Requirements Engineering, vol. 16, no. 2, 2011, pp. 75–99.

[23] H. Wang, X. Wang, X. Hu, X. Zhang, and M. Gu, "A multi-agent reinforcement learning approach to dynamic service composition," Information Sciences, vol. 363, 2016, pp. 96–119.

[24] G. Canfora, M. Di Penta, R. Esposito, and M. L. Villani, "An approach for qos-aware service composition based on genetic algorithms," in Proceedings of the 7th annual conference on Genetic and evolutionary computation. Association for Computing Machinery, 2005, pp. 1069–1075.

[25] M. L. Puterman, Markov decision processes: discrete stochastic dynamic programming. John Wiley & Sons, 2014.

[26] S. Heiler, "Semantic interoperability," ACM Computing Surveys (CSUR), vol. 27, no. 2, 1995, pp. 271–273.

[27] N. F. Noy, A. Doan, and A. Y. Halevy, "Semantic integration," AI magazine, vol. 26, no. 1, 2005, pp. 7–7.

[28] P. Barnaghi, W. Wang, C. Henson, and K. Taylor, "Semantics for the internet of things: early progress and back to the future," International Journal on Semantic Web and Information Systems (IJSWIS), vol. 8, no. 1, 2012, pp. 1–21.

[29] G. Alonso, F. Casati, H. Kuno, and V. Machiraju, "Web services," in Web services. Springer, 2004, pp. 123–149.

[30] IFTTT, "IFTTT." [Online]. Available: https://ifttt.com [retrieved: 2020.09.04]

[31] Tasker, "Tasker for Android." [Online]. Available: https://tasker.joaoapps.com/ [retrieved: 2020.09.04]

[32] openHAB Foundation e.V., "openHAB," 2019. [Online]. Available: https://www.openhab.org/ [retrieved: 2020.09.04]

[33] M. Ganzha, M. Paprzycki, W. Pawłowski, P. Szmeja, and K. Wasielewska, "Semantic interoperability in the internet of things: An overview from the inter-iot perspective," Journal of Network and Computer Applications, vol. 81, 2017, pp. 111–124.

[34] "Linked Open Vocabularies for Internet of Things (LOV4IoT)." [Online]. Available: http://lov4iot.appspot.com/ [retrieved: 2020.09.04]

[35] A. Bröring et al., "The big iot api-semantically enabling iot interoperability," IEEE Pervasive Computing, vol. 17, no. 4, 2018, pp. 41–51.

[36] K. Kurniawan, F. J. Ekaputra, and P. R. Aryan, "Semantic service description and compositions: A systematic literature review," in 2018 2nd International Conference on Informatics and Computational Sciences (ICICoS). IEEE, 2018, pp. 1–6.

[37] F. Burzlaff and C. Bartelt, "Knowledge-Driven Architecture Composition: Case-Based Formalization of Integration Knowledge to Enable Automated Component Coupling," in 2017 IEEE International Conference on Software Architecture Workshops (ICSAW). IEEE, Apr. 2017, pp. 108–111.

Development of a Digital Ecosystem Using the Example of Amazon

Marit Mathiszig
Institute for Software and Systems Engineering,
Clausthal University of Technology
Clausthal-Zellerfeld, Germany
email: marit.elke.anke.mathiszig@tu-clausthal.de

Anna Unterluggauer
Institute of Management and Economics
Clausthal University of Technology
Clausthal-Zellerfeld, Germany
email: anna.unterluggauer@tu-clausthal.de

Abstract— **Economic changes have been driven in recent years due to the digital transformation. Companies like Amazon are adapting to this development by using digital ecosystems. It is assumed by the authors that changing customer needs lead to an adaption at the ecosystem level. Amazon's digital ecosystem expands with the integration of new technologies. These technologies are acquired through company acquisitions. This paper deals with the questions of how the future development of Amazon's digital ecosystem can be predicted and which method could be used to analyse the development of Amazon's digital ecosystem. To answer these questions, the technology-portfolio of Pfeiffer et al. combined with other criteria and modified was applied to the previous and the future development of Amazon. A possible future alternative of Amazon's digital ecosystem was developed.**

Keywords: Amazon; expansion strategies; digital ecosystem; innovationsmanagement; technology-portfolio.

I. INTRODUCTION

In recent years, society and especially the economy have changed dramatically due to digital technologies. This process of change, often described in the literature as digital transformation, will progress even more rapidly in the coming years. Intelligent systems and ever more extensive networks will trigger a process that can help those companies that react flexibly and do not ignore this development to achieve a huge growth [1]. Therefore, digital business models, especially digital ecosystems, are becoming more important in research and practice. Digital ecosystems are changing and developing continuously, forcing companies to analyse their digital ecosystem in order to identify (environmental) changes early and to be able to act and react [1]. There are a large number of studies that discuss (digital) ecosystems. The term business ecosystem was first used by Moore in 1993. Just like a natural ecosystem, a business ecosystem moves progressively from a collection of products and services to a more structured community [2].

As an extension of business ecosystems, digital ecosystems focus on the central importance of the digital technologies that make up the ecosystem [3]. There are some studies that focus on the development of digital ecosystems in general from an economic perspective, e.g., network analysis, the formation of digital ecosystems, and co-evolution, a large part of the studies, however, focuses a technical view of digital ecosystems [3].

Companies like Amazon often acquire new technologies and integrate them into their structures and products. The integration avoids competition between new and conventional products [4]. Amazon's business model consists of a digital ecosystem that includes the entire value chain [5]. In the last few years, there have been some studies that have focused on the development of Amazon towards a digital ecosystem [6]. So far, there are no scientific studies that focus on the future expansion of Amazon's digital ecosystem. For this reason, this paper deals in particular with the following question:

How can the future development of Amazon's digital ecosystem be predicted?

This also leads to the question: Which method could be used to analyse the development of Amazon's digital ecosystem? To answer the research question of how the development of Amazon's digital ecosystem can be predicted, the technology-portfolio of Pfeiffer et al. [7] was used in a modified form as an analytical method. It is assumed by the authors that feedback of the customers and changes in customer needs lead to an adaption of Amazon's service system. These changes might also support an adaption at the eco-system level. The adjustment rules in this context are based on human decisions.

Section 2 of this paper includes the description of Amazon's digital ecosystem and a specific method, the technology-portfolio according to Pfeiffer et al. [7]. Section 3 is about the previous development of Amazon's digital ecosystem. The results are used to forecast the development in the future. Section 4 includes the future development of Amazon and Section 5 deals with the influence on Amazon's digital ecosystem. This paper ends with the limitations of the analysis and a conclusion.

II. BACKGROUND

The following section presents the background of the analysis, including a description of Amazon's digital ecosystem and the explanation of the technology-portfolio according to Pfeiffer et al. [7]. The technology-portfolio analysis is typically used to value new technologies in order to identify the most relevant strategic technology areas and to make an investment decision based on the results [8]. Further criteria used in this analysis, e.g. to determine resource strength and technological attractiveness, are explained in more detail in this section [14].

A. *The digital ecosystem of Amazon*

To analyse the development of Amazon's digital ecosystem, Amazon's digital ecosystem should be described previously. There are many definitions of digital ecosystems in the literature.

In general, a digital ecosystem is defined as a network of businesses, individual stakeholders, institutions, and consumers interacting both physically and electronically to provide combined services and value to each other [9].

From an economic point of view, an ecosystem can be perceived as an association of market participants that are in a certain relationship. The relationship between the participants is basically one of partnership, but competitive situations can also exist [10].

In contrast, digital ecosystems can form limited systems in the technical field, combining hardware, software, content, and services [11]. In the following sections, the term digital ecosystem is based on this description.

Amazon's service offer, which includes products and services in Amazon's core business as well as in its subsidiaries, has been visualized based on the understanding of a digital ecosystem by T. Ammon and A. Brem [11] (Figure 1).

B. *Technology-portfolio according to Pfeiffer et al. and further criteria*

The focus of this analysis should be based on technologies because the related software, hardware, content, and services build the digital ecosystem. For this reason, a technology-portfolio is used in this paper. In the course of the paper, the technology-portfolio according to Pfeiffer et al. [7] is discussed further because it is in contrast with different technology-portfolio approaches empirically proved [13].

In advance, the technology-portfolio according to Pfeiffer et al. [7] is used in a modified state and in combination with other criteria as an analytical method regarding the Amazon case. The technology portfolio according to Pfeiffer et al. originally provides recommendations for investment, selection, and disinvestment [7]. Modified in this context means that the technology portfolio analysis is applied to acquisition decisions. Technology attractiveness and resource strength are determined according to criteria that will be explained in detail in the course of this paper [14]. This paper covers Amazon's acquisitions according to the corresponding technologies. To analyse the technologies, it is important to explain the chosen technology-portfolio [7].

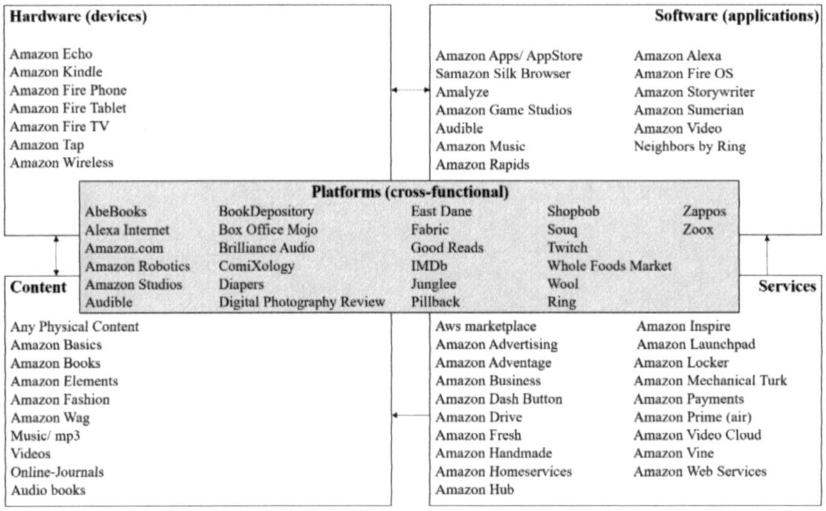

Figure 1. The digital ecosystem of Amazon (adapted from [11])

The allocation was made according to the assessment of the authors. Amazon's digital ecosystem consists of hardware like the Kindle eReader, software for example Kindle Apps, content including eBooks and services [11]. The majority of Amazon's value proposition is bundled on the Amazon platform [12]. In addition, there are other, cross-functional platforms for which it is not obvious at first sight that they belong to Amazon. These are mainly platforms, like Zappos, or Twitch that have been acquired by Amazon.

The objective of a technology-portfolio-analysis is to gain a recommended action based on the position of a specific technology [7].

During this portfolio-analysis, there is a difference between the two dimensions. The first dimension is the attractiveness of technology, whereas the second dimension is the strength of resources. Depending on the position, the technology is located at the investment, the selection, or the disinvestment area of the matrix [7].

A diagonal between the upper left corner and the lower right corner of the matrix symbolizes the selection area. The upper right corner is the investment area and the lower-left corner is called the disinvestment area [7].

In a work of Perspectives4You, criteria were used to determine the attractiveness of the technology and the strength of resources [14]. To determine the attractiveness of the technology and the strength of resources three questions are respectively answered. The answers are consisting of values between zero to four. The answers are weighted with the given percentages [14]. This is the basis to evaluate the general values of the attractiveness of the technology and the strength of resources. During the evaluation of the technology attractiveness, it is determined for example which potential the used technology has regarding the performance enhancement and/or the minimization of the overall cost.

The question of how the technology is mastered flows for example into the determination of the resource strength [14]. The following sections combine the technology-portfolio according to Pfeiffer et al. and the specific criteria [7][14]. The questions will be answered based on data from the literature. It is important to examine if this combination leads to useful results in the case of Amazon.

III. METHOD APPLIED TO THE PREVIOUS DEVELOPMENT

The method applied to the previous development of Amazon is used to identify which companies and corresponding technologies Amazon could acquire. Because of that, the corresponding technologies of Amazon's acquisitions and their competitors are positioned in the matrix of the technology-portfolio. The selection of the technologies includes successful, unsuccessful technology and technologies of companies with different acquisition prices, in order to select a meaningful cross-section.

The input of the analysis is data, which was generated during the time of the acquisition. If there is no data about this time in the literature, the data of the next possible point in time is chosen as input. The positioning regarding the technology-portfolio depends on the criteria of technology attractiveness and strength of resources. If there is no data about the criteria in the literature, data of similar criteria are the basis of the analysis.

The technology of the company Kiva Systems was positioned in the matrix. The company has made a major contribution to improving the goods-to-person concept in the field of warehouse logistics. Robots transport shelves to specific stations [15]. Mick Mountz founded the company in 2003 and Kiva Systems was acquired by Amazon in 2012 [16]. After the acquisition, the company name was changed to Amazon Robotics [17].

Kiva Systems technology in this paper is understood to be any technology used to create, implement, and develop the so-called Kiva Schema. In order to determine the positioning, it should be explained what potential the Kiva technology has. The more efficient design of the process, the use of an improved indoor GPS system, and the use of certain 3D sensors could be further developed in the future [15]. On the basis of the potentials mentioned, the authors assume that the Kiva technology has a very high innovation potential.

In this context, the question of the extent to which Kiva technology can open up further areas of application is also interesting [14]. Kiva's customers have similar demands in the field of logistics. The company's customers are for example part of the shopping industry or pharmaceutical industry [18]. Because companies from different industries are potential customers, a wide range of applications is assumed by the authors [14].

Major customers, such as retailers Toys "R "Us, GAP, and Staples use the Kiva technology [19]. For this reason, it is assumed that Kiva technology was urgently anticipated as a further step towards fully automated warehouses.

The Kiva concept has been imitated by several companies, such as GreyOrange [15]. GreyOrange was founded in 2011 [20]. Since Kiva Systems was already established in 2003, the company can benefit from a lead in the release of the technology of over two years compared to the competitor [14].

Considering the general potential of the Kiva Systems technology it is important to notice the good legal conditions. The company has filed more than 20 patents in the USA and many have been approved [15]. Despite the success of the GreyOrange technology, it is an imitation. For this reason, it is assumed by the authors that the Kiva Systems technology has a higher speed to market entry [14].

Because Kiva Technology and GreyOrange Technology are similar technologies, the innovation potential and the range of applications of these technologies are considered to be equally high. In classifying the technology-portfolio, it is assumed that customers may have reservations about GreyOrange because it is an imitative technology [14].

All the information and decisions lead to a positioning.

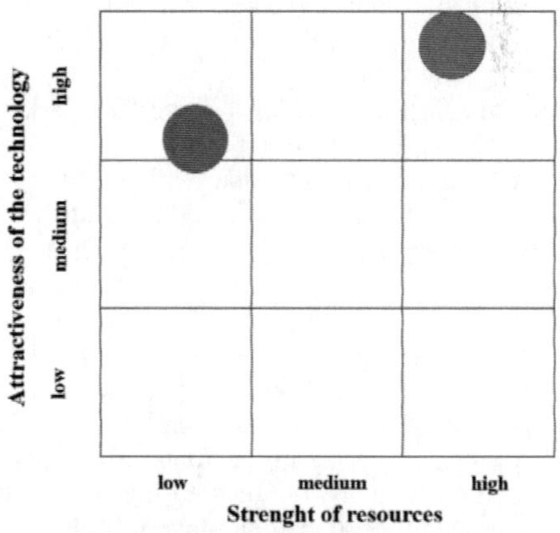

Figure 2. Technology-portfolio of the Kiva Systems technology (adapted from [7][14])

The positioning of the Kiva Systems technology and the GreyOrange technology is shown in Figure 2. The figure includes the two dimensions of the technology-portfolio. It is also shown that the Kiva Systems' technology is clearly in the investment area.

Whereas the GreyOrange technology shown in blue can be found in the selection area. A total of six technologies are compared with selected competitors. All technologies, which have been integrated in the long term in Amazon's digital ecosystem are located at the investment area.

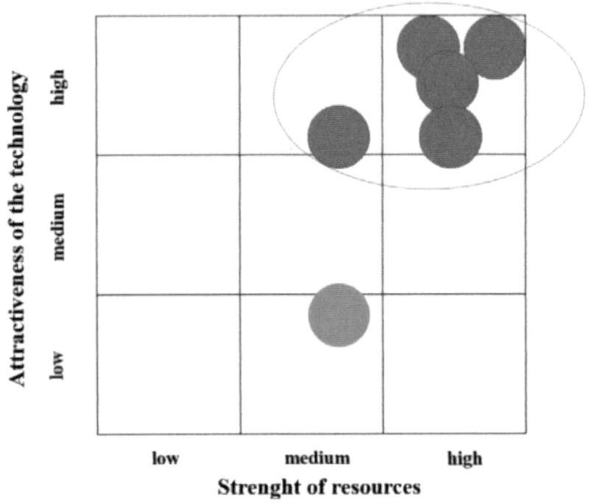

Figure 3. Technology-portfolio of six technologies (adapted from [7][14])

In Figure 3, these technologies are shown in red. One technology is shown in green because it is the only one that was discontinued a few years after the acquisition of Amazon.

IV. Method Applied to the Development in the Future

Using the method applied to the previous development leads to reasonable results. That is why the same method applied to the development in the future is described in Section 4.

In order to select a technology, a specific market is first selected into which Amazon could enter.

L.E.K. Consulting has published why Amazon could be seriously interested in health care. Decreasing health care cost would be a financial advantage for Amazon as a company. There are also a lot of processes in the health care markets that could be improved. The improvement of the health care could be one of the huge challenges that Jeff Bezos is looking for [21]. There has been already a report, that Amazon, Berkshire Hathaway and JPMorgan Chase are working together to decrease spending in the health care sector. One objective is the decreasing of health care expenses of the families of their employees [22].

Furthermore, people in the health industry speculate that Amazon could expand the offers in this sector [23]. Due to these reasons, a company in the healthcare industry is selected for this analysis.

The focus of the analysis lies on a digital physiotherapy of the company Sword Health, which enables a physiotherapy service at the home of the customer [24]. In Figure 4, the possible future technology is shown in red and a similar technology of a competitor is symbolized by a blue circle.

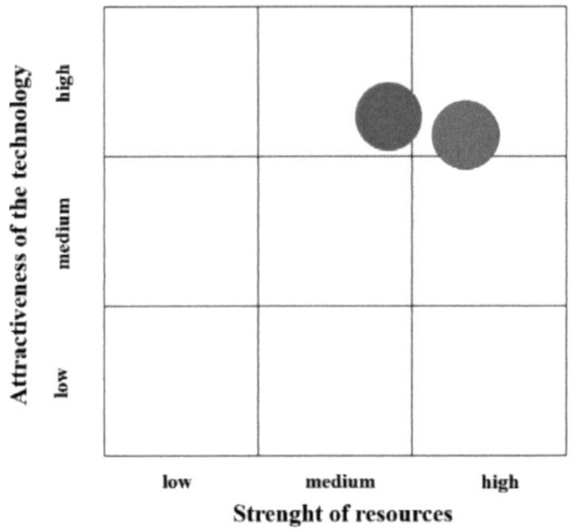

Figure 4. Technology-portfolio of a possible technology (adapted from [7][14])

Both technologies can be found in the investment area, but the position of the chosen technology is marginally better. Based on these results it is assumed in the following sections that the chosen technology might be an alternative in the future. Amazon could perhaps acquire the company that owns the chosen technology. That is why the acquisition of Sword Health might be a possible alternative.

V. Influence on the digital Ecosystem

The company Amazon has started as an online bookstore [25]. That is the reason, why Amazon's digital ecosystems, in the beginning, consisted probably of content like books, services like delivering service, software, and hardware that supported the trading. By integrating the technologies already considered, Amazon's digital ecosystem has become more complex in hardware, software, content and services.

The acquisitions of the company, which offers the online physiotherapy and afterwards the integration of the technology, could extend the digital ecosystem of Amazon. In this context, it is important to understand in which way the technologies were integrated into Amazon's digital ecosystem. It should also be explained how the digital ecosystem could change in the future.

The Kiva Systems robots for example really have been used by Amazon since 2014. This leads to a reduction in costs of the warehouse processes of the company [26]. Kiva combined hardware and software to improve the warehouse processes [27]. Since Amazon already uses Kiva technology, it is expected that the hardware and software of Kiva extend Amazon's digital ecosystem.

Christina Farr describes in an article in which way Amazon could offer health care services. It may be possible for customers to describe their symptoms to a doctor through Alexa. If necessary, the doctor can send tests to the customer [23]. The company Sword Health that is according to this analysis a potential candidate for an acquisition could be integrated in Amazon's ecosystem in a similar way.

Sword Health offers digital physiotherapy. Sensors allow physiotherapists to monitor and adjust the therapy [24]. This service, the software and the associated hardware could be integrated into Amazon's digital ecosystem, e.g. through Alexa.

VI. DISCUSSION

The results of this analysis are not binding and should be viewed as recommendations for actions, suggestions or trends, rather than general rules. The inclusion of more factors or other methods might generate different results. For example, a lot more factors than strength of resources and attractiveness of technology influence acquisition processes. In this specific context the determination leads to comprehensible results.

The appropriateness of this method should be proved with further analysis. Furthermore, the preparation of this work is based on a difficult data situation, because technologies are classified that can only be viewed from an external perspective in this paper. The determination of resource strength and technology attractiveness is based on the answers to certain questions. The answers are consisting of values between zero to four. The determination of the values on the basis of the data could be carried out in further work by different persons to prove whether similar results are obtained. The analysis could also be carried out with more technologies, because other results might be generated.

It could be proved in further investigations if the technology-portfolio according to Pfeiffer et al. [7] is a viable method in this context. It is also important to examine if other methods and data lead to different results or trends.

VII. CONCLUSION

The technology-portfolio according to Pfeiffer et al. [7] combined with other criteria and modified was used to evaluate the development of Amazon. In this paper companies with different acquisition prices and state of success were examined to create a meaningful cross section. Because the long-term successful technologies were positioned in the investment area of the technology-portfolio, the same method is used to forecast the future development of Amazon's expansion. A technology in the health industry was found that is also located at the investment area of the portfolio. The health industry was chosen for several reasons, for example because Amazon has already started activities in this area. The company Sword Health that offers a digital physiotherapy could therefore represent a possible acquisition alternative. For this reason, the technology of Sword Health was positioned in the matrix. The company is assumed as an acquisition alternative, because it is positioned in the investment area of the matrix. The integration of new technologies like the possible alternative could expand the digital ecosystem of Amazon by extending software, hardware, content, and services. The integration of the Sword Health Services in the digital ecosystem of Amazon through Alexa could be a possible alternative in the future. The basis of these results is the use of a method from the field of investment decisions and further criteria with the aim of developing a future prognosis of the digital ecosystem of Amazon. The method leads to reasonable results, since the technologies acquired by Amazon, which have been integrated into the ecosystem in the long term, are positioned in the investment in this analysis. Expanding the sources and technologies that are used during the positioning process could improve the outcome. The number of people carrying out the analysis influences the results and has also potential for improvement.

REFERENCES

[1] R. T. Kreutzer, "Drivers and backgrounds of digital transformation," "Treiber und Hintergründe der digitalen Transformation," in Digital transformation of business models - Basics, instruments and best practices, Digitale Transformation von Geschäftsmodellen, Grundlagen, Instrumente und Best Practices, D. Schallmo, A. Rusnjak, J. Anzengruber, T. Werani and M. Jünger, Wiesbaden: Springer Fachmedien , pp. 33–34, 2017.

[2] J. F. Moore, "Predators and prey: a new ecology of competition," Havard Business Review, 71(3), pp. 75–83, 1993.

[3] P. K. Senyo, K. Liu and J. Effah, "Digital business ecosystem: literature review and a framework for future," International Journal of Information Management. 47, pp. 52–64, 2019.

[4] C. Hoffmeister, "How to assess digital business models correctly," "Digitale Geschäftsmodelle richtig einschätzen," München: Carl Hanser Verlag, p.105 & 106, 2013.

[5] A. Hotz and M. Fost, "The 'amazonisation' of consumption - Game-Changer Amazon," "Die 'Amazonisierung' des Konsums – Game-Changer Amazon," in Digital transformation of business models - Basics, instruments and best practices, Digitale Transformation von Geschäftsmodellen, Grundlagen, Instrumente und Best Practices, D. Schallmo, A. Rusnjak, J. Anzengruber, T. Werani and M. Jünger, Eds. Wiesbaden: Springer Fachmedien, p.681, 2017.

[6] I. Thierry and D. Lescop, "Open innovation within business ecosystems: a tale from amazon.com," Communications & Strategies No. 74, p. 37, 2nd Quart. 2009, 2009.

[7] W. Pfeiffer, G. Metze, W. Schneider, and R. Amler, "Technology portfolio for managing strategic future business areas," "Technologie-Portfolio zum Management strategischer Zukunftsgeschäftsfelder," Göttingen: Vandenhoeck & Ruprecht, 1987.

[8] M. Kayser, L. Wohlfart and F. Wagner, "Dynamic technology assessment," "Dynamische Technologiebewertung," in The digitization hurdle can be mastered - Success factors, tools and examples for medium-sized businesses, Die Digitalisierungshürde lässt sich Meister(n) Erfolgsfaktoren, Werkzeuge und Beispiele für den Mittelstand, T. Knothe, P. Gering, S. O. Rimmelspacher and M. Maier, Eds. Berlin, Heidelberg: Springer Vieweg, p.99, 2020.

[9] M. Schaffnit, "Digital ecosystems," in Digital Business Development The effects of digitalisation on business models and markets, Digital Business Development Die

Auswirkungen der Digitalisierung auf Geschäftsmodelle und Märkte, S. Gatziu Grivas, Ed. Berlin, Heidelberg: Springer Gabler, p.55, 2020.

[10] S. von Engelhardt and S. Petzolt, "The business model toolbook for digital ecosystems," "Das Geschäftsmodell-Toolbook für digitale Ökosysteme," Frankfurt am Main: Campus Verlag, p.85, 2019.

[11] T. Ammon and A. Brem, "Digitalisation and innovation - selected industry-related aspects," "Digitalisierung und Innovation – Ausgewählte branchenbezogene Aspekte," in Digitalisation and Innovation, Digitalisierung und Innovation, F.Keuper, K.Hamidian, E.Verwaayen, Eric T. Kelinowski, and C. Kraijo, Eds. Wiesbaden: Springer Fachmedien, pp. 101, 102, 104 & 110, 2013.

[12] Amazon.com, inc, "amazon" Available from: https://www.amazon.com/ 2020.08.31.

[13] T. Tiefel and M. Frühbeißer, "Portfolio approaches for strategic technology and innovation management - a "state-of-the-art" analysis," "Portfolio-Ansätze für das strategische Technologie- und Innovationsmanagement - Eine "State-of-the-Art"-Analyse," Köln: TÜV Media GmbH, TÜV Rheinland Group, p.38, 2012.

[14] Perspectives4You, Bundesministerium für Wirtschaft und Energie & Zentrales Innovationsprogramm Mittelstand, "Potential analysis overall outcome and overview," "Potenzialanalyse Gesamtergebnis und Übersicht," Available from: https://p4y.informatik.uni-augsburg.de/wp-content/uploads/2015/02/Zusammenfassung-P4You-Präsentation.pdf 2019.10.24.

[15] C. Wurll, "The mobile storage based on a cyber-physical system," "Das Bewegliche Lager auf Basis eines Cyber-physischen Systems," in Handbook industry 4.0, Handbuch Industrie 4.0, B. Vogel-Heuser, T. Bauernhansl and M. ten Hompel, Berlin Heidelberg: Springer Nachschlage Wissen, pp. 1, 5 & 35, 2015.

[16] E. M. Rusli, "Amazon.com to acquire Manufacturer of robotics," Available from: https://dealbook.nytimes.com/2012/03/19/amazon-com-buys-kiva-systems-for-775-million/ 2020.08.31.

[17] About Amazon Staff, "What robots do (and don't do) at Amazon fulfillment centers," Available from: https://www.aboutamazon.com/amazon-fulfillment/our-innovation/what-robots-do-and-dont-do-at-amazon-fulfillment-centers/ 2020.08.31.

[18] C. Kurz, "Robots move forward at Amazon," "Roboter rücken bei Amazon vor," Frankfurter Allgemeine, Available from: https://www.faz.net/aktuell/feuilleton/aus-dem-maschinenraum/aus-dem-maschinenraum-roboter-ruecken-bei-amazon-vor-12685684.html 2019.11.02.

[19] F. Patalong, "Robopackers displace humans," "Robopacker verdrängen den Menschen," Available from: https://www.spiegel.de/wirtschaft/unternehmen/automatisierte-systeme-veraendern-lager-wirtschaft-a-847701.html 2020.08.31.

[20] Business Wire India, "GreyOrange's Samay Kohli recognized as an honoree of MIT Technology Review's 2016 innovators under 35 list," Available from: https://www.businesswireindia.com/greyoranges-samay-kohli-recognized-as-an-honoree-of-mit-technology-reviews-2016-innovators-under-35-list-49848.html 2020.08.31.

[21] J. Haslehurst, Robert Johnson, "As Amazon turns its gaze to healthcare, the industry may be in for a wild ride," L.E.K. Consulting / Executive Insights, Volume XX. Available from: https://www.lek.com/sites/default/files/insights/pdf-attachments/2021-Amazon-Healthcare_R1.pdf, 2020.08.31.

[22] R. S. Huckman, "What Could Amazon's approach to health care look like?," Available from: https://hbr.org/2018/02/what-could-amazons-approach-to-health-care-look-like 2020.08.31.

[23] C. Farr, "Amazon's vision for the future of health care is becoming clear," Available from: https://www.cnbc.com/2018/12/17/amazon-vision-future-health-care.html 2020.08.31.

[24] K. Anderton, "How Sensors are Changing the Way We Deliver Physiotherapy," Available from: https://www.news-medical.net/news/20180926/How-Sensors-are-Changing-the-Way-We-Deliver-Physiotherapy.aspx, 2020.08.31.

[25] B. Stone, "The all-rounder - Jeff Bezos and the empire of Amazon," "Der Allesverkäufer – Jeff Bezos und das Imperium von Amazon, " Frankfurt am Main: Campus Verlag, p.47, 2013.

[26] E. Kim "Amazon's $775 million deal for robotics company Kiva is starting to look really smart," Available from: https://www.businessinsider.com.au/kiva-robots-save-money-for-amazon-2016-6 2020.08.31.

[27] B. Einstein, "Meet the drone that already delivers your packages, Kiva robot teardown," Available from: https://robohub.org/meet-the-drone-that-already-delivers-your-packages-kiva-robot-teardown 2020.08.31.

Analysing the Impact of the Implementation of a Blockchain in an Existing Business Model

Lars Heim
Department of General Management
Clausthal University of Technology
Clausthal-Zellerfeld, Germany
email: lars.heim@tu-clausthal.de

Abstract— **Blockchain technology offers great potential for companies and the number of start-ups whose business models are based on this technology is growing rapidly. However, for many companies already active in their respective markets, the question arises as to whether and how this technology is relevant to their individual business model and what effects an implementation in the company or in the corporate environment would have. These questions can be answered with the help and modification of existing methods and tools. In this paper, we present the method of business model stresstesting, which, with certain adjustments, can help to answer the question of the impact of Blockchain technology on an existing business model. This will help to actively shape and evolve the ecosystem emerging in the area of Blockchain technology. The implementation and further development of the technology based on specific requirements from the business environment is thus facilitated and accelerated.**

Keywords: Blockchain; business model; stresstesting; stressfactor.

I. INTRODUCTION

Companies are typically faced with uncertainties regarding their future environment and their development [1]. In this context, the further development of business models is considered to be of great importance for maintaining competitiveness and economic growth [2]. The redesign of business models with the inclusion of innovations should lead to an increase in the robustness of a business model with respect to uncertainties in the company's environment [1]. Such business model innovations can be defined as systemic changes in the economic and entrepreneurial logic of companies in creating and maintaining value for both customers and companies [3]. Such changes also include modifications of value creation stages and the integration or elimination of partners in the value chain [4]. New technologies are among the external drivers of business model innovation [5]. For example, by creating new technologies or using existing ones, a company's existing resources can be better utilized, and a competitive advantage can be generated [3][5]. One technology in this context is the Blockchain technology [5]. The future effects of implementing this technology are not yet fully foreseeable for companies [6].

Analytical approaches to researching business model innovations deal with how business model components are influenced by the introduction of new technologies [6]. According to Nowiński and Kozma, examples of such analyses can already be found, for 3D printing, life science innovations and cloud technology [6]-[9]. Nowiński and Kozma have already been striving to develop methods to assess the impact of the implementation of Blockchain technology in existing business models [6]. The goal of this paper, as part of a project on evolving ecosystems and services, is to complement this approach with a concrete method to create opportunities for actively building the ecosystem around the Blockchain technology and to support the further evolution of the technology against the background of existing business models. This enables future integration of the Blockchain technology into existing business models, making business processes smoother and more secure.

The second section of this paper first introduces the method of stresstesting for business models in general. In the following third section, the procedure of this method is presented and modified for the concrete application to evaluate business models against the background of the Blockchain technology. In the fourth section a summary and an outlook are given.

II. STRESSTESTS FOR FUTURE BUSINESS MODELS

Technology forecasting provides an overview of existing and emerging technologies and how they influence and replace each other [10][11]. Technology forecasting thus shows developments that begin in the past. As shown in Figure 1, scenario planning begins where technology forecasting stops. To a certain extent, the early detection of scenario planning can provide a range of possible developments [10]. Scenarios represent outlooks on the future, describing how it could develop based on clearly defined assumptions [10]. By presenting possible technical implementations in scenarios, technologies can be brought closer to future users and thus appear more real. Scenarios thus make it easier for decision makers to include future technologies in the decision-making process [10]. They make it possible to better assess the risks of decisions under high uncertainty. Scenario planning recognizes that the future environment of a company is uncertain. This approach helps to assess the robustness of a company against the background of possible scenarios [1]. Scenario planning thus creates a basis for decision-making and, similar to the explicit presentation of a business model, helps to pick up all those involved in the planning process [12]-[14]. The fact that scenario planning can help to tailor business models to specific future scenarios has already been demonstrated [1]. Examples can be found for telecommunications and the Internet of Things [15][16].

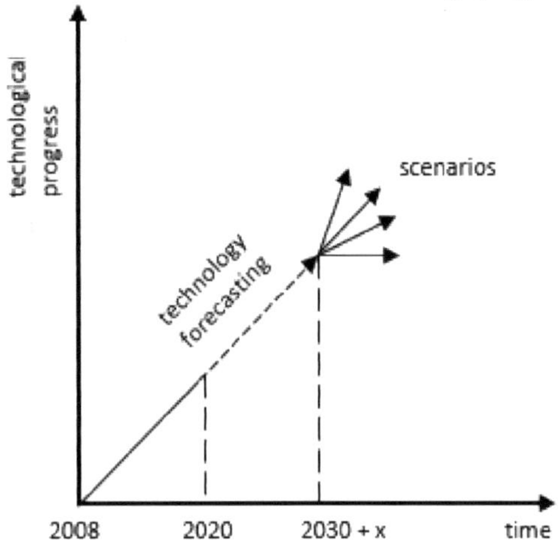

Figure 1. Combination of technology forecasting and scenario planning [10]

The authors Bouwman and van der Duin combine technology forecasting with scenario planning [10]. Consequently, they developed the business model stresstesting method as an approach to operationalize the approaches of business model innovation in connection with scenario planning [1][3][17][18]. They thus create an opportunity to develop scenarios and use them as input for the analysis of business models [18]. This method can be used to demonstrate the robustness of business model components against one or more future scenarios [1]. Business model stresstesting is therefore defined as follows [3]:

> *"[...] a systematic analysis of the robustness (i.e., long- term viability as well as feasibility) of BM components - such as a value proposition, revenues or cost structure – based on different future conditions (or uncertainties)."*

This means business model stresstesting combines future uncertainties by using scenarios with business model ontologies [3]. The resulting analyses and estimates of the effects of scenarios on business model components can be used to identify the components that are particularly affected under the given circumstances and therefore require increased attention in planning. The results enable users to assess whether an existing business model can meet technical, regulatory, or other changed conditions and which business model components may need to be modified. In a three-part case study, Bouwman et al. [3] were able to successfully test the functionality of this still relatively new method. Real business models from the health care and transport sectors, as well as that of a charity organisation were used for this [3]. The applicability of the method for technologies that are still in an early stage of development and for which there are no or only little tested implementations in business models could also be proven [19].

III. STRESSTESTING PROCEDURE FOR BUSINESS MODELS IN ORDER TO IMPLEMENT BLOCKCHAIN TECHNOLOGY

Bouwman et al. developed the business model stresstesting method in the form of a six-step process as a structured approach to identifying robust or non-robust business model components [1][18]. These original steps are (1) the selection and description of a business model, (2) the identification and selection of stressfactors, (3) the comparison of the business model components with the selected stressfactors, (4) the presentation of the influences of the stressfactors on business model components with a heat map, (5) the analysis of the heat map and (6) the drawing of conclusions about weaknesses of the business model.

For the application of the stresstesting method to assess the consequences of implementing the Blockchain technology in an existing business model, adjustments to the known procedure are required. In the following, the process including the changes will be described.

Step 1: Selection and description of a business model

According to Bouwman et al., the first step in the stresstesting procedure consists of describing the business model in an explicit form [3]. If a company operates several business models, one must be selected for the analysis. A possible tool for adequately describing the business model is the Business Model Canvas following Osterwalder and Pigneur [1][22]. De Vrij notes that the Business Model Canvas in combination with the Value Proposition Canvas contributes in particular to the functioning of the stresstesting [21].

Step 2: Identification and selection of stressfactors

In the second step, it is necessary to select those factors that are to be tested for their impact on the business model components. These in general include trends and uncertainties [3]. For each factor, two opposing, extreme characteristics should be defined [1]. In the application considered here, the existence of a Blockchain is predefined as the relevant stressfactor for the procedure. The respective concrete characteristics of this Blockchain variant with regard to user rights and access to the consensus mechanism should fit the underlying business model. Such a Blockchain variant could be, for example, a private-permissioned or a public-permissioned Blockchain.

The two opposing characteristics of this stressfactor are also predefined. The first variant is the implementation of the Blockchain in the existing business model. The second, opposite variant is the decision against an implementation, under the assumption that such a Blockchain nevertheless exists in the environment of the company. The analysis thus shows the effects of the implementation on the one hand and the consequences for the existing company on the other if competitors implement such a model.

The plausible description of this stressfactor plays a decisive role in the procedure and validity of the stresstesting [10]. A further substep for the design and description of this stressfactor therefore appears necessary. For this purpose, the business model ontology is again applied to simulate a hypothetical business model which can be used as a reference for the changes in the original business model components. In this way, the abstraction level of the stressfactor and that of the business model can be raised to the same level [10].

The Business Model Canvas following Osterwalder and Pigneur has already formed the basis for specific applications several times since its initial presentation [9]. There are already several approaches for adapting the Business Model Canvas for the Blockchain technology.

Burgwinkel retains the nine business model components, but develops new guiding questions for each component, which facilitate the application to the Blockchain technology. In order to facilitate the description of a hypothetical, Blockchain-based business model in the stresstesting process, the guiding questions as implemented by Burgwinkel can be applied [23]. The structure of the nine business model components is retained in order to enable a comparison with the business model defined in the first step of stresstesting [3]. These guiding questions are presented in Table 1.

TABLE I GUIDING QUESTIONS FOR THE BUSINESS MODEL CANVAS ACCORDING TO BURGWINKEL

Business Model Component	Guiding Questions
Key Partners	• Who are the partners or industry consortium for the development of the Blockchain application? • Is the new Blockchain application in competition with other traditional partners (such as banks)? • Why do the partners get involved (do they not want to miss a trend or do they see it as an innovative opportunity)? • Are there cross-industry partnerships that generate new benefits? • How are national and international supervisory authorities and industry committees involved? • Will the Use Case become an alternative to traditional approaches or does it offer a completely new benefit?
Key Ressources	• Which services does the Blockchain platform serve as a foundation? • Which special resources or functions/capabilities are realized by the use case?
Key Activities	• Does the application use an existing Blockchain platform (such as Ethereum) or is a standalone application built? • How are customers/users motivated to use the application and possibly pay for it?
Value Proposition	• Which customer problems are solved with the Blockchain application? • What value is created for the customer, e.g. increased trust or the advantage of not being dependent on a central provider? • Why do the participants want to use Blockchain and not a traditional technology? • Why will the Blockchain application establish itself in the market and replace traditional offerings?
Customer Relationships	• Which new relationships does the Blockchain application enable, e.g. direct contact between customer and producer without the involvement of middlemen? • For business-to-business applications: which participants (suppliers, inspection bodies, producers etc.) use the Blockchain for their coordination?
Channels	• Through which channels do customers use the Blockchain application? • Are these channels completely new or is the Blockchain application integrated into existing e-commerce processes? • What is the advantage of omitting the previous central instance which coordinated the market participants and guaranteed trust?
Customer Segments	• For which customers/users does the Blockchain application create value?
Cost Structure	• Why does a Blockchain offer technical advantages in the application scenario or why can costs be saved compared to traditional technologies?
Revenue Streams	• Which business concept/sources of income do the founders of the Blockchain application pursue? • Which business concept does the operator of the Blockchain platform (e.g. Ethereum) pursue?

Step 3: Mapping of the business model components with the stressfactors

The third step is the actual stresstest and consists of a description of how the business model components behave against the background of the stressfactor and its characteristics. This is done by describing in detail the relationship between the stressfactor and the individual business model components [1][3].

Step 4: Presentation of the influence on the business model using a heat map

In the fourth step of stresstesting, the potential impact of the Blockchain stressfactor on the respective business model components must be assessed. Based on this qualitative assessment, a heat map is drawn up using a colour scheme. The colour scheme illustrates the extent of the impact on the component [10]. Bouwman et al. and Haaker et al. define four colour levels for this purpose [1][3]:

- Red: The effect of the stressfactor on the business model component makes this component appear as no longer feasible. The effect of the stressfactor can potentially render the business model as a whole unsustainable.
- Orange: The effect of the stressfactor on the business model component makes this component appear to be no longer feasible. The business model component must therefore be considered separately and adjusted if necessary.
- Green: The stressfactor has an influence on the business model component but does not negatively affect the feasibility and usefulness of the component. If circumstances permit, a positive influence of the stressfactor on the component can be realized.
- Gray: The stressfactor has no relevant influence on the business model component.

The respective classification of the stressfactor in the colour categories must be documented and justified [1].

Step 5: Analysis of the heat map

After the heat map already shows which components are not robust, the fifth step is to analyse the heat map in order to uncover possible overarching weaknesses of the business model. The analysis can be divided into two partial analyses [20]:

Sub-View Analyses

In a Sub-View analysis, individual areas of the heat map are considered separately [1]. Problem areas can thus be identified by a horizontal or vertical view of the heat map [20]. Accordingly, a horizontal view of the columns provides an overview of the effects of all the characteristics of all stressfactors on a business model component. The vertical view of the columns provides a focused view of the effects of one stressfactor on all business model components [1][20].

Pattern Analysis

By taking a holistic view of the heat map, patterns can emerge, e.g., what characteristic of a stressfactor would be the ideal state for the business model. Furthermore, it is possible, for example, to identify whether business model components lose their usefulness under any given scenario [20].

Step 6: Conclusion on weaknesses of the business model

Once the analysis of the robustness and vulnerability of a business model has been completed, the next step is to formulate measures based on the insights gained [1]. This step is broad in scope, but usually includes recommendations for improving weak business model components or improving consistency within the business model [20].

This modified procedure of stress testing for business models provides a concrete tool for analysing existing business models against the background of implementing the block chain technology. It not only evaluates the effects of the implementation in an existing business model, but also the consequences of an implementation in the company's environment.

IV. Conclusion and Future Work

The Blockchain technology still appears to be relatively new when seen from an economical perspective. To enable a wider range of applications for this technology, tools have to be created that make the technology accessible to economists. Using the existing research on the business model ontology offers the possibility to adapt tools for this new application. The combination of the technology forecast with the scenario planning within the business model Stresstesting is such a tool. By extending this approach by a Blockchain use case, economists can analyse their own or hypothetical business models against this emerging technology. The approach presented here provides a first structured roadmap for this purpose. Existing business models can be analysed, and new business models can be planned. Future research could further extend this approach especially with respect to quantifying the analyses. Furthermore, the procedure presented is based on subjective assessments of the impact of the technology on the business model components. Future research work could attempt to make this process more objective by means of further sub-analyses.

References

[1] T. Haaker, H. Bouwman, W. Janssen, and M. de Reuver, „Business model stresstesting: A practical approach to test the robustness of a business model." Futures, vol. 89, pp. 14-25, 2017.

[2] M. Heikkilä, et al., "Business Model Innovation Paths and Tools." In Bled eConference, p. 6, 2016.

[3] H. Bouwman, J. Heikkilä, M. Heikkilä, C. Leopold, T. Haaker, "Achieving agility using business model stress testing." Electronic Markets, vol. 28, no. 2, pp. 149-162, 2018.

[4] B. W. Wirtz and M. J. Thomas, „Design und Entwicklung der business model-innovation." In Kompendium Geschäftsmodell-Innovation, pp. 31-49, 2014, Springer Gabler, Wiesbaden.

[5] W. Nowiński and M. Kozma, „How can Blockchain technology disrupt the existing business models?" Entrepreneurial Business and Economics Review, vol. 5, no. 3, pp. 173-188, 2017.

[6] A. Agrawal, S. Laddha, and M. S. Devi, "Impact and Uncertainty of Blockchain Usage on Supply Chain." Studies in Indian Place Names, vol. 40, no. 68, pp. 438-446, 2020.

[7] J. Brink and M. Holmén, "Capabilities and radical changes of the business models of new bioscience firms." Creativity and Innovation Management, vol. 18, no. 2, pp. 109-120, 2009.

[8] T. Rayna and L. Striukova, "From rapid prototyping to home fabrication: How 3D printing is changing business model

innovation." Technological Forecasting and Social Change, vol. 102, pp. 214-224, 2016.

[9] C. M. DaSilva, P. Trkman, K. Desouza, and J. Lindič, „Disruptive technologies: a business model perspective on cloud computing." Technology Analysis & Strategic Management, vol. 25 no. 10, pp. 1161-1173, 2013.

[10] H. Bouwman and P. van der Duin, P. "Technological forecasting and scenarios matter: research into the use of information and communication technology in the home environment in 2010." Foresight, vol. 5, no. 4, pp. 8-20, 2003.

[11] A. L. Porter, A. T. Roper, T. W. Mason, F. A. Rossini, and J. Banks, "Forecasting and management of technology", vol. 18, 1991, John Wiley & Sons.

[12] M. Godet, "The art of scenarios and strategic planning: tools and pitfalls." Technological forecasting and social change, vol. 65, no. 1, pp. 3-22, 2000

[13] A. Osterwalder and Y. Pigneur, "Business Model Generation: A Handbook for Visionaries, Game Changers, and Challengers.", 2010, Hoboken: Wiley.

[14] C. Leopold, "How do SME's use Business Model Stress Testing?", 2015, TU Delft

[15] U. Killström, et al., "Business models for new mobile applications and services.", MobiLife, 2006.

[16] J. F. Tesch, "Discovering the role of scenario planning as an evaluation methodology for business models in the era of the internet of things (IoT)" In Twenty-Fourth European Conference on Information Systems (ECIS)–AIS, 2016.

[17] M. Niemimaa, J. Järveläinen, M. Heikkilä, and J. Heikkilä, "Business continuity of business models: Evaluating the resilience of business models for contingencies." International Journal of Information Management, vol. 49, pp. 208-216, 2019.

[18] H. Bouwman, et al., „Business models tooling and a research agenda." The first, vol. 25, pp. 1-28, 2012.

[19] L. Klomp, "The impact of Blockchain technology on insurance business models: Stress testing the insurers' business models using the STOF Model", 2018, TU Delft

[20] T. van Beusekom, "Testing Business Model Innovation Tooling for Small and Medium Sized Enterprises: A Multiple Case Study on the Business Model Stress Test.", 2017, TU Delf.

[21] X. de Vrij, "Decentralised Local Energy Markets: Evaluating the Impact of Blockchain Technology on Local Energy Markets.", 2018, TU Delft.

[22] A. Osterwalder, Y. Pigneur, and C. L. Tucci, "Clarifying Business Models: Origins, Present, and Future of the Concept." Communications of the Association for Information Systems, vol. 16, pp. 1–25, 2005.

[23] D. Burgwinkel, „Blockchaintechnologie und deren Funktionsweise verstehen." In D. Burgwinkel, Blockchain Technology: Einführung für Business- und IT Manager. 2016, Basel: De Gruyter Oldenbourg.

Anonymization of Transactions in Distributed Ledger Technologies

Robert Werner, Sebastian Lawrenz, Andreas Rausch
Clausthal University of Technology, Institute for Software and Systems Engineering
Arnold-Sommerfeldstraße 1
Clausthal-Zellerfeld, Germany
email: { robert.werner | sebastian.lawrenz | andreas.rausch}@tu-clausthal.de

Abstract—**Increasing acceptance of transparent cryptocurrencies is leading to more and more publicly traceable financial transactions. This is a problem for civil society due to a lack of privacy, as well as for companies because of public financial data. It could even endanger entire states due to a transparent economy. To solve this problem, private, decentralized currencies have been created, but these prevent prosecution and thus undermine the accountability of citizens. In this paper, existing centralized techniques for ensuring privacy in distributed ledger technologies are presented and evaluated. On this basis, a software is presented which, through its semi-decentralized architecture, guarantees privacy for citizens and the economy when transacting on distributed ledger technologies without preventing state prosecution.**

Keywords—Distributed Ledger; Blockchain; Privacy; Blockchainanalysis; Cryptocurrency

I. Introduction

The idea of cryptocurrencies was introduced by the pseudonym Satoshi Nakamoto in 2008 with the Bitcoin Whitepaper [1]. Since then, cryptocurrencies have become increasingly popular, and both the transaction volume [2] on the Bitcoin blockchain and the trading volume [3] of Bitcoin has increased almost steadily. Besides, many new cryptocurrencies - so-called "altcoins" (alternative coins) - have been created and further developed, which also enjoy increasing usage and forming a new kind of a (software) ecosystem. Just like a natural ecosystem, a software ecosystem describes the relation and balance between organisms and their environment. The Bitcoin ecosystem for example is characterized by the blockchain itself, miners, the market, developers, and applications running on top of Bitcoin. The bitcoin price is influenced by this ecosystem, the market supply, and demand, as well as other external conditions, such as the dollar price [4] . In line with this is the definition of a software ecosystem, which is defined as the interaction of a set of actors on top of a common technological platform that results in several software solutions or services [5].

The usage of cryptocurrencies has also increased rapidly in the Darknet and has reached a new peak in 2019 with a monthly transaction volume of 8-14 million USD in bitcoin (BTC). Overall, illegal transaction volumes in 2019 accounted for approximately 1.1% of all transparent cryptocurrencies [6]. Furthermore, the blockchain hype that occurred in 2017 has also spread to governments and commercial companies. For example, the EU envisages great potential for the blockchain with international financial institutions and supply chains [7]. The blockchain for securing digital identity is seen as another great potential of this technology [8]. Facebook has also set itself the goal of launching a global currency based on the blockchain [9]. From the Bitcoin hype onward, many new cryptocurrencies and innovations in the area of blockchain have come forth and the ecosystem of cryptocurrencies is in continual change and adapting to new user requirements.

In the early years of cryptocurrencies in particular it was assumed that transactions on the blockchain are anonymous since people neither have to register nor have to enter a real name before transacting. As a matter of fact, it has been shown that the blockchain provides a good basis to break the supposed anonymity through data analysis. This results in observers being able to infer from people to their activities or inversely from activities to the participating people with little information from outside of the blockchain. With cryptocurrencies, transparency in our digital world reaches a new level. Financial data is one of the most sensitive pieces of information as it allows conclusions to be drawn about the whereabouts of people, their social environment, buying habits, state of health, and much more. In addition, many users are unaware of the public accessibility of this data. Due to the pseudonymity of many cryptocurrencies, users are often lulled into a false sense of security.

Further far-reaching cuts in the private sphere could severely endanger the basic human right to the free development of one's personality, and thus also the people themselves. The public availability of financial data can not only be threatening for the individual, but also poses a problem for companies as it would be possible for competitors to find out about their revenue, origin of revenue, and partnerships. Likewise, states cannot have any interest in making their own economy and national budget publicly available to the world and thus do the work of hostile intelligence services.

On the other hand, online crime is posing a challenge and is aggravated by new decentralized cryptocurrencies with a focus on privacy. These so-called "privacy coins" conceal transactions and prevent the investigation of crimes financed by such money. The German Federal Ministry of Finance sees privacy coins like Monero as "particularly susceptible to money laundering" and is concerned about "increasing acceptance in the darknet", although they allegedly do not pose a real threat yet [10].

New cryptocurrencies and technologies have emerged not only with a focus on privacy but also with an emphasis on scalability. Networks based on Directed Acyclic Graph (DAG) ledgers promise to scale far beyond bitcoin's limit of seven transactions per second [11] by adding transactions asynchronously to the ledger.

What is needed is an efficient payment system that works reliably, offers users privacy, but still enables state authorities to bring criminals to justice by analyzing their financial flows. At the same time, it must be prevented that this system can be abused, even by the operator herself.

A. *Objective*

The aim of this paper is to find a balance between anonymization and the preservation of law enforcement. Therefor, concepts for anonymization in decentralized and censorship-resistant Distributed Ledger Technologies (DLT) that safeguard criminal prosecution will be evaluated. As part of this, a semi-decentralized anonymization tool for a transparent DAG-based cryptocurrency is proposed. The goal is to provide users of this cryptocurrency with optional privacy via a second layer without obstructing law enforcement. Furthermore, we present a concept of how our tool can be integrated into the modern constitutional state and how it can be protected against abuse.

B. *Outline*

The rest of the paper is structured as follows: Section II presents relevant fundamentals, context, and related work. In Section III we present our software by outlining its requirements, introducing the concept, and giving implementation details. In Section IV we evaluate the limitations of our solution and propose further enhancements to combat these. Finally, we conclude the paper in Section V.

II. Background and Related Work

In the following section, the basics of different DLTs are discussed and blockchain analysis of transparent cryptocurrencies is introduced. Decentralization and centralization in the context of privacy are discussed and general attacks for deanonymizing transactions in DLTs are described. Furthermore, we present related projects.

A. *Distributed Ledger Technologies*

DLT is a technique for managing a decentralized transaction database. This database is stored redundantly by any number of equal participants. Each participant has the same copy of the transaction database, which is continuously synchronized peer-to-peer with all participants. The most prominent DLT is the blockchain technology, which can be implemented in different ways. Some newer DLTs use a DAG, and can also be implemented in different ways. In this paper, the focus of DAGs is on the implementation of the "block-lattice", which was introduced by the cryptocurrency "Nano" [12].

B. *Block-Lattice vs Blockchain*

In contrast to the traditional blockchain, on the DAG-based block-lattice, there is no single blockchain synchronized by all network participants to which new blocks, and thus transactions, are sequentially added by, e.g., miners. Instead, every user exclusively manages her own account-chain, to which only that same user may attach new blocks.

The account balance is stored in stateful blocks. This is in contrast to most blockchain-based cryptocurrencies (including Bitcoin [1] and Ethereum [13]), where the state of an account is not stored on the ledger itself, but has to be derived from it. To find out the balance of an account in Nano, only the last block of this account ("frontier", or "head block") must be considered. In the future, this feature could allow nodes to store only the frontiers by "pruning" the ledger, thus drastically reducing the size of the ledger since the transaction history is no longer being stored.

Unlike the blockchain, a block in the block-lattice contains only one transaction, thus only one state update for one account. Since only the account owner is allowed to attach blocks to her account and can thereby update the account state, the account owner has to create a block for each outgoing and incoming transaction to update her balance. Consequently, there are two basic actions that the blocks can represent: Send and receive. Each fully completed transaction consists of two blocks [12].

C. *Blockchain Analysis*

The first intrinsic contribution to privacy in DLTs lies in the pseudonymity of addresses. A pseudonym is an alias that by itself does not allow conclusions to be drawn about the actual person or entity behind it, but is nevertheless closely connected to it. In contrast to anonymity, i.e., complete namelessness, actions can be assigned to a pseudonym and vice versa. In the case of cryptocurrencies, addresses serve as pseudonyms for a user. Pseudonyms are tied to the user since only the user has access to the coins stored on these addresses. These addresses are automatically generated when a wallet is created. Their pseudonymity is broken as soon as a user receives money from someone or sends money to someone who knows their true identity. This is the case, for example, when a person receives coins from a friend or service with Know Your Customer (KYC) compliance or sends money to a friend, exchange, or online shop.

So far, the identity can only be linked to an address by those involved. However, it is even possible for third parties to obtain this information. This is because DLTs' transactions contain not only the sender and receiver addresses but also the value and time of the transaction. If, for example, a customer pays in a shop with a cryptocurrency, the customer automatically knows the address of the shop. If the customer now wants to find out the address of the person who stood in line after her, all the customer has to do is look at the ledger and check the incoming transaction after her own in the transaction history of the address of the shop. The address of the other customer is then displayed there as the transaction origin. This shows how easy it is, even for private individuals, to break peoples' pseudonymity as a third party. For states, interested companies, or consortia that can benefit from such information and have more data and resources available, this should pose a little hurdle.

Nakamoto,[1] has already known that a global currency needs privacy and has made some suggestions for improving it beyond pseudonymity. One of these suggestions is the use of multiple addresses per person. This way the wallet generates a new receiving address each time coins are requested. Multiple addresses make the scenario described in the previous paragraph much more difficult because the store would generate a new receiving address for each customer, who then would not easily be able to find other customers' addresses.

At first glance, this measure of using multiple addresses per user appears to be very powerful at protecting against prying eyes, but in reality, is far less effective. If funds are spread across multiple addresses and the balance of one is no longer sufficient, a transaction that combines these funds must take place. Consequently, tools exist that are able to find multiple addresses belonging to the same user and other addresses the user has interacted with [14].

D. Decentralization

An important aspect of evaluating DLTs is the degree of decentralization. Decentralization is not a binary state but can be classified on a spectrum from centralized to decentralized in different areas. By definition, all DLTs can be considered "decentralized" because the ledger is stored on several computers. This ensures greater accessibility and reliability compared to centralized alternatives and more resistance to technical failure and DoS attacks against individual actors.

However, decentralization is not only applicable to the way transactions are stored, but also to the creation or authorization of transactions, i.e., the consensus. This is important because a monetary system with guaranteed availability cannot be considered decentralized if only one single party decides which transactions are permitted and which are not. This type of centralization however is desired, especially for permissioned and private blockchains. Projects that focus more on performance and scalability also tend to have a more centralized consensus. For example, the EOSIO blockchain is an open blockchain, but with 21 alternating block producers, it has relatively few consensus creators at a point in time [15].

Another aspect of decentralization is the development of a DLT, because the ongoing development of a project determines its scope, features, and security. For example, centralized development could use software updates to change the inflation rate, disable privacy features [16], or even reverse transactions [17] in the blockchain otherwise known for its immutability.

Availability, security against manipulation, and development - these areas of decentralization influence the permanence, autonomy, and agility of projects. All three are of vital importance when it comes to privacy and thus possibly also to the well-being of people.

E. Attacks against Privacy

Although a definite value is usually desired when evaluating privacy, implementations show that there are various anonymization procedures that differ in the level of privacy they provide. In some cases, it is not yet clear how effective some approaches really are, so that they cannot be evaluated and compared well at this time. In addition, new methods of deanonymization are constantly being researched [18], which makes a final evaluation of different approaches impossible.

A basic principle of anonymization in DLTs is to make transactions indistinguishable to an observer, so that only a set of transactions is visible, which can no longer be assigned to exactly one sending and receiving address. It is important how large this set of indistinguishable transactions, the so-called "anonymity set", is since it is an important indicator for the degree of anonymity. For example, if there are only two sender addresses and two indistinguishable transactions, the anonymity set amounts to only two and the transactions can be attributed with a 50 percent probability. How an anonymity set is constructed depends on the method used and varies greatly between different projects, some of which are introduced in the next subsection.

Attacks designed to deanonymize aim to reduce this anonymity set so that in the end a transaction can be assigned to an address, i.e., a user, with high probability. Anonymization methods try to make the anonymity set as large as possible and at the same time prevent possibilities for reducing this set. In this context, two side-channel attacks play a special role: the "timing attack" and the "value attack".

The timing attack utilizes the behavior of users who act predictably. For example, this is ideally the case when a customer pays for a coffee every morning at exactly 8 o'clock. Even if the addresses are not known to outsiders, they can be assigned to the user through this predictable transaction.

The value attack focuses on the value of transactions. This attack also goes beyond the DLT. For example, if someone sends 121.27€ in BTC to exchange and later withdraws 121.27€ (minus fees) in Ether (ETH), it is easy to associate these two transactions. This way one has created a connection between two addresses on two different networks without the transaction history of a single network indicating this.

Both attacks can be combined to further reduce the anonymity set in case of doubt. Furthermore, there are also attacks carried out off-chain, that is, based on data that does not appear on the ledger. This includes methods to find out the IP address that was used to initially propagate a transaction.

F. Related Work

To create privacy on DLTs there are already many different projects with different properties. Some are centralized, building on top of a DLT, others are decentralized and have privacy built directly into the protocol, at the first layer.

Centralized projects usually require the trust of the user that they are actually protecting the users' privacy and not stealing coins. They are also susceptible to external factors, such as cyberattacks and regulations. They are at the second layer because they build on top of existing transparent DLTs, of which the ledger and circulating supply is verifiable and the transaction history is always observable.

Decentralized projects are often linked to a cryptocurrency or are one themselves. Some projects use mechanisms that no longer store any transaction history and/or in which the circulating supply can no longer be checked.

This paper only covers central methods of anonymization because of their optional property to deanonymize transactions and similarity to the proposed solution. A very simple form of anonymization is to send coins to a central exchange and receive them at a later time from a newly generated address. This can be effective because an exchange serves many users, who make many incoming and outgoing transactions. Therefore the anonymity set is relatively large. However, the anonymity set can be reduced to one with a systematic value attack if used improperly. Figure 1 depicts transactions (TX) made to or from an exchange within a certain period of time. Since TX 3 and TX 4 have the same value, it can be assumed that addresses C and D belong to the same person.

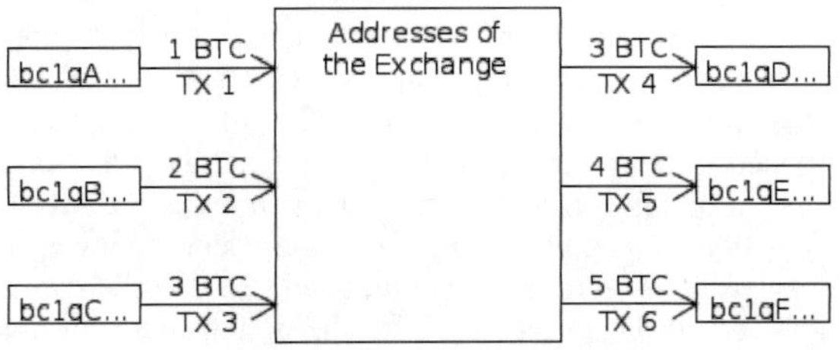

Figure 1. The concept of mixing coins on an exchange.

Another inherent disadvantage of exchanges is that they are a popular target for cyberattacks because they manage a large number of coins. The number of attacks on exchanges has increased almost steadily over the last few years. A total of USD 875 million was stolen by hackers in 2018 [6]. This not only has the consequence that coins may be insecure, but along with the high complexity of exchanges, it also repeatedly causes deposits and withdrawals to be temporarily disabled. Furthermore, there is a risk that the exchange will steal the coins or share the transaction history of its users.

Similar to exchanges are so-called CoinMixers, which are also based on the idea that a large number of users send them coins. The mixer then sends coins back to the user, which have a different history than the user's previously sent in coins. In order to prevent deposits and withdrawals from being associated by the same value, withdrawals can be split up into several transactions of which each is sent to a different address of the user. The mixer can create payouts with uniform values so that the case shown in Figure 1 does not occur. The latter two methods have already been implemented in Dash's PrivateSend protocol in a decentralized manner [19].

The mixer must be trusted, just as with the exchange, to return the coins and not to log and share data of the mixing process [20]. Due to its centralized structure, it is just as susceptible to cyberattacks or DoS attacks, albeit giving hackers a smaller incentive since it is not permanently storing user funds. With dedicated coin mixers, there is the additional risk that the mixed coins will be highly contaminated if they are being used primarily for money laundering.

III. SOLUTION

This section covers our solution that provides privacy in decentralized and censorship-resistant DLTs while maintaining law enforcement. We state the requirements and present a corresponding concept. Based on that concept we present our prototypical implementation.

A. Requirements

Due to their decentralized architecture, DLTs offer the possibility to quickly transfer values without registration and intermediaries. Since DLTs are non-discriminatory, participants are basically on an equal footing in creating and monitoring transactions. If, for example, it is possible for governmental agencies to track financial data, anyone else can also track the data, thus undermining any privacy.

The centralized privacy enhancement concepts introduced in the last section are highly vulnerable to cyberattacks and technical failure. Furthermore, access to deanonymizing data cannot be controlled from the outside, which means that they have a high potential for abuse. Completely centralized anonymization tools are therefore unsuitable for safely and reliably protecting the privacy of companies and citizens.

Another aspect is scalability, which must be taken into consideration in case of possible increasing acceptance of cryptocurrencies. Privacy must not be costly or accessible to only a fraction of users due to technical limitations.

The solution must be able to be built on top of decentralized DLTs and sufficiently protect the privacy of the population. It is also necessary that the executive authority can break this privacy with relatively little effort. This effort must nevertheless be high enough and access must be transparent to prevent mass surveillance and allow only targeted observations.

To solve this problem, a concept is presented below, which was implemented on top of the cryptocurrency Nano. Nano is perfectly suited because it has high scalability due to its block-lattice, transactions do not cost any fees and are confirmed within milliseconds. Nano is exclusively transparent and has no possibility of a decentralized implementation of privacy. So far, there are also no effective anonymization tools for this cryptocurrency. The concept can be applied to other DLTs to a large extent. The implementation, however, is specific to this type of ledger and cannot be adopted by a blockchain.

B. Concept

The anonymization of transactions is carried out via a cluster of centrally administered coinmixers, each of which functions similarly to coinmixers of other cryptocurrencies. To ensure that the mixers are under state regulation, they can be operated by existing banks, for example. Banks are subject to strict banking secrecy, which may only be lifted by the state under certain circumstances. At the same time, banks are relatively trustworthy and can be closely monitored through the transparent ledger, so they cannot effectively steal customer funds.

A high-level overview of the concept is given in the following Figure 2.

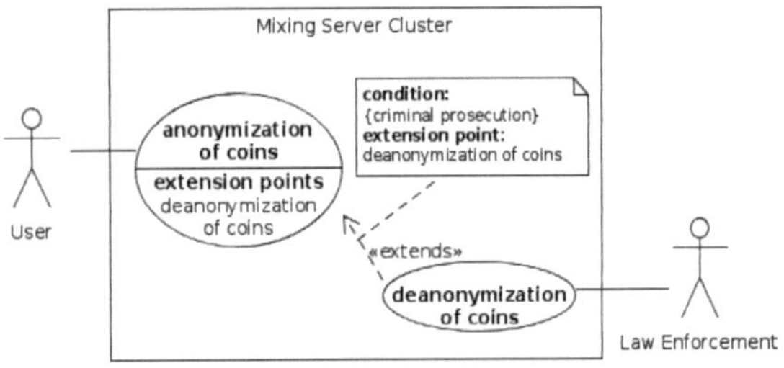

Figure 2. The user and law enforcement interact with the mixing service.

The coinmixers receive NANO from users of a predetermined denomination. After a time specified by the user, which should be as random as possible, the mixer sends back NANO of the same value to another address specified by the user. Because several users go through this process simultaneously, there is an overlap between deposits and withdrawals so that withdrawals can no longer be assigned to a single deposit. This successfully counters the value attack. The process is depicted in Figure 3 below. The coinmixer receives three incoming transactions of the same value from three different users within a certain period of time. The server later sends the coins back to the users to another address. It is no longer traceable which of the new addresses belong to which user.

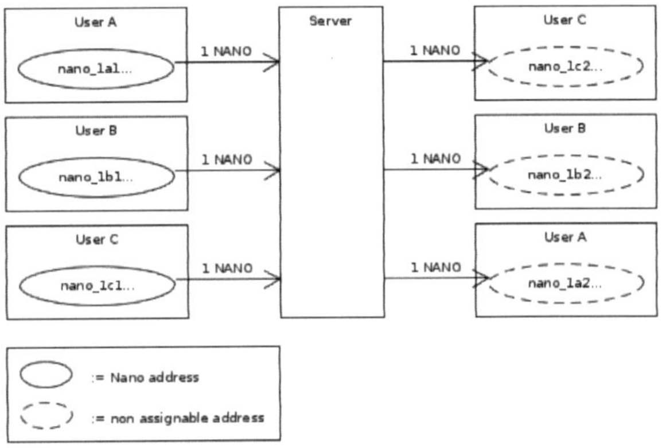

Figure 3. The concept of mixing transactions of the same value.

How large the anonymity set is, i.e., with how many other users a new payout address can be mistaken, depends on the number of deposits into the coinmixer within a common time period before the payout. This time period cannot be determined exactly and depends on the usual time chosen by the user until the Mixer returns the Coins. This consequently makes the timing attack less effective. Figure 4 visualizes the anonymity set of users in different scenarios. User A has an anonymity set of two since two deposits were made before her withdrawal. C has one of three and B and D both have an anonymity set of four since the same number of deposits took place within a common time period before. E only has an anonymity set of 2, as there were only two deposits within a typical time period.

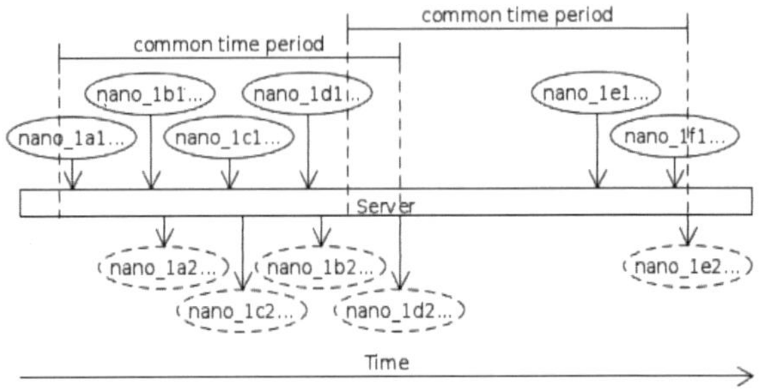

Figure 4. Multiple users deposit and withdraw from the coinmixer over time. The total number of users and their timing affect their anonymity set.

To increase the anonymity set significantly, it is alternatively possible to receive a private key to a "reserved address" from the server instead of being sent back coins. This key is transmitted off-chain, which changes the owner of the reserved address without this transaction being published. The reserved address contains the appropriate number of coins corresponding to the denomination selected by the client. The transaction that initially sent money to this address was made in advance, unrelated to a specific request, by the server. This gives the user the option to spend these coins at any time, as the user does not have to wait for the mixing process. The longer the user waits, the more her anonymity set increases. This is illustrated by the following Figure 5 in which NANO is sent to address d2 in the beginning. However, the associated private key is only transmitted to user D later on. Because D only uses this address after user E has made a deposit, e1 also falls into its anonymity set, which is equivalent to five in this figure. At the same time, e2 cannot be clearly assigned to e1, since e2 could also be a reserved address.

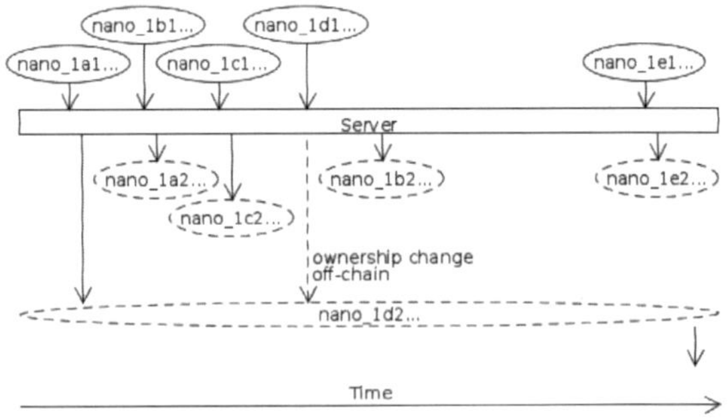

Figure 5. Transmitting ownership of coins off-chain greatly increases the anonymity set.

Since the server coordinates the received payment with a respective payout, it can document all mixing processes and thus remove the anonymity of desired users. This can be used if, for example, the flow of money beyond the mixer has to be tracked in the context of a criminal case. At the same time, however, this logging can also endanger the privacy of the users. To prevent this, several mixing servers are used. A user can now use these mixers sequentially so that her privacy is protected by each individual mixer. Figure 6 shows that by using three mixers for a mixing process, the privacy of user A is not broken even if two of these mixers are compromised.

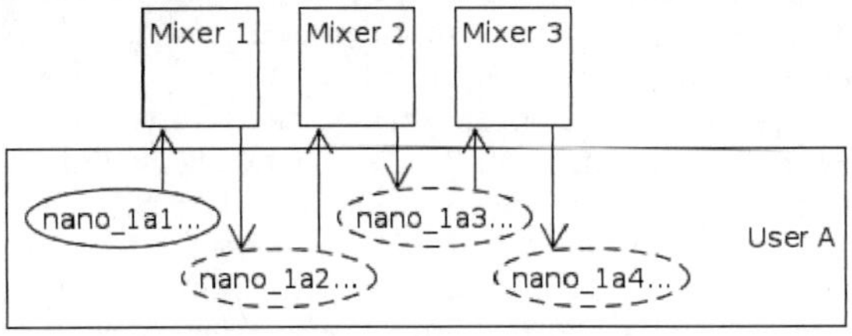

Figure 6. Using multiple mixers sequentially protects against maliciously tracking mixers and further increases the anonymity set.

Due to the sequential use of mixers, the number of required transactions, and the required time increases linearly. Therefore, for less privacy-critical transactions it is possible to use only one mixer per anonymization. This mixer is selected randomly so that all available mixers are used equally. This ensures basic privacy and a malicious mixer only has insight into a small subset of all private transactions taking place on the network.

To ensure sufficient liquidity of the mixer and thus a high anonymity set, it is necessary to promote the use of mixers by integrating them into the crypto ecosystem, such as wallets and enabling them by default. In that way, the coins of used addresses are regularly mixed. The privacy that is thereby strongly promoted serves to protect the general population and economy, even if they would not value privacy themselves. This way, the characteristic of cash to be anonymous by default is inherited.

C. Implementation

Within the scope of this work, the server software was implemented according to the use case shown in Figure 4. The code for this prototype is publicly available [21]. The server must be able to accept mixing orders, which can be placed either via a programming interface or a graphical user interface. In either case, the client sends the server the payout address, the number of coins to be mixed, and the time of the desired payout. The server then assigns the client a unique, newly generated deposit address, to which the client now sends the agreed-upon amount. As soon as this address contains sufficient coins, the funds are forwarded to a central address where they are combined with the coins of other users. As soon as the time for payout is reached, the respective number of coins will be sent from this mixing address to the specified payout address.

This is visualized in Figure 7. Client A and B send an equal amount of NANO to the mixer. Using an address generated for each of them, the mixer can confirm the payment and forward the coins to the mixing address. From there the payout takes place and it is not possible to trace which of these payout addresses belong to A or B.

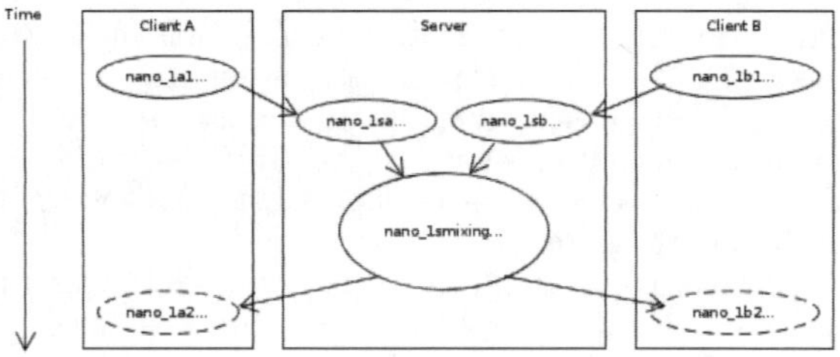

Figure 7. The mixing process of two clients in detail.

A relational database consisting of a single table is used for coordination. For each incoming order, a new row is created, which also reflects the status of the order. A row has the following eleven columns:

	name of row: variable type
1.	order_id: int(11)
2.	account: varchar(65)
3.	denomination: decimal(39,0)
4.	submission_epoch: int(10)
5.	fully_received_epoch: int(10)
6.	mixer_tx: varchar(64)
7.	mixer_epoch: int(10)
8.	fulfillment_account: varchar(65)
9.	fulfillment_tx: varchar(64)
10.	fulfillment_epoch: int(10)
11.	fulfillment_deadline_epoch: int(10)

Figure 8. A row in the database table for a single mixing request.

The column "account" corresponds to the deposit address and is unique. At the time of order creation, only columns 1, 2, 3, 4, 8, and 11 have a value. When the deposit is complete, column 5 is assigned and the mixing is initiated, which sets columns 6 and 7. Finally, when the payment is complete, columns 9 and 10 are filled. The columns ending in "_epoch" each store the corresponding timestamp in Unix time. The columns ending on "_tx" contain the ID of the respective transaction created by the server. Under "fulfillment_account" the payout address of the user is stored. A regularly executed script checks for incoming transactions and due payouts and updates the database accordingly.

IV. Evaluation

The software is working correctly, as can be verified by the block explorer when examining the mixing address [22]. Nonetheless, it's effectiveness depends on actual usage. Without frequent usage of these coinmixers, they do not offer any privacy advantage over exchanges as exchanges are also regulated and have to document all transactions. On the contrary, low usage could lead to an anonymity set of one and thus offer no additional privacy at all. In contrast to exchanges, mixers do not manage large amounts of money at any given time and are far less complex. This makes them more reliable, easier to maintain, and unattractive as a target of a cyberattack. However, mixers are also not given any incentive to process transactions. This jeopardizes the concept that is based on having as many reliable mixers available as possible.

Compared to non-transparent cryptocurrencies, this anonymization does not conceal the transaction values and, due to the transparent underlying cryptocurrency, allows attackers, even with extensive use of the mixers, to perform blockchain analysis and apply the timing and value attack or to observe the merging of addresses.

This can compromise anonymity if the user handles the mixer incorrectly. This is the case, for example, when a user spends the funds of a reserved address immediately after receiving it and thus becomes vulnerable to the timing attack. Such attacks through data analysis can become increasingly sophisticated as soon as statistics on user behavior are available or algorithms can recognize patterns with the help of artificial intelligence.

Equally dangerous can be the combination of remaining funds (change) on an account after an outgoing transaction. This is particularly critical if these funds cannot be further mixed because it is less than the smallest denomination.

The concept of using the exchange of private keys as value transfer is currently difficult to integrate into the existing wallet ecosystem as this type of transaction is not intended and would require new wallet backups by the client with every mixing transaction. Furthermore copying private keys and thus sharing them between multiple people is not reconcilable with the idea of trustless private keys which require a one-to-one relationship between key and user.

Another possible weakness is the constitutional state that the central authority is part of. If for some reason the central authority was no longer subjected to jurisdiction, its access would become uncontrollable and thus the tool meant to bring privacy to the masses could be turned into a tool for mass surveillance. This is not a novel problem and equally applies to current digital money transfer. This mixing concept will not protect users' privacy in an authoritarian regime but instead relies on a stable constitutional state.

If a good integration into the user wallets is achieved, it can be guaranteed that the tool is used correctly and thus offers strong privacy, which can only be lifted by the state in legally justified cases. This privacy is achieved without experimental and computationally expensive encryption. The greatly increased transaction volume resulting from mixing and the resulting growth of the ledger can be compensated for by modern cryptocurrencies that support ledger pruning. Expensive transaction fees and high latencies of transaction confirmations are also eliminated by cryptocurrencies like Nano.

A. Possible Enhancements

The anonymization tool can be improved in efficiency as well as functionality to further enhance privacy. Potential attack vectors can be closed and the user experience improved.

The transactions required by the server for the mixing process can be reduced from two to one by additionally requesting the source address from the client when creating an order and sending its coins directly to the mixing address. This worsens the user experience when used manually but hardly represents any additional effort when mixing in an automated way. In this case, the server checks the receipt of payment by filtering incoming payments to the mixing address according to the specified source address. This feature can coexist with the current system.

To prevent users from having their coins frozen after they have started a mixing order with a long mixing duration, it is possible to request an immediate payout. To do this, the user sends a request to the server with her order ID, whereupon the server ignores the originally set payout time and initiates the immediate payout. This would reduce the anonymity set in that specific case, but gives an incentive to initially specify a longer mixing time, since immediate payout is guaranteed, and thus increase the average anonymity set.

To make use of change without combining it with other addresses, it is possible to create an order with several deposit addresses. The user can then send the remaining coins of each account to one of those deposit addresses until they reach the value of the smallest denomination. To prevent a value attack, this deposit process should be spread over a longer period of time and overpaid. An overpayment not only enables untraceability but also creates a monetary incentive to operate a mixer. The concept of overpayment is illustrated by the following Figure 9 in which one NANO is assumed to be the smallest denomination of the mixer. Client A makes two payments with change to two different addresses of the mixer. Since A is overpaying, it is difficult for attackers to link her two addresses.

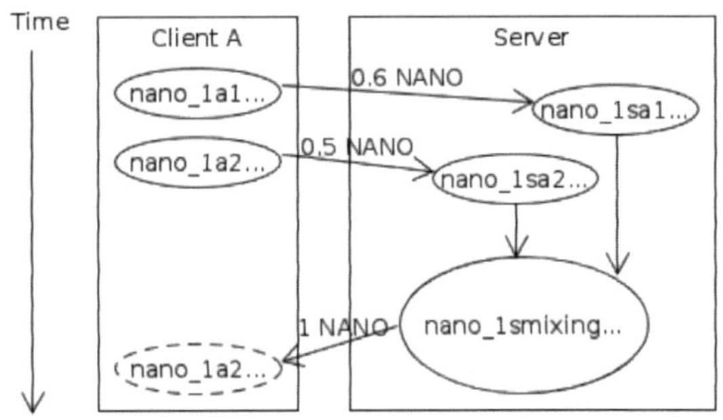

Figure 9. To utilize change without compromising privacy, the mixer supports multiple input addresses per order.

In addition to mixing, the mixer can offer a service requiring registration to manage user coins. The mixer manages all funds of a customer and makes the desired payments directly from the mixing address. This is very similar to a bank account or exchange account and can therefore be very attractive for many users, as they can hand over the responsibility for managing the coins to the bank.

The current implementation is decentralized in terms of anonymization, but still requires trust in the mixers for managing the coins. To decentralize control over the coins, it is possible to split the administration among several parties. Using so-called "multisignature" wallets, it would only be possible to carry out transactions if the majority agrees on them [23]. This prevents a single party from stealing coins. However, it also requires more reliable participants and a more complex system, which tends to work slower and is more prone to failures.

V. Conclusion and Outlook

The spread of DLTs as a means of payment is bringing with it new challenges. Some cryptocurrencies do not provide sufficient privacy, while others by contrast create complete anonymity at the expense of government authority.

In this paper, a concept for the anonymization of transactions on DAG-based cryptocurrencies was presented. A plan is proposed for integrating this concept into the modern constitutional state so that selective deanonymization maintains the possibility of criminal prosecution without being susceptible to abuse. Within the framework of the presented concept, the developed software enables the anonymization of transactions in a decentralized and censorship-resistant DLT while safeguarding criminal prosecution. How well it works in the real-world depends largely on its adoption and integration into the ever-changing crypto ecosystem. It provides a basis to promote and monitor decentralized transparent cryptocurrencies and make them suitable for society.

Semi-decentralized anonymization tools of the kind presented manage the balancing act between crypto-anarchism and state control. They allow states to have insight in decentralized cryptocurrencies without having to suppress them. It also gives them the possibility to introduce their own (complimentary) currencies based on DLTs and to control the use of transparency and anonymity purposefully in selected areas.

The development of such software is far from complete. With new technologies, there will always be new possibilities and limitations for existing implementations to reliably protect privacy. As the analysis of such transparent anonymization tools will progress, existing systems will be challenged again and again. Since DLTs are still in their infancy, there will continue to be a lot of potential in the area of trustless, centrally monitored anonymization in the foreseeable future.

Acknowledgment

This paper evolved from the research project "Recycling 4.0" (digitalization as the key to the Advanced Circular Economy using the example of innovative vehicle systems) which is funded by the European Regional Development Fund (EFRE | ZW 6-85017297) and managed by the Project Management Agency NBank.

References

[1] S. Nakamoto, "Bitcoin: A Peer-to-Peer Electronic Cash System," 2008. https://bitcoin.org/bitcoin.pdf (accessed Sep. 19, 2020).

[2] "Bitcoin Sent in USD Chart," 2020. https://bitinfocharts.com/comparison/bitcoin-sentinusd.html#log (accessed Sep. 19, 2020).

[3] "Bitcoin price today, BTC marketcap, chart, and info | CoinMarketCap," 2020. https://coinmarketcap.com/currencies/bitcoin/ (accessed Sep. 19, 2020).

[4] P. Ciaian, M. Rajcaniova, and d'Artis Kancs, "The economics of BitCoin price formation," *Appl. Econ.*, vol. 48, no. 19, pp. 1799–1815, 2016, doi: 10.1080/00036846.2015.1109038.

[5] K. Manikas and K. M. Hansen, "Software ecosystems-A systematic literature review," *J. Syst. Softw.*, vol. 86, no. 5, pp. 1294–1306, 2013, doi: 10.1016/j.jss.2012.12.026.

[6] Chainalysis, "The 2020 State of Crypto Crime," no. January, 2020.

[7] E. Davradakis and R. Santos, "Blockchain, FinTechs and their relevance for international financial institutions," *Econ. - Work. Pap. 2019/01*, 2019, doi: 10.2867/11329.

[8] T. Lyons, L. Courcelas, and K. Timsit, "Blockchain and digital identity," p. 27, 2019, [Online]. Available: https://www.eublockchainforum.eu/sites/default/files/report_identity_v0.9.4.pdf (accessed Sep. 19, 2020).

[9] E. Kühl and M. Laaff, "Einmal mit Facebook zahlen, bitte! [Just pay with Facebook please!]," *Zeit online*, 2019.

[10] Bundesministerium der Finanzen, "Erste Nationale Risikoanalyse Bekämpfung von Geldwäsche und Terrorismusfinanzierung [First National Risk Analysis Combating money laundering and terrorist financing]," 2019.

[11] S. Elnaj, "The Problems With Bitcoin And The Future Of Blockchain," 2018. [Online]. Available: https://www.forbes.com/sites/forbestechcouncil/2018/03/29/the-problems-with-bitcoin-and-the-future-of-blockchain/#1a05067f68dc (accessed Sep. 19, 2020).

[12] C. Lemahieu, "Nano: A Feeless Distributed Cryptocurrency Network," *White Pap.*, p. 8, 2018.

[13] G. Wood et al., "Ethereum: A secure decentralised generalised transaction ledger," 2019. [Online]. Available: https://ethereum.github.io/yellowpaper/paper.pdf (accessed Sep. 19, 2020).

[14] R. Werner, S. Lawrenz, and A. Rausch, "Blockchain Analysis Tool of a Cryptocurrency," *ACM Int. Conf. Proceeding Ser.*, pp. 80–84, 2020, doi: 10.1145/3390566.3391671.

[15] "Consensus Protocol | EOSIO Developer Docs," 2020. https://developers.eos.io/welcome/v2.0/protocol/consensus_protocol (accessed Sep. 19, 2020).

[16] Furszy and Random.Zebra, "Report: 'Wrapped Serials' Attack," 2019. https://medium.com/@dev.pivx/report-wrapped-serials-attack-5f4bf7b51701 (accessed Sep. 19, 2020).

[17] V. Buterin, "Hard Fork Completed," 2016. [Online]. Available: https://blog.ethereum.org/2016/07/20/hard-fork-completed/ (accessed Sep. 19, 2020).

[18] T. de Balthasar and J. Hernandez-Castro, "An Analysis of Bitcoin Laundry Services," 2017, pp. 297–312.

[19] E. Duffield and D. Diaz, "Dash: A Payments-Focused Cryptocurrency," 2014. [Online]. Available: https://github.com/dashpay/dash/wiki/Whitepaper (accessed Sep. 19, 2020).

[20] J. Bonneau, et al., "Mixcoin: Anonymity for bitcoin with accountable mixes," *Lect. Notes Comput. Sci. (including Subser. Lect. Notes Artif. Intell. Lect. Notes Bioinformatics)*, vol. 8437, pp. 486–504, 2014, doi: 10.1007/978-3-662-45472-5_31.

[21] "rw501/nanonymity," 2020. https://github.com/rw501/nanonymity (accessed Oct. 20, 2020).

[22] "Account – nano_3ikhg5yxkcpjcsrj7zyepzntpqzebe6qt6b8wy5k967wf49y7eei1cjtygg8," 2020. https://nanocrawler.cc/explorer/account/nano_3ikhg5yxkcpjcsrj7zyepzntpqzebe6qt6b8wy5k967wf49y7eei1cjtygg8/history (accessed Sep. 19, 2020).

[23] V. Buterin, "Bitcoin Multisig Wallet: The Future of Bitcoin," *Bitcoin Magazine*, 2014.

Towards an Evolving Software Ecosystem in the Mining Industry

Mirco Schindler
Institute for Software and System Engineering
Technische Universität Clausthal
Clausthal-Zellerfeld, Germany
e-mail: mirco.schindler@tu-clausthal.de

Sunny Schoone, Elisabeth Clausen
Institute for Advanced Mining Technologies
RWTH Aachen University
Aachen, Germany
e-mail: sschoone@amt.rwth-aachen.de,
e-mail: eclausen@amt.rwth-aachen.de

Abstract— **How will the data provider and consumer come together? Towards a mining 4.0, research is being conducted on innovative technologies for digitalization and automation. In addition to data transport on the technical infrastructure level, there are many challenges in the area of integration of different sensor and actuator data sets, as well as already existing isolated applications from different stakeholders. The defined goal is to reduce the gap between the existing system boundaries, on a technical level as well as among the involved persons.**

Keywords Digital-Ecosystems; cloud-based Systems; Data-driven architectures; Software Engineering approaches for ecosystems and Services; Ecosystem Architecture

I. INTRODUCTION

The sector of the primary resources industry and especially the sub-sector of raw material extraction is subject to a technological change in a facsimile to Industry 4.0 - Mining 4.0. This also includes, with regard to mining, new social demands on this sector of industry [16] and [18]. Thus, technology transfer and implementation not only lead to problems in dealing with existing interfaces aimed at process optimization and thus increasing economic efficiency, but also to the desire for more transparency, sustainability and security [16] and [18]. These two trends must progress harmoniously, and can be supported by flexible, innovative and modern technologies and IT solutions. High-level architectures enable a new type of software design, which is described by the approach of development and IT operations (DevOps), and enable the use of new tools for the optimization of software solutions [14] and [19].

In order to implement these trends, a new role model for the use of platform-based cloud solutions was developed. For this purpose, in Section II an underground mining system is roughly transferred into an ecosystem. In doing so, rudimentary aspects of underground mining and the special features of this use case and its rough structures are also described. In particular, in Section III, the belt conveyor is explained and presented as a subsystem of an entire mining ecosystem. In Section IV is exemplarily described what challenges can influence the implementation of new models in the mining industry, in order to go into the utilization structures of the data generated in the subsystem in Section V. These data utilization structures are extended by the introduction of cloud-based platforms. Based on this, Section VI presents the role and process model developed to reduce or overcome dynamically existing system boundaries. Section VII summarizes the findings and gives an outlook on future next steps and work

II. THE MINE AS IT ECOSYSTEM

The increasing complexity of software-intensive systems has led to the fact that the classical approaches of software engineering have shown difficulties with scalability. Software-intensive systems are systems, in which software development and/or integration are dominant considerations, which includes computer-based systems ranging from individual software applications, information systems, embedded systems, software product lines and product families and systems-of-systems. Consequently, software systems should no longer be considered in isolation due to their high degree of interconnectedness, as otherwise the exchange of information and thus the synchronization, actuality and consistency between the systems is inhibited. Instead, they should be designed as part of a larger IT ecosystem [13].

In analogy to biological ecosystems, IT ecosystems are based on the balance between individuals (autonomy) and rules (control) that define equilibria within an IT ecosystem. The maintenance and continuous development of IT ecosystems requires a deep understanding of this balance [8] and [26]. In addition to these aspects, the mixture of interdisciplinarity and technology and non-technology-driven perspectives plays an important role [7]. The aim of an IT ecosystem is therefore to establish and ensure a balance between autonomous subprocesses and systems for greater controllability and optimization of the overall system by gaining a better understanding of the influencing components and actors [10] and [11].

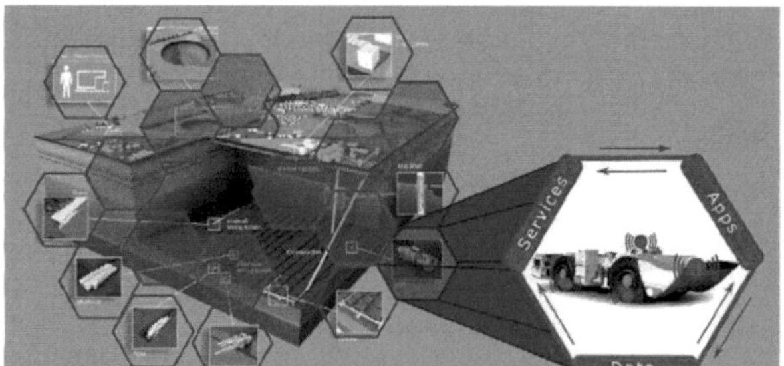

Figure1. Exemplary elements, based on an underground mining ecosystem.

Analogous to the term IT ecosystem, economic industrial companies/mines can also be described as ecosystems [7].

A. *Short introduction to underground mining*

The term mining infers development and extraction of valuable primary mineral resources from natural deposits. In particular, the underground mine, shown here in Figure 1, describes the development and extraction via shafts and extensive drift systems. Based on the geological conditions, there may be a difference in the implementation of the respective mining method. Due to the different possibilities of the mining method, different technologies and machines can be used. Nevertheless, underground mines are subject to difficult conditions, a constant change of position of machines due to the progress of the mining site, the influence of dust, temperature, limited access to the machines in use and often long distances, to name but a small number of influencing factors. Due to the constant increase in size and a frequently very long working time, different machines from different manufacturers with different state of the art technology are often used, which makes it difficult to overcome the interfaces between the machines.

In principle, underground mining can be divided into several processes for simplified presentation. The Extraction of Raw Materials refers to the extraction of valuable mineral resources and waste rocks from the natural deposit. Following this, the Haulage and Transportation of the dissolved materials takes place. This is done by underground logistics and the various machines required for this. The aim of loading and transport logistics is to transfer the extracted rocks to the Mineral Processing. In mineral processing the concentration of the targeted valuable minerals should be enriched by separating from the waste rocks. The supply of sufficient fresh air must be ensured in order to guarantee the work in underground mining. This section is grouped together in the Ventilation work area. These fields of work are supported by other fields of work, such as Safety, Maintenance and Logistics and several others, which will not be discussed further here [22].

When transferring the ecosystem understanding to a mining company, the individual supply and process chains play an important and specific role in order to ensure optimized mining operations. The independently acting subsystems extend along these chains and thus define very clear system boundaries with a defined goal and set of rules. As shown schematically in Figure 1, a section can consist of participating subsystems, actors and mutually influencing dependencies. The real representation of a mining ecosystem depends on the underlying implementation of an operation and is not subject to a superordinate definition or delimitation.

An entire operational ecosystem is made up of many interactive or parallel systems, which system boundaries are characterized by great dynamics. Nevertheless, an attempt can be made to idealize these individual systems and to delimit them by "virtual" system boundaries into their areas of activity, such as extraction, haulage and transportation, processing and ventilation.

These systems are further subdivided into subsystems, which can be defined within system boundaries in analogy to the previous description. In transport logistics, for example, these are subsystems, such as Load Haul Dump Vehicles (LHD) and conveyor belts. These subsystems provide data obtained by sensor technologies in different ways, which can be used in the higher-level systems to gain new information about the underlying processes by recombining these collected data with the aim of building virtual sensors. The entire system structure and hierarchy is shown as an example in Figure 2. The macrosystems in the third level of the system structure cluster the sensor technologies used on the acting machines according to their data technological end-use. Depending on the configuration, these respective macrosystems are composed of many microsystems. Representatives for these microsystems are the individual sensor technologies.

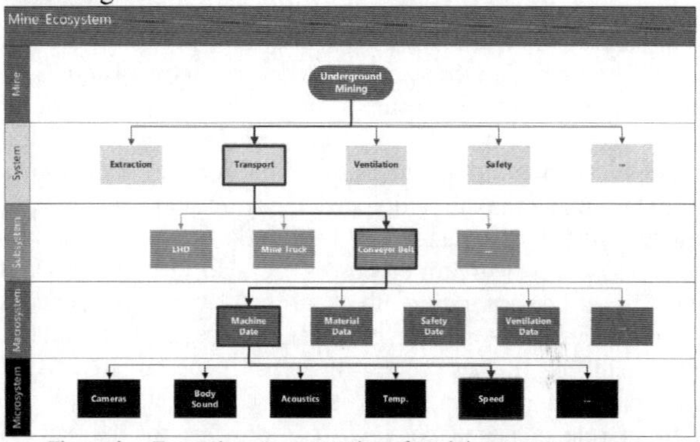

Figure 2. Exemplary representation of a mining system structure.

III. SUBSYSTEM BELT CONVEYER

As described in the previous Sections, the overall ecosystem of a mine is made up of subordinate systems and these in turn are made up of many subsystems. From the system of haulage and transport, the belt conveyor (Figure 3) was chosen as a consistent example to illustrate the system structural complexity [5].

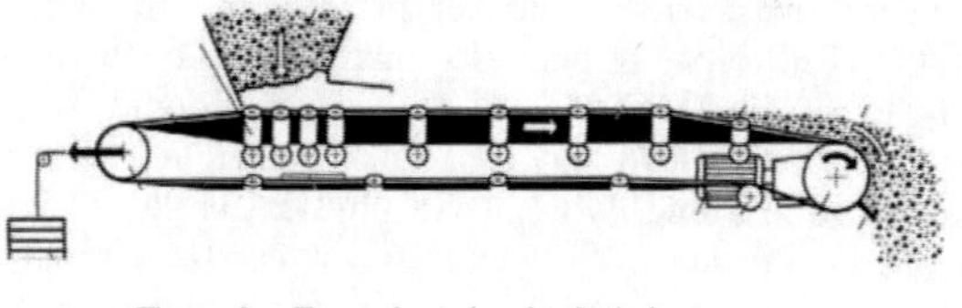
Figure 3. Exemplary sketch of a belt conveyor.

The conveyor belt is a central component of underground mining and combines extraction with further processing steps like hoisting or mineral processing. It supports the haulage and transport of the rock extracted during the mining process. The distances to be conveyed from extraction to mineral processing can range from a few hundred meters to several kilometers. Due to this central location in a mine, uninterrupted operation of this subsystem is essential [1]. The subsystem conveyor belt can be seen as a Cyber-Physical System [26].

IV. Particular Challenges Exemplified by Data Quality and Model Validation

In an extensive industrial ecosystem, a large number of systems act and react in a network to guarantee cross-process and process-specific functionality. In the Section described above, an infinitesimal part of a hierarchy in a mine is shown and divided into several levels according to the data and communication hierarchy. This Section briefly outlines the increased requirements and demands placed on a subsystem (see Figure 2) if the operated machines are compared to the target concept of the digital mine.

A basic prerequisite for the vertical integration of processes into a higher architecture is the digitalization and automation of the machines used within the specific processes [16]. The operational requirements of the target system, i.e., stable system states to ensure a link to the equilibrium of an ecosystem, must never be ignored [16]. For process-central systems, such as a logistics system (belt conveyor) within a mine, permanent availability, efficiency and no loss of work quality must be guaranteed [16]. When a belt conveyor system stops, the upstream processes are also interrupted [17]. This has a corresponding effect on the downstream process steps in the mine like for example, that without a mineral processing no further processing steps of the targeted value mineral to a product are possible. This strategically important role of a belt conveyor can only be maintained by applying robust machines that can operate in a constantly changing environment. In addition, due to the frequent local changes in the mining industry, digitalization measures specializing in a particular application must be recalibrated again and again in order to ensure that the quality of the new application does not deteriorate [16]. The resulting constantly changing environmental conditions mean that systems can rarely be mirrored or flexibly transferred to "similar" applications. This is made even more difficult by the fact that the systems are not always up to date and combined with the fact that with an increasing number of different suppliers, the number of different systems also increases. The evolution of such long-living cyber-physical systems should be performed in a managed way. A formal description technique for modelling long-living cyber-physical systems is described in [24] and [25], which guarantees the consistency between the system evolution requirements and system implementation.

This general importance of logistic systems in mining also led to the specific content of the Use Case design in the EIT Raw Materials funded project Maintained Mine and Machine (MaMMa)[21]. Here, an interface-neutral, cloud-based MaMMa platform for the optimization of maintenance cycles is to be developed using a belt conveyor in an underground mine as a use case. In order to optimize individual sub-areas, such as a belt conveyor, of a superordinate operational system, such as an underground mine. For this purpose, the data producer and usage structure of such a described subsystem had to be analyzed [21].

V. Data Use and Role Structure of a Subsytem In Mining

The current state of data usage and the role structure are presented in the following. For this purpose, a subsystem is divided into the respective macro and micro systems.

A. *Collected Sensor Data of a Subsystem (Belt Conveyer) Divided into Macrosystems*

As previously described mining operations are characterized by versatility and variability. Therefore, a lot of data can be generated to describe processes and their environment [2] and [6]. These possibilities include not only extensive machine data sets, which can be derived from the belt conveyer usage alone, but also a large number of other microsystems, which are conducive to transparency of the subsystem. This leads to the fact that a target horizon of data collection and thus the data consumer of the different sensor data has been divided into different macrosystems.

When considering the data technology environment of a machine-related subsystem, the available sensors and data sets can be divided into two categories. On the one hand, the existing machine data and those included in the machines are to be used. The advantage of these data is that they can be acquired in real time without any sensor-technical extension. On the other hand, the sensor-technical acquisition of machine data, as described in the previous Section, is possible by means of additional sensors that are specifically applied to the machine environment. In addition, there are further sensor-technical investigations that are active in the periphery of the subsystem under consideration and address different data sets and data consumers as their main goal. These data can be used, for example, for quality control, control engineering, safety engineering, ventilation engineering and process optimization. This multitude of generated data sets is supplemented by the number of data sets of the upstream and downstream machines and systems for the respective subsystem. The belt conveyor, as a single system is separated from the overall process by system boundaries, is shown in Figure 3. In their technical use the described possibilities of sensor-technical data collection, which are grouped into individual macrosystems in different cases of data collection, are very dependent on the respective degree of technology, the conveyor system, the machine manufacturer and the mine operator. Even within one company there can be different degrees of technology or fixed physical system boundaries. Irrespective of this, the data collected in the subsystem belt conveyor should be made available for process analysis. The complexity of the process analysis can be shown more completely by an increased information density.

Figure 4 refers to the singular data usage according to the respective thematic macrosystem. The different sensor data collected are used by the respective data specialist for process optimization or maintenance. Often, coordinated systems and structures are used for this purpose. An exchange of information within the system structure between the data usage paths is neither planned nor made possible. Thus, a change in the system structure of data use aims at enabling flexible data and information exchange [3].

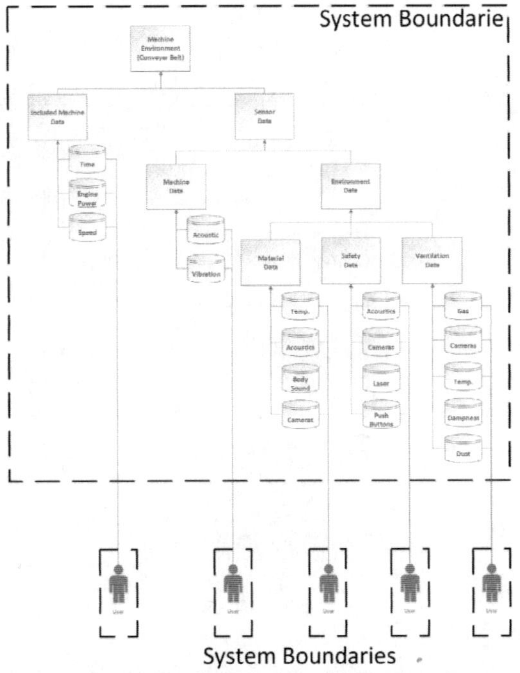

Figure 4. Example of a reduced data hierarchy of a subsystem.

B. *Introduction of a Cloud and Service Based Platform – MaMMa*

Figure 5 picks up the data usage structure defined in Section V-A. Based on this, a comprehensive data usage string is derived. As an example, for the presentation of the structural change and problem definition, the data input is shown singularly for one sensor from the structural points - machine data / material data / system data. Here, the data usage is extended by the individual acting roles in the development of IT solutions for sensor technical data collection.

The **Sensor Specialist** is responsible for the configuration and design of the sensor technologies used. He has a deep understanding of the domain and detailed knowledge of the microsystem.

The **Data Analyst** is a specialist for processing and evaluating data. He has a high level of domain knowledge. He interacts with the sensor specialist, to increase or optimize data quality. The data analyst does not work directly with sensor data, but with the data provided by any kind of infrastructure. If the data analysis has reached a stage where these findings should be made available to the user or third parties, the data analyst passes these findings on to the Software Developer.

The **Software (SW) Developer** is an IT specialist and developer, who implements new Services or Applications to make data or processed data available. For this he only needs a rudimentary domain understanding, but a very high IT understanding.

The **User** is the person who uses the product, which was created during the development.

Over the entire data value chain, which was described by means of the acting roles, a data point reduction is carried out with each processing step. In each step, information is lost, perhaps unimportant for the end-user in this context, but presumably important in another context. The introduction of platform-based cloud solutions and the resulting expansion of system boundaries means that extended, flexible and extensive data use can be enabled. The system boundaries between developer and user (or between data supplier and consumer) are softened and/or dissolved. By feeding existing and newly developed products into a platform-based system, new possibilities for their use arise. This enables the development of virtual sensors by deriving the final products and the information included for new applications and information bases [3].

The presented open system is a tool for a comprehensive high-level architecture. Not only the linear feeding and provision of pre-processed data or the combined provision of different end products, related to the macrosystems, shall be enabled in this way. Interaction of the user with the platform for flexible retrieval of the different analyzed data sets and end products via flexible/interactive dashboards is used to create an increased value of the existing data. This should lead to a more comprehensive process analysis to improve process optimization and also maintenance [4].

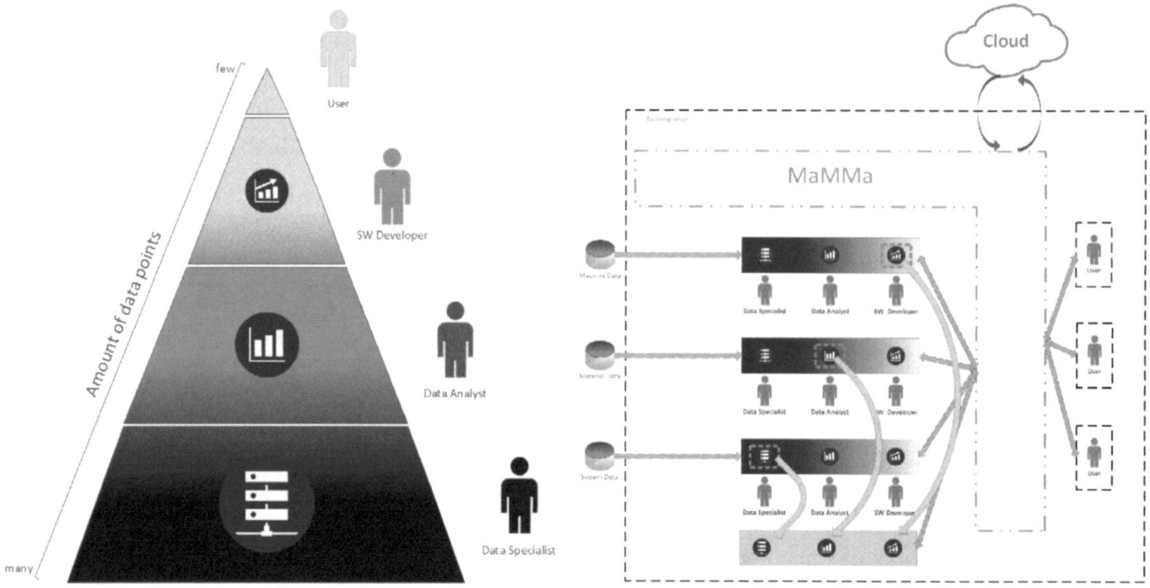

Figure 5. MaMMa-Solution and data reduction.

VI. STRUCTURAL DEVELOPMENT OF SOFTWARE FOR IT ECOSYSTEMS

Based on the stringent and linear data usage and the associated role structure derived from the current state of practice, the benefits of platform-based systems to bridge the technical gapwas demonstrated. In the following, a new concept for a role structure enabled in this way is presented.

A. *Overall Approach*

The innovation of a cloud-based platform in contrast to the classical monolithic IT concepts is the shift of the system boundaries from a closed to an open one, as shown in Figure 5. The solution presented here not only allows to combine already existing products, but also to break the described linear paths of usage. However, this can only be done in a managed way and process. An IT ecosystem in the mining industry is subject to clearly structured processes and operational limitations on the one hand, but must also ensure creative, flexible and fast changes in the process structure on the other hand. The visualization of the described transformation process is shown in Figure 6. Here, a clear role model is used to define responsibilities in relation to processes, data, applications and the goals pursued. To achieve this, clear communication channels must be created across the existing system boundaries and limiting interfaces.

This model can be used as a blueprint for all software-intensive processes regardless of their complexity and level of abstraction (see Figure 2). Scalability and implementation are discussed in detail in the following Section VI-B. In contrast to common process models, the one presented does not have a defined sequence of execution. The interaction is rather to be interpreted as synchronization points, where the arrow direction describes the initiation of synchronization. For this purpose, the roles already introduced in previous Sections are extended by the roles Operator and Integrator.

The **Operator** has a very high understanding of the IT infrastructure, its use and design. He interacts indirectly with every other role through the data and services he manages. During the interaction / communication between the other roles involved, the operator has a special position. If the role of the operator does not coincide with another role, the interaction takes place only via the integrator. From the complexity level onwards, where this role is occupied as an independent role, the topic of infrastructure will also be cross-sectional and concern more than one usage path.

The **Integrator** has a superordinate understanding of all areas and controls the cooperation of all roles. Furthermore, he is responsible for integration beyond the system boundaries, i.e., both on the same hierarchical level and between different usage threads.

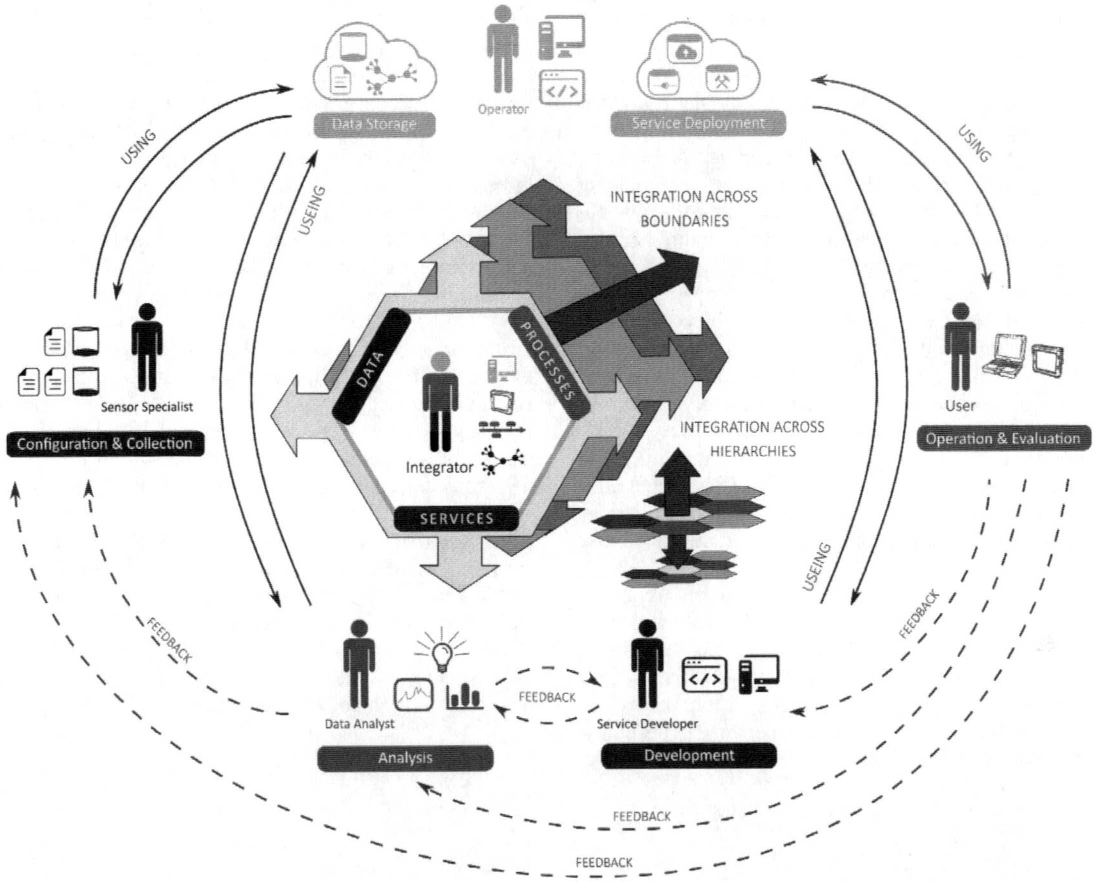

Figure 6. Role- and process model.

His role is not only to be regarded as a technical integrator, but also as a mediator, since he is the one who brings together the triad of data, service and process.

Basically, there are three types of interaction,

i.) the mediation and integration within the system, between systems and between hierarchy and abstraction level is responsible through the role of the integrator.

ii.) usage relationships with the infrastructure as a central element.

iii.) feedback channels that allow iterative and incremental development. The interaction / communication is either directly through the cycles implied by the feedback channels or through the integrator.

The following Section will deal with this role and process model can be adapted to the different needs in a mining ecosystem.

B. *Scalability and Mapping to Software Engineering Processes*

Considering a macrosystem and its usage paths as shown in Figure 2, such software-intensive systems can be modelled very well to proven and classical waterfall models [9] and classical concepts of software engineering. The disadvantage resulting from these process models are the long project durations, which are predominant due to the placing of orders. By developing cloud and service-based technologies a technical infrastructure is created, which allows integrating systems or components in different ways. However, this results in new challenges in the context of an ecosystem that requires new methodologies, concepts and mechanisms on higher levels of abstraction [9] [15].

These challenges not only result in a change regarding the role of the data specialist, the analyst and also the developer in the context of a mining operation but also, to a greater emphasis on agile development methodologies [12], so that shorter release cycles can be achieved and smaller projects can be established in a quick and dynamic way. Furthermore, the user comes as an essential part of an IT ecosystem comes to the fore. The IT ecosystem must represent a benefit for the user. Otherwise, the role of the user or the development must be questioned at this point. The proposed approach also allows flexibility regarding fusion roles to be combined in one person. This can be done depending on the complexity or the involved usage paths. This can range from the extreme case that all roles are combined in one person, which can be the example in the case of experimental prototype development and testing, to a distribution of all roles even beyond the company borders. Figure 5 shows how such a dynamic adaptation of roles and thus a scaling of the approach across several abstraction levels and system boundaries can be designed.

Looking at the utilization path in Figure 2, the scenario shown in Figure 7 case i. could represent the development and installation of the speed sensor in the belt conveyor engine. This can also be done by or at the manufacturer. In this case the sensor is only used to control the drive of the machine. Therefore, the roles of developer and operator coincide, since the deployment is carried out on the control system of the machine itself. The roles of sensor specialist and analyst also coincide here, since the generated data output is designed for this special application and is therefore used for automated control. In this case, the user would be synonymous with the client, or the designer of the machine, and would thus implicitly represent the role of the integrator. However, the role of the integrator can also be fulfilled by the other two people/roles depending on the focus of the use case.

Case ii. of Figure 7 represents the scenario of making data available via a cloud infrastructure. Previously this data was only used for controlling the machine. This means that the role of the operator is occupied independently, since a central infrastructure is now accessed. In addition, the role of the developer will be newly occupied in person, because now it is no longer a question of developing a piece of software in an embedded system, but of writing a new service for the infrastructure. This leads to a new profile of the role of the developer. Also, in case ii), depending on the interpretation, the role of the integrator can be performed by one of the other roles. The integrator now has a special responsibility, as he is responsible for ensuring that added value is created through cloud integration. This does not have to be done in person by the integrator of the cloud integration project but can also be done by an integrator from the material analysis path of use, who could initiate case iii). Based on his/her domain expertise and the active exchange with the integrators of other utilization paths, it can be determined, that a virtual scale can be realized through the now available speed values, so that the original sensor data of the machine can now also be used for the utilization path of the material analysis. As shown in Figure 7 iii), each role is now the responsibility of a separate person, with the role of the analyst being more dominant over the sensor specialist, in contrast to cases i) and ii).

In summary, there is no single profile for the roles, nor for the combination of individual roles. This depends rather on the level of abstraction, the required domain and expertise and the context in the ecosystem. It is crucial that in every project the role affiliation and thus the responsibility is made explicit, and that the integrator can spread impulses and best practices through an active exchange across usage paths.

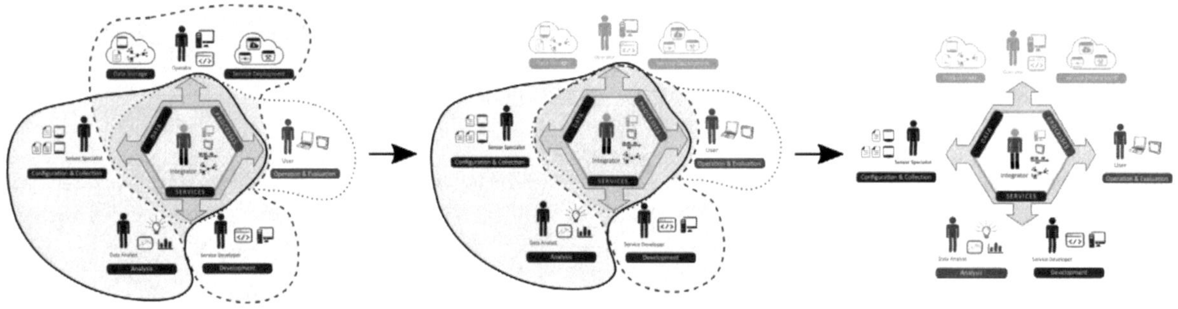

i.) ii.) iii.)

Figure 7. Dynamic role decomposition.

VII. Conclusion, Future Challenges and Further Work

In this article a case study was considered, which gives an impression of the existing complexity and at the same time that this complexity is still detectable and hand-able. Exemplary the data collection possibilities and usage structures were worked out. Therefore, the cyber-physical subsystem conveyer belt was used as a case study. By introducing a cloud-based platform, data usage could be made more flexible and extensive for the whole IT ecosystems. The described approach offers an important technical basis and reduces the hurdle to carry out small, agile and user-oriented software development projects.
In a first step, the approach presented here has focused on modelling the actual state and the necessary changes in relation to the process and role model in to reduce existing barriers. The differentiation from existing technology solutions / technology stack was not considered in depth, as this is highly influenced by the existing solutions and could only be answered with the help of a comprehensive study.

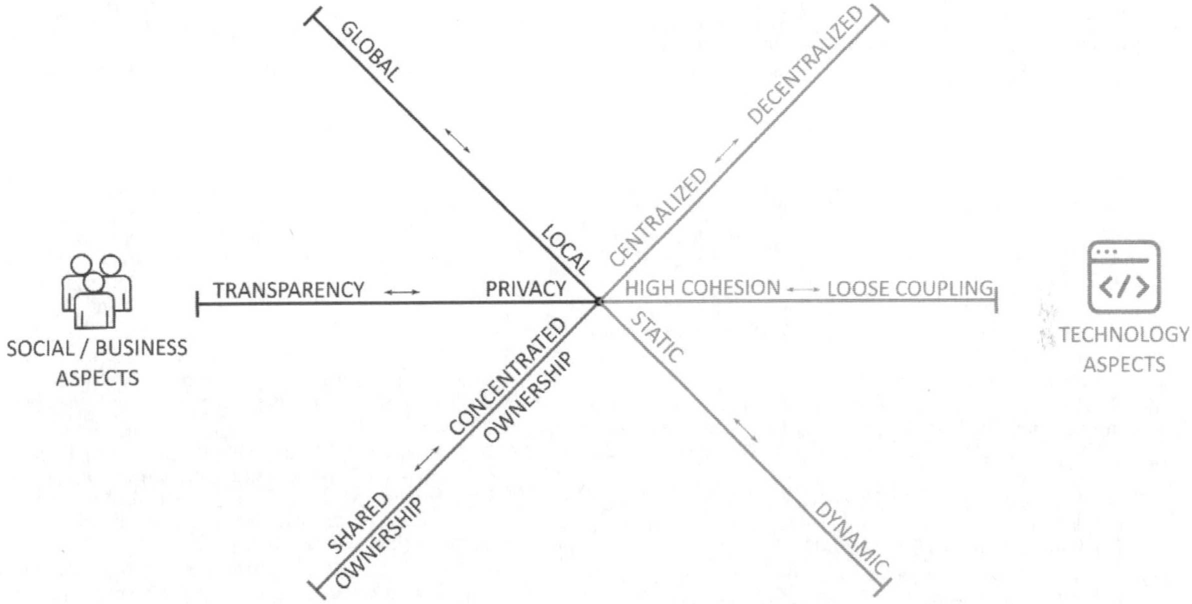

Figure 8. Classification of IT ecosystem.

Future research, necessary for integration into active mining operations may include following questions:

1) What role will employees play in future mining ecosystems?

2) What methodology and mechanisms can be used to create a balance for the social and business aspects, so that obstacles can be removed in this area as well?

In order to classify this challenge, systems can not only be classified into macro- or microsystems due to their complexity but can also be evaluated with regard to their technological, social and business aspects. Figure 8 describes six dimensions that can be used for this purpose. Also, from practical experience (reference to project MaMMa) it is known that the hurdles are not purely technical in nature. In order to create emergent system behavior, a high level of transparency and data availability beyond the system's own boundaries is necessary. The resulting areas of conflict cannot, however, be decided at a purely technical level, but the approach described here attempts to ensure a controlled process by introducing a specific role model and, in particular, the cross-cutting role of the integrator. The aim is to build and refine the necessary understanding between the individual actors and to contribute to the stability of the ecosystem. Another future challenge is the implementation of the model described to an active mining operation, since technological transformation must be accompanied by a cultural change in the company.

Furthermore, the specification of the individual activities, their initiation and their lifecycle will be part of further research. As shown in Figure 7, a comparison with the general definition of a DIN 69901 concept is obvious. The dynamic formation of teams pursuing a common goal fulfils the project character. But our approach goes one step further as we explicitly do not speak of a development project anymore. Hereby the evolution of the system and the shutdown or replacement of a system within the IT ecosystem is an integral part of this approach and had to be part of further research [20].

ACKNOWLEDGMENT

This work was partially funded under the auspices of the EIT - KIC Raw materials program within the project "Maintained Mining Machine" (MaMMa) with the grant agreement number: [EIT/RAW MATERIALS/SGA2018/1, 17031]

REFERENCES

[1] H. Wotruba, H. Knapp, K. Neubert and C. Schropp, "Application of sensor-based sorting for the processing of mineral resources," Chemie Ingenieur Technik 86, Nr. 6, pp. 773-783, ISSN 0009286X, 2014

[2] T. Vraetz, „Development and application of an innovative concept for inline characterisation of mixtures of substances in continuous mass flows using Acoustic Emission Technology," RWTH Aachen, Diss., 1. Auflage Aachen: Verlag R. Zillekens, Aachener Schriften zur Rohstoff- und Entsorgungstechnik, Band 96 ISBN: 978-3-941277-36-6, 2018

[3] M. Jaekel, „The power of digital platforms," Springer Verlag Wiesbaden GmbH, ISBN: 978-3-658-19178-8, 2017

[4] B. Vogel-Heuser and T. Bauernhansl, „Manuel Industry 4.0," Bd.4; Springer Verlag Deutschland, ISBN: 978-3-662-53254-6, 2017

[5] I. Schindler, „Belt conveyor technology - state of the art and current development," Studienarbeit, Institut für Bergwerks- und Hüttenmaschinenkunde, Rheinisch-Westfälische Technische Hochschule Aachen, 1998

[6] K. Nienhaus, T. Pretz and H. Wotruba, „Sensor Technologies: Impulses for the Raw Materials Industry," Schriftenreihe zur Aufbereitung und Veredlung 50, RWTH Aachen, Shaker Verlag, 2014

[7] D. G. Messerschmitt and C. Szyperski, „Software ecosystem. Understanding an indispensable technology and industry," Cambridge, Mass.: MIT Press., 2003

[8] A. Rausch and D. Niebuhr: "DemSy - A Scenario for an Integrated Demonstrator in a Smart City."NTH Focused Research School for IT Ecosystems, Science Report, TU Clausthal, Clausthal-Zellerfeld, 2010

[9] H. D. Benington, "Production of Large Computer Programs," in Annals of the History of Computing, vol. 5, no. 4, pp. 350-361, Oct.-Dec. 1983.

[10] H. Balzert, „Textbook of software technology: Basic concepts and requirements engineering," Springer-Verlag, 2010.

[11] F. Wortmann and K. Flüchter, "Internet of things." Business & Information Systems Engineering 57.3,2015, p. 221-224

[12] K. Beck, M. Beedle, A. Bennekum, A. Cockburn, M. Fowler, J. Grenning, J. Highsmith, A. Hunt, R. Jeffries, J. Kern, B. Marick, R. C. Martin, S. Mellor, K. Schwaber, J. Sutherland, D. Thomas, "Manifesto for agile software development.", [Online] Available from www.agilemanifesto.org, 2006, retrieved: March, 2020.

[13] R. Bachmann, G. Kemper and T. Gerzer, „Big Data - Curse or blessing?", mitp/bhv, Verlag C. H. Beck, 2014, ISBN: 978-3-8266-9690-9

[14] R. Jabbari, N. Ali, K. Petersen and B. Tanveer, "What is devops? A systematic mapping study on definitions and practices." Proceedings of the Scientific Workshop Proceedings of XP2016. ACM, 2016

[15] M. Gharbi, A. Koschel, A. Rausch and G. Starke, „Basic knowledge for software architects. Training and further education according to iSAQB standard to become a Certified Professional for Software Architecture - Foundation Level. 3.", revised and updated edition. Heidelberg: dpunkt.verlag, 2018

[16] O. O'Neill, "Digitisation in mining – Industry 4.0," Mining Report 153, ISSN. 2195-6529.101.106, 2017

[17] B. Eichentopf, T. Wendel R. Baltes and K. Nienhaus, „Application examples of LWIR cameras for process monitoring and automation," AKIDA, Aachener Kolloquium für Instandhaltung, Diagnose und Anlagenüberwachung, 1. Aufl. Stolberg Zillekens, 19./20. November 2014, pp. 27-36 ISBN: 978-3-941277-21-2

[18] P. Hopwood "Tracking the trends 2018," Deloitte Design Studio, Canada 17, 2018,

[19] M. Hüttermann, "DevOps for Developer," Springer Science and Business Media New York, 2012, ISBN 978-1-4302-4569-8,

[20] Deutsches Institut für Normung, „DIN 69901-5, Projektmanagement –Teil 5: Begriffe," Deutsche Norm, 2009

[21] EIT Raw Materials, "Maintained Mine & Machine," [Online] available from www.mamma-project.eu, retrieved: 01.06.2020

[22] K. Nienhaus, T. Pretz and H. Wotruba, „Sensor Technologies: Impulses for the Raw Materials Industry," Schriftenreihe zur Aufbereitung und Veredlung, Shaker Verlag, Aachen, 2014

[23] D. Wang, C. Knieke, H. Fischer and A. Rausch, "An Approach for Configuration of the Industry 4.0 Technologies on Production Systems," ICONS 2020: The Fifteenth International Conference on Systems, Copyright (c) IARIA, 2020, February 23-27, 2020, Lisbon, Portugal, Page(s): 84-87, ISBN: 978-1-61208-771-9

[24] D. Wang, C. Knieke, and A. Rausch, "Data-driven Component Configuration in Production Systems," Adapt. 2019 Elev. Int. Conf. Adapt. Self-Adaptive Syst. Appl., no. c, pp. 44–47, 2019.

[25] J. Fitzgerald, C. Gamble, P. G. Larsen, K. Pierce, and J. Woodcock, "Cyber-Physical Systems Design: Formal Foundations, Methods and Integrated Tool Chains," in Proceedings - 3rd FME Workshop on Formal Methods in Software Engineering, 2015, pp. 40–46.

[26] A. Rausch, J. P. Müller, D. Niebuhr, S. Herold and U. Goltz, "IT ecosystems: A new paradigm for engineering complex adaptive software systems," 2012 6th IEEE International Conference on Digital Ecosystems and Technologies (DEST), Campione d'Italia, 2012, pp. 1-6, doi: 10.1109/DEST.2012.6227908.

Effective Self-Healing Networks against Attacks or Disasters in Resource Allocation Control

Yukio Hayashi
Graduate School of Advanced Institute of Science and Technology, Japan Advanced Institute of Science and Technology
Nomi-city, Ishikawa 923-1292
Email: yhayashi@jaist.ac.jp

Atsushi Tanaka
Department of Informatics and Electronics
Faculty of Engineering, Yamagata University
Yonezawa-city, Yamagata 992-8510
Email: tanaka@yamagata-u.ac.jp

Jun Matsukubo
Department of Creative Engineering, National Institute of Technology Kitakyushu College
Kitakyushu-city, Fukuoka 802-0985
Email: jmatsu@apps.kct.ac.jp

Abstract—**With increasing threats by large attacks or disasters, the time has come to reconstruct network infrastructures such as communication or transportation systems rather than to recover them as before in case of accidents, because many real networks are extremely vulnerable. Thus, we consider self-healing mechanisms by rewirings (reuse or addition of links) to be sustainable and resilient networks even against malicious attacks. In distributed local process for healing, the key strategies are the extension of candidates of linked nodes and enhancing loops by applying a message-passing algorithm inspired from statistical physics. Simulation results show that our proposed combination of ring formation and enhancing loops is particularly effective in comparison with the conventional methods, when more than half damaged links work or are compensated from reserved ones.**

Keywords–Self-Healing; Complex Network Science; Connectivity; Enhancing Loops; Message-Passing Algorithm; Resource Allocation; Resilience.

I. INTRODUCTION

In contemporary world, network infrastructures, such as communication, trading, transportation, energy and water supply systems are crucial for supporting social activities, economy, industrial production, etc., while increasing the frequency of large disasters or military conflicts turn threats by destroying the functions into reality. To confront the serious problems, a new supple approach *resilience* [1][2] attracts much attention in system engineering, biology, ecology, and sociology. Resilience means the ability to sustain basic objective and integrity even in encountering with the extreme change of situations or environments (e.g., by disasters or malicious attacks) for technological system, organization, or individual [1]. However, to be resilient system, the concept of safety against accidents or disruptions should be extended from *Safety-I* to *Safety-II* [3]: from "as few things as possible go wrong" to "as many things as possible go right", from "reactive, respond when something happens" to "proactive, continuously trying to anticipate developments and events", and so on, in these two complementary views, which do not conflict. Safety-II requires to adjust, adapt, develop, and design better processes with technological or human resource allocations. Moreover, the concept of resilience includes reorganization or reconstruction of the system with adaptive capacity beyond the conventional recovery [4], as shown in Table I. Such paradigm shift has affinity to self-adaptive mechanism or system. Thus, we focus on developing new mechanism to lead to (social-ecological) resilience with reconstruction as far as accepting innovation rather than finding and decreasing weak or wrong parts in a network system.

TABLE I. A SEQUENCE OF RESILIENCE CONCEPTS WHICH ARE PARTIALLY EXTRACTED FROM [4].

Resilience concept	*Characteristics*	*Focus on*
Engineering resilience	Return time, efficiency	Recovery, constancy
Ecological/ecosystem resilience	Buffer capacity, withstand shock, maintain function	Persistence, robustness
Social−ecological resilience	Interplay disturbance and **reorganization**, sustaining and developing	**Adaptive capacity**, transformability, learning, innovation

In this paper, we study how to reconstruct a sustainable network under limited resource, and propose effective self-healing methods based on enhancing loops through a local process around damaged parts. The motivations for enhancing loops are as follows. There is a common topological structure called Scale-Free (SF) in many social, biological, and technological networks [5][6]. Although the SF networks have an extreme vulnerability against malicious attacks [7], it has been found that onion-like structure with positive degree-degree correlations gives the optimal robustness of connectivity [8][9]. Onion-like structure can be generated by whole rewiring [8][10] in enhancing the correlations under a given degree distribution. Moreover, since dismantling and decycling problems are asymptotically equivalent at infinite graphs in a large class of random networks with light-tailed degree distribution [11], a tree remains without loops at the critical state before the complete fragmentation by node removals. Dismantling (or decycling) problem known as NP-hard [12] is to find the minimum set of nodes in which removal leaves a graph broken into connected components whose maximum size is at most a constant (or a graph without loops). It is suggested that the robustness becomes stronger as many loops exist as possible. In fact, to be onion-like networks, enhancing loops by copying or intermediation is effective for improving the robustness in incrementally growing methods [13][14] based on a local distributed process. Thus, we remark that loops make bypasses and may be more important than the degree-degree correlations in order to improve the connectivity in a network reconstruction after large disasters or attacks. However, identifying the necessary nodes to form loops is intractable due to combinatorial NP-hardness, we effectively apply an approximate calculation based on a statistical physics approach in our proposed self-healing. We assume that rewirings (reuse of undestroyed links) are performed by changing directions or ranges of flight routes or wireless beams in the healing process, though we do not discuss the detail realization that depends on the current or future technologies and target systems.

The organization of this paper is as follows. In Section 2, we introduce the conventional methods for recovery and healing of a damaged network, and newly discuss some limitations and extensions of the resource for connecting nodes. In Section 3, we explain our proposed self-healing method. In Section 4, we show the effect of healing on the connectivity and the efficiency of paths in damaged real networks by malicious attacks through computer simulation. In Section 5, we summarize the obtained results and mention a future work.

II. Related Work

We briefly review recent progress of typical methods for recovery and healing of a network in complex network science (inspired from fractal statistical physics) and computer science.

In complex network science, several recovery and healing methods have been proposed. As one of the recovery methods, the strategies of random, greedy (for regaining the largest connectivity), and preferential recovery weighted by population have been considered in taking into account the order of recovered links [15]. The effectiveness of recovery from localized attacks is investigated on a square lattice. Against link failures, a simple recovery method has been also introduced to reconstruct an active tree for delivering from a source node by using back-up links [16]. However, it is unclear which pairs of two nodes should be prepared for back-up links in advance.

On the other hand, a self-healing method has been proposed by establishing new random links on interdependent (two-layered) networks of square lattices [17], and the effect against node attacks is numerically studied. In particular, for adding links by the healing process, the candidates of linked nodes are incrementally extended from only the direct neighbors of the removed node by attacks until no more separation of components occurs. In other words, the whole connectivity is maintained except the isolating removed parts (known as induced sub-graphs for removed nodes in computer science). Note that such an extension of the candidates of linked nodes is a key idea in our proposed self-healing method as mentioned later.

Furthermore, the following self-healing methods, whose effects are investigated for some data of real networks, are worthy to note. One is a distributed local repair in order of a priority to the most damaged node [18]. In the repair by linking from the most damaged node to a randomly chosen node from the unremoved node set in its next-nearest neighbors before attacks, the order of damaged nodes is according to the smaller fraction k_{dam}/k_{orig} of its remained degree k_{dam} and the original degree k_{orig} before the attacks. The selections are repeated until reaching a given rate f_s controlled by the fraction of nodes whose k_{dam}/k_{orig} exceeds a threshold. Another is a bypass rewiring [19] on more limited resource of links (wire cables, wireless communication or transportation lines between two nodes) and ports (channels or plug sockets at a node). To establish links between pair nodes, a node is randomly chosen only one time in the neighbors of each removed node. When k_i denotes the degree of removed node i, only $\lfloor k_i/2 \rfloor$ links are reused. Note that a degree represents the number of using ports at the node. In the bypass rewiring, reserved additional ports are not necessary: they do not exceed the original one before attacks. Moreover, greedy bypass rewiring [19] is proposed in order to improve the robustness, the selection of pair nodes is based on the number of the links not yet rewired and the size of the neighboring components.

In computer science, ForgivingTree algorithm has been proposed [20]. Under the repeated attacks, the following self-healing is processed one-by-one after each node removal, except when the removed node is a leaf (whose degree is one). It is based on both distributed process of sending messages and data structure, furthermore developed to an efficient algorithm called as compact routing [21]. In each rewiring process, a removed node and its links are replaced by a binary tree. Note that each vertex of the binary tree was the neighbors of the removed node, whose links to the neighbors are reused as the edges of the binary tree. Thus, additional links for healing is unnecessary. It is remarkable for computation (e.g., in routing or information spreading) that the multiplicative factor of diameter of the graph after healing is never more than $O(\log k_{max})$, where k_{max} is the maximum degree in the original network, because of the replacing by binary trees. However, the robustness of connectivity is not taken into account in the limited rewiring based on binary trees, since a tree structure is easily disconnected into subtrees by any attack to the joint node. In other research, a recovery strategy with resource allocation of bandwidth in a communication network is discussed at several service levels from full to partial with respect to what and how optimization [22], although considering the link's thickness (e.g., defined by bandwidth or transportation amounts) is out of our current scope.

TABLE II. Reserved resource at a node in self-healing methods.

Method	*Additional links*	*Additional ports*
ForgivingTree [20]	Unnecessary, enough by the original under the reuse	Two or three at most in a binary tree
Bypass Rewiring [19]	Unnecessary, if about half is reusable from the original	Unnecessary, enough by the original
Simple Local Repair [18]	Controllable by $f_s(1-q)N$	Necessary according to f_s and attack rate q
Our Proposed Method	Controllable by M_h	Necessary according to r_h and attack rate q

The characteristics of resource allocation are summarized in Table II for the above conventional and our proposed methods, although there has been no discussion about resource of links and ports. ForgivingTree or bypass rewiring methods is not controllable but strongly depending on the reuse of all or half links before attacks. We assume that some links emanated from a removed node i can be reused for healing by local rewiring between the neighbors. These links (cable lines) work at the neighbor's sides, even though they are disconnected at the removed node's side. As a control parameter in our simulation, we set the reusable rate r_h according to the damage, on the assumption $k_i(1-r_h)$ links do not work in the removed node's degree k_i. In the two kinds of resource, we consider that ports work independently from connection links, as similar to a relation of airport runaway (or plug socket) and flight by airplane (or cable line). As one of the added values from the conventional heuristic methods, we consider a new design strategy by enhancing loops to improve the effect on healing in the next section.

III. Effective Self-Healing

A. Outline of Proposed Methods

We assume that almost simultaneously attacked nodes are not recoverable immediately, therefore are removed from the network function for a while. In case of emergency for healing, unconnected two nodes are chosen and rewired as the reconstruction assistance or reuse of links emanated from removed qN nodes, when the fraction of attacks is q. The healing process in each of the following 1), 2), and 3) is initiated just after detecting attacks and repeated by $M_h \stackrel{\text{def}}{=} r_h \times \tilde{\sum}_{i \in D_q} k_i$ links. Here, $\tilde{\sum}_{i \in D_q} k_i$ means the number without multiple counts of lost links by attacks. D_q denotes the set of removed nodes, $|D_q| = qN$. The key strategies are 1) enhancing loops contributes to improve the robustness [14][23], 2) forming a ring that encloses damaged parts is able to maintain the connectivity on the edges of extended neighbors, and 3) complementary effects of 1) and 2) in the limited resource of M_h links. Any one of them is performed as the healing process.

1) Enhancing loops for smaller $q_j^0 + q_{j'}^0$
To select two nodes in the neighbor nodes $j, j' \in \partial i$ in the increasing order of $q_j^0 + q_{j'}^0$ for all $i \in D_q$, as shown in Figure 1.
2) Extended ring
To make a ring of simple cycle without crossing, the neighbors are extended from the first damaged, the second damaged, etc., to the last damaged area in this order, as shown in Figure 2.
3) Combination of extended ring & enhancing loops for smaller $q_j^0 + q_{j'}^0$
After using $M_r \leq \tilde{\sum}_{i \in D_q} k_i$ links for the ring, if $M_h > M_r$, then the selections of two nodes in the extended neighbors on ring are repeated in the increasing order of $q_j^0 + q_{j'}^0$ for $M_h - M_r$ links. Else a ring is incomplete and an open chain is generated among the extended neighbors. In this case, additional rewirings between the nodes j, j' with smaller $q_j^0 + q_{j'}^0$ are not performed due to lack of links.

Enhancing loops is performed by applying the values of q_i^0 (introduced in next subsection) for estimating Feedback Vertex Set (FVS) whose nodes are necessary to form loops. Since a node i with small q_i^0 belongs to a dangling subtree with high probability, by connecting such nodes, it is expected that a new loop on which a part of the subtree is included is added. From left to right in Figure 1, the original red links emanated from the removed node i (marked by filled circle) are reused as the blue ones for the healing. When there is at least a path between the nodes j and j' in Figure 1, a new loop is created. Note that the attacked node i is isolatedly removed as breakdown.

A ring is generated as follows. In Figure 2, the process is initiated in order of removals of three nodes from left to right. Filled and open circles denote removed and active nodes, red and magenta lines denote removed and virtually added links, respectively. From top left to top right in Figure 2, a red node and its links are damaged, a ring formation around the 1st removal node at the left is tried to the direct neighbors of it. A green link is established, while virtual magenta links are considered by sending messages to active neighbors. From middle left to middle right in Figure 2, the ring formation around the 2nd removal node at the center is tried again to the neighbors which include the extended ones by the virtual links. Light blue links are added, but virtual magenta links are considered. From bottom left to bottom right in Figure 2, the ring formation around the 3rd removal node at the right is tried similarly. Finally, a ring is established by green, light blue, and blue links. The connections between neighbors on a ring are in random order except through the extension process.

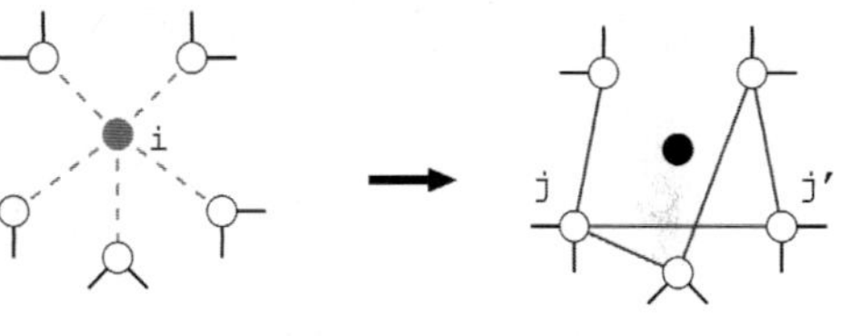

Figure 1. Rewiring between nodes with small $q_j^0 + q_{j'}^0$.

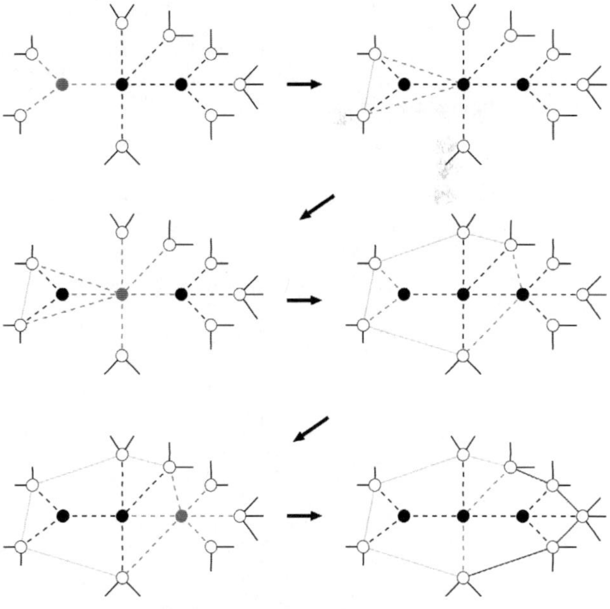

Figure 2. Generation process of a ring.

B. Applying Belief Propagation Algorithm

We review the following approximation algorithm [24][25] derived for estimating FVS known as NP-hard problem [12]. It is based on a cavity method in statistical physics in the assumption that nodes $j \in \partial i$ are mutually independent of each other when node i is removed. The joint probability is $\mathcal{P}_{\backslash i}(A_j : j \in \partial i) \approx \Pi_{j\in\partial i} q^{A_j}_{j\to i}$ by the product of independent marginal probability $q^{A_j}_{j\to i}$ for the state A_j as the index of j's root. In the cavity graph, if all nodes $j \in \partial i$ are either empty ($A_j = 0$) or roots ($A_j = j$), the added node i can be a root ($A_i = i$). There are the following exclusive states.

1) $A_i = 0$: i is empty (removed). Since i is unnecessary as a root, it belongs to FVS.
2) $A_i = i$: i becomes its own root. The state $A_j = j$ of $j \in \partial i$ is changeable to $A_j = i$ when node i is added.
3) $A_i = k$: one node $k \in \partial i$ becomes the root of i when it is added, if k is occupied and all other $j \in \partial i$ are either empty or roots.

The corresponding probabilities to the above three states are represented by

$$q_i^0 \overset{\text{def}}{=} \frac{1}{z_i(t)}, \tag{1}$$

$$q_i^i \overset{\text{def}}{=} \frac{e^x \Pi_{j\in\partial i(t)} \left[q^0_{j\to i} + q^j_{j\to i}\right]}{z_i(t)},$$

$$q_i^k \overset{\text{def}}{=} \frac{e^x \frac{(1-q^0_{k\to i})}{q^0_{k\to i}+q^k_{k\to i}} \Pi_{j\in\partial i(t)} \left[q^0_{j\to i} + q^j_{j\to i}\right]}{z_i(t)},$$

$$q^0_{i\to j} = \frac{1}{z_{i\to j}(t)}, \tag{2}$$

$$q^i_{i\to j} = \frac{e^x \Pi_{k\in\partial i(t)\backslash j} \left[q^0_{k\to i} + q^k_{k\to i}\right]}{z_{i\to j}(t)}, \tag{3}$$

where $\partial i(t)$ denotes node i's set of connecting neighbor nodes at time t, and $x > 0$ is a parameter of inverse temperature. The normalization constants are

$$z_i(t) \overset{\text{def}}{=} 1 + e^x \left[1 + \sum_{k\in\partial i(t)} \frac{1-q^0_{k\to i}}{q^0_{k\to i}+q^k_{k\to i}}\right] \Pi_{j\in\partial i(t)} \left[q^0_{j\to i} + q^j_{j\to i}\right], \tag{4}$$

$$z_{i\to j}(t) \overset{\text{def}}{=} 1 + e^x \Pi_{k\in\partial i(t)\backslash j} \left[q^0_{k\to i} + q^k_{k\to i}\right] \tag{5}$$

$$\times \left[1 + \sum_{l\in\partial i(t)\backslash j} \frac{1-q^0_{l\to i}}{q^0_{l\to i}+q^l_{l\to i}}\right], \tag{6}$$

to be satisfied for any node i and link $i \to j$ as

$$q_i^0 + q_i^i + \sum_{k\in\partial i} q_i^k = 1,$$

$$q^0_{i\to j} + q^i_{i\to j} + \sum_{k\in\partial i} q^k_{i\to j} = 1.$$

The message-passing iterated by equations (1)-(6) is called Belief Propagation (BP). These calculations of q_i^0, q_i^i, q_i^k, $q^0_{i\to j}$, $q^i_{i\to j}$, and $q^k_{i\to j}$ are locally executed through the message-passing until to be self-consistent in principle but practically to reach appropriate rounds from initial setting of $(0, 1)$ random values. The unit time from t to $t+1$ for calculating a set $\{q_i^0\}$ consists of a number of rounds by updating equations (1)-(6) in order of random permutation of the total N nodes. The distributed calculations can be also considered.

IV. Simulation Results

We evaluate the effect of healing by two measures: the ratio $\frac{S(q)}{(1-q)N}$ [18] for the connectivity and the efficiency $E \overset{\text{def}}{=} \frac{1}{N(N-1)} \sum_{i\neq j} \frac{1}{L_{ij}}$, where $S(q)$ and L_{ij} denote the size of GC (giant component or largest connected cluster) and the length of the shortest path counted by hops between i-j nodes, respectively, for a network after removing qN nodes by attacks with recalculation of the highest degree node as the target. We investigate them for Open Flight between airports and Internet AS Oregon as examples of real networks [26], whose number of nodes and links are $N = 2905$, $M = 15645$, and $N = 6474$, $M = 12572$. The following results are averaged over 10 samples with random process for tie-breaking in a node selection or ordering of nodes on a ring.

TABLE III. Number of additional ports in our proposed combination method for the fraction q of attacks and the reusable rate r_h of links.

Open Flight: $k_{max} = 242$

r_h \ q	0.1	0.2	0.3	0.4	0.5	0.6	0.7	0.8	0.9
0.05	1.0	1.0	1.0	1.0	1.0	1.0	1.0	32.8	73.2
	(0.3)	(0.4)	(0.5)	(0.5)	(0.5)	(0.5)	(0.5)	(1.4)	(4.6)
0.1	1.0	1.0	1.0	1.0	18.2	80.8	194.1	246.7	203.5
	(0.4)	(0.5)	(0.5)	(0.5)	(0.7)	(1.4)	(2.3)	(4.1)	(9.0)
0.2	89.2	84.7	294.3	347.0	362.0	446.5	412.5	341.1	228.2
	(1.0)	(1.5)	(1.7)	(2.3)	(3.1)	(4.0)	(5.8)	(9.0)	(19.1)
0.5	253.1	244.0	636.4	671.6	726.6	584.1	539.8	407.9	233.0
	(4.8)	(6.3)	(6.3)	(7.5)	(9.2)	(11.8)	(15.9)	(24.3)	(50.8)
1.0	403.0	449.4	807.8	822.1	755.8	626.7	571.2	422.4	249.2
	(10.9)	(13.8)	(14.1)	(16.1)	(19.5)	(24.6)	(33.3)	(50.9)	(103.4)

As Oregon: $k_{max} = 1458$

r_h \ q	0.1	0.2	0.3	0.4	0.5	0.6	0.7	0.8	0.9
0.05	1.0	1.0	1.0	1.0	1.0	1.0	1.0	1.0	1.0
	(0.4)	(0.5)	(0.5)	(0.5)	(0.5)	(0.6)	(0.6)	(0.5)	(0.5)
0.1	1.0	1.0	1.0	1.0	1.0	1.0	1.0	1.0	147.4
	(0.5)	(0.6)	(0.5)	(0.5)	(0.5)	(0.5)	(0.5)	(0.5)	(2.5)
0.2	1.0	1.0	1.0	1.0	1.0	1.0	176.9	440.1	473.7
	(0.5)	(0.5)	(0.5)	(0.5)	(0.5)	(0.5)	(1.1)	(2.4)	(6.1)
0.5	70.1	289.1	509.4	824.6	1112.4	1252.7	1122.7	820.1	485.1
	(0.7)	(1.0)	(1.3)	(1.8)	(2.4)	(3.3)	(4.9)	(8.1)	(17.7)
1.0	248.9	2275.3	2002.8	1801.2	1575.7	1343.0	1068.0	822.8	494.6
	(3.0)	(3.3)	(4.0)	(4.9)	(6.2)	(8.2)	(11.4)	(17.8)	(37.1)

TABLE IV. Number of additional ports in the conventional simple local repair method for the fraction q of attacks and the reusable rate r_h of links.

Open Flight: $k_{max} = 242$

r_h \ q	0.1	0.2	0.3	0.4	0.5	0.6	0.7	0.8	0.9
0.05	14.9	8.1	8	8.7	8.3	9.1	10.6	9.2	7.1
	(2.5)	(1.5)	(1.3)	(1.5)	(1.4)	(1.5)	(1.5)	(1.5)	(1.4)
0.1	14.6	8.2	11.6	9.2	8.5	10.1	8.9	7.7	6
	(2.0)	(1.5)	(1.5)	(1.5)	(1.5)	(1.5)	(1.5)	(1.5)	(1.4)
0.2	7.6	9.3	10.3	11.8	11.1	10.8	8.8	8.6	6.7
	(1.4)	(1.5)	(1.5)	(1.5)	(1.5)	(1.5)	(1.5)	(1.5)	(1.4)
0.5	7.6	9.3	10.3	11.8	11.1	10.8	8.8	8.6	6.7
	(1.4)	(1.5)	(1.5)	(1.5)	(1.5)	(1.5)	(1.5)	(1.5)	(1.4)
1.0	7.6	9.3	10.3	11.8	11.1	10.8	8.8	8.6	6.7
	(1.4)	(1.5)	(1.5)	(1.5)	(1.5)	(1.5)	(1.5)	(1.5)	(1.4)

AS Oregon: $k_{max} = 1458$

r_h \ q	0.1	0.2	0.3	0.4	0.5	0.6	0.7	0.8	0.9
0.05	4.5	4.4	4.3	5.3	5	5.2	6.4	7.6	6.6
	(1.1)	(1.2)	(1.2)	(1.2)	(1.3)	(1.3)	(1.4)	(1.5)	(1.5)
0.1	5.8	5.9	5.8	6	7.1	7.1	7.6	7.9	6.9
	(1.3)	(1.3)	(1.4)	(1.4)	(1.4)	(1.5)	(1.5)	(1.5)	(1.5)
0.2	7.9	7.8	7.9	8.7	9.5	9	7.4	7.3	7.3
	(1.4)	(1.5)	(1.5)	(1.5)	(1.5)	(1.5)	(1.5)	(1.5)	(1.5)
0.5	8.6	9	9.5	9.2	9.1	9	7.4	8.2	6.9
	(1.5)	(1.5)	(1.5)	(1.5)	(1.5)	(1.5)	(1.5)	(1.5)	(1.5)
1.0	8.6	9	9.5	9.2	9.1	9	7.4	8.2	6.9
	(1.5)	(1.5)	(1.5)	(1.5)	(1.5)	(1.5)	(1.5)	(1.5)	(1.5)

Figure 3 shows the ratio of GC in the surviving nodes which may be divided into isolated clusters after attacks. The number M_h of rewiring is controlled by a parameter r_h in the healing. Red, green, blue, orange, and purple lines correspond to the reusable rate of links $r_h = 0.05$, 0.1, 0.2, 0.5, and 1.0. Black line shows the result for no healing. In comparison with

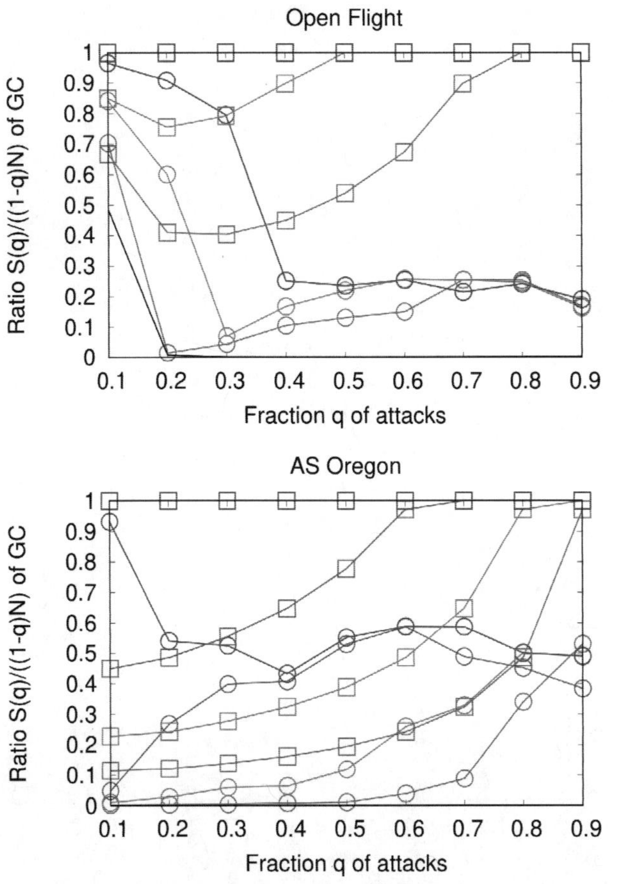

Figure 3. Communicable or transportable size with healing by our proposed combination (square) and conventional simple local repair (circle). Red, green, blue, orange, and purple lines correspond to the reusable rate $r_h = 0.05$, 0.1, 0.2, 0.5, and 1.0. Black line shows the result for no healing.

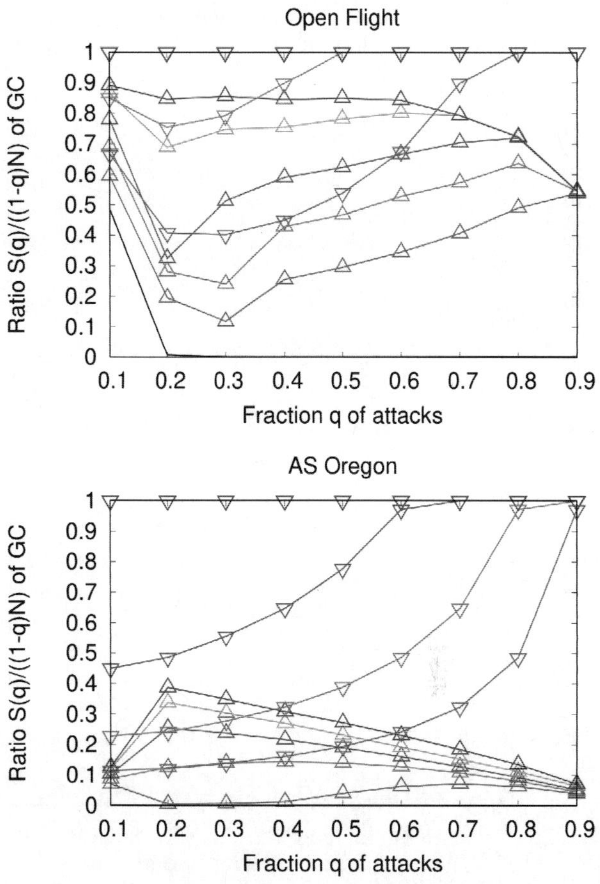

Figure 4. Communicable or transportable size with healing by only enhancing loops (up triangle) or extended ring (down triangle). Red, green, blue, orange, and purple lines correspond to the reusable rate $r_h = 0.05$, 0.1, 0.2, 0.5, and 1.0. Black line shows the result for no healing.

same color lines, our proposed combination method (marked by square) of extended ring and enhancing loops is superior with higher ratio than the conventional simple local repair [18] method (marked by circle) with a priority of rewirings to more damaged nodes, whose healing works only for weak attacks in small q. We remark that in our proposed combination method the cases of $r_h \geq 0.5$ (overlapped orange and purple lines marked by square) maintains the almost whole connectivity in the surviving $(1-q)N$ nodes. In other words, the network function can be revived completely, if more than half of links emanated from removed nodes work. In $r_h \leq 0.1$ (green and red lines marked by square), making a ring is unfinished, the ratio is dropped. Moreover, since the ratio in Figure 4 is lower than the ratio marked by square in Figure 3, only enhancing loops (marked by up-pointing triangle) or extended ring (marked by down-pointing triangle) has weaker effect than the combination. However, enhancing loops increase the ratio of GC moderately in $r_h \leq 0.1$ for $q \leq 0.5$ (green and red lines marked by up-pointing triangle) in Figure 4.

As shown in Figures 5 and 6, our proposed combination method (marked by square) has higher efficiency of paths than the conventional simple local repair method (marked by circle) in comparison with same color lines, although the effect in the method by only enhancing loops (marked by up-pointing triangle) or extended ring (marked by down-pointing triangle) becomes weaker with $E < 0.3$. Dotted line shows the efficiency in the original network before attacks.

On the other hand, we investigate the number of additional ports which should be prepared in advance besides reusable ports. It is reasonable to consider that the original ports at neighbors of a removed node remain and can be reused at undamaged locations, even if the links from the neighbors are disconnected on the way. Thus, we assume that there exist active ports of a node at least as many as its degree in the original network before attacks. Note that the minimum, average, and maximum degrees are $k_{min} = 1$, $\langle k \rangle = 10.77$, and $k_{max} = 242$ in Open Flight, $k_{min} = 1$, $\langle k \rangle = 3.88$, and $k_{max} = 1458$ in AS Oregon. Table III shows the maximum number of reserved additional ports in our proposed combination method. The number tends to be larger ranging from a few to nearly $2k_{max} \sim 3k_{max}$, as the fraction q of attacks and the reusable rate r_h increase. Shown in parentheses are averaged values over the nodes that require additional ports in each network with healing. The averaged number of

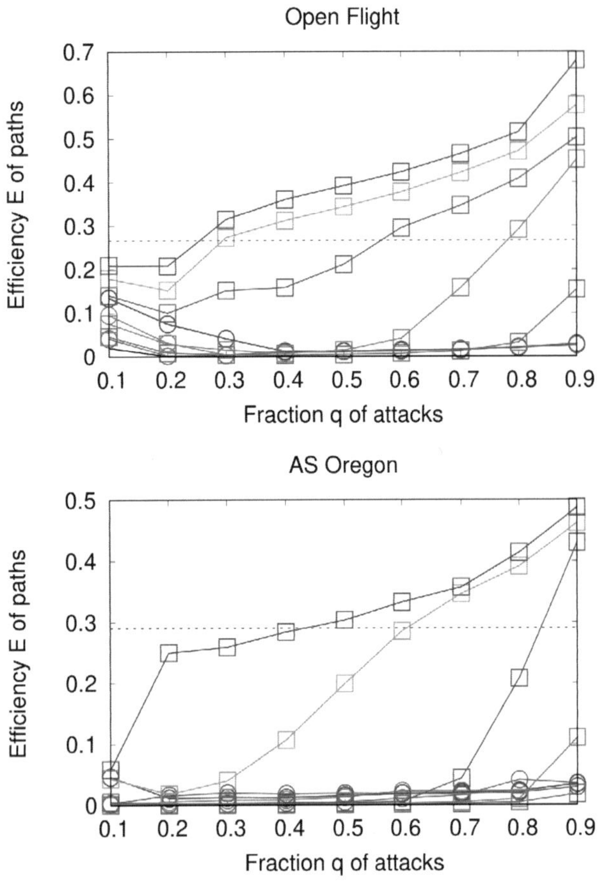

Figure 5. Efficiency of paths in the network with healing by our proposed combination (square) and conventional simple local repair (circle). Red, green, blue, orange, and purple lines correspond to the reusable rate $r_h = 0.05, 0.1, 0.2, 0.5$, and 1.0. Black line shows the result for no healing. Dotted line is the original level before attacks.

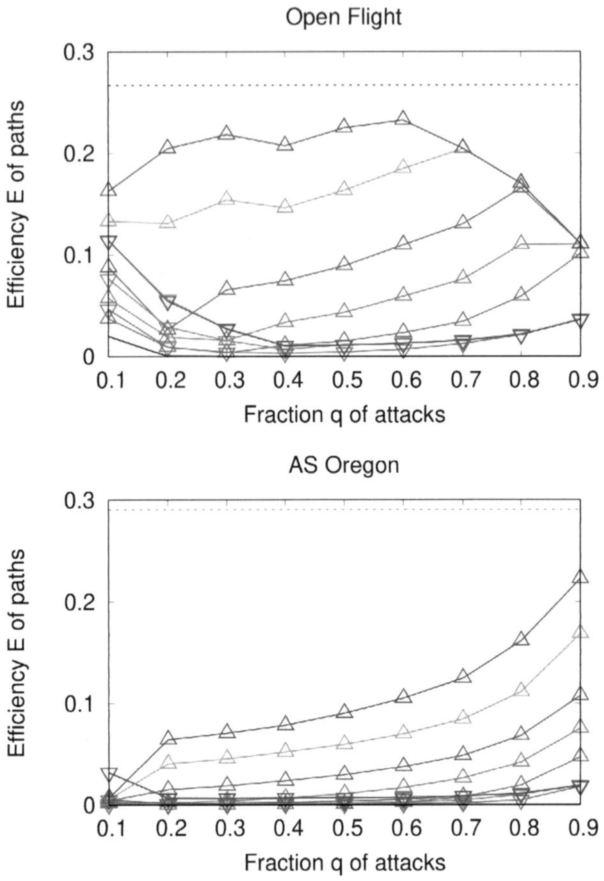

Figure 6. Efficiency of paths in the network with healing by only enhancing loops (up triangle) or extended ring (down triangle). Red, green, blue, orange, and purple lines correspond to the reusable rate $r_h = 0.05, 0.1, 0.2, 0.5$, and 1.0. Black line shows the result for no healing. Dotted line is the original level before attacks.

additional ports is small, thus the cost of resource is so much inexpensive. While the number is small even for the maximum in the conventional simple local repair method as shown in Table IV. It is almost constant for varying r_h and q.

V. Conclusion and Future Work

We have proposed self-healing methods for reconstructing a sustainable network by rewirings against attacks or disasters in the meaning of resilience with adaptive capacity. The fundamental rewiring mechanisms are based on maintaining the connectivity on a ring and enhancing loops for improving the robustness by applying BP algorithm inspired from statistical physics. As the resource allocation, the rewirings are controlled by a parameter r_h for reuse or addition of links between the extended neighbors of attacked nodes. We have shown that our proposed method is better than the conventional simple local repair method [18] with a priority of rewirings to more damaged nodes, although reserved additional ports are required much more. In particular, the whole connectivity can be revived with high efficiency of paths in our proposed method, when more than half links emanated from attacked nodes work. Thus, such amount of links are necessary for sustaining network function. If there is lack of the resource, the shortage parts should be compensated according to the damages. Under the same resource, further improvement for both connectivity and efficiency with fewer additional ports by a modification of the proposed healing method will be a future work.

Acknowledgment

This research is supported in part by JSPS KAKENHI Grant Number JP.17H01729.

References

[1] A. Zolli and A. Healy, Eds., Resilience -Why Things Bounce Back-. Free Press, Jul. 2012, ISBN: 10: 1451683804.

[2] E. Hollnagel, D. Woods, and N. Leveson, Eds., Resilience Engineering - Concepts and Precepts-. CRC Press, Jan. 2006, ISBN: 10: 0754646416.

[3] E. Hollnagel, Ed., Safety-I and Safety-II -The Past and Future of Safety Management-. CRC Press, Apr. 2014, ISBN: 10: 13: 978-1472423054.

[4] C. Folke, "Resilience: The emergence of a perspective for social-ecological systems analyses," Global Environmental Change, vol. 16, 2006, pp. 253–267, DOI: 10.1016/j.gloenvcha.2006.04.002.

[5] L. Amaral, A. Scala, M. Barthelemy, and H. E. Stanley, "Classes of small-world networks," Proc. Natl. Acad. Sci. USA, vol. 97, no. 21, 2000, pp. 11 149–11 152, DOI: 10.1073/pnas.200327197.

[6] A.-L. Barabási, "Scale-Free Networks," Scientific American, vol. 288, no. 5, 2003, pp. 60–69, DOI: 10.1038/scientificamerican0503-60.

[7] R. Albert, H. Jeong, and A.-L. Barabási, "Error and attack tolerance of complex networks," Nature, vol. 406, 2000, pp. 378–382, DOI: 10.1038/35019019.

[8] C. M. Schneider, A. A. Moreira, J. Andrade, Jr., and H. J. Herrmann, "Mitigation of malicious attacks on networks," Proc. Natl. Acad. Sci. USA, vol. 108, no. 10, 2011, pp. 3838–3841, DOI: 10.1073/pnas.1009440108.

[9] T. Tanizawa, S. Havlin, and H. E. Stanley, "Robustness of onion-like correlated networks against targeted attacks," Physical Review E, vol. 85, no. 046109, 2012, pp. 1–9, DOI: 10.1103/PhysRevE.85.046109.

[10] Z.-X. Wu and P. Holme, "Onion structure and network robustness," Physical Review E, vol. 84, no. 026106, 2011, pp. 1–5, DOI: 10.1103/PhysRevE.84.026106.

[11] A. Braunstein, L. Dall'Asta, G. Semerjiand, and L. Zdeborová, "Network dismantling," Proc. Natl. Acad. Sci. USA, vol. 113, no. 44, 2016, pp. 12 368–12 373, DOI: 10.1073/pnas.1605083113.

[12] R. M. Karp, Reducibility among combinatorial problems. Springer, Boston, MA, 1972, pp. 85–103, the IBM Research Symposia Series, ISBN: 978-1-4684-2003-6.

[13] Y. Hayashi, "Growing Self-organized Design of Efficient and Robust Complex Networks," IEEE Xplore Digital Library SASO (Self-Adaptive and Self-Organizing systems) 2014, 2014, pp. 50–59, DOI: 10.1109/SASO.2014.17.

[14] Y. Hayashi, "A new design principle of robust onion-like networks self-organized in growth," Network Science, vol. 6, no. 1, 2018, pp. 54–70, DOI: 10.1017/nws.2017.25.

[15] F. Hu, C. H. Yeung, S. Yang, W. Wang, and A. Zeng, "Recovery of infrastructure networks after localized attacks," Scientific Reports, vol. 6, no. 2452, 2016, pp. 1–10, DOI: 10.1038/srep24522.

[16] W. Quattrociocchi, G. Caldarelli, and A. Scala, "Self-Healing Networks: Redundancy and Structure," PLOS ONE, vol. 9, no. 2, 2016, pp. 1–7, DOI: 10.1371/journal.pone.0087986.

[17] M. Stippinger and J. Kertész, "Enhancing resilience of interdependent networks by healing," Physica A, vol. 416, 2014, pp. 481–487, DOI: 10.1016/j.physa.2014.08.069.

[18] L. K. Gallos and N. H. Fefferman, "Simple and efficient self-healing strategy for damaged complex networks," Physical Review E, vol. 92, no. 052805, 2015, pp. 1–9, DOI: 10.1103/PhysRevE.92.0528058.

[19] J. Park and S. G. Hahn, "Bypass rewiring and robustness of complex networks," Physical Review E, vol. 94, no. 022309, 2016, pp. 1–4, DOI: 10.1103/PhysRevE.94.022310.

[20] T. Hayes, N. Rustagi, J. Saia, and A. Trehan, "The Forgiving Tree: A Self-Healing Distributed Data Structure," in Proceedings of the 27th ACM Symposium on Principles of Distributed Computing. ACM NY, USA, Aug. 2008, pp. 203–212, ISBN: 978-1-59593-989-0, DOI: 10.1145/1400751.1400779, URL: https://dl.acm.org/citation.cfm?doid=1400751.1400779 [accessed:2020-03-02].

[21] A. Castañeda, D. Dolev, and A. Trehan, "Compact routing messages in self-healing tree," Theoretical Computer Science, vol. 709, 2018, pp. 2–19, DOI: 10.1016/j.tcs.2016.11.022.

[22] S. S. Savas, M. F. Habib, M. Tornatore, F. Dikbiyik, and B. Mukherjee, "Network Adaptability to Disaster Disruptions by Exploiting Degraded-Service Tolerance," IEEE Communications Magazine, vol. 52, 2014, pp. 58–65, DOI: 10.1109/MCOM.2014.6979953, https://ieeexplore.ieee.org/abstract/document/6979953 [accessed:2020-03-02].

[23] Y. Hayashi and N. Uchiyama, "Onion-like networks are both robust and resilient," Scientific Reports, vol. 8, no. 11241, 2018, pp. 1–13, DOI: 10.1038/s41598-018-29626-w, Author Correction: https://www.nature.com/articles/s41598-018-32563-3 [accessed:2020-03-02].

[24] H.-J. Zhou, "Spin glass approach to the feedback vertex set problem," Eur. Phys. J. B, vol. 86, no. 445, 2013, pp. 1–9, DOI: 10.1140/epjb/e2013-40690-1.

[25] S. Mugisha and H.-J. Zhou, "Identifying optimal targets of network attack by belief propagation," Physical Review E, vol. 94, no. 012305, 2016, pp. 1–8, DOI: 10.1103/PhysRevE.94.012305.

[26] Open Flight: http://konect.uni-koblenz.de/networks/opsahl-openflights AS Oregon: http://snap.stanford.edu/data/as.html [accessed:2020-03-02].

SensAI+Expanse
Adaptation on Human Behaviour Towards Emotional Valence Prediction

Nuno A. C. Henriques
BioISI
Faculdade de Ciências
Universidade de Lisboa
Portugal
nach@edu.ulisboa.pt

Helder Coelho
BioISI
Faculdade de Ciências
Universidade de Lisboa
Portugal
hcoelho@di.fc.ul.pt

Leonel Garcia-Marques
CICPSI
Faculdade de Psicologia
Universidade de Lisboa
Portugal
garcia_marques@sapo.pt

***Abstract*—An agent, artificial or human, must be continuously adjusting its behaviour in order to thrive in a more or less demanding environment. An artificial agent with the ability to predict human emotional valence in a geospatial and temporal context requires proper adaptation to its mobile device environment with resource consumption strict restrictions (e.g., power from battery). The developed distributed system includes a mobile device embodied agent (SensAI) plus Cloud-expanded (Expanse) cognition and memory resources. The system is designed with several adaptive mechanisms in the best effort for the agent to cope with its interacting humans and to be resilient on collecting data for machine learning towards prediction. These mechanisms encompass homeostatic-like adjustments, such as auto recovering from an unexpected failure in the mobile device, forgetting repeated data to save local memory, adjusting actions to a proper moment (e.g., notify only when human is interacting), and the Expanse complementary learning algorithms' parameters with auto adjustments. Regarding emotional valence prediction performance, results from a comparison study between state-of-the-art algorithms revealed Extreme Gradient Boosting on average the best model for prediction with efficient energy use, and explainable using feature importance inspection. Therefore, this work contributes with a smartphone sensing-based system, distributed in the Cloud, robust to unexpected behaviours from humans and the environment, able to predict emotional valence states with very good performance.**

Keywords*—*emotional valence prediction; context adaptation; memory; human-agent interaction.

I. INTRODUCTION

The scientific evidence of epigenetics reveal on/off mechanisms inside chromosomes of human agents and reinforces the importance of any entity continuous adaptation to its environment. Additionally, some natural entities such as human individuals with self-consciousness and emotion-driven cognition developed a bond between the evolutionary way of emotions and their supporting physical structure as proposed by Damásio [1]. In a sense, it is clear that an agent's behaviour will not develop independently of the environment and that its affective states are paramount in the adjustment. Further, a developed behaviour may be the result of an ongoing, bidirectional interchange between inherited traits (e.g., parameter initial value) and the environment (e.g., data collected from an interacting human). Therefore, it may be envisioned an artificial agent adjusting empathetically towards the interacting human current behaviour and affective state [2][3]. The concept of empathy [4] may be used as a starting point for social glue bringing better interaction, communication and mutual helping. Human-Agent Interaction (HAI) should be based on the way each entity perceives contact, together with the perception of human's affective states in a multimodal approach [5][6]. Hence, the affect sensing using wearable or mobile devices, such as a smartphone seems appropriate. The American College of Medical Informatics (ACMI) has already envisaged this path. In the 1998 Scientific Symposium, one of the informatics challenges for the next 10 years was "Monitor the developments in emerging wearable computers and sensors — possibly even implantable ones — for their potential contribution to a personal health record and status monitoring" [7]. Twenty years have passed since this awakening for the mobile device as a sensing tool. Smartphone sensing for behavioural research is thriving with active discussions [8][9] including exploration on correlates between sensors' data and depressive symptom severity [10].

This paper describes the SensAI+Expanse system and its adaptive mechanisms towards emotional valence prediction ability on humans. The individuals may be diverse in behaviour, age, gender and place of origin. Accordingly, the developed system encompass a mobile device embodied agent SensAI and its Cloud-expanded (Expanse) cognition and memory resources. SensAI collects data from several sources including (a) device sensors, such as Global Positioning System (GPS) and accelerometer; (b) current timestamp in user calendar; and (c) available text writings from in-application diary and social network posts (Twitter status). These written texts in (c) will be subjected to sentiment analysis [11] in order to collect emotional valence from this modality source. The ground truth is obtained from the user when reporting about current sentiment (positive, neutral, negative). On the other hand, the artificial agent will be subjected to a simple adaptive process by means of interaction with humans. An empathy score value is presented during this interaction. The score decays over time, it also changes with some factors, such as the frequency of human reporting. This visual adaptive metric should be perceived by the human as current human-agent empathetic score. The Expanse complementary resources comprise several heuristics and algorithms, such as unsupervised location clustering parameters auto discovery and supervised learning hyperparameters auto tuning. These are continuously adapting to the data set of each human entity. Further, preliminary results from a running study with the agent in the wild, publicly available for installation, are presented. This methodology contributes to avoid a well-known Western, Educated, Industrialized, Rich, and Democratic (WEIRD) society bias in research studies involving human subjects exclusively from academia. Moreover, performance results of a comparison study between state-of-the-art machine learning algorithms are presented and a model is elected as the best for future studies.

The first section introduced the purpose of this investigation and the work done so far. Next, Section II will describe the mechanisms in place for the developed mobile agent system adaptive capabilities. Section III describes the research study including the followed method and the achieved results. Finally, Section IV summarises the outcomes and presents a future perspective.

II. SensAI+Expanse Adaptive Mechanisms

This section describes the adaptive mechanisms in place for the developed SensAI+Expanse as a distributed, fault-tolerant, mobile, and Cloud-based system from scratch. The platform is used as a research tool for continuously, online, gather and process sensory data. Figure 1 depicts the general data flow between the SensAI agent and its expanded resources. The collected data from mobile sensors and HAI is processed and stored locally. Additionally, data is periodically synced in order to feed the learning process and prediction service.

The general HAI is initially restricted by its parameter values which drives SensAI. This behaviour may be influenced by the agent's context along the interaction timeline and changes may emerge as adjustment details. Complementary, SensAI Expanse contains a myriad of adaptive mechanisms regarding collected data from human behaviour. These actions work towards Automated Machine Learning (AutoML) and efficient prediction. The emotional valence ground truth values used for prediction performance measurement are reported by humans. The main interface includes three emoticons as depicted in Figure 2. Moreover, this mechanism is robust to interaction bias, such as high-frequency repeated button (emoticon) clicks. Also, on cases of mistaken valence promptly corrected by an additional hit on a different emoticon. It includes a simple yet effective heuristic of accounting only for the last hit during a defined time interval. All these actions are contextualised, i.e., the location and timestamp of the event are collected.

SensAI has two ways of collecting data by doing it (a) passively using several sensors, such as accelerometer and GPS; and (b) actively by interacting with the human using

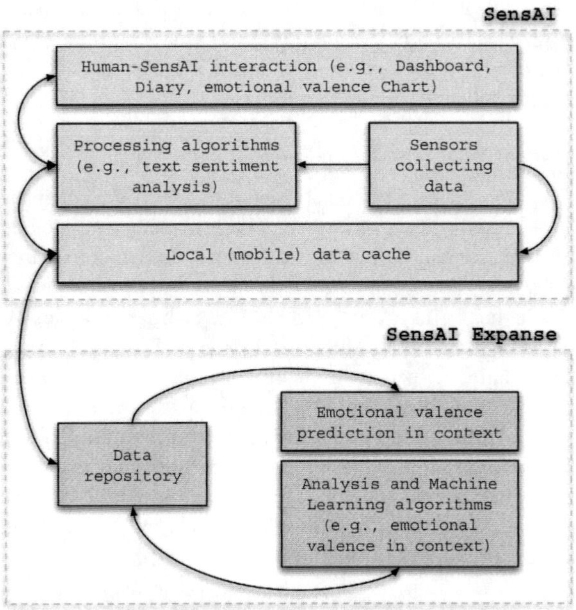

Figure 1. SensAI+Expanse general data flow.

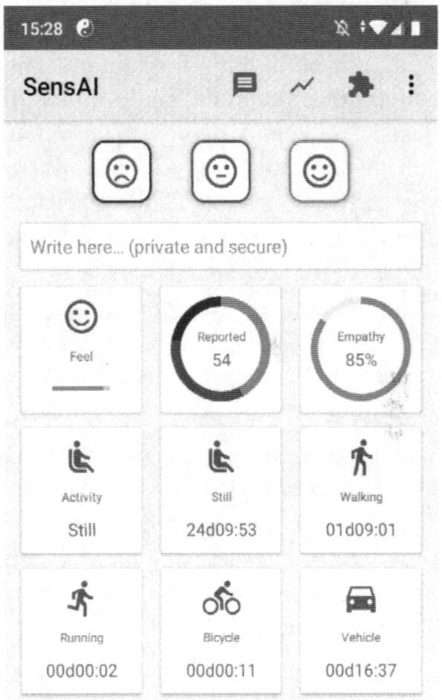

Figure 2. SensAI main user interface and system notification bar.

display notifications and buttons for emotional valence reporting. Moreover, SensAI displays information about the human physical activity aggregated time by each recognisable type (e.g., running), current emotional valence status, self-report statistics, and agent empathy score as depicted in Figure 2. Additional displays are available with (a) sentiment chart with the chronology of reporting and messaging emotional valence values; (b) private diary for writing messages to self where text is subjected to sentiment analysis [11], including a SensAI report of current averaged emotional valence status and physical activity every three or so hours; and (c) several statistics about sensors event count, last Expanse data sync, and data collecting uptime.

A. *SensAI*

The mobile device embodied agent has several mechanisms in place for specific adjustments. These workings are included in different modules. Each one of those is autonomously managed although orchestrated by `Homeostasis` module with periodic health checks. `SenseiStartStop` is a fail-safe last resort to deal with device start/stop and also unexpected SensAI failures such as asynchronous illegal states causing the application to crash, i.e., be removed from running state. Activity, service and special modules are instantiated objects from code developed classes. Some run on demand, others periodically, as services and activities on dedicated threads or the main user interface thread. The relevant activities and services for SensAI embodiment are described below.

`Homeostasis` is paramount to guarantee some tolerance to failures and keep the agent in a good health, it is a scheduled, service designed to regulate the embodiment. Every run checks for critical aspects, such as database health and data feed. It takes proper actions to solve some common failures, such as sensor data `Feed` not running. Moreover, adapt itself to the interaction state, i.e., if at rest then database optimisations and fix actions may run, conversely, updating notifications, such as empathy level only happen when the human user is paying attention. This mechanism prevents potentially disturbing events, such as too frequent device's screen awaking just for an empathy value adjustment. The homeostasis-like solution for the SensAI application is complemented with `SenseiStartStop` required to protect and guarantee `Homeostasis` service to run as expected.

`SenseiStartStop` is a system event receiver to assure persistence and robustness against the device failures and reboots. It does a system registration at SensAI first start to be called on device boot and on application upgrade dealing with those special states. This registration also signals Android operating system to revive SensAI in case of unexpected crash and removal from running state.

`Feed` is a started service running autonomously in the background. Several other services run on demand in an adaptation to save mobile device resources consumption, such as battery. This module encompasses and manages all data collecting from sensors, such as Android-device hardware types (e.g., accelerometer). Moreover, a balanced data acquisition rhythm, such as $active = 2s$, $inactive = 8s$, $f = 1/5Hz$, and $D = 20\%$ is devised and in place for relevant data to be acquired without draining too much power. This rhythm as well as other thresholds may be subjected to automatic adaptation in the future. Furthermore, Figure 3 depicts a persistent notification message which includes empathy level adjustment in a progress bar triggered by emotional valence reports (using emoticon buttons). Also, a dashboard is available with relevant information including empathy level. An active SensAI main user interface dashboard was already depicted in Figure 2.

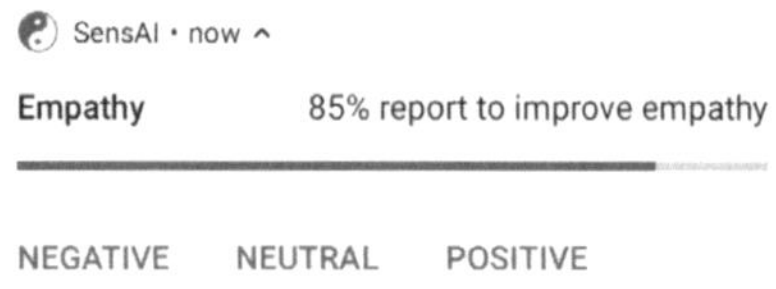

Figure 3. Empathy notification including valence report buttons.

`Sentiment` analysis utility including integration with language detection, translation and more is provided by specific libraries and services included in SensAI. All contributing for the best effort to get the sentiment value along with the language. A heuristic is in place to adapt the analysis to human idiosyncratic aspects, such as mixed languages (English and Portuguese supported) and emoticons amongst other abbreviations when writing short messages. To deal with this rich and sometimes creative written content the best effort approach is depicted in Figure 4.

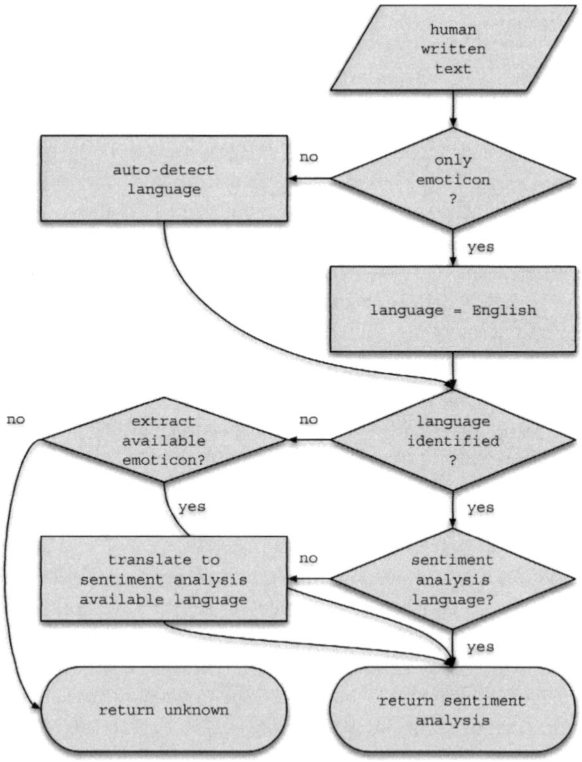

Figure 4. Sentiment analysis heuristic.

`Expanse` is a periodic and scheduled service for data syncing with a memory aggregator in the Cloud — SensAI Expanse. It is robust to failures using a mechanism similar to a transaction, i.e., only successfully transferred data is marked as such (able to be deleted after cache persistence time limit). Moreover, on lack of a suitable data connection available it will adapt by increasing verification frequency for later try to sync. This mechanism of local cache and Cloud sync is paramount to restrict memory resources consumption and guarantee proper data collection.

B. *SensAI Expanse*

The agent Cloud-expanded resources — Expanse — are the augmentation spread of the SensAI limited smartphone resources (e.g., data persistence, processing and power). Expanse stores data from all SensAI agents anonymously to guarantee that the human's privacy is kept when the data flows to analysis. It includes a repository with historical data, processing algorithms, services of machine learning towards prediction of emotional valence in context, i.e., SensAI augmented memory and cognition. Moreover, processing all eligible data through available algorithms towards AutoML requires (a) adaptation to the diverse human behaviours reflected in the data set; and (b) Bayesian efficient auto discovery on parameters. Software architecture modules and services are depicted in Figure 5.

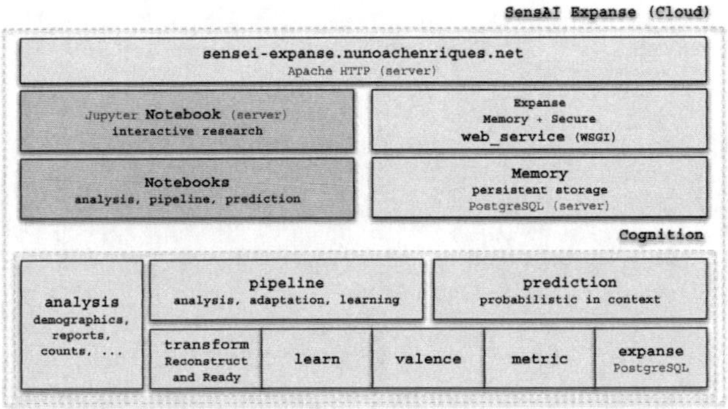

Figure 5. Expanse software architecture modules and services.

Adaptive actions start, amongst other things, with `analysis` on gathering data aggregations and filtering eligible human entities. This eligibility selection has more steps through the `pipeline` process until reaching the final data samples for machine learning. Before the final step, `transform` acts on cleaning, reconstructing and fixing collected data such as upsampling data within proper boundaries related to collecting parameters previously used to save resources in SensAI. The Expanse developed custom `pipeline` for SensAI learning uses a myriad of heuristics and other algorithms. These include a data class (negative, neutral, positive) imbalance (reports count) degree from [12]. Also, a custom valence class count check and restrict in order to adapt the learning process in cases such as emotional valence reported for only two (or even one) classes. The final eligible entities are achieved after these valence class count and imbalance degree processing.

The `learn` module integrates several state-of-the-art algorithms from two main categories of (a) unsupervised ones, such as HDBSCAN for clustering location coordinates and accurately drop outliers; and (b) supervised for multi-class classification, such as Extreme Gradient Boosting by XGBoost and a custom multilayer Perceptron using Keras in TensorFlow.

Additional steps are in place towards AutoML by making use of (a) the learn process calling a function for running HDBSCAN clustering algorithm on the different `min_samples` provided in order to find the best `min_cluster_size` parameter; and before each call to one of the classification algorithms learning process (b) an auto search is in place for the best cross validation N splits regarding the algorithm minimum number of accepted classes. Next, a hyperparameter auto tuning with cross validation for each specific model uses Bayesian optimisation. Finally, the model with parameters fit for each human current data is achieved and performance metrics such as F1 score are computed. The current knowledge from the learning process is stored using the `expanse` module and the `Memory` component. The `prediction` module is serving answers from Web service requests in the Cloud. These responses are for contextualised (location and moment) emotional valence prediction requests for the requiring human, as depicted in Figure 6.

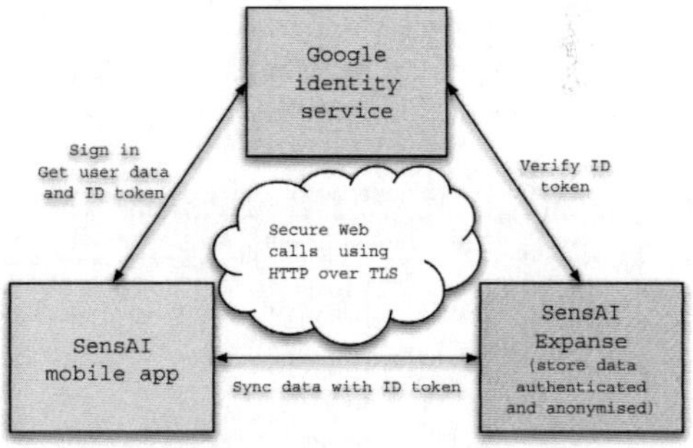

Figure 6. End-to-end secure communication.

All communications are end-to-end secured and digitally signed, restricted to the owner available data, i.e., a human A cannot obtain the prediction for a human B.

III. Study

In this section, it will be described the applied method and the outcomes of a research study comprising a population of human individuals interacting with SensAI in the wild.

A. *Method*

The participants are gathered from all kinds and creeds, i.e., avoiding the laboratory usual limitations, such as sampling only from WEIRD societies known as a frequent bias [13]. This goal is accomplished by choosing to collect data using smartphone sensing [14] by means of an Android application. SensAI has already been installed by users from ten different countries and four continents (Africa, America, Asia, Europe). A total of 57 participants installed SensAI, eight were discarded for not sharing demographic data thus 49 (18 female, 31 male) remained eligible. The pipeline process further reduces the population to 31 eligible individuals after valence class imbalance restrictions are applied. Moreover, demographic data comprises birthdate and gender at this stage, extending the collection to other aspects such as income and education level is foreseen as of interest for future studies.

Regarding the system prediction performance, a comparison study assessing a few state-of-the-art algorithms and two metrics was in place. The set of estimators comprises linear (Logistic Regression), non-linear (Extreme Gradient Boosting), and connectionist (TensorFlow Keras MLP) distinct approaches. Also, one more estimator is used as baseline (Dummy) generating predictions by respecting the training set's class distribution (option `strategy=stratified`). The two metrics studied were F1 score (option `average=weighted`) and Matthews Correlation Coefficient (MCC) prepared for multi-class ($n = 3$) case from `scikit-learn` package. Both metrics are very popular and with good software support for machine learning.

B. Results

The preliminary results were achieved by first using the MCC metric on four estimators. The performance statistics depicted in Figure 7 revealed unexpected overly high values (e.g., baseline median near 0.8) raising red flags about possible issues, such as estimators overfitting.

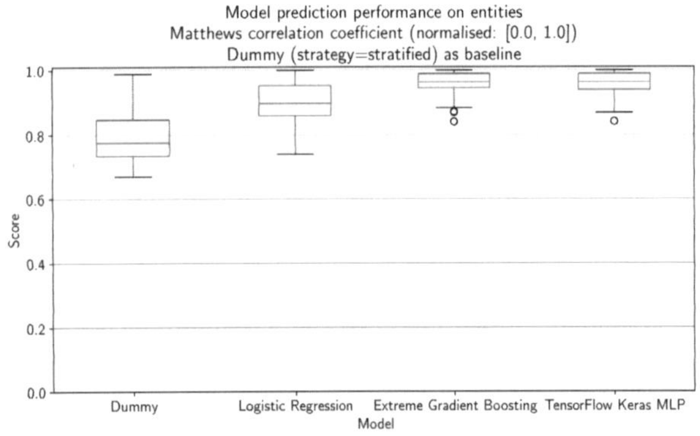

Figure 7. Model prediction performance statistics using MCC.

In order to verify the overfitting issue possibility on the first results (after several runs to sustain the achieved values) a different score metric is used. F1 score is selected for performance evaluation within the same experimental conditions. The results are depicted in Figure 8.

There is evidence of measurement discrepancies between F1 versus MCC over the population datasets, as depicted in Figure 9. In order to assess the significance of these differences, a Mann-Whitney U test is applied on F1 versus MCC and the results presented in Table I show that the null hypothesis (H_0: two sets of measurements are drawn from the same distribution) can be rejected, i.e., evidence of significant differences on F1 versus MCC results.

As a result, F1 measurements seem reasonably nearer to the expected baseline statistics than MCC. Further inspection

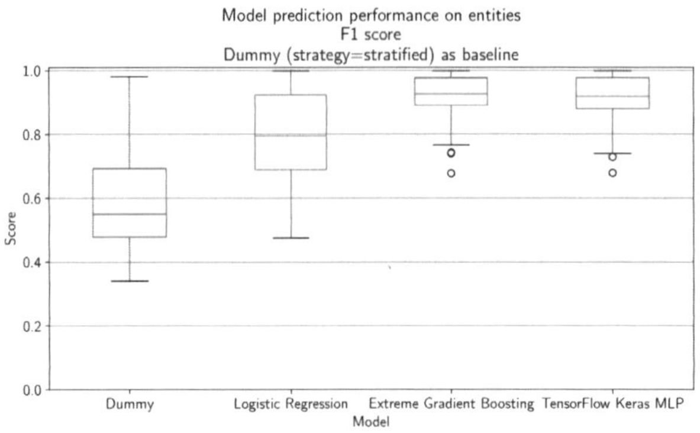

Figure 8. Model prediction performance statistics using F1 score.

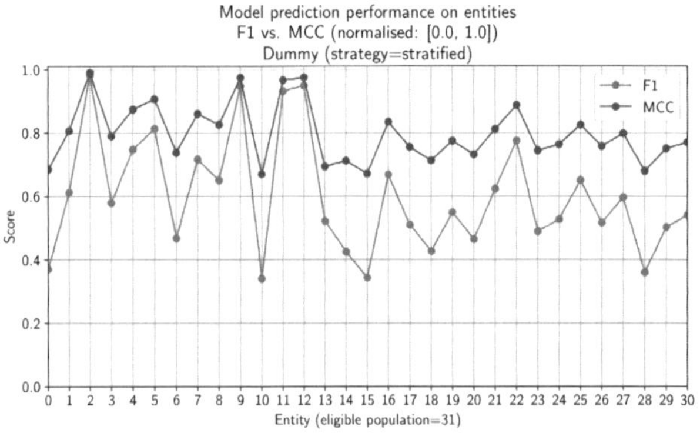

Figure 9. Model prediction performance on entities: F1 vs. MCC.

using the confusion matrix for some cases from the $26/31$ (83%) with more than 10 percentage points difference uphold F1 score as more accurate than MCC. Moreover, making use of the classification report no pattern was identified correlating the inspected cases, i.e., all distributions have distinct data shapes. Although the MCC is considered to have advantages over the F1 score, specifically in the binary classification case, such claim [15] was not evidenced in this research with the current eligible population and datasets. The results of this study using F1 score for each model are summarised in Table II and depicted in Figure 8.

The Extreme Gradient Boosting model is elected as best

TABLE I. F1 VS. MCC (FIGURE 9): MANN-WHITNEY U TEST RESULTS

Metrics	p value	Meaning ($\alpha = 0.05$)
F1 vs. MCC	2.237×10^{-2}	H_0 can be rejected ($p < \alpha$)

TABLE II. ALL FOUR ESTIMATORS AVERAGE F1 SCORE AND TOTAL DURATION

Model	F1 average	Duration
Dummy	0.600	00:00:46
Logistic Regression	0.795	01:46:22
Extreme Gradient Boosting	**0.910**	**01:54:34**
TensorFlow Keras MLP	0.907	24:35:11

option amongst the other two additional models plus baseline also available. The choice for this model is further supported by an interest towards (a) Explainable Artificial Intelligence (XAI) predictions; and (b) efficient energy use besides overall score achievement. Regarding (a) the Extreme Gradient Boosting includes feature importance scores for each entity model thus proper explainable context (e.g., the specific location feature with the highest score). As for (b) evidence already presented in Table II show Extreme Gradient Boosting as the best performer although marginally to the second yet for less than a tenth of the processing duration. Therefore, Extreme Gradient Boosting is simultaneously on average the best model for prediction with efficient energy use and also easy explainable by feature importance inspection.

IV. Conclusion and Future Work

This paper has described the SensAI+Expanse smartphone sensing-based system, distributed in the Cloud, robust to unexpected behaviours from humans and the mobile demanding environment, able to predict emotional valence states with very good performance. The SensAI agent adapts to the restricted resources and volatile environment of a mobile device where an operating system dictates behaviour rules. Any ill-behaved application is automatically stopped by the system and may even be excluded from restarting. These cases where processing takes too long usually result in the application being stopped and declared Application Not Responding (ANR). There is no evidence of any ANR in the Google Play Console used to monitor all events from SensAI. Conversely, there is evidence of a few "Illegal State" crashes from which the agent recovered and continued to interact after a maximum of fifteen-minute delay (interval for periodic scheduled checks). Furthermore, battery consumption is kept at one digit percentage (e.g., 1%) for a day-long use in several devices laboratory and regular testing. The outcomes presented show evidence, restricted to population and data samples in this research, of SensAI+Expanse ability to adapt and learn to predict emotional valence states with a high score of $F1 = 0.910$ on average (Table II and Figure 8). Therefore, SensAI+Expanse contributes as a novel platform for studies about human emotional valence changes in context of location and moment. Moreover, it reinforces smartphone sensing contribution as a tool for continuous, passive, and personalised health check, such as emotional disturbances, in spatial and temporal context. Furthermore, all the source code is published as free software under the Apache License 2.0. Future work should investigate emotional valence report discrepancies amongst population demographics, such as age and gender. Furthermore, an assessment over the agent robustness to those differences would be of interest. Thus, studies about the agent's neutrality to distinct age ranges and gender combinations should be in place by means of the elected Extreme Gradient Boosting model with F1 score.

Acknowledgement

N.A.C.H. thanks Jorge M. C. Gomes for the precious contributions. This work is partially supported by *Universidade de Lisboa* [PhD support grant May 2016–April 2019]. Partially supported by *Fundação para a Ciência e Tecnologia* [UID/MULTI/04046/2019 Research Unit grant from FCT, Portugal (to BioISI)]. This work used the European Grid Infrastructure (EGI) with the support of NCG-INGRID-PT.

References

[1] A. Damásio, *Self Comes to Mind: Constructing the Conscious Brain*, 1st ed. ["O Livro da Consciência: A Construção do Cérebro Consciente", Círculo de Leitores, ISBN:9789896441203], 2010.

[2] R. W. Picard, *Affective Computing*. Cambridge, MA, USA: MIT Press, 1997. ISBN:0-262-16170-2

[3] G. Castellano, I. Leite, A. Pereira, C. Martinho, A. Paiva, and P. W. McOwan, "Affect recognition for interactive companions: Challenges and design in real world scenarios," *Journal on Multimodal User Interfaces*, vol. 3, no. 1, pp. 89–98, 2010. DOI:https://doi.org/10.1007/s12193-009-0033-5

[4] K. Stueber, *Empathy*, winter2014 ed., E. N. Zalta, Ed. Metaphysics Research Lab, Stanford University, 2014. URL:http://plato.stanford.edu/archives/win2014/entries/empathy

[5] L. Tavabi, "Multimodal Machine Learning for Interactive Mental Health Therapy," in *2019 International Conference on Multimodal Interaction on - ICMI '19*. New York, New York, USA: ACM Press, 2019. DOI:https://doi.org/10.1145/3340555.3356095 pp. 453–456.

[6] C. Tsiourti, "Artificial agents as social companions: design guidelines for emotional interactions," phdthesis, Université de Genève, 2018.

[7] R. A. Greenes and N. M. Lorenzi, "Audacious Goals for Health and Biomedical Informatics in the New Millennium," *Journal of the American Medical Informatics Association*, vol. 5, no. 5, pp. 395–400, 1998. DOI:https://doi.org/10.1136/jamia.1998.0050395

[8] K. Denecke, E. Gabarron, R. Grainger, S. T. Konstantinidis, A. Lau, O. Rivera-Romero, T. Miron-Shatz, and M. Merolli, "Artificial Intelligence for Participatory Health: Applications, Impact, and Future Implications," *Yearbook of Medical Informatics*, 2019. DOI:https://doi.org/10.1055/s-0039-1677902

[9] I. R. Felix, L. A. Castro, L.-f. Rodriguez, and O. Banos, "Mobile sensing for behavioral research: A component-based approach for rapid deployment of sensing campaigns," *International Journal of Distributed Sensor Networks*, vol. 15, no. 9, pp. 1–17, 2019. DOI:https://doi.org/10.1177/1550147719874186

[10] S. Saeb, M. Zhang, C. J. Karr, S. M. Schueller, M. E. Corden, K. P. Kording, and D. C. Mohr, "Mobile Phone Sensor Correlates of Depressive Symptom Severity in Daily-Life Behavior: An Exploratory Study." *Journal of medical Internet research*, vol. 17, no. 7, p. e175, 2015. DOI:https://doi.org/10.2196/jmir.4273

[11] C. J. Hutto and E. Gilbert, "VADER: A Parsimonious Rule-based Model for Sentiment Analysis of Social Media Text," in *Proceedings of the Eighth International AAAI Conference on Weblogs and Social Media*, Ann Arbor, Michigan, USA, 2014, pp. 216–225.

[12] R. Zhu, Z. Wang, Z. Ma, G. Wang, and J. H. Xue, "LRID: A new metric of multi-class imbalance degree based on likelihood-ratio test," *Pattern Recognition Letters*, vol. 116, pp. 36–42, 2018. DOI:https://doi.org/10.1016/j.patrec.2018.09.012

[13] J. Henrich, S. J. Heine, and A. Norenzayan, "The weirdest people in the world?" *Behavioral and Brain Sciences*, vol. 33, no. 2-3, pp. 61–83, 2010. DOI:https://doi.org/10.1017/S0140525X0999152X

[14] V. P. Cornet and R. J. Holden, "Systematic review of smartphone-based passive sensing for health and wellbeing," *Journal of Biomedical Informatics*, vol. 77, pp. 120–132, 2018. DOI:https://doi.org/10.1016/j.jbi.2017.12.008

[15] D. Chicco, "Ten quick tips for machine learning in computational biology," *BioData Mining*, vol. 10, no. 1, pp. 1–17, 2017. DOI:https://doi.org/10.1186/s13040-017-0155-3

SOBA: A Self-Organizing Bucket Architecture to Reduce Setup Times in an Event-Driven Production

Martin Krockert, Marvin Matthes, Torsten Munkelt
Faculty of Computer Science
Dresden University of Applied Sciences
Dresden, Germany
Email: *firstname.lastname*@htw-dresden.de

***Abstract*—Modern industry prefers self-organization in production over central production planning for the sake of greater flexibility, faster response to disruptions and to deviations, and less effort. The strategy also propagates highly customizable products. These products mostly require different group technologies and therefore cannot be grouped into lots. This leads to a huge number of operations that have to be scheduled and processed, which in turn leads to high computation times for scheduling algorithms and high setup costs for production due to frequent setup changes. To ensure high flexibility and robust planing, we present a self-organizing bucket architecture (SOBA) to group equal operations which require the same group technology to reduce setup times and even maintain high flexibility and robust planning for any scheduling algorithm. In this paper, we explain our approach and show an implementation of the approach in our self-organizing production. Furthermore, we show a set of empirical studies that compares our approach to simple and exhaustive queuing rules. The tests show the superiority of our approach and indicate further development opportunities.**

***Keywords*—Self-Organization; Self-Adaptation; Production; Group Technology; Job Shop; Setup Time Reduction**

I. INTRODUCTION

Industry 4.0 propagates a lot size of one for modern production of piece goods, because customers more often expect individual products and there is no reason to combine individual products into conventional lots, because machines process individual products differently and have to be setup for every individual product [1]. If a machine only processes lots the size of one in no specific sequence and the products differ from each other, more frequent setups are necessary which lead to longer overall setup times. Irrespective of all measures to shorten setup times technologically, setup times of considerable length still occur [2]. It is well known that long setup times extend throughput times and reduce effective capacity utilization [3]. In order to reduce the number of setups, thereby shortening the overall setup time and ultimately reducing their negative effects, we propose our Self-Organizing Bucket Architecture (SOBA) that combines separate operations into so-called buckets. All operations in a bucket require the same setup, but can belong to different products. SOBA only combines operations to be processed on the same machine successively in a certain period of time. The machine processes the operations from the bucket successively according to urgency. Buckets exist only temporarily: Before SOBA creates a bucket and fills it with operations, the operations are independent of each other; and after the machine processed all operations from the bucket, the bucket dissolves and its operations are then independent of each other again. In this way, SOBA differs from conventional lot sizing, which usually keeps lots together during the processing of their production orders (although it sometimes splits and overlaps lots). In this paper, we present the implementation of SOBA and some results of an empirical study. SOBA is part of our event-driven, self-organizing production, and SOBA itself is driven by events and organizes itself.

The paper is organized as follows: The next section classifies the problem and provides a review of related work. Section III declares the concept including architecture and algorithms of SOBA. Subsequently, Sections IV and V describe the implementation of SOBA into our self-organizing production system and our empirical study. Finally, Section VI concludes and gives an outlook on further work.

II. PROBLEM CLASSIFICATION

In job shop production, an efficient and reactive scheduling for a given set of machines and jobs is essential to meet the economical objectives. In the context of manufacturing each product is represented by a job, which contains a sequence of operations. In job shop scheduling every operation has to be processed without interruption on any capable machine, while a machine can only process operations one by one. The job shop problem considering more than two machines is known to be NP-complete [4]–[6].

Operations with similar characteristics, which require the same machine setups are called group technology (GT), as they share the same technology requirements but are assigned to different products [7], [8].

Consequently, the operations combined to one group can be seen as a horizontal cross-linked aggregation of different products over the same GT. The optimization problem for scheduling job shop systems reaches another dimension of complexity by integrating setup times [9]. By grouping operations requiring the same technology, the schedule becomes more efficient, because operations of the same group can be processed without intermediate machine setups, which eliminates additional setup times compared to pure priority heuristics. In real-world manufacturing, especially simple dispatching rules become the most applied solution to solve the scheduling problem in a highly unpredictable and dynamical environment [10]. Dispatching rules are applied to queues to prioritize the operation to be processed next.

Moreover, *Dispatching rules* can be divided into two groups, exhaustive and non-exhaustive rules. While exhaustive rules perform all operations of a GT existing in one queue, non-exhaustive rules allow splitting of grouped operations and therefore switching of setups even though there are still operations remaining requiring the same setup. In previous research from Frazier, exhaustive rules prove to be superior to non-exhaustive rules in flow shop production [11]. As our research focuses on high flexibility and robustness in a job shop scenario, we developed a non-exhaustive approach and compare it with an exhaustive rule. Therefore, the problem is classified as a job shop scheduling problem including setup times and it differs from the flow shop problem analyzed by Frazier. But like Frazier, we cover uncertainty: Customer orders/Sales orders/Jobs arrive after exponentially distributed inter-arrival times, and processing times of operations are log-normally distributed. Because of this uncertainty, it is impossible to generate a optimal schedule. In order to still gain a robust schedule, we need a dynamic grouping and scheduling of operations. Therefore, we create dynamic time scopes based on forward and backward scheduling, then apply the dynamic time scopes to group operations within one GT, and delegate the group to a scheduling mechanism afterwards.

Under the term of group planning heuristics, dispatching rules resulted in approaches that solve the planning problem of operations that require the same technology. Those heuristics have received increasing attention. They reduce setup times and increase processing efficiency in production [11]–[14]. Several studies with focus on flow cell manufacturing and group heuristics already exists [10], [11], [15] and were an inspiration to this paper. Aside from dispatching rules, mixed integer linear programming (MILP) can be used to solve the GT-based scheduling. For our research, we do not consider MILP as it requires complete knowledge of all operation instances to find a solution; and using a suitable algorithm already leads to high computational costs, even for small instances of scheduling problems as [16] showed.

To sum up, our approach to reduce setup times combines non-exhaustive dispatching rules with a dynamic time scope to solve the job shop scheduling problem under uncertainty. Our approach differs from previous research, as the focus lies on a job shop scheduling problem. Most previous concepts focus on cell manufacturing, where the queuing of operations happens in front of a cell with identical machines [10]. Forward and backward scheduling is a well known technique, but to the best of our knowledge, we are not aware of other research applying forward and backward scheduling to group operations in a job shop production.

III. The Concept of SOBA

A. Structure of the self-organizing bucket architecture

Figure 1 shows the structure of SOBA. It consists of three elements: a set of jobs, one or more "SOBA - Bucket Managers" and a set of machines. Each *job* contains a sequence of operations. Thus, alternative and parallel operations are not considered yet. Moreover, all operations contain the following information: estimated processing time, due time of the job, average transition time, required setup time, and earliest start as well as latest start obtained by forward and backward scheduling.

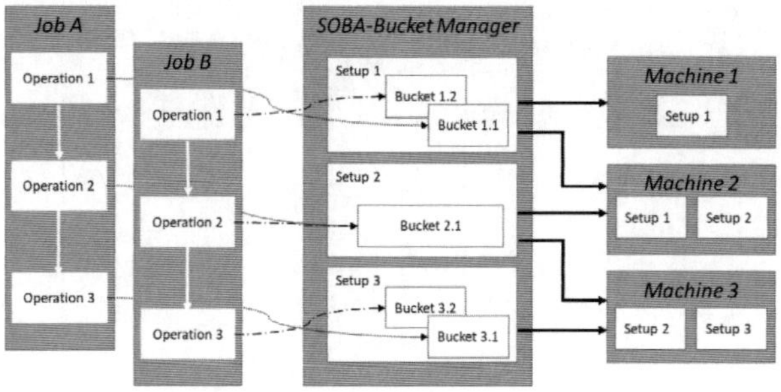

Figure 1. Self-organizing bucket architecture

The resources are represented by machines in the context of our production. Each resource can be assigned to one or more setups, but only be equipped with one setup at a time. Each setup represents a certain group technology to process an operation, i.e., drill a hole with a diameter of 4 mm. The same group technology can be provided by different resources. As shown in Figure 1, *Setup 1* is assigned to *Machine 1* and *Machine 2*. Thus, setups can be assigned to more then one machine and each machine can be equipped with one of the assigned setups. This way, it is possible to have multiple machines equipped with the same setup at the same time.

The bucket manager is a persistent instance. It assigns open operations requiring the same group technology to buckets linked to the same setup. If there is no suitable bucket for an operation, the bucket manager creates a bucket and assigns the operation to this bucket. After creating a bucket, the allocation of the bucket to the resource can start. How the allocation is carried out is irrelevant for the creation of the buckets. The bucket manager organizes the varying number of *buckets*, which are created upon or filled with incoming operations. As the number of potential operations in a bucket can be equal to the number of all operations of the same group technology, multiple buckets can be created for each setup to maintain flexibility by splitting or merging operations into new buckets. But each bucket must contain at least one operation. This is the operation the bucket manager originally created the bucket for. After the initial creation of the bucket, further operations can be added depending on the time scope. To determine the time scope we use forward and backward scheduling when the job and its operations enter the production initially. After processing the last operation of the bucket and removing it from the bucket, the bucket dissolves.

B. Creating the scope for buckets

Considering industry 4.0, materials become smart by giving them not only essential information about their current status.

TABLE I
SYMBOL DEFINITION

Symbol	**Definition**
gt	group technology with $gt \in GT$
d	duration with $d > 0$, $d \in \mathbb{N}$
dt	due time with $dt > 0$, $dt \in \mathbb{N}$
sbt	start time from backward scheduling
sft	start time from forward scheduling with $(sbt > sft)$
o	is a column vector with $(gt, d, dt, sbt, sft)^T$
O	is a set $\{o_1, \cdots, o_n\}$ of operations sorted by $sft(o)$
b	is a vector with $\begin{pmatrix} O \\ gt \leftarrow gt(o_1) \\ d \leftarrow \sum_{o \in O} d(o) \\ dt \leftarrow dt(o_1) \\ sbt \leftarrow sbt(o_1) \\ sft \leftarrow sft(o_1) \\ scp \leftarrow sbt(o_1) - sft(o_1) \end{pmatrix}$

Moreover, the materials get digital twins providing them with further details, i.e., their locations, their bills of materials and their operations. We aim to calculate a time scope from the processing and transition times for each operation.

The bucket manager should assign the operation to the bucket which is the most suitable bucket regarding processing and completion time. The procedure to find a suitable bucket is shown in Figure 2.

While exploding the bill of material, each operation is scheduled individually. Crucial for the scheduling, the operation's duration includes the processing and transition time. After calculating the schedule both, the start and end times for the backward schedule and the forward schedule for each operation, are set. As example, Operation 1 in Figure 3 has an earliest start time of 0 from forward scheduling and a latest start time of 9 from backward scheduling. The resulting time frame is the scope, in which the operation shall be processed in order to finish the product in time.

Let us assume an empty production without any bucket. By scheduling the first operation, the Bucket Manager responsible for the group technology required by the operation would create a new bucket with the earliest start time 0 and the latest start time 9. The scope of the bucket would be a total of 9 time units. Usually scopes between earliest start time and latest start time can be very large, if the orders enter the production immediately. Therefore, we apply a maximum bucket scope, to avoid blocking of resources. We suggest a setup-specific maximum bucket size depending on working shifts, such as 8 hours, 4 hours, 2 hours or less. To ensure high flexibility, we do not set a minimum bucket size, as we want single urgent operations to be processed as fast as possible. In our experiment we make sure, that the start time from backward scheduling is always higher then the start time from forward scheduling. Thus, a time scope can be determined. Otherwise buckets would only contain single operations.

Data: S is a set of all existing buckets
A is a priority queue of operations ordered by $\rightarrow sft(o)$
T is a set of buckets requiring equal gt

Input: An operation o

1 **Procedure:** ManageBuckets(o)
2 $A \leftarrow \{o\}$
3 **while** $A \neq \emptyset$ **do**
4 `// take the most important`
5 `// operation and remove it from` A
6 $o \leftarrow o_1 \in A$
7 $A \leftarrow A \setminus \{o\}$
8 `// create a set of possible`
9 `// matching buckets`
10 $T \leftarrow \{b \in S | gt(o) = gt(b)\}$
11 `// find all buckets with later`
12 `// start to dissolve them and`
13 `// remove them from T`
14 $tmp \leftarrow \{b \in T | sft(b) > sft(o)\}$
15 $A \leftarrow A \cup \{o | (o \in b) \wedge (b \in tmp)\}$
16 $T \leftarrow T \setminus tmp$
17 `// find fitting buckets in T`
18 `// and take one bucket with the`
19 `// least start time from forward`
20 `// scheduling`
21 $tmp \leftarrow \left\{ b \in T \middle| \left(\sum_{p \in b} d(p) \right) + d(o) \leq scp(b) \right\}$
22 **if** $tmp \neq \emptyset$ **then**
23 $b \leftarrow$ an arbitrary $b \in \arg\min_{t \in tmp} sft(t)$
24 $O(b) \leftarrow O(b) \cup \{o\}$
25 **else**
26 new b with $O(b) \leftarrow \{o\}$
27 $S \leftarrow S \cup \{b\}$
28 **end**
29 **end**

Figure 2. Procedure assign operation to bucket

C. Procedure to create, find and modify buckets

As mentioned before, buckets are virtual elements organized by the bucket manager. The buckets are created, modified or deleted if any event occurs concerning the involved group technology. All properties of a bucket shown in Table I are calculated based on the operations assigned to the bucket. As shown in Algorithm 2, by receiving a new operation, the bucket manager determines the matching buckets depending upon their group technology (see line 10).

All buckets with an earliest start higher than the earliest start

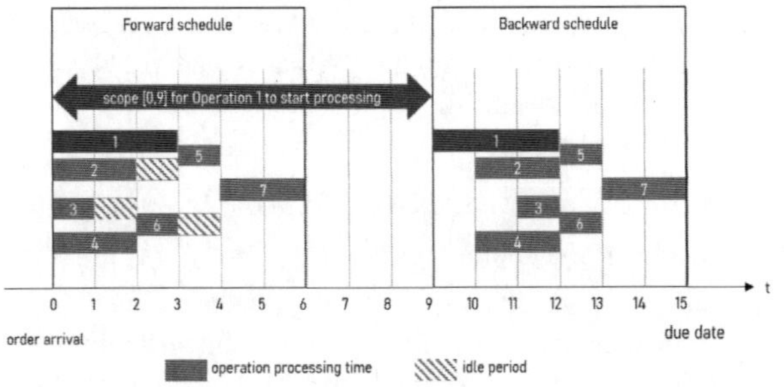

Figure 3. Scope definition by forward and backward scheduling

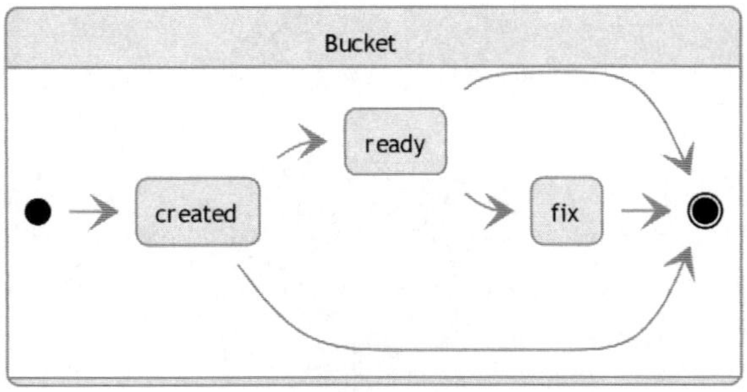

Figure 4. The main status flow for one bucket.

of the newly arrived operation dissolve into their operations (see lines 14 to 16). These operations are rescheduled during the next loop. Then, the bucket manager calculates for all remaining buckets whether the new operation still fits in the bucket scope or not and returns a set of fitting buckets (see line 21). If at least one fitting bucket can be found, the bucket manager chooses the bucket with the smallest earliest start time to assign the operation to the bucket (see lines 22 to 24). If no fitting bucket can be found, a new bucket will be created for the operation (line 26).

After assigning an operation to a bucket, this newly created or modified bucket can be scheduled at any of the capable resources. Scheduled buckets can still be rescheduled in case the bucket is modified afterwards.

D. Releasing buckets to production

Crucial for the event-driven production, we use a releasing mechanism to process buckets on shop floor. After assigning the bucket to a machine, the bucket remains in a planning queue in front of the machine. The machine picks the next bucket from the planning queue using the Least Slack Time (LST) rule. LST is known to be the best due date criteria based rule for timeliness and throughput [17]. Of course this rule can be replaced with any other priority rule, but that is not part of this contribution. Our approach includes the setup time into the calculation of the LST.

All buckets are queued regardless of their precondition. It is likely that a bucket contains operations that are not ready to be processed as their materials are not yet in stock or preceding operations of the same job are not yet completed. We solve the issue by giving buckets a state. When operations of a bucket receive material and their predecessors are completed, we set the state of the bucket to *ready*. Once setting the bucket *ready*, we enable the machine to select the bucket from the planning queue in front of the machine. At this time, new operations can still be inserted into the bucket. The bucket reaches the status *fix* when the machine selects the bucket as the next bucket to be processed. At that moment, all operations of the bucket without satisfied preconditions, are sent back to the bucket manager and trigger the algorithm in 2 to find or create a new bucket. Moreover, it is not possible to insert new operations into the bucket in status *fix*. The transitions between the states are shown in Figure 4.

After the resource chooses the bucket and sets its status to *fix*, the resource organizes the handling of the operations from the bucket. In general the operations in the bucket are unsorted. However, the operations of the bucket are processed applying again the LST-rule.

IV. Adaptation of SOBA to our event-driven production

ACATECH promotes self-organizing production systems with "intelligent" resources and "intelligent" materials in their Industry 4.0 concepts to meet all upcoming challenges of future production [1], [18]. In our self-organizing production, resources and materials are agents and can be physically attached to the product or have a virtual representation known as digital twin [19]. Our agents communicate asynchronously and cooperate based on an event-driven system [20]. Thus, we created a robust and reactive multi-agent production that we named SOPA - 'Self Organizing Production Architecture' shown in Figure 5. Each symbol represents one type of agent. Each arrow is a communication path between two types of agents. In the text below, the numbers (#number) refer to the communication paths. The letters in brackets describe the type of the agents according to their lifetime: (P) for persistent and (T) for transient. [21] introduced the self organizing production in detail. Therefore, it is only described in short here.

The "intelligent" resources and materials of Industry 4.0 suggest multi-agent systems (MAS) to realize self-organization in production. Figure 5 shows the agents and their communication. At the beginning there are the supervisor agent (SA), the warehouse agents (WA), the imparting agents (IA), the resource agents (RA), and the hub agents (HA). The SA is responsible for communication with the system's environment. The HA manages a resource group. The IA imparts knowledge about resource capabilities between HA and production agents (PA). When a customer order arrives, the SA creates a new contract agent (CA) (1). For each sales order item, the CA creates a disposition agent (DA) (2) that represents the product of the sales order item. Each DA asks the corresponding WA if the material is available (3). If the material is not available and is manufactured externally, the WA transmits a purchase order for the required material via the SA (4). Then the WA informs the DA about the availability (5) of the requested material. If

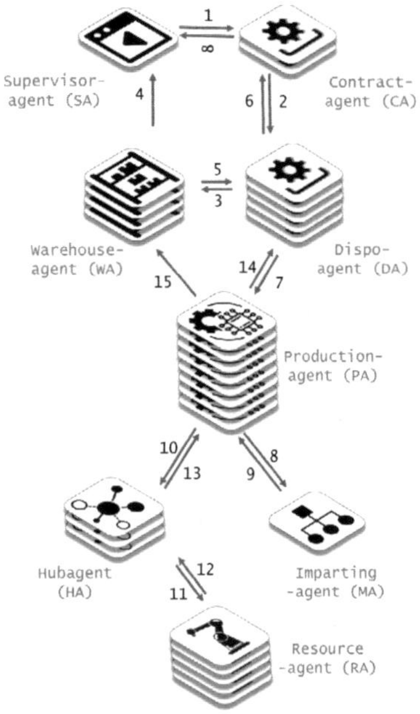

Figure 5. Architecture of our multi-agent-based self-organizing production

the material is available, the DA send a completion notification (6) to the CA. Otherwise, the DA creates a PA for the material (7). The PA creates a new DA for each of its BOM items, and the process described starts again until all BOM elements have been completely exploded. During BOM explosion, a backward scheduling is carried out. Each PA requests an HA from the IA for each of the PA's containing operations (8), and the IA returns the responsible HA (9). Now, the PA sends a request to the HA (10) for the next time slot in which the resources can execute the operation. The HA forwards the request to each of its RAs (11). Each RA calculates a start time based on his current workload and returns it as an offer to the HA (12), which chooses the best offer, sends a confirmation to the corresponding RA, and informs the requesting PA of the start time of the operation (13). The RA queues the operation according to its start time, removes those operations from the queue that are delayed by the newly queued operation, and asks the HA to reschedule these operations (12), as this enables other RAs to submit better offers. If the processing time of an operation deviates from its expected duration, the same mechanism reorganizes subsequent operations so that the self-organizing production always reacts to deviations immediately, which is one of its superior advantages. After a resource carried out an operation, its RA sends a completion message to the HA (12), which forwards the message to the PA of the operation (13), whereupon the PA sets the status of the following operation to *"ready"*, so that the assigned resources can start processing the operation. If no subsequent operation exists, the PA sends its completion message to its DA (14) and informs the WA about incoming material (15). The WA supplies that DA with the material (5) which needs it most urgently. After all DAs of the PA have been received their materials, the production of the PA starts and the described process starts again until the end product is finished and the sales order can be fulfilled.

V. Empirical Study

A. *Structure of the simulation model*

In order to test SOBA, we use simulation model of a production with three machine types as shown in Figure 6. The main production flow involving two cutting machines, one drilling machine, and two assembly units. The production allows different routings for every material. The drilling machine is the bottleneck. Each machine is able to yield at least two different kind of tools. The production is able to produce two types of wooden toy trucks. The bill of material of each product is three levels deep and contains approximately 30 materials, were each material is either produced or purchased. Each material to be produced is manufactured in up to three operations. The operations of one material can seize a machine more than once.

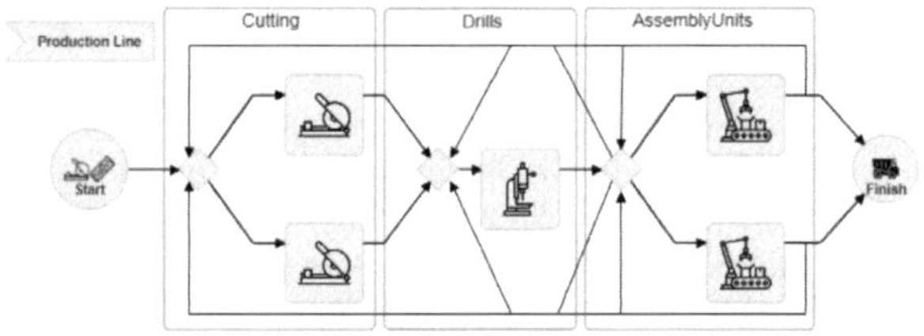

Figure 6. Production line of our simulation model

The operations sum up to 20 per product. Transportation times are not considered yet, but can be represented by an additional operations assigned to the material. In our empirical study, we compare SOBA with two different approaches and thus compare three approaches in total:

1) **Default:** No rules for setup time improvement are applied. Therefore, the resources do not group any operations and only process operations from the queue applying shortest slack time rule.
2) **Stacked:** All operations in the resource queue which are matching the current setup and having all preconditions satisfied, will be processed before the resource decides which group technology to setup next. The selection of the next technology and the selection of the next operation both apply the shortest slack time rule.
3) **Bucket (SOBA):** In order to determine an appropriate value for a maximum bucket size we increase the value step by step. To take the proportions of usage of group technologies into account and to force a more frequent change of group technology on the resources, we use different proportions based on the average required usage in our production. The proportions per category are shown in Table III. For instance, for all resource groups, we define the same overall bucket size of 1440 time units. The maximum bucket size for each group technology is

determined by proportion of its usage shown in Table III. Therefore we calculate: $1440 * 50\% = 720$ and gain the maximum bucket size for the screwdriver in resource group assembly. To ensure a reasonable bucket creation, the maximum bucket size cannot drop below 60 minutes, so at least 4 operations with the maximum processing duration of 15 minutes can join a bucket. Creating and processing buckets with only one operation should be possible to ensure fast processing of urgent operations. Therefore we do not set a minimum bucket size.

TABLE II
SIMULATION PARAMETERS

Value	Unit	Description
28	days	simulation end time
2	days	settling time
36	hours	average time from order placement to delivery
20	%	deviation of estimated operation processing time
80	%	target machine utilization

TABLE III
PROPORTIONS OF USAGE OF GROUP TECHNOLOGIES IN BUCKET MANAGER

Category	Group technology	Proportion Group Usage
Cutting	Blade Big	50%
	Blade Small	50%
Drill	Drill Head M4	25%
	Drill Head M6	75%
Assembly	Screwdriver	50%
	Holding	33%
	Hammer	17%

During the simulation of the production, new customer orders arrive continuously at the production. The inter-arrival time of customer orders is exponentially distributed as suggested in [22] and [23]. We choose an inter-arrival time, which leads to a well-utilized production but does not cause an overload. The production runs for four weeks, 24 hours a day. The production will produce approximately 33 products per day if the processing times do not deviate. To examine the flexibility of the production, we vary the processing times of the operations. According to [22], processing times are distributed log-normally. The inter-arrival times, the processing times, the capacity of the machines as well as the duration of the simulation can be configured separately for each simulation run. All simulation parameters of our empirical study are listed in Table II. However, the production have to dynamically adapt upon fluctuating effects. Those effects are caused by varying arrival rates and delivery dates of orders as well as deviations in processing time of operations. The production reaches its steady state after approximately 24 hours. We add another 48 hours before we start the measurement of the KPIs. All our simulations run with a deviation of processing times of ± 20 % and an average time to delivery of 36 hours.

B. *Simulation results*

Table IV, *Bucket* shows overall good results. In comparison, *Bucket* is superior to *Stacked* in work in progress and average setup time, which indicates less capital commitment and fewer setups. However, using *Bucket* with unlimited bucket size creates significant bigger buckets which lead to the expected phenomenon of potentially blocking bottlenecks in the production. Thus, our results indicate that finding a suitable maximum bucket size is crucial for SOBA. By reducing the maximum bucket size, we obtain smaller buckets which force the machine to setup different group technologies more frequently. Consequently the setup time increases significantly. Moreover, using a suitable bucket size such as *Bucket 1200* leads to better results in terms of throughput time. Generally for our simulation model, bucket sizes from *Bucket 720* to *Bucket 960* are superior to *Stacked* in terms of work in progress and setup times, while delivering almost the same results at timeliness and throughput time. *Default* as our reference behaviour is inferior in all KPIs. Although *Default* results in the smallest amount of work in progress and therefore less capital commitment, the simulation run for four weeks only completes 652 orders in total, which is by far the worst result for completed orders regarding all experiments. However, using *Stacked* already leads to significant better results. These results are consistent with [11], which demonstrates that exhaustive rules are superior to non-exhaustive rules in terms of timeliness.

VI. CONCLUSION

The target of our research was to develop a concept to group operations requiring the same group technology and prove SOBA empirically. We developed the concept and implemented a prototype of SOBA in our self-organizing production. Then, we simulated a four week production cycle and were able to prove the viability of SOBA. The results show that the production system is still as robust as before in terms of disruptions and deviations. We were also able to reduce the work in progress, throughput times and average setup times by completing the same amount of orders. The trade off for these savings is a slightly lower timeliness. For now, our approach is limited to a single scenario with focus on discrete manufacturing. In general, the concept can be adapted to any production size in terms of machines, setups and production structure. To cope with this, we will investigate further simulation parameters like different priority rules, load dependent delayed production starts and different bucket limitations. Furthermore, we will experiment with larger production models to gain more general results and afterwards transfer the solution to a real world scenario with production data from different cooperating companies.

ACKNOWLEDGEMENT

The authors acknowledge the financial support by the German Federal Ministry of Education and Research within the

TABLE IV
TEST SCENARIO FOR BUCKET

Behaviour	Timeliness	Work in Progress	Throughput time	Average machine utilization time	Average machine setup time	Completed orders	Comparison to Stacked △ Timeliness	△ Work in Progress	△ Average setup time
Default	21.00%	25.81	6882.27	52.00%	41.60%	652	-79.29%	-65.49%	118.95%
Stacked	99.28%	92.43	476.72	78.82%	18.74%	931	0.00%	0.00%	0.00%
Bucket 600	92.64%	83.08	483.84	78.94%	15.26%	931	-6.69%	-10.12%	-18.57%
Bucket 720	96.09%	85.37	503.93	78.82%	15.24%	931	-3.21%	-7.64%	-18.68%
Bucket 840	95.35%	82.87	509.79	78.94%	15.02%	931	-3.96%	-10.34%	-19.85%
Bucket 960	96.63%	79.41	522.64	78.94%	17.60%	931	-2.67%	-14.09%	-6.08%
Bucket 1080	94.35%	80.58	520.21	78.96%	14.80%	931	-4.97%	-12.82%	-21.02%
Bucket 1200	94.65%	80.07	506.82	78.96%	15.04%	931	-4.66%	-13.37%	-19.74%
Bucket 1320	94.49%	81.73	509.93	79.08%	14.64%	931	-4.83%	-11.57%	-21.88%
Bucket 1440	94.38%	83.48	493.03	78.98%	14.84%	931	-4.93%	-9.68%	-20.81%
Bucket 1920	93.63%	83.29	448.69	79.06%	14.74%	931	-5.69%	-9.88%	-21.34%
Bucket 2400	91.42%	83.59	443.22	79.34%	14.52%	931	-7.92%	-9.57%	-22.52%
Bucket ∞	88.68%	77.02	448.27	79.94%	14.14%	931	-10.68%	-16.68%	-24.55%

funding program "Forschung an Fachhochschulen" (contract number: 13FH133PX8).

REFERENCES

[1] acatech, *Recommendations for implementing the strategic initiative INDUSTRIE 4.0 (Abschlussbericht Industrie 4.0).* Munich: acatech, 2013.

[2] S. C. Kim and P. M. Bobrowski, "Impact of sequence-dependent setup time on job shop scheduling performance," *International Journal of Production Research*, vol. 32, no. 7, pp. 1503–1520, 1994.

[3] A. M. Spence and E. L. Porteus, "Setup reduction and increased effective capacity," *Management Science*, vol. 33, no. 10, pp. 1291–1301, 1987.

[4] M. R. Garey, D. S. Johnson, and R. Sethi, "The complexity of flowshop and jobshop scheduling," *Mathematics of Operations Research*, vol. 1, no. 2, pp. 117–129, 1976.

[5] W. Domschke, A. Scholl, and S. Voß, *Production planning: aspects of industrial engineering (Produktionsplanung: Ablauforganisatorische Aspekte)*, 2nd ed., ser. Springer-Lehrbuch. Berlin: Springer, 1997.

[6] F. Herrmann, *Operational planning in IT systems for production planning and control(Operative Planung in IT-Systemen für die Produktionsplanung und -steuerung).* Wiesbaden: Vieweg+Teubner, 2011.

[7] I. Ham, K. Hitomi, and T. Yoshida, *Group technology: Applications to production management*, ser. International series in management science/operations research. Boston: Kluwer-Nijhoff, 1985.

[8] R. W. Brennan, "Modeling and analysis of manufacturing systems. isbn 0-417-51418-7 [pp.461]," *International Journal of Computer Integrated Manufacturing*, vol. 8, no. 2, pp. 155–156, 1995.

[9] C. T. Ng, T. C. E. Cheng, A. Janiak, and M. Y. Kovalyov, "Group scheduling with controllable setup and processing times: Minimizing total weighted completion time," *Annals of Operations Research*, vol. 133, no. 1-4, pp. 163–174, 2005.

[10] A. Klausnitzer, J. S. Neufeld, and U. Buscher, *Scheduling dynamic job shop manufacturing cells with family setup times: a simulation study.* U. Logist. Res., 2017.

[11] G. V. Frazier, "An evaluation of group scheduling heuristics in a flow-line manufacturing cell," *International Journal of Production Research*, vol. 34, no. 4, pp. 959–976, 1996. accessed: November 2019. [Online]. Available: https://www.tandfonline.com/doi/pdf/10.1080/00207549608904945

[12] R. A. Ruben, C. T. Mosier, and F. Mahmoodi, "A comprehensive analysis of group scheduling heuristics in a job shop cell," *International Journal of Production Research*, vol. 31, no. 6, pp. 1343–1369, 1993.

[13] B. Grabot and L. Geneste, "Dispatching rules in scheduling dispatching rules in scheduling: a fuzzy approach," *International Journal of Production Research*, vol. 32, no. 4, pp. 903–915, 1994.

[14] D.-J. van der Zee, G. J. Gaalman, and G. Nomden, "Family based dispatching in manufacturing networks," *International Journal of Production Research*, vol. 49, no. 23, pp. 7059–7084, 2011. [Online]. Available: https://hal.archives-ouvertes.fr/hal-00669040/document

[15] G. Egilmez, E. M. Mese, B. Erenay, and G. A. Süer, "Group scheduling in a cellular manufacturing shop to minimise total tardiness and nt: a comparative genetic algorithm and mathematical modelling approach," *International Journal of Services and Operations Management*, vol. 24, no. 1, p. 125, 2016.

[16] D. Giglio, "A milp model for single machine family scheduling with sequence-dependent batch setup and controllable processing times." [Online]. Available: http://arxiv.org/pdf/1501.07396v2

[17] H. Corsten and R. Gössinger, *Production management (Produktionswirtschaft): Introduction to industrial production management(Einführung in das industrielle Produktionsmanagement)*, 13th ed., ser. Lehr- und Handbücher der Betriebswirtschaftslehre. München: Oldenbourg, 2012.

[18] C.-C. Kuo, J. Z. Shyu, and K. Ding, "Industrial revitalization via industry 4.0 – a comparative policy analysis among china, germany and the usa," *Global Transitions*, vol. 1, pp. 3–14, 2019.

[19] R. Stark and T. Damerau, "Digital twin," in *CIRP Encyclopedia of Production Engineering*, S. Chatti and T. Tolio, Eds. Berlin, Heidelberg: Springer Berlin Heidelberg, 2019, vol. 66, pp. 1–8.

[20] G. Di Marzo Serugendo et al., "Self-organisation: Paradigms and applications," in *Engineering Self-Organising Systems*, ser. Lecture Notes in Computer Science, G. Goos et al., Ed. Berlin, Heidelberg: Springer Berlin Heidelberg, 2004, vol. 2977, pp. 1–19.

[21] T. Munkelt and M. Krockert, "Agent-based self-organization versus central production planning," in *2018 Winter Simulation Conference (WSC).* [Piscataway, NJ]: IEEE, 2018?, pp. 3241–3251.

[22] G. Zäpfel and R. Braune, *Moderne Heuristiken der Produktionsplanung: Am Beispiel der Maschinenbelegung*, ser. WiSo-Kurzlehrbücher Reihe Betriebswirtschaft. München: Vahlen, 2005.

[23] J. Košturiak and M. Gregor, Eds., *Simulation of production systems (Simulation von Produktionssystemen).* Vienna: Springer Vienna, 1995.

Adaptation of Schedules and Scheduling Parameters in Cybernetic Systems

Andreas Heimrath
and Joachim Froeschl

BMW Group
R & D electronics
Munich, Germany
Email: andreas.heimrath@bmw.de

Jan Ahlbrecht
and Uwe Baumgarten

Technical University of Munich
Department of Informatics
Garching, Germany
Email: baumgaru@in.tum.de

***Abstract*—In the automotive domain, components are increasingly based on software that is being integrated through fewer and more powerful connected computing systems. With the main focus being the control of hardware with actuators and the monitoring of sensors, such systems are inherently complex. Additionally, their functions have both static and dynamic dependencies. Functions appear in a huge number with a large variety of dependencies. For decades, cybernetic approaches have been used to handle the complexity of dynamic systems in a natural manner. They have proven effective in different scientific domains like economics and management, governance, social sciences, and technical systems. Based upon the experience with a flexible energy and power management in the automotive industry (fEPM) we transfer those findings to software systems of sophisticated cars integrating more and more functions and components. We have identified Stafford Beer's Viable System Model (VSM) as a promising approach. We follow this approach step by step, starting with a basic VSM-based system/component. Using the principle of recursivity, we build horizontal and vertical combinations of systems resulting in powerful computational nodes with dynamic load depending on the individual feedback control systems and the control loops of all layers. Having the whole software stack in mind, we started to investigate modern microkernels (like seL4, Fiasco.OC and other) with their components. The scheduling, besides others, is the most promising component, where a VSM structure can be established. Here, we introduce an adaptive scheduler for the scheduling of an automotive workload, in which a machine learning process could exist. This is in line with other approaches in the field of autonomic or organic computing. A simplified energy and power management serves as an example for illustrating the applicability and usefulness of Beer's VSM in technical software systems.**

***Index Terms*—Software Cybernetics; Microkernel; Adaptive Scheduling.**

I. INTRODUCTION

In the automotive domain, components are increasingly based on software and are integrated in a few powerful connected computing systems. Nevertheless, their main focus is controlling hardware, sensors and actuators. Intelligent power and energy management for a car is a good example, where we have made encouraging experiences with cybernetics in the development and operation of a complex system.

For the purpose of controlling the main components, a cybernetic approach is used. Following the ideas of the Viable System Model (VSM) [1] the fEPM [2] was built in a successful manner.

With the growth of software-intensive components and services within a connected car, the basic software system gains importance. Therefore, we started investigating software cybernetic approaches for building the basic systems software blocks. On the one hand we analyzed software cybernetic approaches in the context of microkernel construction. On the other hand we examined the approaches of organic computing. Together with the experience of the energy and power management fEPM, we identified a VSM-based approach for constructing complex systems, that combines the best ideas of different worlds.

The rest of the paper is structured as follows. Section II will introduce the concepts of cybernetics, VSM, and microkernels, while discussing some related work. Later, in Section III we present our approach in constructing a complex (automotive) system along the ideas of VSM, putting special emphasis on adaptive scheduling. After introducing the workload to be scheduled in Section IV, we present our current solution for scheduling for a simplified energy and power management in Section V. Trying to prove the concepts presented in our current solution Section VI focuses around the creation and evaluation of a prototype and we then draw our conclusions and suggest future work in Section VII.

II. BACKGROUND WITH RELATED WORK

The application of cybernetics has a long tradition in handling complex systems. Looking at computer systems, embedded systems, internet of things (IoT) or cyber physical systems the initiatives of autonomic and organic computing have shown remarkable impact on systems architecture - both in hardware and in software - and modeling. With autonomic computing IBM developed first very fundamental steps [3] including self-configuration, self-healing and self-optimization. The paradigm shift with organic computing and further ideas and details may be found in [4]. Paradigms of biology with respect to self-organization will be applied there.

In the area of complex technical systems the cybernetic approach found its way in terms of organic computing and others.

The transition to distributed control with a strengthening of autonomy of systems and their components can be seen, for example, in [5]. A clear consequence was the development of the cyber organic system model (see [6]) with its application in the automotive domain. Further approaches taking operating systems into account may be found using the example of ubiquitous computing (see [7]). Similarly, software cybernetics occurs in the area of complex software systems. Yang et. al. (see [8]) take lots of approaches into consideration including Stafford Beer's Viable System Model.

A. Cybernetics and VSM

The science of cybernetics was founded in 1948 by the results of research of Norbert Wiener [9]. For Wiener's original work see [10]. Based around these ideas the research of Beer resulted in his VSM [11]. The VSM is an abstract model of the nervous system. It combines five subsystems to create a management model for business applications. The subsystem 1 (named as system level 1 in Figure 1) represents an operational unit. The subsystem 2 (system level 2) creates a metasystem for the coordination of all subsystems of type 1 (operational units). The function of stabilization is the main task of subsystem 3 (system level 1). The information input is given by the subsystems 4 and 5 and the metasystem of subsystem 2. The regulation function is similar to the autonomic nervous system as a cooperation of the sympathetic and parasympathetic nervous system. At least the subsystems 1 to 3 create a functionality called homeostasis. This means that all activities and procedures result in an intrinsic behavior to reach always a balanced system state or equilibrium. Beer called it "autonomics". The subsystem 4 (system level 4) combines the information of the system environment with the system information built in subsystem 3. Finally, the subsystem 5 (system level 5) has the purpose to make decisions and to give instructions to the lower instances within the model. Beer called the subsystems 3 to 5 "corporate management". Figure 1 in the next section presents the VSM solution for the fEPM.

Advancing this concept, Malik includes the principle of recursivity to couple more than one VSM to manage more extensive systems, e.g., big companies in an evolutionary way [12]. Recursivity means that an operational unit is implemented with a VSM in a similar way depending on the local tasks and their abstraction.

In addition, the VSM will be applied in various domains, like economics, governance with a sustainable equilibrium [13] and software systems (see section II-C).

B. OC, E/E, and fEPM

There are several applications of the VSM. One implementation is the flexible energy and power management as a technical approach for coordinated power supply systems. The basic model of the fEPM is shown in Figure 1. The fEPM features all five system levels [2].

- SL1 Contains the system values, the physical connection control and the control functions.
- SL2 Condenses the system values into operating figures and has to combine the level 1 functionalities in a fast way.
- SL3 Determines the operating figures and tendencies with deposited knowledge into system states. This level contains the autonomous, state based system modifications for the purpose of system stabilization. Compared to biological systems, it works like a reflex system.
- SL4 Combines the internal system states and diagnostic information from the system itself with the external system states based on environment information. The instruction of a higher hierarchy level is included here. The coupling of the environment information is made of filtered, relevant information out of the system specific environment.
- SL5 Contains the operating strategy. Compared to the biological system it works like a conscious behavior. In this level the regulation values, so called modificators, are calculated.

The fEPM was originally designed for automotive systems. Another use case for VSM and its implementation for the management of stationary energy storage systems is described in [14].

From a point of view in computer science, the organic computing (OC) initiative had a bio-inspired look into aspects of systems and their implementation. A comparison of the OC-model, the fEPM-model and a combination of both called Cyber Organic System model (COS) was published by Adam et. al. in 2015 in [6]. The COS contains several layers for the basic objects, reflex, strategy, intelligence, and communication including observer/controller mechanisms. For a more detailed discussion within the topic of electric and electronic systems design E/E see [15].

A promising approach is the combination of the cybernetic modeling and artificial intelligence (see [16]).

C. VSM and Software Systems

Stafford Beer's Viable Sytem Model can be applied to software systems. The introduction as a first part in this section is based upon [17]. The second part describes our automotive example (see [18]).

Herring and Kaplan [17] are among the first scientists who applied the VSM to software with the idea of building better software systems. A complex software system, here a Viable System Architecture, integrates viable components (VC) in an overall system. Viable components are structured along the principles of VSM (see section II-A and fEPM) and provide interfaces for managing viability.

For our purpose, building a microkernel-based automotive power management, the system's characterization by Herring fits in a perfect manner. "These systems are characterized by large numbers of heterogeneous components with a high degree of interconnections, relationships and dependencies.

They exist in a dynamically changing environment that demands dynamically responding behavior. In other words, these systems must adapt to their environment."[17].

The integration of the control paradigm to (object oriented) software was postulated by Shaw [19] in a sense that a component does its own work, whereas being controlled by others. Later in section III we will use this statement for scheduling, where the creation and execution of a schedule might be adopted depending on various influences.

Corresponding to the former sections about cybernetics and VSM the principles, which will be applied to software, are autonomy, adaption, recursivity, hierarchies, invariants, and self-reference. In order to use the appropriate features and attributes of the above mentioned principles, a set of object's interfaces are introduced. These interfaces enable the objects itself, their controller and all other related components to influence each other.

The second part of this section gives an example, how the software system for automotive power management can profit from machine learning techniques, here in terms of reinforcement learning. The architecture of the VSM and of the fEPM as its extension paved the way for the development of reflex-augmented reinforcement learning (RARL) [16]. RARL extends the concept of standard reinforcement learning by integrating the biologically-inspired reflex of the fEPMs system level 3 into the learning process. This makes reinforcement learning (RL) accessible to safety-critical applications such as automotive electrical energy management. The reflex ensures that only safe actions suggested by the agent of RL are executed and efficient training as well as operating the system are guaranteed in a defined range of safe system states. In automotive energy management for example, the reflex can reject actions that could lead towards states of undervoltage causing a severe breakdown of the cars steering assistance system. RARL based on deep Q-learning fulfilled major requirements of a real automotive electrical energy management system in a vast simulation study [18]. Furthermore, RARL suggests a way to fuse RL and cybernetic management systems. This makes it possible to realize structured learning management systems even for future systems of very high complexity.

D. Microkernels

Even in the automotive domain hardware/software systems are becoming increasingly connected, software-defined and complex. Therefore, the demand for microkernels undergoes a revival. Their philosophy is (a) to try and keep the kernel as small and lightweight as possible, (b) execute almost all code in user space / user mode, and (c) establish a tiny trusted code base for secure, reliable, and resilient systems. Microkernels like L4, seL4 [20], Fiasco.OC [21] or Minix 3 (see [22]) have a long history, but new kernels, like Zircon [23], show up on the horizon. They all have in common similar function blocks, like basics for scheduling, inter process communication (IPC), the basics for security, and some basic memory or address space management. Further aspects and performance evaluation for communication may be found in [24]. With respect to cybernetics, scheduling is most appropriate and many contributions (in particular from organic computing, MAPE cycle (Monitor/Analyze/Plan/Execute from [3]) can be found in this direction. Security has some closeness, but IPC is far away from cybernetics, because of the huge requirements for performance. Some examples, where cybernetic approaches appear, are self-management in Minix 3 [22] or Fiasco.OC [21]. The monitoring of drivers in Minix 3 can discover, that a driver is inhibited in his processing and the scheduler may react on this observation. Like the MAPE cycle the scheduler in Fiasco.OC can monitor the execution of tasks and may change the strategy depending on the analysis, planning and execution steps.

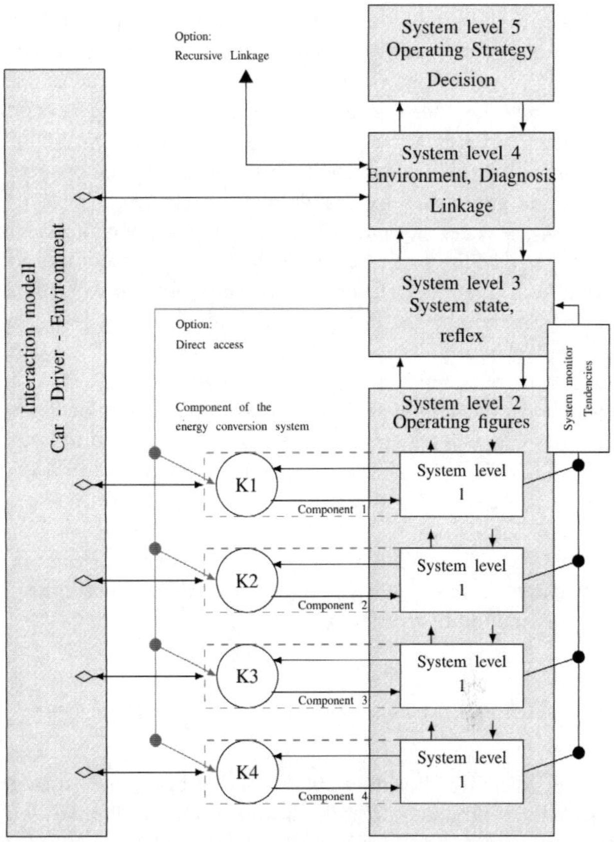

Fig. 1. fEPM.

III. Approach

In the former sections, we explained the origins and ideas of VSM and shown how VSM is used within an automotive energy and power management and how it is applied to software. The next step will be its application in the area of adaptive scheduling for the energy and power management system. This example illustrates the general approach.

The five layers of the cyber organic system model (see [6]) are adopted with respect of our scheduling approach. Starting from bottom to top the object layer includes the real (hardware) components of the energy system (generator of energy, storage for energy, and its consumers including sensors and actuators) and the necessary software components (workload and basics for scheduling/dispatching). The layer above is the reflex layer which includes first and fast analysis of the state of the real components (some of the processes in Table I). The strategy layer is responsible for the execution of the schedule by the dispatcher and the shortterm learning for the scheduler. The intelligence layer tries to learn the long term operating strategy, which is at the moment not included in our prototype. The communication layer includes the interplay with the environment (again one of the processes in Table I). For our scheduling approach, the given workload has to be scheduled and this is done in an adaptive manner. The structure of the COS shows the way to implement the scheduling. The MAPE cycle is applied and includes an appropriate learning strategy. Details including the workload are presented in chaper IV.

IV. Model of the workload and its parameters

The scheduler should operate in a non-interactive, mixed criticality environment. This means that it consists of processes that have strict check-up intervals every couple of milliseconds, which we will refer to as processes with a deadline, and other processes without deadlines. However, these check-up intervals are not strict, i.e., not a hard deadline, in the sense that if processes are missed their calculations become obsolete. Therefore, processes continue their calculation even if they miss their check-up time. Additionally, during the normal execution of the schedule, we want to train a neural network every couple of cycles, where each cycle is one execution of all our periodic processes. The neural network is itself a process and is implemented in OpenNN version 3.1. The network has two hidden layers with 25 neurons and uses simple sigmoid activations. When the process gets to run, it trains for around half a second and tries to approximate a 28 dimensional polynomial. This is done since, currently, we do not require any kind of output from the network and simply want a realistic load emulation.

The processes themselves perform operations ranging from very simple arithmetic operations like subtractions, over read out sensor data or to check if values are within a certain range, to more time intensive tasks like higher dimension matrix multiplications. The exact processes that make up the workload to be scheduled can be seen in Table I and are inspired by the tasks the fEPM has to full-fill. The whole workload consists of lots of these process types with a fixed distribution. The distribution is a based on expert knowledge, examples for possible values are 20% for Model Calculation and 25% for Risk Assessment.

TABLE I. THE PROCESSES THAT ARE PART OF THE WORKLOAD. PRIORITIES MAY BE VARIABLE (VAR) OR FIXED (FIX). THE MAXIMAL PRIORITY IS NAMED AS mpr.

Process	Check-Up Interval	Priority	Calculation
Fault Management	Yes	VAR and $\geq \frac{mpr}{2}$	$\mathbb{R}^{5\times5} \times \mathbb{R}^{5\times5}$
Range Check	Yes	VAR and $\geq \frac{mpr}{2}$	$\mathbb{R} - \mathbb{R}$
Risk Assessment	No	VAR and $< \frac{mpr}{2}$	$\mathbb{N} - \mathbb{N}$
Error Calculation	Yes	FIX and $\geq \frac{mpr}{2}$	$\mathbb{R} - \mathbb{R}$
Functional Safety	No	FIX and $< \frac{mpr}{2}$	$\mathbb{R}^{100\times100} \times \mathbb{R}^{100\times100}$
Model Calculation	Yes	FIX and $\geq \frac{mpr}{2}$	$\mathbb{R}^{30\times30} \times \mathbb{R}^{30\times30}$
Training a Neural Network	No	FIX at $\frac{mpr}{4}$	$\mathbb{R}^{28} \rightarrow \mathbb{R}$
Using a Neural Network	No	FIX and $< \frac{mpr}{2}$	$\mathbb{R}^{28} \rightarrow \mathbb{R}$

V. Solution

In this section we describe the scheduling aspects and our proposed scheduler.

A. Scheduling Method

There were two real options we considered for scheduling approaches. On the one hand, a multi-level priority scheduler [25], which assumes that two processes are not equally important and assigns them a priority. It then orders processes by their priority and, starting with the highest priority, starts to dispatch processes within the same priority using another scheduling method, for example, round-robin.

On the other hand, a batch scheduler [25] that just takes processes that are ready and packages them into a batch. This batch represents the plan that is then handed to the dispatcher and is executed one after another, without interruptions.

Our scheduler needs to able to differentiate between more or less important processes, based on their criticality. But, our domain (i.e. automotive) still consists of a large subset of processes with predictably static behaviour. Therefore, we decided to go for a mix between a multilevel and a batch scheduler.

B. The Proposed Scheduler

The scheduler tries to automatically adapt parameters to keep process execution within check-up intervals. It schedules in batches using MAPE [3] like cycles. After monitoring some parameters such as the amount of check-up intervals missed after every execution of a batch, the performance during the last cycle is evaluated and, if needed, adaptations are made for the next scheduling cycle.

Despite the usual inflexibility of a batch scheduler, it fits our needs since there is no outside interaction necessary and the processes calculations are short enough that the scheduler does not have to be preemptive. However, certain processes, like the one responsible for the training of the neural network, still have hard to predict run times. Therefore, our scheduler requires the ability to differentiate the importance of processes, to create a good batch. As a result, we assign a priority variable to processes, allowing us to influence the kind of batches our scheduler creates and to combat some of the downsides that come with batch scheduling.

Currently, there are two main adaptations our scheduler can make to improve performance in either the amount of check-up intervals held or fair service. One of them we call the minimum priority barrier and the other priority boosts. The first, as the name suggests, attempts to handle higher load situations by simply increasing the minimum priority required to be added to the next batch. Higher load situations are detected by monitoring the amount of check-up intervals kept. If a certain number of check-ups happens too late, the scheduler increases the minimum priority to avoid further check-up intervals being missed, by cutting out non-critical processes.

With the introduction of a system that cuts less important processes, there is the risk of starvation [26]. Starvation is when less important processes do not get to run for longer time periods. If the minimum priority has been increased, the scheduler offers two different ways of avoiding starvation:

The first is for the minimum priority to be decreased again, this happens if check-up intervals are being kept. The scheduler would then decrease the minimum priority and lower priority processes would get to run again.

The second relies on another variable that is being kept by each process called hunger. It determines how many cycles, so batch creations and dispatches, in a row a process had to be excluded from the batch despite being ready. If this variable reaches a certain threshold the priority of the process gets a one time only increase. In our current implementation this means it will have its priority increased to the minimum priority necessary to be included in the next batch. Other versions of the priority increase, like always increasing it by a fixed amount, are also possible. This way we avoid starving lower priority processes while still staying focused on keeping check-up intervals.

The scheduling approach proposed has been inspired by the Fiasco.OC microkernels scheduling approach. Fiasco.OC uses a so called context [27] to store parameters that can be monitored for MAPE like cycles. We also created such a context for our processes to make parameters easy to monitor.

VI. Evaluation with our Prototype

As a proof of concept, we built a prototype in C++ that emulates the execution of the processes controlled by the proposed scheduler and a dispatcher. The current implementation is not directly directly on hardware and therefore suffers from overhead through the underlying operating system (Ubuntu 18.04). However, we deemed this sufficient to determine the feasibility of our approach before an actual implementation.

The processes that make up the workload are deployed by pthreads. The dispatcher uses locks for their coordination. Each process is represented by a pthread that executes an operation which is similar to the computation the components would execute. We did not model the physical components, but only the processes that approximate their behaviour in the real world. Dispatching is simulated through locks, that get unlocked if a process has been assigned calculation time. The dispatcher holds all the locks in the beginning and then unlocks a certain number of locks at the same time to enable processes to run parallel to each other. In our prototype we assumed that a fixed number of threads could run simultaneously. The plan how to dispatch the processes is created by the scheduler as mentioned before.

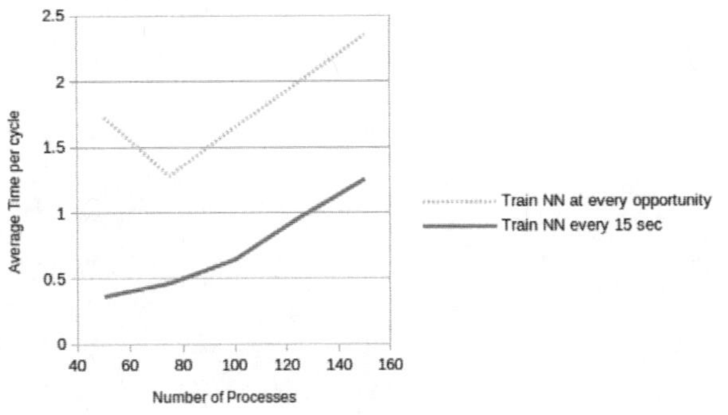

Fig. 2. Variation between neural network training intervals and their effect on the average time per cycle.

We then ran a couple of tests with a different number of total processes while always keeping a singular process responsible for training the neural network and one for using it. First, we wanted to variate some of the parameters of the workload to see the impact on the time per cycle. We started of by testing how the training intervals of the neural network affected the scheduler's performance. For this purpose, we ran two tests, one where we tried to train the neural network as often as the minimum priority barrier allowed, i.e., at every opportunity, and another one where we only scheduled the neural network less frequently, here every fifteen seconds. After executing the processes for 100 cycles for 20 experiments, we looked at the average time it took for our scheduler to complete one cycle. The results can be seen in Figure 2. As we can see, training the neural network in intervals instead of constantly results in more than half the time per cycle and therefore better scheduling performance. The dip in time per cycles for constant training at around 75 processes is due to the minimum priority barrier and will be explained later on.

Next, we fixed the neural network training interval to 15 seconds and changed the percentage of functional safety processes in the total number of processes. We then once again ran for 100 cycles for 20 times and observed the time taken per cycle. While there was a visible difference of around 0.1 seconds for each cycle (see Figure 3), the impact of changing the neural network training interval was a lot greater.

We also wanted to observe the effect the minimum priority barrier had on the percentage of check-up intervals missed.

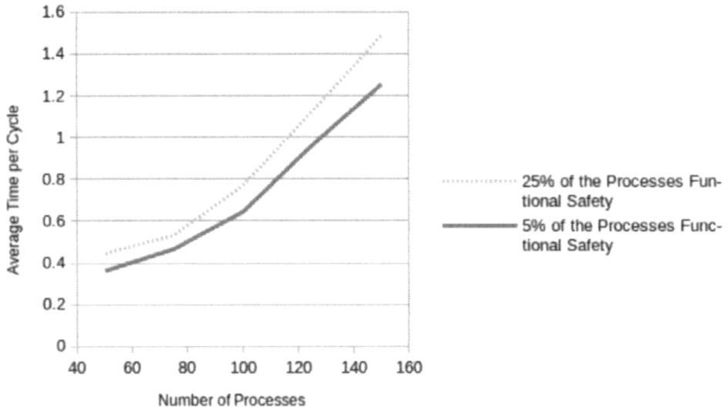

Fig. 3. Impact of the amount of functional safety process on the average time per cycle.

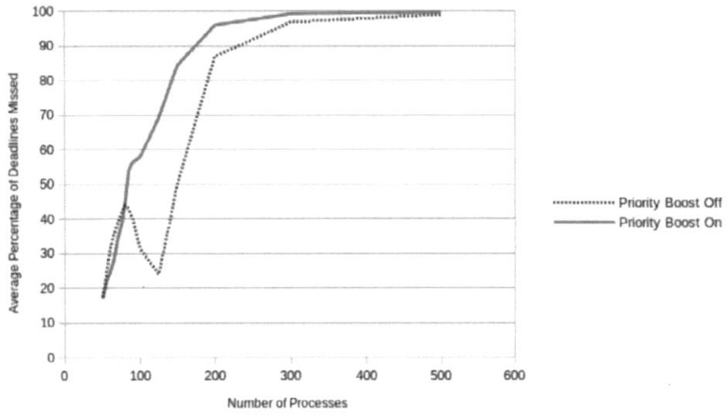

Fig. 4. The graph shows the average percentage of missed check-up intervals per cycle for a certain number of processes.

Figure 4 shows the relationship between the percentage of check-up intervals missed and the number of processes that are currently being scheduled. As to be expected, with an increase in the number of processes the scheduler eventually overloads and the amount of check-up intervals missed increases dramatically. However, before that occurs, at around 80 to 125 processes the amount of check-up intervals missed decreases again. This can be explained through the minimum priority barrier taking effect. It reacts to the higher load and starts cutting processes to maintain the check-up intervals. The reason the amount of check-up intervals missed drops so drastically is due to how the workload is made up. Only less critical processes without check-up intervals can be cut, which in our workload are the processes that require the most time to execute. During an increase in the minimum priority required, more and more of the processes without check-up intervals get cut until eventually, at around 125 processes, the minimum priority barrier is constantly maximized, meaning that all processes that could have been excluded from being scheduled, have been excluded. Now, with an increase in the total number of processes the percentage of check-up intervals missed increases again.

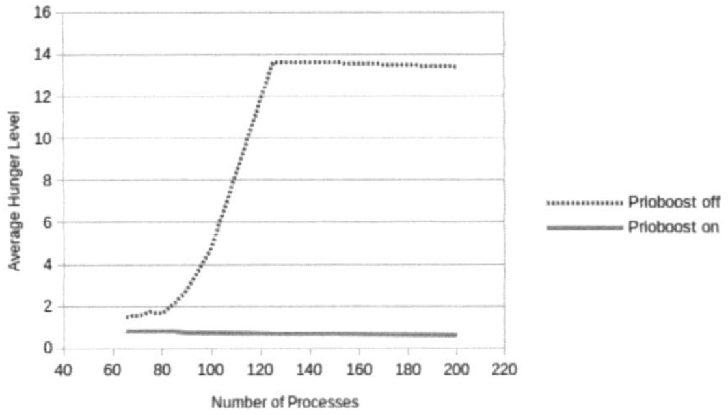

Fig. 5. The graph shows the average hunger level of the processes for a certain number of processes.

Next we wanted to see if the priority boosts had the intended effect of keeping a fair service to all processes. While Figure 4 might give the impression that having the priority boost enabled is solely a disadvantage, a look a Figure 5 shows otherwise. Figure 5 displays a close up of the average value of the hunger variable described earlier, in the area where the dip in the percentage of check-up intervals missed happened in Figure 4. From the graph we can observe a drastic increase in the hunger variable around that time, meaning that processes without check-up intervals are no longer being assigned processor time, essentially starving them. Meanwhile, the curve with priority boosts enabled keeps the hunger variable at a constant level showing that priority boosts can be used to ensure fair service.

VII. Conclusion and Future Work

Concluding, we have shown that methods such as the minimum priority barrier and priority boosts have the intended effect of making the scheduler adaptive to changes in the load, while being able to maintain the intended goals of keeping check-up intervals, fair service or a mix of both.

Due to its adaptability our scheduling approach enables the design of complex systems without previous extensive knowledge of process parameters. This, while not providing the error rate needed for safety-critical systems, paves the way for a wide variety of applications not limited to automotive energy management to keep soft deadlines without any previous knowledge of the run time of other tasks in the system.

In the future, it would be interesting to experiment with a reinforcement learning approach to set parameters such as the one for the priority barrier dynamically based on the current processes ready for scheduling. This could lead to even more adaptable scheduler.

Currently, the scheduler struggles due to its non-native performance and the resulting increase in time needed for a context switch. Implementing a prototype of the scheduler in an operating system and testing it using native performance would definitely be among the next steps.

Additionally, further tuning of the parameters for the minimum priority barrier and priority boosts is necessary to better serve the current workload. Furthermore, the scheduler could be extended to be able to tell if it is barely able keep check-up intervals and as a result to avoid unnecessary decreases in the minimum priority. But, a lower-level implementation with native performance is required for any kind of fine tuning, otherwise cycles are too unreliable.

REFERENCES

[1] S. Beer, *Cybernetics and Management.* Wiley, 1959.

[2] J. Fröschl, S. Kurtz, M. Winter, J. Taube, T. Nuritdinow, and H.-G. Herzog, "Concept of a decision system for an operating strategy in a cybernetic energy and power management," in *EEHE2016*, 2016.

[3] IBM, "An architectural blueprint for autonomic computing," https://www-03.ibm.com/autonomic/pdfs/AC%20Blueprint%20White%20Paper%20V7.pdf (Visited on 28.02.2020), IBM, Tech. Rep., 2005.

[4] C. Müller-Schloer, H. Schmeck, and T. Ungerer, *Organic Computing A Paradigm Shift for Complex Systems.* Basel: Birkhäuser, 2011.

[5] S. Tomforde, B. Sick, and C. Müller-Schloer, "Organic computing in the spotlight," *arXiv:1701.08125 [cs.MA]*, 2017.

[6] D. Adam, J. Froeschl, U. Baumgarten, A. Herkersdorf, and H.-G. Herzog, "Cyber Organic System-Model New Approach for Automotive System Design," in *ADAPTIVE 2015:The Seventh International Conference on Adaptive and Self-Adaptive Systems and Applications*, 2015, pp. 92–97.

[7] M. Mattos, "Organic computing and operating systems: The big challenge," *2015 Ninth International Conference on Complex, Intelligent, and Software Intensive Systems*, pp. 392–1397, 2015.

[8] H. Yang, F. Chen, and S. Aliyu, "Modern Software Cybernetics: New Trends," *Journal of Systems and Software*, vol. 124, pp. 169–186, 2017.

[9] N. Wiener, *Kybernetik.* Duesseldorf: Econ, 2. Auflage, 1963.

[10] ——, *Cybernetics.* New York: John Wiley u. Sons, 1948.

[11] S. Beer, *Kybernetik und Management.* dt. Ausgabe, Fischer Verlag, 1962.

[12] F. Malik, *Strategie des Managements komplexer Systeme.* Haupt Verlag, 9. Auflage, 2006.

[13] S. Barile, B. Quattrociocchi, M. Calabrese, and F. Iandolo, "Sustainability and the viable systems approach: Opportunities and issues for the governance of the territory," *Sustainability*, vol. 10, pp. 1–17, 2018.

[14] H.-G. Herzog and et. al., "Applications of the viable system model in automotive and battery storage systems," in *2016 IEEE International Conference on Systems, Man, and Cybernetics; SMC 2016 — October 9-12, 2016; Budapest, Hungary*, 2016, pp. 1714–1752.

[15] D. Adam, *Concept of bionic E/E architecture for future vehicles based on the model of the human body (in German).* Dissertation at TUM, 2016.

[16] A. Heimrath, J. Froeschl, and U. Baumgarten, "Reflex-augmented reinforcement learning for electrical energy management in vehicles," in *Proceedings of the 2018 International Conference on Artificial Intelligence, CSREA Press*, 2018, pp. 419–430.

[17] C. Herring and S. Kaplan, "The Viable System Model for Software," *4th World Multiconference on Systemics, Cybernetics and Informatics (SCI'2000)*, 2000.

[18] A. Heimrath, J. Froeschl, R. Rezaei, M. Lamprecht, and U. Baumgarten, "Reflex-augmented reinforcement learning for operating strategies in automotive electrical energy management," in *Proceedings of the 2019 International Conference on Computing, Electronics & Communications Engineering (iCCECE), IEEE*, 2019, pp. 62–67.

[19] M. Shaw, "Beyond objects: a software design paradigm based on process control," *ACM SIGSOFT Software Engineering Notes*, vol. 20, no. 1, pp. 27–38, 1995.

[20] G. Klein and et. al., "sel4: Formal verification of an os kernel," in *Proceedings of the ACM 22nd Symposium on Operating Systems Principles, ACM*, 2009, pp. 207–220.

[21] FIASCO, "The fiasco.oc microkernel," http://os.inf.tu-dresden.de/fiasco/ (Visited on28.02.2020).

[22] A. S. Tanenbaum, "Lessons learned from 30 years of minix," *Communications of the ACM*, vol. 59, p. 3, 2016.

[23] FUCHSIA, "The zircon microkernel," https://fuchsia.dev/fuchsia-src/concepts/kernel (Visited on28.02.2020).

[24] Z. Mi, D. Li, Z. Yang, X. Wang, and H. Chen, "Skybridge: Fast and secure inter-process communication for microkernels," in *EuroSys 19, March 2528, 2019, Dresden, Germany*, 2019.

[25] A. S. Tanenbaum, *Operating Systems Design and Implementations.* Pearson, 2006.

[26] A. S. Tannenbaum, *Modern Operating Systems.* Prentice Hall, 2001.

[27] D. A. Krefft, "Flexible task management for self-adaptation of mixed-criticality systems with an automotive example," Ph.D. dissertation, Technische Universitaet Muenchen, 22.08.2018.

Validation of Self-Adaptive Systems' Safety Requirements at Design Time

Rasha Abu Qasem
Chair of Software Engineering: Dependability
University of Kaiserslautern, Germany
email: abuqasem@cs.uni-kl.de

Peter Liggesmeyer
Chair of Software Engineering: Dependability
University of Kaiserslautern, Germany
email: liggesmeyer@cs.uni-kl.de

***Abstract*—Self-Adaptive Systems (SAS) are becoming more evident in our lives. By definition, these systems are supposed to adapt to changes in their context without human interference. It is essential that they are trusted to autonomously perform critical tasks in changing environmental conditions. That makes assuring their safety a vital task, and because of their complexity, a challenging one. In this work, our goal is to identify potential safety vulnerabilities of SAS at design time. We start by addressing safety requirements of SAS and transferring their natural language description to a guided template then to a formal description. After that, we aim to automatically generate adequate test cases. At the same time, we build the initial models of the system and with the help of a powerful simulator, we run the generated test cases against the system models. This way, we can validate the safety requirements of SAS at design time.**

Keywords*— *Self-Adaptive Systems; Safety Requirements; Test cases; Auto-generation; Design time

I. Introduction

Self-adaptive systems usually have high levels of automation which present new risks to the surroundings. To minimize the risk to a residual value, we came up with a new approach to represent and test safety requirements of SAS. Knowing that, the bigger the gap between error introduction and error detection, the bigger the cost of development. We designed our approach to validate SAS safety requirements at design time, which will facilitate early detection of failures in the system and subsequently reduce the time and effort of the development.

We start by requirements elicitation process of SAS, which is still not a solved problem because of the uncertain behavior of these systems. Although there are some proposed solutions for the requirements problem of SAS as in [1] [2] [3], we are convinced there is no solution that specifically targets the representation of safety requirements of SAS. That is why we start by investigating how safety requirements are managed in the first place.

The Parametrized Safety Requirements Templates (PSRTs) defined by Oliveira in [4] can be used as the basis of safety requirements elicitation of SAS. PSRTs are used to check the safety requirements for conflicts and completeness by translating the natural language description to a controlled structured natural language.

We propose a possible representation of the safety requirements of SAS by extending PSRTs to Extended PSRTs (E-PSRTs). PSRTs already focus on how to reflect the safety analysis results and failure propagation models on the system's requirements and architecture. By extending PSRTs, we adjust the PSRTs templates to incorporate the managing and control requirements, the environment's conditions and the expected behavior of SAS. We will also extend the definition of safety requirements in the PSRTs to elaborate the concepts of guaranteed safety and demanded safety requirements form the conditional safety certificates (ConSerts) introduced in [5].

Creating E-PSRTs would provide a promising structure to manage safety requirements of SAS and subsequently facilitate their validation. It would also give a clear insight on how the concepts in ConSerts can be exhibited in the requirements engineering phase of SAS. That summarizes our first contribution in this work.

Later on, we define a domain specific language rules to implement the E-PSRTs templates into a formal structure. Then we use this structure to auto-generate test cases by injecting faults to the normal or expected behavior of the system. The auto-generated test cases are used besides the test cases designed by domain experts to validate the safety requirements of the system.

Finally, we run the all the test cases against the preliminary system models in a simulation environment to evaluate and check the validity and completeness of the safety requirements of SAS before the actual development. We carefully monitor the system response in risky situations and its adherence to the defined guards in safety requirements.

This would provide an early estimation of the SAS behavior at design time. If a risky or unsafe behavior is identified, we can easily trace the architecture elements, safety requirements as well as the failure propagation model to reassess them and perform the needed changes. This would be our second contribution in this work.

The remainder of this paper is structured as follows: In Section II, we discuss the problem we are targeting and identify the gaps in literature. In Section III we present our proposed approach to validate the safety requirements of SAS at design time. In Section IV, we provide the realization and validation plan of our approach with an introduction of the chosen case study. Finally, in Section V, we conclude and discuss future work.

II. Motivation - Problem

The motivation behind our approach is to find a rigorous solution to solve problems we have located through practise and research gaps we have identified in the literature. Mainly, we can classify our motivation into three categories, knowing that, more specific problems can arise in these categories as the research progresses.

A. Specification of Safety Requirements of SAS

There are several attempts of targeting uncertainty in SAS requirements, for example, in [3] probabilistic and fuzzy relaxation have been used to represent the adaptive properties of SAS's requirements. Different types of SAS requirements have been distinguished namely, monitoring, control and evolution requirements. The concept of the Configurable Specification (CP) has been introduced. CP is a set of interrelated configurations where the system can start from a configuration in which the domain assumptions are consistent with the system environment. This concept sounds a promising start to solve the problem of requirements engineering of SAS. However, the safety requirements are not addressed at all, and even the non-functional requirements are vaguely mentioned.

Another try to tackled uncertainty of SAS is with RELAX [1], which is a requirements language for SAS that explicitly addresses uncertainty inherent in adaptive systems. Its formal semantic is represented in terms of fuzzy logic, thus it enables a rigorous treatment of requirements that include uncertainty. Regarding non-functional requirements, they are dealt with in a conventional way, meaning they have their quantification of the minimum acceptable levels and are not changed by RELAX process. RELAX doesn't provides any specifics about safety requirements.

Other attempts, like in [2][6][7], focus mainly on the process of requirements elicitation and/or management of SAS without giving enough focus on the overall safety of the system or the safety requirements themselves.

On another scope, we know that the lack of guidance on how to specify safety requirements that are properly traceable to the architecture design and to failure propagation models is one of the main reasons for their incompleteness and inconsistency, which turns out to be a root cause of safety incidents [4]. That implies the importance of specifying traceable and consistence safety requirements of a system.

The fact that, to our best knowledge, there exists no clear methods neither recommendations on how to elicit or manage safety requirements of SAS, is a big drive behind our approach.

B. Validation of Safety Requirements of SAS at Design time

It has become a rule of thumb in software development, that the earlier the error is detected the less impact it has on the development's cost and effort. That is why we are targeting in our approach the safety requirements of SAS during the system design phase. By using a proper simulator to run the system models against the test cases, we can validate the safety requirements of the SAS at early stages and we can trace errors and locate potential design flows before the actual implementation takes place.

C. Auto-generation of Test Cases to verify the Safety of the SAS

Documented test cases are essential for testing large and complex systems such as SAS or the embedded systems in the automotive domain. ISO-26262 [8], an automotive safety standard, states that all system requirements should be properly tested by corresponding system test cases. Usually test cases are derived manually from the textual requirements, that is why it is a time consuming and error-pron process. Automatic test generation proved to be a powerful approach to reduce the cost of testing as well as to assure the requirements' coverage.

The benefits of automatic test generation are widely acknowledged today and there are many proposed approaches to conduct it in the literature. For instance, in [9] and [10] they proposed approaches to auto-generate UML behavioral diagrams such as, activity diagrams and sequence diagrams from use case descriptions. The generated models can be used to auto-generate test cases. However, the generated test cases are not executable and need manual intervention.

There are some other approaches which generate executable test cases such as [10] and [11]. They require that the requirements specifications are written according to a Controlled Natural Language (CNL). The input specifications are translated into formal specifications, which are later used to automatically generate test input data (e.g., using constraint solving). The problem with these approaches is that the CNL language supported by them is very limited which reduces their usability.

The researchers in [12] generated test cases from the use case specifications of the system. They combined Natural Language Processing (NLP) and constraint solving to extract behavioral information from use case specifications. They have achieved promising results but it was not clear how to tackle the non-functional requirements of the system.

Non of the previously mentioned approaches has specifically addressed the safety requirements of the system nor was designed to handle the specifications of a self-adaptive systems, which have to describe the adaptation strategies of the system against the uncertainty of the domain. With our proposed approach, we will find a feasible method to auto-generate test cases from SAS system specifications to test and verify the safety requirements as we maintain traceability to the safety analysis entities.

To summarize, we form the main questions we answer as the following:

1) How to mitigate safety requirements in adaptation strategies representations of SAS?
2) How to assure that the safety requirements of SAS are consistent and traceable through the design time?
3) How to auto-generate test cases that can validate the safety requirements of SAS at design time with the help of a simulator?

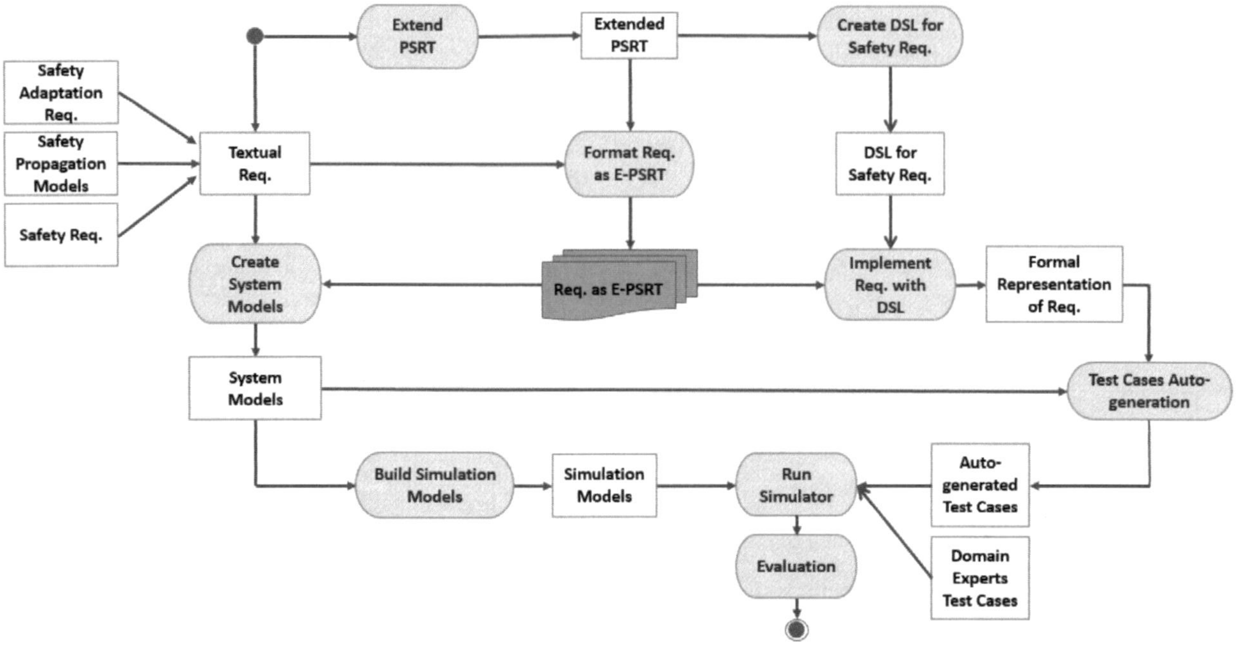

Figure 1. Proposed Approach for Validating Safety Requirements of SAS at Design Time

III. Proposed Solution

Our proposed solution to the problems described in Section II, is a comprehensive approach which consists of nine steps. Each step depends on the intermediate result from a predecessor step as illustrated in Figure 1. The main goal of this approach is to provide a means to evaluate the safety requirements of a self-adaptive system at design time and to assess the system behavior in critical events. That also gives a clear guidance about the quality of the architecture design and its adherence to the overall safety requirements of SAS. In the following, a clearer description of each of the steps is provided:

- Extend PSRTs: originally, PSRTs explained in [4], are templates which provide guidelines on how to specify the safety requirements of a system. The proper usage of PSRT templates assures consistency and establishes traceability between the safety requirements, the failure propagation models, and the system architecture. However, PSRTs weren't designed with self adaptation in mind. That is why, we start by extending the PSRTs to Extended PSRTs (E-PSRTs). E-PSRT would provide a thorough template to help specifying the safety requirements of the different adaptation scenarios and strategies of SAS systems.
- Format Requirements as E-PSRTs: in this step, we format the safety requirements of the self-adaptive system as E-PSRTs. This enable us, at design time, to identify the inconsistent safety requirements and then to update the requirements document, failure propagation models, and the system's architecture, accordingly.
- Create a Domain Specific Language (DSL): DSL is usually created to solve specific problems in a particular domain. In this step, we aim at designing a language which facilitates the representation of adaptation scenarios as well as the rules and accepted patterns of the safety requirements of a self-adaptive system. That will enable us to precisely parse the safety requirements from the E-PSRT templates to a formal structure. We can inject failures to specified safety guards requirements.
- Implement Requirements with a DSL: In this step, we implement the requirements that we formatted as E-PSRTs using the DSL that we have created. The output of this step is a formal representation of the adaptation strategies of SAS. Later on, we use the resulted representation to auto-generate test cases for testing the system along with test cases proposed by domain experts.
- Create System Models: in this step, we create the system models and architecture starting from the system requirements. This step can be conducted manually or in a semi-manual fashion. It is out of the focus of our approach to provide an automation of this step.
- Build Simulation Models: in this step, we build the simulation models that we can later run by a simulator. We build the simulation models based on the system models we created form the previous step. This step is conducted manually.
- Auto-generate Test Cases: in this step, we use the formal representation of the safety requirements and adaptation strategies of SAS and the manually created system models to auto-generate adequate test cases. The automation of the test case generation process provides a means

to ensure that the test cases have been derived in a consistent and objective manner and that all system's safety requirements have been covered.
- Run Simulator: in this step, we run the simulation models of the system in a simulator. Then, we feed the simulator with the auto generated test cases along with the domain experts' test cases and monitor the system's behavior.
- Evaluation: finally, we compare the expected behavior of the system with the resulted/simulated behavior. The found deviations, if any, raise an alarm that the system could encounter unpredicted and hazardous behaviors. We can trace the behaviors back to the initial requirements and perform the needed updates.

By performing the previous steps, we can validate the safety requirements of a SAS at design time. When locating design flows, they could be traced back to either the requirements of the system or to its safety analysis.

IV. Research Validation

We need a proper use case to validate our proposed approach. In the world of self-adaptive and smart systems, there exist a lot of exemplary benchmarks especially for testing object detection and object tracking algorithms. This type of benchmarks are designed to test the end behavior of an implemented system, since we are focusing on design time validation of the system. They are not appropriate to validate our approach. We need a comprehensive use case that fully describes the requirements and the system architecture.

A. Use Case

Safe Adaptive Software for Fully Electric Vehicles (SafeAdapt) is a project conducted by Fraunhofer IKS [13]. The main concept behind SafeAdapt is to develop a novel Electric/Electronic architecture based on adaptation to achieve safety, reliability, and cost efficiency in future Fully Electric Vehicles (FEVs). SafeAdapt has the goal of building adaptable systems in safety-critical environments that comprises methods, tools, and building blocks for safe adaptation.

Side by side through SafeAdapt project, a detailed use case has been built to verify the architecture of the end system. This use case is fully described through several deliverables of the project and it evolves as the project progresses. That makes it a perfect fit to evaluate our approach since it clearly covers the first two phases of the system development, namely requirements elicitation and system design.

B. Approach Validation

To properly validate our approach, we need to run the simulator twice. The first run would assess the system behavior and its hazardous encounters without applying the approach. The inputs of the simulator in this run are the simulation models and the domain experts' test cases. The second simulator run would have the system models and the auto generated test case along with the domain experts' test cases. In both runs, we will assess the design flows of the system and the unpredicted hazards that the system could encounter. The comparison between the simulator runs would provide a good gaudiness of the applicability of the approach and the improvements that it adds to the validation of safety requirements of SAS at design time.

V. Conclusion

Building adaptable systems in safety-critical environments is a challenging task. Our proposed approach addresses some of these challenges in requirements elicitation and system design phases. We first tackle the problem of specifying safety requirements of SAS and how we reflect them in the adaptation strategies while keeping them traceable to the safety analysis models and architecture components. Then we generate adequate test cases to test the expected behavior of the system. To get an early feedback before starting with system implementation, we run the generated test cases at design time with the help of a powerful simulator.

References

[1] J. Whittle, P. Sawyer, N. Bencomo, B. H. C. Cheng, and J.-M. Bruel, "Relax: a language to address uncertainty in self-adaptive systems requirement," *Requirements Engineering*, vol. 15, no. 2, pp. 177–196, 2010.

[2] Y. Zhuoqun, Z. Li, Z. Jin, and Y. Chen, "A systematic literature review of requirements modeling and analysis for self-adaptive systems," in *Requirements Engineering: Foundation for Software Quality*. Springer International Publishing, 2014, pp. 55–71.

[3] I. J. Jureta, A. Borgida, N. A. Ernst, and J. Mylopoulos, "The requirements problem for adaptive systems," *ACM Trans. Manage. Inf. Syst.*, vol. 5, no. 3, 2014.

[4] P. O. Antonino, M. Trapp, P. Barbosa, and L. Sousa, "The parameterized safety requirements templates," in *2015 IEEE/ACM 8th International Symposium on Software and Systems Traceability*. IEEE, 2015, pp. 29–35.

[5] D. Schneider and M. Trapp, "Conditional safety certification of open adaptive systems," *ACM Trans. Auton. Adapt. Syst.*, vol. 8, no. 2, 2013.

[6] H. J. Goldsby *et al.*, "Goal-based modeling of dynamically adaptive system requirements," in *15th Annual IEEE International Conference and Workshop on the Engineering of Computer Based Systems (ecbs 2008)*, 2008, pp. 36–45.

[7] S. J. Cunning and J. W. Rozenblit, "Automatic test case generation from requirements specifications for real-time embedded systems," in *IEEE SMC'99 Conference Proceedings. 1999 IEEE International Conference on Systems, Man, and Cybernetics (Cat. No.99CH37028)*, vol. 5, 1999, pp. 784–789 vol.5.

[8] ISO, "Road vehicles – Functional safety," 2011.

[9] T. Yue, S. Ali, and L. Briand, "Automated transition from use cases to uml state machines to support state-based testing," in *Modelling Foundations and Applications*. Springer Berlin Heidelberg, 2011, pp. 115–131.

[10] T. Yue, L. C. Briand, and Y. Labiche, "An automated approach to transform use cases into activity diagrams," in *Modelling Foundations and Applications*. Springer Berlin Heidelberg, 2010, pp. 337–353.

[11] G. Carvalho *et al.*, "Nat2testscr: Test case generation from natural language requirements based on scr specifications," *Science of Computer Programming*, vol. 95, pp. 275 – 297, 2014.

[12] C. Wang, F. Pastore, A. Goknil, L. Briand, and Z. Iqbal, "Automatic generation of system test cases from use case specifications," in *Proceedings of the 2015 International Symposium on Software Testing and Analysis*, ser. ISSTA 2015. Association for Computing Machinery, 2015, p. 385–396.

[13] F. IKS. (2019) Project SafeAdapt safe adaptive software for fully electric vehicles. [Online]. Available: http://www.safeadapt.eu

Towards an Adaptive Lévy Walk Using Artificial Endocrine Systems

Hugo Sardinha[†*], Mauro Dragone[*] and Patricia A. Vargas[†]

[*]School of Engineering and Physical Sciences
[†]School of Mathematical and Computer Sciences
Edinburgh Centre for Robotics, Heriot-Watt University
Email: {hs20, m.dragone, p.a.vargas}@hw.ac.uk

***Abstract*—Behavioural adaptation is often observed in foraging animals via coupling periods of localized search and long straight forward motions, a well-known strategy named *Lévy* Walk. In this paper we propose an adaptive *Lévy* Walk model to control an autonomous agent. The model is comprised of a Lévy-based controller modulated by an artificial endocrine system optimised through evolutionary techniques. This new approach enables the agent to control the transition between localized search and long relocation when exposed to external stimulus. The model is tested in exploration tasks where environments have resources clustered into patches. Further tests incorporated environments with different patch characteristics, such as patch size or resource distribution within patches. Our model has shown to outperform the benchmark approach in terms of search efficiency, highlighting the benefits of combining a Lévy Walk based controller with a biologically inspired strategy for adaptation.**

Keywords*–*Artificial Endocrine Systems; Adaptation; Lévy Walk; Biologically Inspired Algorithms; Foraging; Autonomous Agents.

I. Introduction

Foraging animals in nature have long been observed to exhibit adaptive search strategies in order to find beneficial environmental conditions, such as water or food sources [1]. To describe this motion of animals in the wild, computational ecologists firstly attempted to use Brownian models to fit empirical data, over large spatial scales and long temporal scales, with relative success [2]. However, these uncorrelated models of motion did not account for the tendency that animals show to continue moving in the same direction [3]. To better describe this behaviour, two major models have been employed, the Correlated Random Walk (CRW) [4] and the Lévy Walk (LW) [5]. As in Brownian motion, the CRW considers a Gaussian distribution of walk lengths, but unlike its predecessor, draws the re-orientation angle from a non-uniform distribution, centered around the current heading, thus generating a directional persistence. Conversely, the LW model considers an uniform distribution to draw new orientations but, unlike the previous models, draws length walks from a power law distribution instead. Since power laws are heavy tailed, this leads to occasional *long* walks, effectively coupling periods of localized random search with periods of ballistic relocation across the domain [6]. Figure 1 shows an example of trajectories generated by Browanian and Lévy motions. Consequently, several works used these models to develop robot controllers in foraging scenarios, corroborating theoretical results [7] [8]. In fact, LWs have become regarded as the optimal foraging strategy by subsequent works [9], particularly when points of interest, or resources, are sparse and randomly distributed [10]. However, different scenarios exist where such resources may not materialize in this manner; for example, in agricultural tasks such as the mapping of weeds in a field, where resources (weeds) tend to be clustered

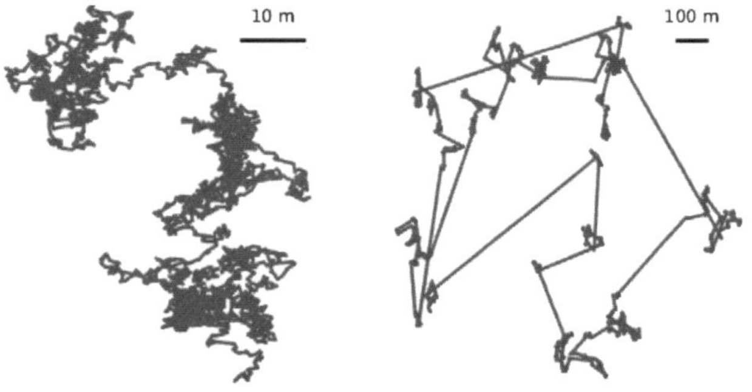

(a) Brownian Motion (b) Lévy Motion

Figure 1. Examples of trajectories generated by Brownian and Lévy motions

together in *patches* [11]. Danchin's [12] definition of a *patch* —"*an homogeneous resource containing area (or part of habitat) separated from others by areas containing little or no resources*"—is of crucial importance for the solution we here present. Since resources are not distributed uniformly, but exist in regions of locally high density there is an imposing drive for an autonomous agent to be able to adapt its behaviour in order to find them efficiently [13]. In fact, one could interpret LWs observed in nature as a consequence of an underlying adaption mechanism, switching to localized search when inside a patch, and switching back to ballistic motions once no new resources are found. To interpret adaptation in the context of either natural or artificial autonomous agents we recall Ashby's definition by which *a form of behaviour is considered* ***adaptive*** *if it maintains the essential variables within physiological limits* [14]. Such an ability to maintain an internal equilibrium, known as *homeostasis*, is ubiquitous in the animal kingdom [15], and depends strongly on the endocrine systems these animals developed over the course of their evolution [16]. These systems are responsible for the production of hormones that regulate a myriad of bodily functions such temperature, heart-rate, or the desire to hunt, and have also inspired researchers to synthesise Artificial Endocrine Systems (AES) for robot control [17]. Drawing inspiration from hormone-based regulation in natural systems, this work proposes an Endocrine-based Lévy Walk (ELW) model for foraging in patchy environments, by which the observable Lévy process is modulated by an underlying AES endowing the forager with the ability to change its behaviour in the presence of favourable environmental conditions.
The paper is divided as follows: Section II highlights the most relevant models for our work; Section III describes in detail our proposed model; Section IV presents our results and how they compare to the benchmark, and finally Section V summarizes our findings.

II. Random Walk Models

Random walks are a class of stochastic processes used to model empirical data. Existing processes arise from the intuitive idea of taking successive steps, each in random direction. Therefore, they consist of displacement events (i.e., walk lengths) interspersed by reorientation events [18]. This section explores the basic concepts of Lévy walks and, in particular, the biological fluctuation method proposed by Nurzaman *et al.* [19], which will be used as a benchmark for our model.

A. Lévy walks

Lévy Walks are a random walk process characterized by drawing each step length (l_s) from a power law distribution:

$$P(l_s) \sim l_s^{-\mu}, \quad 1 < \mu \leq 3 \tag{1}$$

where the parameter μ controls the shape of the distribution's tail, making ballistic relocations more (or less) common. Previous work has shown that for $\mu \geq 3$ the motion becomes Brownian, whereas when $\mu \to 1$, it becomes a series of straight motions with negligible local searches [6]. At each reorientation step, a new heading τ is generated such that $\tau \sim \mathcal{U}(-\pi, \pi)$. Some authors have proposed replacing an uniform turning angle, and instead use a correlated reorientation, which has shown to produce some improvement in search efficiency, particularly in environments where resources are sparsely distributed [3] [20]. In our work, the proposed adaptive model will be tested both with and without correlation, to study its effect on patchy environments. Correlation is achieved by drawing τ from a wrapped Cauchy distribution, whose probability density function, given in [20], is as follows:

$$C(\rho, \tau) = \frac{1}{2\pi} \frac{1 - \rho^2}{1 + \rho^2 - 2\rho \cos(\tau)} \tag{2}$$

where the parameter ρ represents how correlated the direction of consecutive walks is. On the one hand, when $\rho = 1$, correlation is complete and therefore the entire motion is a continuous straight line, while on the other hand, when $\rho = 0$, reorientations are in fact not correlated and τ assumes an uniform distribution.

B. Biological Fluctuation

An alternative to distribution-based random walk models was proposed by Nurzaman *et al*, where the transition between local searches and ballistic motions happens based on the concept of *yuragi* or biological fluctuation [19]. This mechanism is one by which certain bacteria are able to alter their gene expression (and therefore their behaviour) in the presence, or absence, of nutrients. A formal description of such behaviour is given by the attractor selection model, represented by the Langevin equation:

$$\dot{\mathbf{x}}(t) = -\nabla U(\mathbf{x}(t))A(t) + \epsilon(t) \tag{3}$$

where $\mathbf{x}$ and $-\nabla U(\mathbf{x}(t))$ are respectively the state and dynamics of the attractor model, $\epsilon(t)$ is a noise term, and $A(t)$ represents a variable *activity* which indicates how well the current state fits the environment, chosen in Nurzaman's work to be respectively:

$$U(\mathbf{x}(t)) = (\mathbf{x}(t) - h)^2 \tag{4}$$

$$A(t) = R \cdot A(t-1) + f(t) \tag{5}$$

where $f(t)$ represents the number of resources sensed, and R is a decaying coefficient with respect the previous value of A(t). The way the system changes from continuously straight motions to local search is modeled by a finite state machine with two states: *swimming* or *gliding*, which corresponds to a forward motion, and *tumbling* which corresponds to a reorientation. One can observe, from the depiction of in Figure 2, that the transition from the *gliding* state $\mathcal{G}$, to the *tumbling* state $\mathcal{T}$ depends on a probability P(t). On one hand, if P(t) is small the gliding motion continues and long relocations are expected, whereas on the other hand, for high values P(t) a *tumbling* step is more likely to occur, immediately followed by another *gliding* step leading to a local search behaviour.

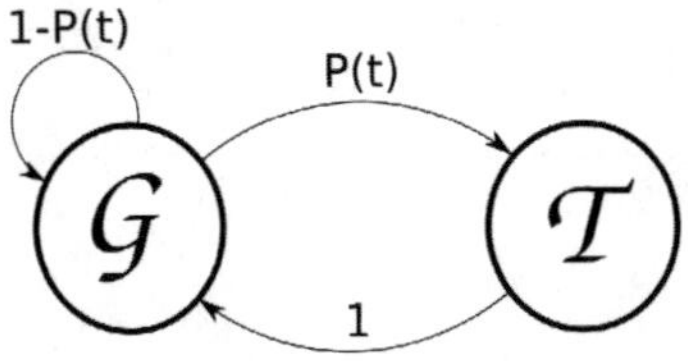

Figure 2. Finite state machine for behaviour

Based on the state of the system, the probability of transitioning between states is computed using (6). One can see, from (3), that when $A(t)$ increases, the first term becomes dominant and the value of the system's state $\mathbf{x}$ decreases towards attractor h (with $0 < h < 1$), therefore leading to a high probability transitioning from $\mathcal{G}$ to $\mathcal{T}$.

$$P(t) = e^{-\mathbf{x}(t)} \tag{6}$$

On the other hand, when $A(t)$ is very small, the dominant term of (3) is the noise term $\epsilon(t)$, which, due to being applied to $\dot{\mathbf{x}}$, gradually makes the state $\mathbf{x}$ diverge from the attractor leading to small value of $P(t)$, and therefore a continued gliding motion.

III. Endocrine-based Adaptive Lévy Walk

The underlying Lévy controller of most (if not all) artificial agents, or foragers, can be considered to have two stages: *Generation* and *Execution*. At the *Generation* stage a tuple (τ, l_s) is selected depending on μ and, if correlated, on ρ. This tuple is used in the *Execution* stage to move the agent in the direction τ while $l(t) < l_s$, where $l(t)$ is the distance travelled since the beginning of the current walk. Our work proposes that, in order to achieve adaptation, both μ and l_s need to change dynamically according to sensory input. Firstly, as the forager enters a patch it is straightforward to envision that μ should increase, so that the behaviour converges to a local search. However, only changing the value of μ will have little or no effect if the current step is not completed within the patch in time for another tuple (τ, l_s) to be generated. In order to harness this intuition we introduce a *desire* to interrupt the current walk, which will translate to a gradual decrease of l_s for the ongoing step. The specific AES proposed for Lévy walk adaption is built upon the concepts put forward by Wilson *et al.* [21] and Stradner *et al.* [22], where the level of a hormone H at time t can be modelled by the following:

$$H(t) = c_0 + c_1 H(t-1) + c_2 S(t) \tag{7}$$

where c_0, c_1, c_2 are constant coefficients, $H(t-1)$ represents the previous hormone level and $S(t)$ is the stimulus received from sensory input. The first term, c_o, represents a base increment simulating a default and constant hormone production, the second term $c_1 H(t-1)$ acts as decay over time, and $c_2 S(t)$ represents the contribution from the sensory stimulus to the overall level of $H(t)$. Wilson [21] highlights that one could calculate the settling point of $H(t)$, when no stimulus is received, as $H_s = c_0/(1-c_1)$. Using (7) we model the variation of μ as the hormone level itself and define:

$$\mu(t) = a_0 + a_1 \mu(t-1) + a_2 S_\mu(t) \tag{8}$$

where $S_\mu(t)$ assumes a binary value depending on the variation of number of resources sensed according to (9). Therefore, as the forager enters a patch of resources, μ tends to increase, while if there are no new resources $\mu(t) \rightarrow \mu_s = a_0/(1-a_1)$.

$$S_\mu(t) = \begin{cases} 1, & \Delta f(t) > 0 \\ 0, & \Delta f(t) \leq 0 \end{cases} \tag{9}$$

Modelling the aforementioned *desire* to interrupt the current walk is done in a similar fashion, by considering the hormone level β defined as:

$$\beta(t) = b_1 \beta(t-1) + b_2 S_\beta(t) \tag{10}$$

Note that there is no b_0 term, allowing in fact the value of $\beta(t)$ to decrease to zero. The stimulus function for β is given in (11), where if $f(t)$ is increasing, there is no stimulus to the *desire* to interrupt the current walk since this means the current walk step is providing a good strategy to find resources. Conversely, if the $f(t)$ is decreasing this *desire* increases, and does so proportionally to the normalized value of $\mu(t)$ between its settling point (μ_s) and its maximum value ($\bar{\mu} = 3$), creating an interdependence of these two artificial hormone quantities as it also the case in several natural systems [16].

$$S_\beta(t) = \begin{cases} 0, & \Delta f(t) \geq 0 \\ \dfrac{\bar{\mu} - \mu(t)}{\bar{\mu} - \mu_s}, & \Delta f(t) < 0 \end{cases} \tag{11}$$

As one can see, when $\mu(t) \rightarrow \mu_s$ then the stimulus $S_\beta \rightarrow 1$ and when $\mu(t) \rightarrow \bar{\mu}$ $S_\beta \rightarrow 0$. In practical terms this means that if the forager is finding fewer resources but the its $\mu(t)$ value is large, it is already performing a local search and the *desire* to interrupt that walk is irrelevant since it would already be a local step. On the other hand, if $\mu(t)$ is small in the presence of a varying number of resources then the *desire* is relevant and it is stronger as $\mu(t)$ is further from $\bar{\mu}$. Updating the target step length is, in our model simply done by computing (12).

$$l_s = l_s\Big(1 - \beta(t)\Big) \tag{12}$$

In summary, we can consider our endocrine-based model, depicted in Figure 3, to have three main components, namely:

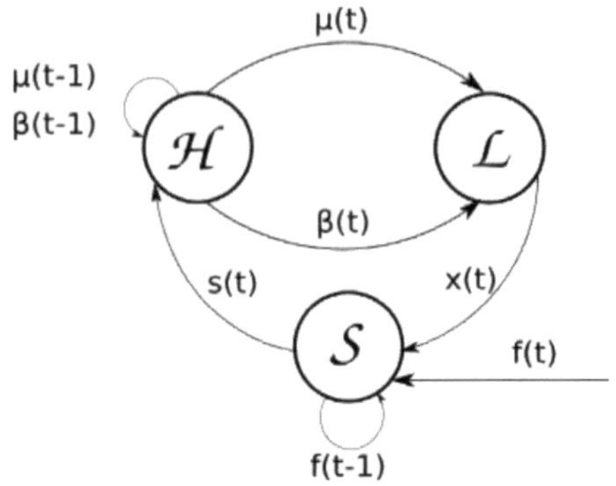

Figure 3. Endocrine-based Lévy Walk model.

the Hormone production module ($\mathcal{H}$) that updates the values of $\mu(t)$ and $\beta(t)$; the Lévy controller ($\mathcal{L}$) which controls the pose of the forager, generates l_s depending on μ and updates it depending on β; and finally the sensory input module, $\mathcal{S}$, which given the new pose $x(t)$ and the previously sensed resources updates the stimulus functions.

IV. Experiments & Results

The performance of our proposed model is assessed by a series of experiments in different environments. The first of which is the one chosen by Nurzaman et al, (Environment I) and comprises an arena of 1000x1000m where 10 patches are randomly distributed. These patches are 10x10m and contain 100 rewards each, also uniformly distributed. As in Nurzaman's work, we consider an agent whose field of view is 2x2m travelling at a speed of 1m/s over 10000s. Furthermore we expand testing to environments where patches are 50x50 (Environment II) and 100x100 (Environment III) maintaining reward density, and use these three environments to test the influence of correlation ρ in our model. Figure 4 depicts these environments. To choose the parameters for our model, namely the coefficients in (8) and (10), we implemented a Real-Coded Genetic Algorithm (RCGA) where each solution is represented by a generic chromosome of the type:

$$\mu_s \quad a_1 \quad a_2 \quad b_1 \quad b_2 \quad \rho$$

Choosing μ_s as a decision variable makes for a more straightforward analysis of the solution, since μ_s represents the settling point for μ, and a_0 can be obtained from $\mu_s = a_0/(1-a_1)$. To optimize the model without correlation, ρ is set to 0 and dropped from the chromosome. Parameters are evolved to maximize search efficiency defined in (13), where P is the total number of rewards found and D the total distance travelled. Individuals for crossover are selected by tournament and an arithmetic crossover operator is used.

$$\eta = P/D \tag{13}$$

Mutation is done by selecting a random allele and changing its value randomly between its predefined limits, i.e., $\mu_s \in (1,3]$ and $a_1,\ a_2,\ b_1,\ b_2\ ,\rho \in [0,1]$. The RCGA runs over 250 generations with a randomly initialized population of 100 and a 5% elitism. Results of the optimization process are shown in Table I, with and without correlation. The first observation we can make is that, as the size of patches increases from environment I to III, the value of μ_s decreases. In fact, this was an expected result, since in an environment where patches

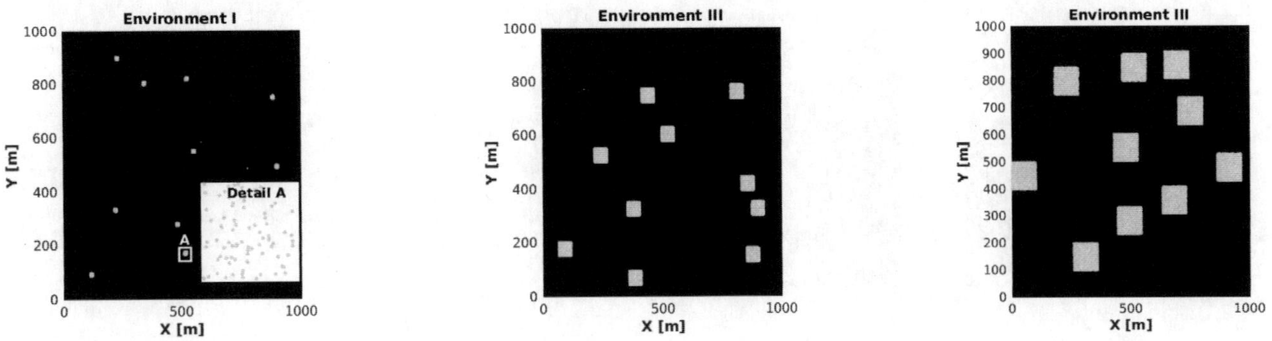

Figure 4. Environments with uniformly distributed rewards.

TABLE I. PARAMETERS OPTIMIZED FOR ENVRIONMENTS I,II AND III.

Environment	μ_s	a_1	a_2	b_1	b_2	ρ
I	2.344	0.196	0.179	0.995	0.235	—
	2.422	0.216	0.599	0.962	0.424	0.073
II	1.625	0.503	0.254	0.976	0.185	—
	1.809	0.507	0.354	0.917	0.563	0.029
III	1.129	0.841	0.619	0.918	0.191	—
	1.428	0.758	0.681	0.904	0.153	0.077

TABLE II. COMPARISON BETWEEN ELW AND CELW OVER 100 RUNS.

Search Behaviour	Efficiency (10^{-2})	Rewards Found (10^{2})	Patches Found
ELW-I	0.42±0.12	4.18±1.13	7.48±1.56
CELW-I	0.41±0.15	3.98±1.22	7.04±1.73
ELW-II	15.02±2.14	126.50±11.32	9.58±0.58
CELW-II	11.70±1.70	104.24±13.39	9.66±0.55
ELW-III	39.93±4.78	372.39±42.00	9.95±0.21
CELW-III	36.71±3.48	351.60±31.93	9.98±0.14

TABLE III. P-VALUE FOR THE 2-SAMPLE KOLMOGOROV-SMIRNOV TEST, FOR ALL METRICS BETWEEN ELW AND CELW BEHAVIOURS.

Search Behaviours	Efficiency	Rewards Found	Patches Found
ELW-I / CELW-I	0.443	0.432	0.893
ELW-II / CELW-II	$\ll$0.01	$\ll$0.01	0.987
ELW-III / CELW-III	$\ll$0.01	$\ll$0.01	0.998

are of considerable size, a strategy that favours more frequent ballistic motions, will tend find new rewards more efficiently. On the other hand, in an environment where patches are very small, more frequent changes of direction are necessary to find these rewards, and therefore the μ_s is higher. We also observe that parameter a_1 increases with the increasing size of patches. Recalling (8), the higher a_1 becomes the slower is the decay of $\mu(t)$. An increasing value a_1 with patch size shows that it is beneficial to not let the value of $\mu(t)$ decay too abruptly, sustaining more localized search for a longer period. Concurrently a_2, the weight of the stimulus to the value of $\mu(t)$, also increases. Since μ_s is smaller for such environments, the change of $\mu(t)$ to a point that translates into local search needs to occur at a higher rate, and thus the stimulus has a bigger weight. As for the coefficients that modulate β, we see that b_1 always maintains a high value, but decreases only slightly with increasing patch size, showing that a slow decay of the *desire* to interrupt the current walk is always desirable regardless of the size of patches. As for the stimulus to this *desire*, i.e., the b_2 parameter, has a higher value when patches are smaller. Naturally, given the smaller size of patches, the weight of the stimulus must be stronger so that the current walk is interrupted sooner. Perhaps the more interesting result is the one concerning the correlation ρ. These results show that ρ always converges to very small values, hinting that, in patchy environments, directional correlation between steps might not play a significant role. To confirm this hypothesis we show in Table II the average values for *Efficiency*, number of *Rewards Found* and number of *Patches Found*, for both the Endocrine-based Lévy Walk (ELW) and its correlated version (CELW). These results show that, in fact, even a negligible correlation can have an apparent negative impact on the overall performance of the system, since the ELW tends to outperform its correlated counterpart for most metrics in all environments. To further investigate the statistical difference between models, we calculate the p-value for the 2-sample Kolmogorov-Smirnov (KS) goodness-of-fit hypothesis test. For the 2-sample KS test, the null hypothesis is that *"two data vectors belong to the same continuous distribution"* and therefore, the hypothesis is rejected, at the 99% confidence level, if the p-value < 0.01. Table III summarizes the p-values between each uncorrelated and respective correlated model, for each different metric. These results show that for the models optimized for Environment I, there is no statistical difference in results for any of the metrics, confirming that including correlation, for small patch environments, does not have any impact on the system's performance. However, for Environments II and III the respective optimized models are in fact statistically different for both the *Efficiency* and *Rewards Found*. In these particular cases it shows that including correlation actually has a detrimental effect to the system's performance, since metrics' values shown in Table II are higher for the ELW. Having established that correlation either does not affect or worsens the performance of the system, the next set of results will only compare the ELW and the Yuragi approaches. To also test the flexibility of both approaches, to scenarios where rewards within patches are distributed differently we further extend our analysis to Environments IV and V (Figure 5) where rewards within patches have Gaussian distributions.

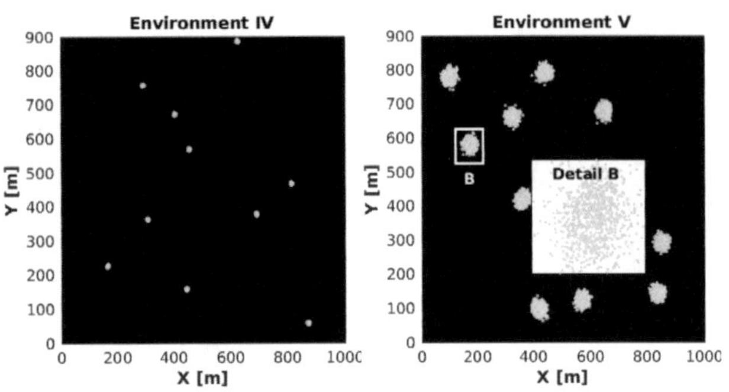

Figure 5. Environments with Gaussian distributed rewards.

TABLE IV. PARAMETERS OPTIMIZED FOR ENVIRONMENTS IV AND V

Environment	μ_s	a_1	a_2	b_1	b_2
IV	1.659	0.152	0.511	0.940	0.499
V	1.445	0.489	0.495	0.980	0.194

The parameters of our model for these environments were also obtained via the aforementioned RCGA, and are shown in Table IV. For a fair comparison with the Yuragi model, we conduct the same sensitivity analysis as Nurzaman *et al.* to select the value of R in (5), which maximizes *efficiency*. These results are summarized in Table V, where we include the values reported by Nurzaman, in brackets, to validate our own implementation. In the following analysis, we refer to Yuragi A/B or C depending on which R is best suited for a particular environment. Table V shows that Yuragi-A is best suited for Environments II, IV and IV, and Yuragi-B for Environments I and III. We also note that the values obtained with our Yuragi implementation yield very close results to those reported by Nurzaman, validating our implementation for the subsequent analysis. Finally, the comparison between the ELW and Yuragi approaches is presented in Table VI. This table compares the results obtained with the optimized ELW model for each particular environment (ELW-I, ELW-II, etc.) with the corresponding Yuragi model chosen from the sensitivity analysis in Table V. Highlighted values for each metric show that the ELW always yields best performance both across the different metrics and different environments. However, one could still argue that our model requires prior knowledge in order to select optimal parameters for the task. To address this question, we perform a cross-testing analysis and run each ELW model (ELW-I, ELW-II, etc.) in every environment, and compare those results, both with the optimal results for such environment, and with those achieved with the Yuragi approach. This comparison is made in Table VII, where the optimal efficiency values for each environment are highlighted in green and the best Yuragi approach for each environment is highlighted in red. Furthermore, we also highlight the performance obtained with ELW-II and ELW-IV, since these are able to consistently outperform the best Yuragi solution, even in those environments for which the ELW was not specifically optimized. The existence of sets of ELW parameters that lead to a higher performance, in comparison to the Yuragi approach, and regardless of the environment is an important evidence of the superiority of the

TABLE V. SENSITIVITY ANALYSIS ON EFFICIENCY WITH VARYING R

Model	R	Env I	Env II	Env III	Env IV	Env V
A	0.99	0.26±0.11 (0.23±0.11)	8.98±2.38	19.74±3.51	0.35±0.13	3.93±0.99
B	0.90	0.29±0.10 (0.28±0.11)	7.41±1.98	24.07±4.48	0.29±0.11	3.19±0.89
C	0.50	0.21±0.09 (0.17±0.06)	6.72±1.61	20.70±4.69	0.24±0.10	2.49±0.79

TABLE VI. METRIC COMPARISON BETWEEN YURAGI AND ELW

Search behaviour	Efficiency (10^{-2})	Rewards Found (10^{2})	Patches Found
ELW-I	**0.42±0.12**	**4.18±1.13**	**7.48±1.56**
Yuragi-B	0.29±0.10	2.61±1.01	5.20±1.53
ELW-II	**15.02±2.14**	**126.50±11.32**	**9.58±0.58**
Yuragi-A	8.98±2.38	64.40±14.50	6.03±1.30
ELW-III	**39.93±4.78**	**372.39±42.00**	**9.95±0.21**
Yuragi-B	24.07±4.48	180.59±29.03	6.07±1.48
ELW IV	**0.39±0.01**	**3.83±0.97**	**6.89±0.97**
Yuragi-A	0.35±0.13	3.03±1.12	4.45±1.37
ELW V	**6.22±0.85**	**56.71±7.13**	**9.73±0.48**
Yuragi-A	3.93±0.99	29.91±6.67	6.19±1.41

ELW model, and its inherent increased adaptation ability. It is also interesting to point out that the performance, with respect to every metric, of ELW-II and ELW-IV in environments I,III and V is considerably closer to the optimal value, than to the Yuragi approach, often lying within the standard deviation of the former. This is yet another evidence that improvement in performance can be achieved mostly due to the model itself and that RCGA optimization is mostly useful in fine-tuning.

V. CONCLUSION AND FUTURE WORK

This work proposes an Endocrine-based Lévy Walk (ELW) model for autonomous agents, that modulates the parameters of a Lévy controller for foraging in patchy environments. Firstly, we analysed the hypothesis that angular correlation between steps can benefit the search efficiency, and have shown that in fact, it either does not have any statistical impact on results, or slightly decreases the efficiency of the model in environments with larger patches. Secondly, we compared our model with a one based on biological fluctuation, across environments where rewards were either uniformly or normally distributed within patches. Both models were compared using three different metrics: *Efficiency*, *Rewards Found* and *Patches Found*. Results show that ELW outperforms the benchmark model in all scenarios. Future work will look into the gap in performance by studying the difference in trajectories, as well as a heatmap analysis of the probability density of visited areas within the environment, and the temporal evolution of hormone levels $\mu(t)$ and $\beta(t)$. We further aim to conduct experiments using real and simulated mobile robots to test how suitable these controllers are to swarm robotics and the control of collective behaviours [23]. We envision that these behaviours could contribute to tackling real-world applications, both in agricultural and environmental domains, such as weed mapping or forest fire prevention, to name a few.

TABLE VII. CROSS-TESTING OF ELW PARAMETERS ACROSS ENVIRONMENTS.

Search Behaviour	Metric	Environment I	Environment II	Environment III	Environment IV	Environment V
ELW-I	Efficiency (10^{-2})	0.42±0.12	10.09±1.74	20.64±2.63	0.37±0.15	4.40±0.81
	Rewards Found (10^{2})	4.18±1.13	72.70±9.97	124.68±12.17	3.59±1.30	34.00±5.42
	Patches Found	7.48±1.56	6.01±1.04	3.91±1.73	5.18±1.62	6.83±1.17
ELW-II	Efficiency (10^{-2})	0.40±0.10	15.02±2.14	38.81±3.74	0.38±0.11	6.17±0.92
	Rewards Found (10^{2})	3.92±0.99	126.50±11.32	266.51±18.25	3.73±1.05	55.92±7.74
	Patches Found	7.27±1.43	9.58±0.21	8.59±1.08	7.08±1.38	9.80±0.47
ELW-III	Efficiency (10^{-2})	0.24±0.07	9.98±1.73	39.93±4.78	0.21±0.07	3.82±0.64
	Rewards Found (10^{2})	2.36±0.69	98.12±16.84	372.39±42.00	2.18±0.78	37.82±6.35
	Patches Found	7.56±1.32	9.85±1.03	9.95±0.21	7.10±1.57	9.93±0.32
ELW-IV	Efficiency (10^{-2}	0.41±0.10	12.92±2.02	38.22±3.46	0.39±0.01	5.20±0.79
	Rewards Found (10^{2})	4.16±0.95	113.35±15.87	276.95±18.67	3.83±0.97	48.12±6.85
	Patches Found	7.32±1.29	9.87±0.37	9.49±0.67	6.89±1.29	9.85±0.36
ELW-V	Efficiency (10^{-2}	0.36±0.11	15.01±1.87	39.01±3.61	0.35±0.11	6.21±0.85
	Rewards Found (10^{2})	3.60±1.12	127.10±13.51	274.55±17.48	3.56±1.11	56.71±7.13
	Patches Found	6.98±1.50	9.66±0.55	8.87±0.87	7.12±1.45	9.73±0.46
Yuragi-A	Efficiency (10^{-2})	0.26±0.11	8.98±2.38	19.74±3.51	0.35±0.13	3.93±0.99
	Rewards Found (10^{2})	2.01±1.01	64.40±14.51	121.61±16.64	3.03±1.12	29.91±6.67
	Patches Found	4.81±1.16	6.03±1.31	3.86±1.4	4.45±1.37	6.19±1.41
Yuragi-B	Efficiency (10^{-2})	0.29±0.10	7.41±1.98	24.07±4.48	0.29±0.11	3.19±0.89
	Rewards Found (10^{2})	2.61±1.01	61.80±15.68	180.59±29.03	2.58±0.95	27.17±7.29
	Patches Found	5.20±1.53	7.19±1.41	6.07±1.48	4.85±1.45	7.43±1.65

REFERENCES

[1] A. M. Reynolds and C. J. Rhodes, "The lévy flight paradigm: random search patterns and mechanisms," Ecology, vol. 90, no. 4, 2009, pp. 877–887.

[2] H. C. Berg, Random walks in biology. Princeton University Press, 93.

[3] F. Bartumeus, M. G. E. da Luz, G. M. Viswanathan, and J. Catalan, "Animal search strategies: a quantitative random-walk analysis," Ecology, vol. 86, no. 11, 2005, pp. 3078–3087.

[4] P. Bovet and S. Benhamou, "Spatial analysis of animals' movements using a correlated random walk model," Journal of theoretical biology, vol. 131, no. 4, 1988, pp. 419–433.

[5] G. Viswanathan et al., "Lévy flights in random searches," Physica A: Statistical Mechanics and its Applications, vol. 282, no. 1-2, 2000, pp. 1–12.

[6] O. Bénichou, C. Loverdo, M. Moreau, and R. Voituriez, "Intermittent search strategies," Reviews of Modern Physics, vol. 83, no. 1, 2011, pp. 82–127.

[7] G. M. Fricke, F. Asperti-Boursin, J. Hecker, J. Cannon, and M. Moses, "From microbiology to microcontrollers: Robot search patterns inspired by t cell movement," in Artificial Life Conference Proceedings 13. MIT Press, 2013, pp. 1009–1016.

[8] V. Fioriti, F. Fratichini, S. Chiesa, and C. Moriconi, "Levy foraging in a dynamic environment–extending the levy search," International Journal of Advanced Robotic Systems, vol. 12, no. 7, 2015, pp. 98–110.

[9] M. E. Wosniack, M. C. Santos, E. P. Raposo, G. M. Viswanathan, and M. G. da Luz, "The evolutionary origins of lévy walk foraging," PLoS computational biology, vol. 13, no. 10, 2017, pp. 1–31.

[10] V. K. Jandhyala and S. B. Fotopoulos, "Applications of random search methods to foraging in ecological environments and other natural phenomena–a review," Environmetrics, vol. 29, no. 5-6, 2018, pp. 1–12.

[11] F. Castaldi, F. Pelosi, S. Pascucci, and R. Casa, "Assessing the potential of images from unmanned aerial vehicles (uav) to support herbicide patch spraying in maize," Precision Agriculture, vol. 18, no. 1, 2017, pp. 76–94.

[12] E. Danchin, L.-A. Giraldeau, and F. Cézilly, Behavioural ecology, 2008.

[13] J. Wawerla and R. T. Vaughan, "Robot task switching under diminishing returns," in IEEE/RSJ ICIRS, 2009, pp. 5033–5038.

[14] W. Ashby, Design for a brain: The origin of adaptive behaviour. Springer Science & Business Media, 2013.

[15] P. L. deFur, "Use and role of invertebrate models in endocrine disruptor research and testing," ILAR journal, vol. 45, no. 4, 2004, pp. 484–493.

[16] P. A. Vargas, R. C. Moioli, F. J. Von Zuben, and P. Husbands, "Homeostasis and evolution together dealing with novelties and managing disruptions," Int. J. Intel. Comp. and Cyb., 2009, pp. 435–454.

[17] P. Vargas et al., "Artificial homeostatic system: a novel approach," in ECAL. Springer, 2005, pp. 754–764.

[18] F. Bartumeus, "Lévy processes in animal movement: an evolutionary hypothesis," Fractals, vol. 15, no. 02, 2007, pp. 151–162.

[19] S. G. Nurzaman et al., "An adaptive switching behavior between levy and brownian random search in a mobile robot based on biological fluctuation," in 2010 IEEE/RSJ International Conference on Intelligent Robots and Systems. IEEE, 2010, pp. 1927–1934.

[20] C. Dimidov, G. Oriolo, and V. Trianni, "Random walks in swarm robotics: an experiment with kilobots," in International Conference on Swarm Intelligence. Springer, 2016, pp. 185–196.

[21] J. Wilson, J. Timmis, and A. Tyrrell, "A hormone arbitration system for energy efficient foraging in robot swarms," in Annual Conference Towards Autonomous Robotic Systems. Springer, 2018, pp. 305–316.

[22] J. Stradner, H. Hamann, T. Schmickl, and K. Crailsheim, "Analysis and implementation of an artificial homeostatic hormone system: A first case study in robotic hardware," in IEEE/RSJ ICIRS, 2009, pp. 595–600.

[23] V. Trianni, E. Tuci, C. Ampatzis, and M. Dorigo, "Evolutionary swarm robotics: A theoretical and methodological itinerary from individual neurocontrollers to collective behaviors," The Horizons of Evolutionary Robotics, 2014, pp. 153–178.

Ant Colony Optimization for an Adaptive Transportation System: A New Termination Condition Definition Using an Environment Based Approach

1st Pierre Romet
CIAD (UMR 7533)
UTBM
Belfort, France
pierre.romet@utbm.fr

2nd Franck Gechter
CIAD (UMR 7533) and MOSEL LORIA UMR CNRS 7503
UTBM and Universite de Lorrain
Belfort and Vandoeuvre, France,
franck.gechter@utbm.fr

3rd El-Hassane Aglzim
ISAT-DRIVE
Univ. Bourgogne Franche-Comte
Nevers, France
el-hassane.aglzim@u-bourgogne.fr

4th Olivier Grunder
NIT-O2S
Univ. Bourgogne Franche-Comte
Belfort, France
olivier.grunder@utbm.fr

5th Sidi-Mohammed Senouci
ISAT-DRIVE
Univ. Bourgogne Franche-Comte
Nevers, France
sidi-mohammed.senouci@u-bourgogne.fr

***Abstract*—The delivery of the packages following the online purchase of goods trough web giants platforms is growing faster each years. To meet the demand of the growing quantity of packages and their delivery, the algorithm used to resolve the Vehicle Routing Problem (VRP) has to be efficient and adaptive. The algorithms used to solve the VRP algorithm still provide better turn, but do not deal with situation adaptation at delivery point. Seeking to fit into this adaptive feature, the commitment of this paper is to lay solid groundwork for the development of an adaptive transportation system. Exploring various strategies taking care of the possibilities of delivery at delivery point, our objective is to define a strategy minimizing the time and the distance travelled by packages and maximizing the satisfaction of the customers.**

***Index Terms*—Ant Colony convergence; Adaptive delivery**

I. Introduction

The research presented in this paper is part of the development of a new urban and rural freight transportation system. Each year, the amount of packages bought on web market places grows, to the detriment of local urban and rural shopkeepers. Our freight transportation system aims to revitalize urban and rural areas by providing to the customer the possibility to buy online goods from local shops and restaurants and to benefit from delivering services similar to those proposed by traditional web market places. Moreover, our project is intended to be more than a classical transportation system. Seeking to revitalize the urban area and to draw the attention of as many customers as possible, the delivery of goods has to be as close as possible to customers in city center and rural area. The project try to provide adaptive feature to the delivery services, to consider the customer as the most important part of the system.This delivery transportation system is described in detail in [3]. The main principle of this system is based on small electrical vehicles able to follow the buses or the tramways of the already existing public transportation system using platoon control algorithm. As soon as one of these vehicles arrives to a stop near a delivery target, it can park near the bus stop and then wait for the customer. The main interest of this system is to have a potential ability to adapt to the load (the number of goods to be delivered) and to the dynamical constraints of the customers. Thus, to implement this kind of freight transportation system, we will need to adopt and implement applications of Vehicle Routing Problem. First of all, we need to define a good base structure on which to implement our transportation system. Our choice focused on the Ant Colony to performed on the VRP algorithm, thanks to its intrinsic ability of adaptation to the dynamic update of the graph. This ability provides us the capacity to include real time adaptation to the demand of delivery and pickup of packages. However, wishing to develop an adaptive freight transportation system, the ant colony algorithm needs to be self-adaptive convergent. In this context, the ant colony algorithm defined in [1] does not fit directly in this self-adaptive convergent feature. Thus, the first part of our work is to identify if the self-convergence of the ant colony algorithm can be characterized by an environment based approach. This research work is developed in the first Section II of this paper. Then, after having defined the self-adaptive convergent property of the ant colony algorithm, the next step is to focus on the implementation of the VRP application to our freight transportation system. Basing our application on the VRP, a way to bring an adaptive feature to it is to find one. To do so, we include in the VRP application different strategies to adapt the possibility of delivery at city point according to the adaptive possibility of customers to be present to pickup the package(s). Thus, those strategies are not limited to deliver or not a package(s) according to the presence of the customer, it must provide the customer the possibility to redefine his point of delivery and its time of delivery during the same turn of the vehicle. According to this fact, the delivery turn, defined by the VRP application has to self-adapt its path to deliver package(s). This research work is defined in Section III of this paper.

The paper is structured as follows: Section II provides the overview of the basics of ant colony optimization and concludes with the environment based approach to define the self-adaptive convergent property of the algorithm. Section III gives an overview of the Vehicle Routing Problem approach and develops self-adaptive reconfiguration to adapt its turn to the availability of the customer. Finally, we will present our experimentation, results and analyses in Section IV and then Section V concludes the research conducted in this paper.

II. Ant Colony Algorithm Convergence

This section provides an overview of the Ant colony Algorithm before introducing the work on the convergence criterion of this algorithm.

A. Ant colony for operational research

This section is intended as a review of the main features of the ant colony optimization algorithm, that Dorigo synthesized in [6]. To do this, we will support our demonstration by the determination of the shortest path between two points; a combinatory optimization problem already widely covered in the specific literature. For a set of "n" cities, a shorter path search allows to determine the smallest distance between two cities, passing through each of them once. The shorter path search is based on the implementation of a graph $G = (N, L)$, with N all cities and L all paths connecting cities. Each arc $li \in L$ having a d_{ij} value that characterizes the distance between two cities i and j. Optimization by ant colony is the study of how work guides the worker [4]. Ant agents use pheromones that guide them on the paths with the shortest distance between the anthill and the food source. This solution is built by a succession of turns in which an agent travels guided by a pheromone trace and a search heuristic. Then, when all ant agents have finished their turn, they come back to the anthill by updating their pheromone trace. Ant agents thus seek a better solution within the paths that have the highest pheromone rate.

1) Iteration construction: When the algorithm is initialized, all ants (the number of ants being equal to the number of cities in the [5] graph) are dropped to the common starting point. Then, each ant agent applies a stochastic search, called the "random choice rule," to determine which to which city it will move on thereafter. Taking k agent ants, in a city i, the next city will be chosen with the probability defined below.

$$P_{ij}^{k}(t) = \begin{cases} \frac{[\tau_{ij}(t)]^{\alpha}.[\eta_{ij}(t)]^{\beta}}{\sum\limits_{r \in N_j^k} [\tau_{ir}(t)]^{\alpha}.[\eta_{ir}(t)]^{\beta}} & if \quad j \in N_i^k \\ 0 & otherwise \end{cases} \quad (1)$$

With $n_{ij} = \frac{1}{d_{ij}}$ a heuristic value, $T_{ij}(t)$ the value of the pheromone trace, with t the iteration counter. Side and Side parameters determine the influence of pheromone trace and the heuristic value. Finally N_{ik} represents the direct neighborhood of the ant agent k, being in city i.

2) Pheromones update : Once all the ants have completed an exploration, they must return to their starting town and will at the same time update the pheromones rate of the paths forming their route during the last round. The pheromones are updated using the following equation:

$$\tau_{ij}(t+1) = [(1-\rho) * \tau_{ij}(t) + \sum_{k=1}^{m} \Delta\tau_{ij}^{k}(t)] \quad (2)$$

With $p(0 < p <= 1)$ evaporation rate, $\Delta\tau_{ij}^{k}$ the amount of pheromones that the agent k repents on the path visited, as follows:

$$\Delta\tau_{ij}^{k}(t) = \begin{cases} \frac{1}{f(S^k)} \text{if the edge belong to } S^k \\ \text{0 otherwise} \end{cases} \quad (3)$$

where $f(S^k)$ is the size of the path constructed by the ant k agent, for the current iteration.

TABLE I. PROCEDURE ACO ALGORITHM

```
Procedure ACO algorithm
  set parameters, initialize pheromone trails
  while (termination condition not met) do
    construct ants solutions
    update pheromones
  end
end
```

The pheromones act as a strengthening position, encouraging other ants to use an already marked path, amplifying the positive reinforcement effect as more and more ants go along the path.

3) Termination condition: Since the development of optimization algorithms by ant colony, the efforts made through various research projects have focused on the development of iteration construction and pheromone updating. However, very few have sought to develop new approaches on how to end algorithms. In addition, it is legitimate to ask which methods to put in place, since the number of optimal solutions available is infinite.

B. State of the art of termination criteria

By the stochastic property of ant colony algorithms, the emergence of a solution for a given problem is guaranteed, with a probability of reaching 1, for an infinite time of exploration. Such application is not possible, therefore it is necessary to agree on the number of iterations to end ACO, to enable the emergence of an optimal result that best characterizes the exploited problem. The number of iterations being the key, the higher the iteration, the better the quality of the solution. However, arbitrarily setting a very high number of iterations is very inefficient in terms of resources, whether they are energy and/or computational. Therefore, it appears to be possible to use as little iteration as possible to determine the best solution. In addition, this search by means economy is adequate within this meta-heuristics, as illustrated by [7] through the "Stalling effect", which they define as the following: "the problem of stalling effect in fitness function is related to the non improvement of the fitness value during the evolutionary process". Since this phenomenon has been observed through many algorithm run, it appears that a better solution emerges at a given point in the research. However, the latter tends to stagnate before the simulation stops, without a better solution emerging again.

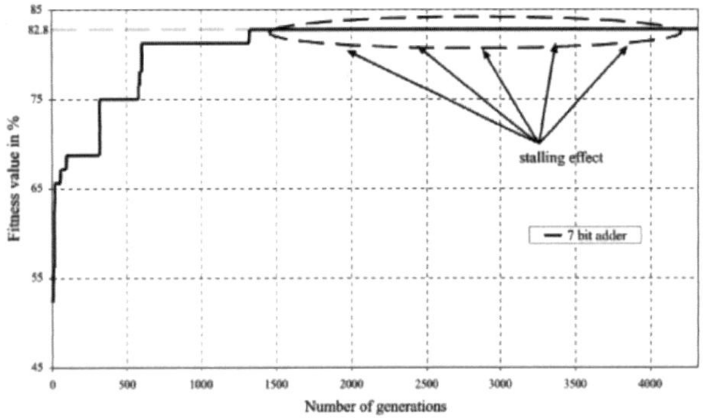

Fig. 1: Stalling effect

The optimization of the resources of ACO is entirely based on the way in which the termination criteria will be set. There are various methods in the scientific literature that we will now explain. Currently one of the most common approaches is to use an arbitrarily set termination criteria. This results in a high number of iterations, but above all,they are defined randomly. When the specified number of iterations is reached by the algorithm, the algorithm will return the best solution found [13]. Another, but similar, approach is to stop the iteration of the algorithm after it has exceeded a pre-defined execution time, always randomly [10]. In the end, these two approaches, although easy to put in place, reveal a complete decorrelation between the agents (ants) and their environment, cutting them off from the influence of the latter. In addition, they translate in a highly resource-intensive implementation, which is antinomic with the principle of optimization sought through meta-heuristics. Statistical approaches using evolutionary factors, are then used to evaluate the termination criteria of the algorithm to terminate its execution. Nicolas et al. [9] have developed an iterative solution that involves launching their ant colony algorithm several times conditioned by a minimum number of iterations to reach. Then they determine a percentage of success by comparing the different solutions obtained according to the parameters of each execution. Zhaojun et al. [14] propose a solution characterizing the evolution of the system using three factors. The first two assess whether the termination criteria is met and the last one is also an assessment factor based on the convergence of path with pheromone around the shortest path. In addition to the above methods based on the use of an arbitrarily fixed termination criteria, solutions based on decision trees were also developed. Kate et al. [2] have developed a decision tree that determines the best heuristics to be implemented to solve the problem facing the latter. Kate et al. [12], have also worked on the ontology engine allowing to choose the best stop condition, allowing to optimize the termination criteria. Moreover, by exploring the literature to find advanced methodologies for our problem, a physics-centered solution was found. This solution proposes to implement the mechanics of the point through the observation of position curves, speed and acceleration. The study of these curves is supposed to help in the decision-making process to stop the execution of the algorithm [8]. To finish this review of various approaches available in the literature, we will now discuss the search for the local minimum. The solution provided by [11], proposes to stop this search for a solution when a better solution is found, coupled with an arbitrary stop criteria in case the algorithm does not converge. However, nothing is defined as to how a better solution is evaluated, or even how it is correlated with the environment in which the research is conducted. Finally, the approach that we propose in this article is also based on this idea of local minimum exploration, like the solution of Silvia et al. [11]. However, unlike the latter, we strive to correlate the depth of exploration of the local minimum with the environment in which our agents operate. By doing so, we seek dynamic behavior for the algorithm, giving it an adaptation to its environment to help it make decisions about its termination criteria. By doing so, we are trying to demonstrate that a good knowledge of the studied environment can bring real added value in the search for solutions.

C. Environment based approach for the ant colony convergence

The objective of this section is to provide a self adaptive convergence to the Ant Colony algorithm. As seen previously, there is many different approach used to stop the ACO, but most of those amount to end up with a termination criteria arbitrarily set, to limit the solution. Wishing to provide an adaptive feature to the Ant Colony algorithm, the question was: "How to determine an adaptive termination condition and on what it can be based on?". Each project on which an ACO can be applied is different from an other, but they all have pieces in common, the structure of their graph. The uniqueness of each graph can be reflected through its number of vertices, its number of edges or even its complexity. Thanks to the last research, we could demonstrate that the number of edges ant the number of vertices do not characterize the convergence of the Ant Colony algorithm. Finally, the only lead we left to study for an adaptive termination condition is the complexity of the graph. To conduct this study, we implement two different benchmark tests on which to base our research. The first one is a small graph, made of 10 vertices, but with a significant complexity compared to its small number of vertices. The second is a reproduction of the public transportation system of the city of Belfort. This graph, although very voluminous, with 150 vertices, has a low complexity. Thanks to those graphs, we conducted experiments that generated raw data to exploit. In the last section IV we will see if the generated raw data allow us to correlate graph complexity and adaptive Ant Colony termination.

III. Adaptive transportation system at delivery point

This section provides an overview of the Vehicle Routing problem and introduce different strategies to provide an adaptive feature to this classical problem.

A. Vehicle Routing Problem overview

As introduced previously, our commitment trough this paper is to provide adaptive delivery feature to the Vehicle Routing Problem. But first of all, we will define the Vehicle Routing Problem application. Thank to the previous section II-A, we already describe the Ant Colony part of the VRP application such as choice of a new point to reach, and update of the pheromone trails. However, the VRP obeys to additional rules that we will introduce now. For each customer v_i, a non-negative demand q_i is given ($v_i = 0$). The aim is to find a minimum cost vehicle routes where:

- Every customer is visited exactly once by exactly one vehicle
- All vehicle routes begins and end at the same depot
- For every vehicle route, the total demand does not exceed the vehicle capacity Q

The VRP is a very complicated combinatorial optimization problem that has been studies since the late fifties because of its central meaning in distribution management. Problem specific methods as well as meta-heuristics like tabu search, simulated annealing, have been proposed to solve the VRP. VRP and TSP are closely related. As soon as the customers of the VRP are assigned to vehicle, the VRP is reduced to several TSPs. For that reason, our approach is highly influenced by the TSP ant system algorithm by Dorigo [1]. To solve the VRP, the artificial ants construct vehicle routes by successively chosing cities to visit, until each city has been visited. Whenever the choice of another city would lead to an infeasible solution for reason of vehicle capacity or an already visited point, the depot is chosen and a new VRP turn is started. Concerning the initial placement of the artificial ants, it was found that the number of ants have to be equals to the number of vertices [5] (for the TSP and VRP) and each ant should start its turn at different vertices of the graph.

B. Strategies for adaptive delivery

As defined previously, our application is based on the VRP, but with the need to providing it adaptive feature. To do so, we paired the VRP application with different strategies to adapt the possibility of delivery, at city point, according to the adaptive possibility of customers to be presented to pickup his package(s). Thus, those strategies are not limited to deliver or not a package(s) according to the presence of the customer, it has to provide to the customer the possibility to redefine its delivery time at its delivery point during the same turn of the vehicle. According to this fact, the vehicle processing the delivery turn, define by the VRP application, has to self-adapt the scheduling of his set list of city points to deliver package(s).

1) First Strategy: The first strategy is a classical VRP turn to have a point of reference to compare the results with those of the second strategy. This strategy is common to all delivery city points, is defined as: "deliver the package(s) and continue".

2) Second Strategy: The second strategy is defined as follow:

- Upon arrival at delivery point, the vehicle has two choices:
  - If the customer is present, the vehicle delivers the package(s) and continue
  - If the customer is not present, the vehicle waits 10 minutes
    * If the customer arrives, the vehicle delivers the package(s) and continues
    * If the customer do not arrive, the vehicle continues and has to come back at the end of its VRP turn.

Furthermore, we implement two variants for this strategy. At the end of a turn, if all the packages were not delivered we organize the second part of the turn to be sure to deliver them.

First variant:

- The current VRP turn is ending at the depot (its starting point)
  - A possibility is create a new turn thank to the VRP algorithm
  - A other one is to link all points with a shortest path algorithm

Second Variant:

- The current VRP turn stop at the last delivery point of its turn
  - A possibility is create a new turn thank to the VRP algorithm
  - A other one is to link all points with a shortest path algorithm

3) Evaluation Criteria: For this work, the evaluations criteria will be the following:

- The total time:
  - of the VRP turn
  - for a delivery
- The total distance:
  - of the VRP turn
  - for a delivery

IV. Experiments and Results

As presented at the beginning of this paper, the development of our transportation system is based on an adaptive Vehicle Routing Problem to self adapt to the possibility of delivery of goods at city points. Our transportation system being based on an Ant Colony to support VRP algorithm, the first stage is to improve the Ant Colony Algorithm to bring it an adaptive convergence. This point will be developped following this paragraph, in IV-A. Next, to bring a self-adaptation to the possibility of delivery at city point, we have to develop an adaptive VRP in order to answer our needs of improvement for our transportation system. This part will be analyzed and develop in the section IV-B.

A. Environment based approach for the ant colony convergence

In a previous work, we explored two different paths to characterize the convergence of the Ant Colony algorithm. Searching to exploit an environment based approach, the objective was to identify if the number of vertices or the number of edges could be the key for the self convergence of the Ant Colony Algorithm. However, as we demonstrate it, those parameters were not the key. In this section, the objective is to identify if the last parameter of an environment based approach, being the graph complexity, can solve the self convergence of the Ant Colony Algorithm.

We defined the graph complexity as the average number of edges connecting a vertex to others in the graph. As said previously, our test bench is based on two graph, the first being a small graph, but with a significant complexity. The second one, being a reproduction of the public system transport of the city of Belfort, with a low complexity.

The first step was to define the complexity of any of our graph. To do that, we calculate the complexity of our two graphs, calculating the following value:

$$\theta = \frac{\sum_{v=1}^{n} \omega_i}{k} \tag{4}$$

with v the number of vertices into the graph, ω_i the number of edges starting to the current vertex and connecting it to an other vertex and k the number of edges into the graph.

Thus, thanks to θ, we determined that $G_1(v, e)$ has a complexity of 1.25, and $G_2(v, e)$ has a complexity of 1.05. Having been able to determine the complexity of any of our graph, we will now search a way to define the number of iteration ϵ of the Ant Colony, according to the graph complexity previously calculated. So, to identify ϵ, we took inspiration from work we previously performed in which we tried to identify if the number of algorithm iterations can be reflected by the number of ants into the graph. Starting with one ant and increasing the number of ants until it reach the number of vertices (according to [5], the number of ants should be equals to the number of vertices in a graph).

Those results gave us the followings graphics:

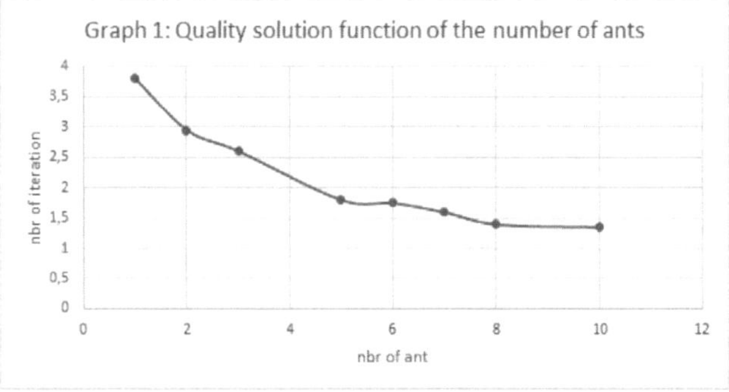

Fig. 2: Quality solution of the test graph

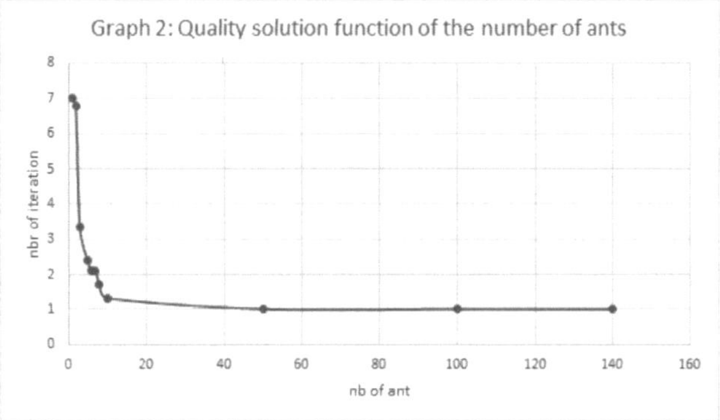

Fig. 3: Quality solution of the graph of Belfort

The "Quality solution" illustrate the number of algorithm iterations according to the number of ants. For the tow previous simulations, the number of iteration was arbitrarily set to a high value. This allow us to identify the stagnation point of the stalling effect curve and determine the best number of iterations for the explored problem. Thanks to previous work, we refuted the claim saying that the convergence of the ACO can be defined by a number of ants equals to the number of vertices. As it can be observed in Figure 4 and 5, the two curves function of our two graphs do not have the same equation. However, as it can be observed in Figure 2 and 3, the graph complexity is the key. Considering the graph complexity as the optimisation point to reach, paired with the Dorigo criterion [5], we obtain the convergent point for our two curves which characterizes the self-convergence of the Ant Colony algorithm.

B. Adaptive transportation system at delivery point

As introduce it earlier, simulations was leads on two strategies. The first one being a classical VRP application allowing to find the best turn according to the set list of city points, paired to the obligation of delivery at each city point. This first simulation gave us a reference total distance travelled and a reference total time for the vehicle turn. Those distance and time references are used as benchmark to analyse the performance of the second strategy. The second strategy being composed of two variants to explore different possibilities

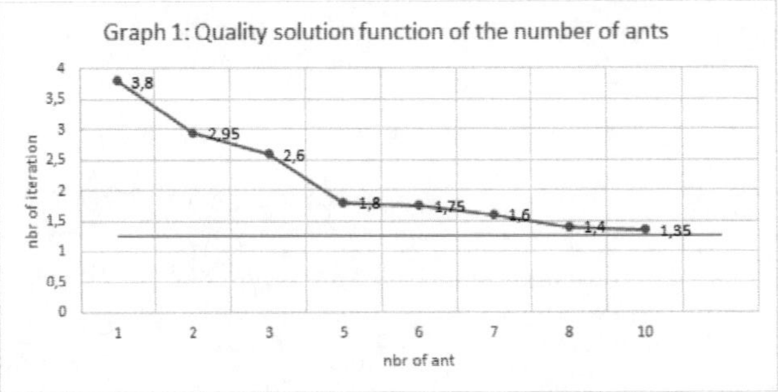

Fig. 4: Quality solution test graph compare to complexity solution

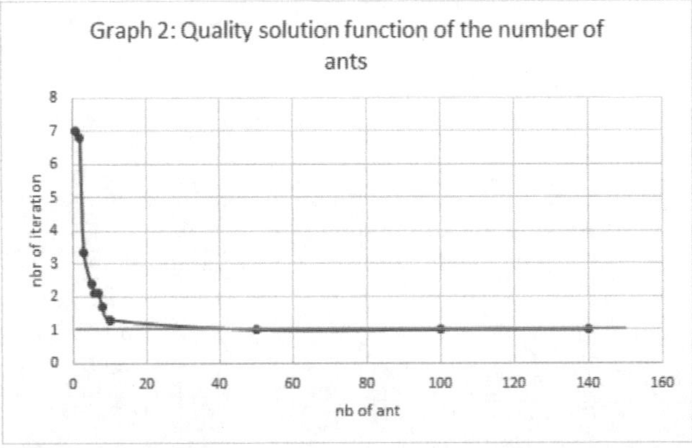

Fig. 5: Quality solution Belfort graph compare to complexity solution

through an adaptive VRP algorithm. Simulations was lead on $G_1(v, e)$, (previously defined in this paper) with one package delivered by vertex.

TABLE II. Procedure ACO algorithm

Strategies	total distance (km)	total time (min)
Strategy 1	44	29
Strat2: frst variant		
cascading VRP	52	114
VRP and ShP	49	110
Strat2: scd variant		
cascading VRP	44	102
VRP and ShP	41	98
VRP = Vehicle Routing Problem, ShP = Shorstest Path		

According to Table 2, the first strategy provides the best indicators in terms of distance, with a travel distance of 44 km and time, with a turn time of 29 min. However, the classical VRP is not adaptive, so it does not take into account the un-delivery possibility of package(s). Thus, at the end of a turn, the total percentage of un-delivered package(s) will necessary impact the next turn, by overloading the delivery delivery turn and/or postpone the delivery of future package(s). So, wishing to perform an adaptive application, the objective of the second strategy is to be able to ensure the delivery of the totality of packages for a given turn. The second strategy explores two variants for the "re-starting" point of the un-delivered package(s) turn. The first variant is to come back to the goods deposit. After that, the last turn is define either with a reload of the VRP algorithm of with a shortest path, linking all un-delivery city points. Regrettably, this variant violently deteriorates distance and time indicators. The second variant offers to start the un-delivered package(s) turn at the last city point visited by the vehicle. After that, the last turn is define either with a reload of the VRP algorithm of with a shortest path, linking all un-delivery city points. As can be seen in Table 2, this variant clearly proves his interest. Although this solution deteriorates the time indicators (reflecting a longer use of the vehicle), the distance indicator stays stable in the worst case (44 km) and is even improved, with a gain of 7%, while paired with the use of shortest path algorithm, all that with a delivery rate of 100%.

V. CONCLUSIONS

Following the re-contextualization of the ant colony algorithm in the section II-A, we provide a non-exhaustive state of the art regarding the criterion termination of the ant colony algorithm in the section II-B. Then, we search to know if an environment based approach can characterize the self-adaptive convergence of the ant colony. In previous work, we concluded that the others parameter of the graph for an environment based approach was not conclusive. Thus, into the section II-C, thanks to the study, we could demonstrate that the graph complexity was the good way to illustrate self-adaptive convergence of the algorithm. Then, with the section III we explored different strategies to provide self-adaptive ability for the VRP turn, to be more flexible and to match as well as possible to the availability of customers to pick-up their package(s). Finally, into the section IV we present our results for the self-convergence of the ant colony algorithm in section IV-A and for the adaptive delivery VRP turn in the section IV-B. Furthermore, even if the time indicator is deteriorated, the improvement of the distance indicator support the use of electric vehicle for future research. The next step will be to combine the Vehicle Routing Problem with the capacity of the vehicle to characterize VRP turns and to define feasible adaptation during VRP turn.

VI. ACKNOWLEDGMENT

This work is done with the support of the Région Bourgogne-Franche-comté, through the SURATRAM Project.

REFERENCES

[1] V. Maniezzo A. Colorni, M. Dorigo. Distributed optimization by ant colonies. In *Proceedings of the First European Conference on Artificial Life*, 01 1991.

[2] J. Giffin Y. Tu A. Kate, R. James. A knowledge discovery approach to understanding relationships between scheduling problem structure and heuristic performance. In *Learning and Intelligent Optimization*, 2009.

[3] S. Senouci N. Kroichvili C. Cappelle D. Fass F. Gechter, E. Aglzim. Transportation of goods in inner-city centers: Can autonomous vehicles in platoon be a suitable solution? In *2017 IEEE Vehicle Power and Propulsion Conference (VPPC)*, pages 1–5, 2017.

[4] P. Grassé. La reconstruction du nid et les coordinations interindividuelles chezbellicositermes natalensis etcubitermes sp. la théorie de la stigmergie: Essai d'interprétation du comportement des termites constructeurs. *Insectes Sociaux*, 6:41–80, 2005.

[5] A. Colorni M. Dorigo, V. Maniezzo. Ant system: optimization by a colony of cooperating agents. *IEEE Transactions on Systems, Man, and Cybernetics, Part B (Cybernetics)*, 26(1):29–41, 1996.

[6] T.Stützle M. Dorigo. Ant colony optimization algorithms for the traveling salesman problem. *Ant Colony Optimization*, pages 65–119, 2004.

[7] P. Broomhead M. Veluscek, T. Kalganova. Improving ant colony optimization performance through prediction of best termination condition. In *2015 IEEE International Conference on Industrial Technology (ICIT)*, pages 2394–2402, 2015.

[8] P. Broomhead M. Veluscek, T. Kalganova. Improving ant colony optimization performance through prediction of best termination condition. In *2015 IEEE International Conference on Industrial Technology (ICIT)*, pages 2394–2402, 2015.

[9] I. Stéphan P. Nicolas, F. Saubion. Answer set programming by ant colony optimization. In *Logics in Artificial Intelligence*, 2002.

[10] A. Rizzoli A. Donati R. Montemanni, L. Gambardella. Ant colony system for a dynamic vehicle routing problem. *Journal of Combinatorial Optimization*, 10:327 – 343, 2005.

[11] I.Loiseau S. Mazzeo. An ant colony algorithm for the capacitated vehicle routing. *Electronic Notes in Discrete Mathematics*, 18:181 – 186, 2004.

[12] X. Lim S. Miles, J. Hemert. Understanding tsp difficulty by learning from evolved instances. In *Learning and Intelligent Optimization*, 2010.

[13] P. Abad Y. Gajpal. An ant colony system (acs) for vehicle routing problem with simultaneous delivery and pickup. *Computers Operations Research*, 36(12):3215 – 3223, 2009.

[14] Z. Ren Z.Zhang, Z. Feng. Approximate termination condition analysis for ant colony optimization algorithm. In *2010 8th World Congress on Intelligent Control and Automation*, pages 3211–3215, 2010.

Performance Predictions for Adaptive Cloud-Based Systems using FMC-QE

Stephan Kluth
FOM University of Applied Sciences
Berliner Allee 7, 30175 Hannover
Email: mail@stephankluth.de

Abstract—**This paper presents an application of an analytical performance prediction approach to (self-)adaptive cloud-based systems. The methodology called Fundamental Modeling Concepts for Quantitative Evaluation (FMC-QE) uses three perspectives to hierarchically describe the performance behavior of a system. This methodology is now applied to cloud-based systems with infinite and parallel server capacities and further, the ideas are ported to the world of (self-)adaptive systems. Furthermore, a case study is shown as an example of such models.**

Keywords-FMC-QE; cloud; adaptive.

I. Introduction

Cloud technology is more and more used to process parts of every kind of business process [1] [2]. This paper shows a way to performance modeling and performance predictions in these distributed scenarios. Especially the performance predictions of the Fundamental Modeling Concepts for Quantitative Evaluation (FMC-QE) [3] [4] called FMC-QE Tableau could be used to implement algorithms for (self-)adaptive cloud-based workflow handlers. In this paper, this methodology is applied to cloud-based systems with infinite and parallel server capacities and further, the ideas are ported to the world of (self-)adaptive systems. These ideas are furthermore shown in a case study as an example of such models.

In the following, the methodology FMC-QE is shortly described as a repetition in Section II. Afterward, some related work is described in Section III. Then the linkage to (self-)adaptive systems is given in Section IV along with an example in Section V. Finally, some conclusions and future work are described in Section VI.

II. Background: FMC-QE

FMC-QE [3]–[7] is a performance modeling and analysis methodology in which the systems are modeled from the perspective of the hierarchical service requests based in FMC [8]. In FMC-QE, these hierarchies are the key to complexity in the modeling and evaluation of complex systems. Furthermore, the complexity is reduced through three different modeling perspectives, the service request structures, the server structures, and the dynamic behavior including the control flow. Furthermore, the service requests are modeled as a tuple of value and unit like physical units. This enables hierarchical service request transformations through the Forced Traffic Flow Law [9].

The hierarchical service request structures are the entry point of the modeling in FMC-QE. An exemplary service request structure, modeled in FMC-QE in Entity-Relationship-Diagrams, is shown in Figure 1. Here one service request is decomposed into two sub-requests, an initialization, and an execution.

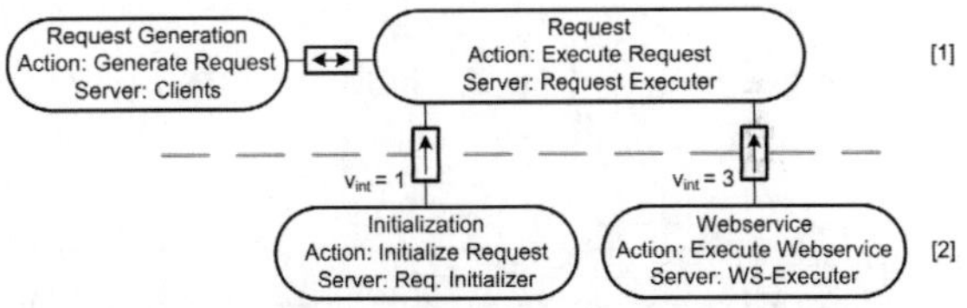

Figure 1. Service Request Structures [7].

In the modeling of the server structures, there is a distinction between logical and real servers with parallelism on every hierarchical layer. This enables the modeling of complex software systems running on distributed and shared hardware. The server structures in FMC-QE are modeled in Block Diagrams, as shown in Figure 2. In the example, there is one application server and an infinite number of web servers available (e.g., in a cloud-based approach).

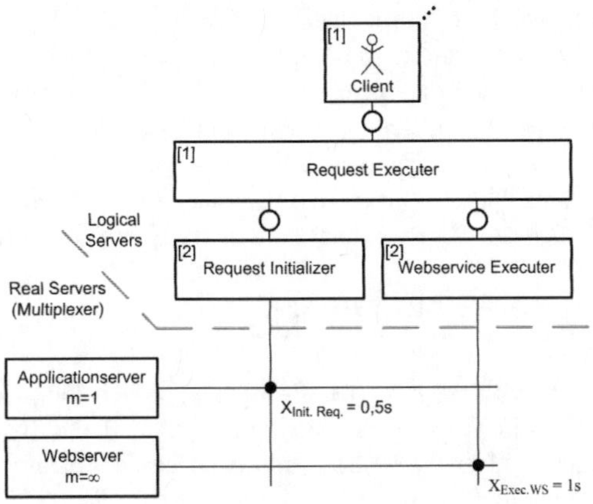

Figure 2. Server Structures [7].

The dynamic behavior and the control flows are modeled in Petri Nets [10]. This allows the modeling of parallel,

TABLE I. FMC-QE TABLEAU EXAMPLE [7].

Experimental Parameters:	
n_{ges}	30
λ_{bott}	2,0000
f	0,8000
λ	1,6000

Service Request Section							Server Section					Dynamic Evaluation Section						
[bb]	$SRq_i^{[bb]}$	$p_{[bb-1],i}$	$v_{i,ext}^{[bb-1]}$	$v_{i,int}^{[bb]}$	$v_i^{[bb]}$	$\lambda_i^{[bb]}$	$Server_i$	$X_{i,measured}^{[bb]}$	$m_{i,ext}^{[bb-1]}$	$m_{i,int}^{[bb]}$	$m_i^{[bb]}$	$X_{i,mpxed}^{[bb]}$	$\mu_i^{[bb]}$	$\rho_i^{[bb]}$	$n_{i,q}^{[bb]}$	$n_{i,s}^{[bb]}$	$n_i^{[bb]}$	$R_i^{[bb]}$
2	Webservice	1	1	3	3	4,8000	Webserver	1,0000	1	1	1	1,0000	1,0000		0,0000	4,8000	4,8000	1,0000
2	Initialization	1	1	1	1	1,6000	App. Server	0,2000	1	1	1	0,5000	2,0000	0,8000	3,2000	0,8000	4,0000	2,5000
1	Request	1	1	1	1	1,6000			1	1	1		2,0000		3,2000	5,6000	8,8000	5,5000
1	Request Generation	1	1	1	1	1,6000			1	1	1	13,2500	0,0755		0,0000	21,2000	21,2000	13,2500

Multiplexer Section				
$Multiplexer_j$	m_j	$X_j^{[1]}$	$\mu_j^{[1]}$	$\mu_j^{[1]} * m_j$
App. Server	1	0,5000	2,0000	2,0000
Webserver	∞	1,0000		

serial, branch, loop, and synchronization structures. The complexity of the state-space is further reduced through the distinction of operational and control states [11]. An exemplary FMC-QE Petri Net is illustrated in Figure 3.

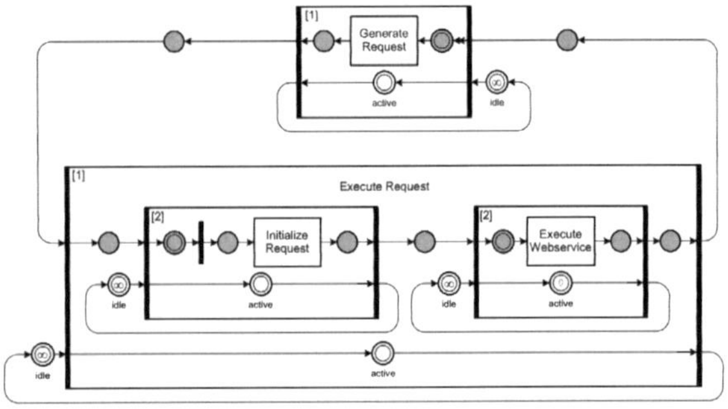

Figure 3. Dynamic Behavior and Control Flow [7].

The performance values of the modeled system are predicted in the FMC-QE Tableau. This hierarchical balance sheet is based on Little's Law [12] for relations within a hierarchical layer (horizontal) and the Forced Traffic Flow Law [9] for relations among layers (vertical). It extracts the performance parameters from the model and calculates predictions. The different system- and load-parameters are easy to change to compute a broad range of possible configurations. Table I shows an exemplary FMC-QE Tableau.

III. RELATED WORK

This work relates to the Palladio approach [13]. While the focus in Palladio is on simulation, here the focus is on numerical analysis. This approach could be integrated into Palladio to provide another numerical analysis beside Queuing Petri Nets (QPN) and Layered Queuing Networks (LQN) as described in [14] and shown in Figure 4. FMC-QE also uses ideas from LQN [3] and therefore cooperation in this field would be interesting to benefit from each other.

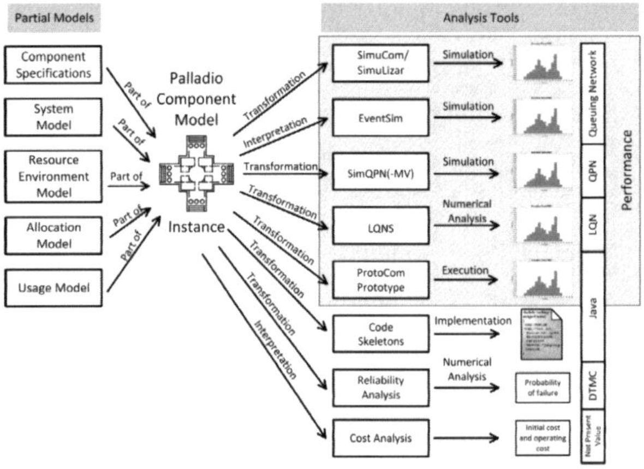

Figure 4. Palladio overview [13], [14].

As in earlier papers described [7], FMC-QE also uses model transformations to transform the non-hierarchical system models into the strictly hierarchical FMC-QE approach. In very new contributions of Palladio, similar transformations are described [15] and shown in figure 5.

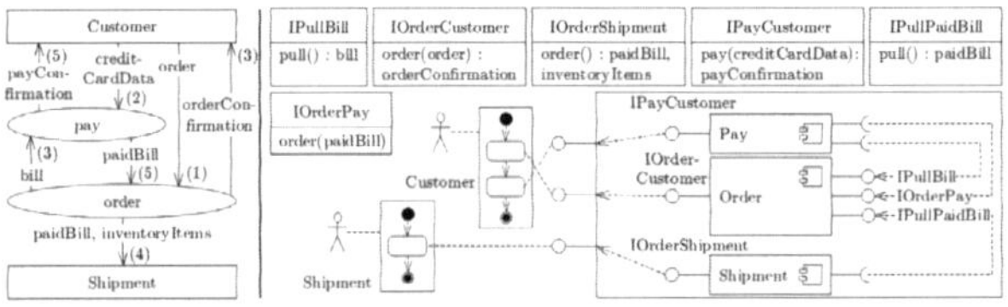

Figure 5. Palladio Transformations [15].

In contrast to this representation, FMC-QE uses the hierarchical service request as the central perspective and precise or approximated calculations as described in [16] and in section IV. Nevertheless, there are similarities in the hierarchical decomposition of the service request in FMC-QE [7] and the data flow transformations from Data Flow Models (DFM) into Palladio Component Models (PCM) in Palladio [15].

Furthermore, there are numerous simulation approaches

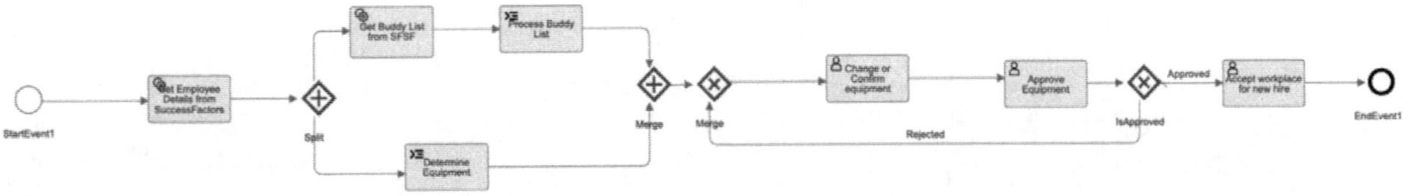

Figure 6. Example SAP Cloud Platform Workflow [17]

like [18]. FMC-QE delimits from these approaches, as it is based on numerical analysis. Nevertheless, comparison case studies of simulations and numerical analysis (in special FMC-QE) are very interesting as already done in [7].

IV. Applying FMC-QE to (Self-)Adaptive Cloud-based Systems

FMC-QE could be used to predict the performance behavior of the system processing the modeled business process. Therefore, the business process is transformed into the hierarchical request structure of FMC-QE [7] and if there are no inter-server control flows (and therefore, the underlying system is of type Product-Form-Network (PFN) [19] [16]) FMC-QE could predict the performance in a very fast (no simulation) and precise (if PFN) way. If the business process and the underlying system is not of type PFN, FMC-QE could provide approximations [16].

Business processes processed on cloud-based systems or systems, where parts of the whole business process are processed on cloud-based systems are the ideal use case for FMC-QE, because the processing unit could often be assumed as an infinite server as shown in Figure 7. This is the case if the closed Service-Level-Agreement is of type: *No matter how many requests will come, we will respond in x sec per request.*

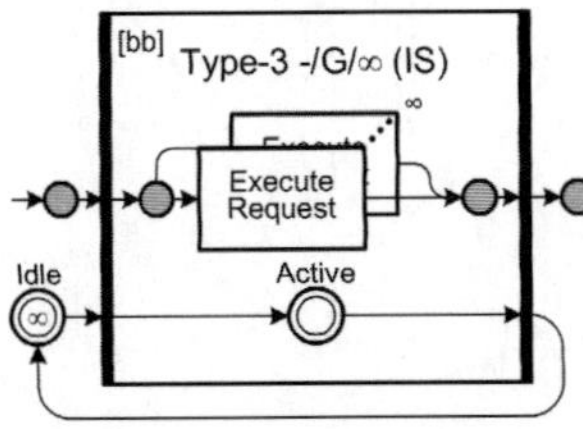

Figure 7. Infinite Server [3]

If the closed Service-Level-Agreement is of type: *We will provide x compute units each with a speed of y.*, the underlying system (multiplexer) could be assumed as a parallel server with exponentially distributed service times as shown in Figure 8 or with other service time distributions such as deterministic [3].

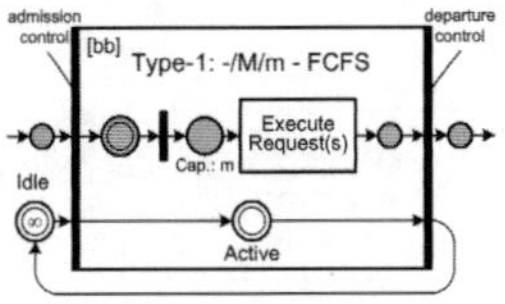

Figure 8. Infinite Server [3]

Another advantage of FMC-QE is, that the methodology is based on hierarchical service requests as shown in Figure 1. This reduces the complexity of the whole calculations and could therefore be implemented quite easily.

The performance predictions of FMC-QE could then be taken to adaptively (self-)adjust the allocated cloud computation performance based on the actual number of service requests or to compute a broad range of possible load scenarios to be aware of performance adaptations in the future.

V. Case Study

The approach was applied to an SAP case study [17], shown in Figure 6 with an example of ordering a notebook for a new employee.

In this section, the workflow of Figure 6 is transformed into the three perspectives of FMC-QE and the computations of the performance predictions in the FMC-QE Tableau. For other implementations of (self-)adaptive systems, this is not essential. The algorithms of the self-adaptive systems could just use the ideas of FMC-QE in terms of hierarchical service requests and the corresponding performance predictions [3] [16].

A. Dynamic Behavior and Control Flow (Petri Net)

In Figure 9, the dynamic behavior of the workflow is shown. The main difference between the original workflow [17] designed as BPMN-Diagram [20] [21] is the transformation to four hierarchical levels.

B. Service Request Structure and Static Structure

The corresponding service request structures of the example are shown in Figure 10. The service request is partitioned into the same 4 hierarchical levels. In this diagram the increased traffic flow realizing the retransmission of the *Equipment Negotiation Request* ($v_{int} = 1, 2 \frac{[OrderNotebookfornewEmployee-Request]}{[EquipmentNegotiationRequest]}$) is visualized.

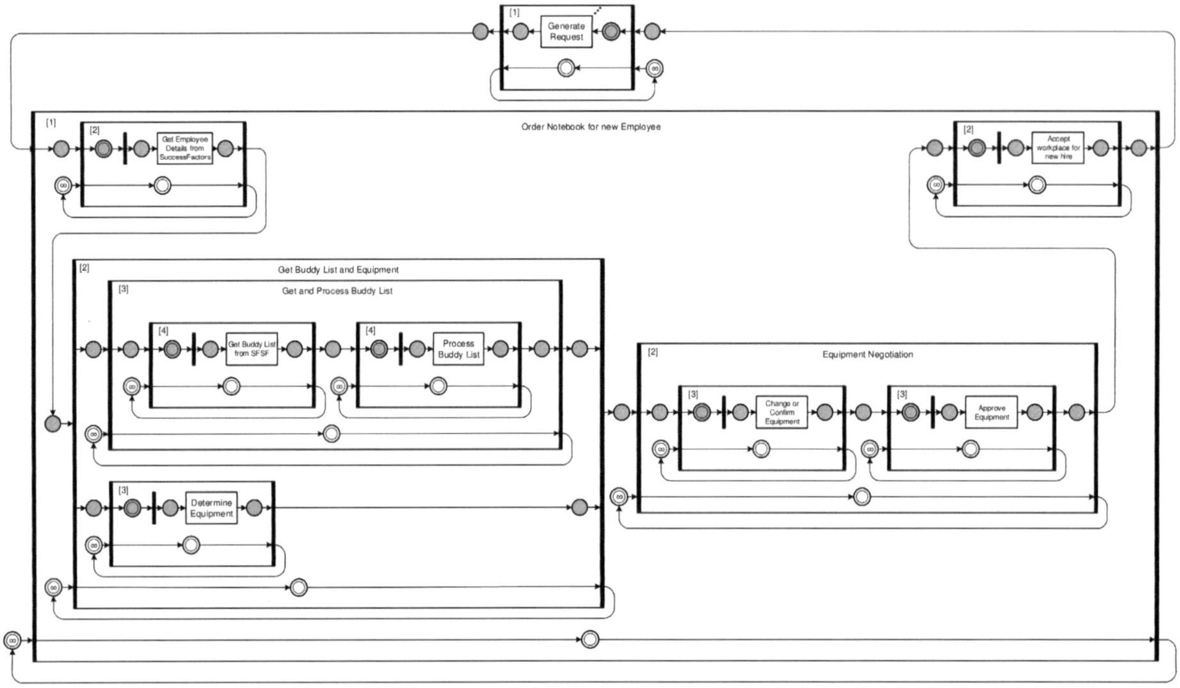

Figure 9. Case Study - Petri Net.

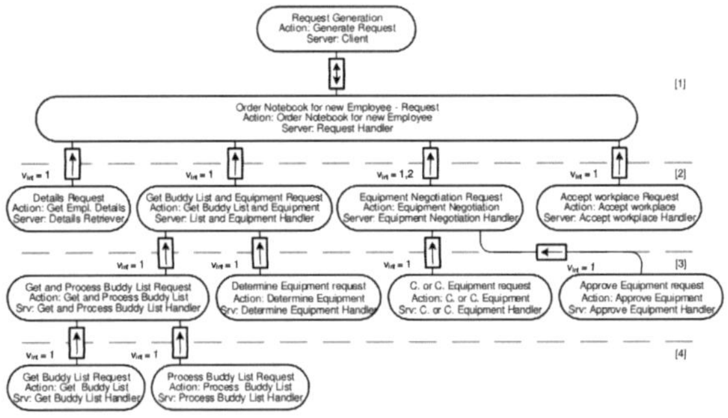

Figure 10. Case Study - Service Request Structures.

C. Static Structure

In the third diagram of the model, the server structures are represented in the Block Diagram, as shown in Figure 11. In this model, the four hierarchies of the logical server structures and the mappings to the multiplexer servers are defined. The different service times for the basic servers are also defined in this diagram. In contrast to the original use case [17] the human actors are replaced by AI to have more widely performance predictions (otherwise the humans would be the bottleneck) - this is only done for these performance calculations. In the real workflow, human actors are not replaced by AI.

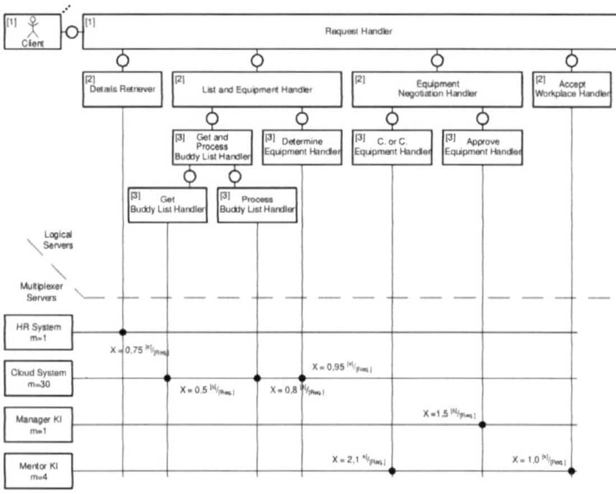

Figure 11. Case Study - Server Structures.

D. Tableau

FMC-QE delivers exact solutions for open Product From Queueing Networks. Through transformations, the flat example could be transformed into a hierarchical model. After this transformation, a broad range of performance values could be calculated in the FMC-QE Tableau, as shown in Table II. On every hierarchical level $[bb]$, this includes values like queue lengths $n_{i,q}^{[bb]}$, waiting times $W_i^{[bb]}$, service durations

TABLE II. CASE STUDY - TABLEAU.

Experimental Parameters	
$n_{ges}^{[1]}$	80
$\lambda_{bott}^{[1]}$	0,5556
f	0,9500
$\lambda^{[1]}$	0,5278

Service Request Section								Server Section						Dynamic Evaluation Section								
[bb]	i	$SRq_i^{[bb]}$	$p_{p(i),i}$	$v_{p(i)}^{[bb-1]}$	$v_{i,int}^{[bb]}$	$v_i^{[bb]}$	$\lambda_i^{[bb]}$	$Server_i^{[bb]}$	$m_{p(i)}^{[bb-1]}$	$m_{i,int}^{[bb]}$	$m_i^{[bb]}$	Mpx_i	$X_i^{[bb]}$	$m_{i,mpx}^{[bb]}$	$\mu_i^{[bb]}$	$\rho_i^{[bb]}$	$n_{i,q}^{[bb]}$	$W_i^{[bb]}$	$n_{i,s}^{[bb]}$	$Y_i^{[bb]}$	$n_i^{[bb]}$	$R_i^{[bb]}$
2	1	Get Employee Details from SuccessFactors	1,00	1,00	1,00	1,00	0,528	Details Retriever	1	1	1	1	0,750	1,000	1,333	0,396	0,259	0,491	0,396	0,750	0,655	1,241
4	2	Get Buddy List from SFSF	1,00	1,00	1,00	1,00	0,528	Get Buddy List Handler	1	1	1	2	0,500	30,000	60,000	0,009	0,000	0,000	0,009	0,017	0,009	0,017
4	3	Process Buddy List	1,00	1,00	1,00	1,00	0,528	Process Buddy List Handler	1	1	1	2	0,800	30,000	37,500	0,014	0,000	0,000	0,014	0,027	0,014	0,027
3	4	Get and Process Buddy List	1,00	1,00	1,00	1,00	0,528	Get and Process Buddy List Handler	1	1	1				37,500		0,000	0,001	0,023	0,043	0,023	0,044
3	5	Determine Equipment	1,00	1,00	1,00	1,00	0,528	Determine Equipment Handler	1	1	1	2	0,950	30,000	31,579	0,017	0,000	0,001	0,017	0,032	0,017	0,032
2	6	Get Buddy List and Equipment	1,00	1,00	1,00	1,00	0,528	List and Equipment Handler	1	1	1				31,579		0,001	0,001	0,040	0,075	0,040	0,076
3	7	Change or Confirm Equipment	1,00	1,20	1,00	1,20	0,633	C. or C. Equipment Handler	1	1	1	4	2,100	4,000	1,905	0,333	0,166	0,262	0,333	0,525	0,498	0,787
3	8	Approve Equipment	1,00	1,20	1,00	1,20	0,633	Approve Equipment Handler	1	1	1	3	1,500	1,000	0,667	0,950	18,050	28,500	0,950	1,500	19,000	30,000
2	5	Equipment Negotiation	1,00	1,00	1,20	1,20	0,633	Equipment Negotiation Handler	1	1	1				0,800		18,216	28,762	1,283	2,025	19,498	30,787
2	6	Accept workplace for new hire	1,00	1,00	1,00	1,00	0,528	Accept Workplace Handler	1	1	1	4	1,000	4,000	4,000	0,132	0,020	0,038	0,132	0,250	0,152	0,288
1	7	Order Notebook for new Employe	1,00	1,00	1,00	1,00	0,528	Request Handler	1	1	1				0,667		18,496	35,044	1,850	3,505	20,345	38,549
1	8	Request Generation	1,00	1,00	1,00	1,00	0,528	Client	1	1	1		113,030		0,009		0,000	0,000	59,655	113,030	59,655	113,030

Multiplexer Section			
j	$Name_j$	m_j	$X_j^{[1]}$
1	HR System	1	0,750
2	Cloud System	30	1,300
3	Manager KI	1	1,800
4	Mentor KI	4	2,250

$Y_i^{[bb]}$ and response times $R_i^{[bb]}$.

Through the dependencies in the FMC-QE Tableau, some parameters, such as the service times $X_j^{[1]}$ or multiplicities m_j of the multiplexers or the overall arrival rate $\lambda^{[1]}$, could be adjusted to predict the described values. An example of such a calculation is shown in Figure 12.

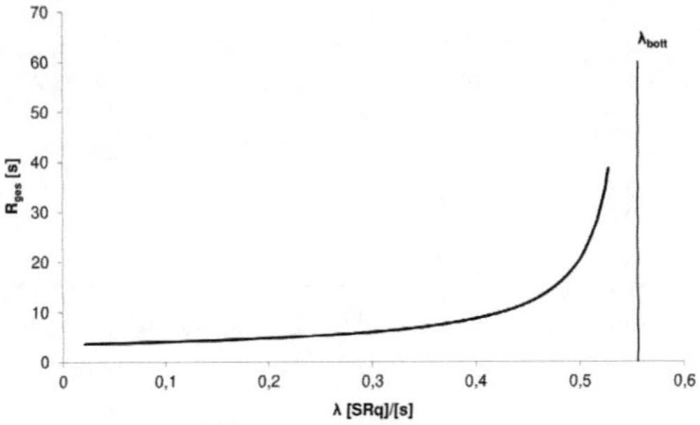

Figure 12. Case Study - Performance Prediction

This shows the dependency on the response time R from the arrival rate λ, as the arrival rate is increased towards the maximum bottleneck arrival rate λ_{bott}. In a possible real use case, a threshold for R could be defined from which for example further virtual servers would be allocated.

VI. CONCLUSION AND FUTURE WORK

With the help of FMC-QE including its hierarchical modeling and the underlying hierarchical performance calculations performance values, such as response times or queue lengths could be predicted even for distributed cloud-based systems. These performance predictions could be used to adapt the Service-Level-Agreements (SLAs) of the connected cloud-systems, while one of the main components of FMC-QE is the service request. These predictions could be further integrated into the algorithms of self-adaptive systems while the hierarchical approach reduces the complexity dramatically. In this publication, the performance predictions are integrated into a spreadsheet program, but as said, it is not limited to this.

In the future, it is planned to further integrate calculations of the FMC-QE Tableau to BPMN as BPMN is a widely used modeling notation. Therefore, patterns for the hierarchical modeling will be defined to transform BPMN Diagrams or further annotate it.

Furthermore, as already described in Section III the Palladio approach seems to address similar problems, therefore, cooperation would be from interest. One possible connection point could be the integration of the FMC-QE calculation (FMC-QE Tableau) into Palladio, another could be an exchange of experience in the area of model transformations, as it is said, that this a current research question in Palladio [15].

Also, a more extensive comparison to the predictive

process monitoring approaches such as mOSAIC [18] or [22], which are often simulations in contrast to the numerical analysis shown here, would further sharpen the results, as already done in [7].

ACKNOWLEDGMENT

The author would like to thank Prof. Dr.-Ing. Werner Zorn for countless useful discussions during the development of FMC-QE. The author would furthermore thank Dr. Helge Fischer for encouraging to this publication.

REFERENCES

[1] M. Chui *et al.*, "Ten it-enabledbusiness trends for the decade ahead," McKinsey Global Institute, Tech. Rep., May 2013.

[2] D. W. Cearley, "Top 10 strategic technology trends for 2019," Gartner, Tech. Rep., 2019.

[3] S. Kluth, "Quantitative Modeling and Analysis with FMC-QE," Ph.D. dissertation, Hasso Plattner Institute for Software Systems Engineering at the University of Potsdam, Potsdam, Germany, July 2011.

[4] W. Zorn, "FMC-QE - A New Approach in Quantitative Modeling," in *Proceedings of the International Conference on Modeling, Simulation and Visualization Methods (MSV 2007) within WorldComp '07*, H. R. Arabnia, Ed. Las Vegas, NV, USA: CSREA Press, June 2007, pp. 280 – 287.

[5] T. Porzucek, S. Kluth, F. Copaciu, and W. Zorn, "Modeling and Evaluation Framework for FMC-QE," in *Proceedings of the 16th IEEE International Conference on the Engineering of Computer-Based Systems (ECBS2008)*. Los Alamitos, CA, USA: IEEE Computer Society, April 2009, pp. 237–243.

[6] M. Seelig *et al.*, "Comparison of Performance Modeling and Simulation - a Case Study," in *Proceedings of the 15th IEEE International Conference on Engineering of Computer-Based Systems (ECBS 2008 - Belfast, UK)*, D. W. Bustard and R. Sterritt, Eds. Los Alamitos, CA, USA: IEEE Computer Society, March 2008, pp. 49–56.

[7] T. Porzucek, M. Fritzsche, S. Kluth, and D. Redlich, "Combination of a Discrete Event Simulation and an Analytical Performance Analysis through Model-Transformations," in *Proceedings of the 17th IEEE International Conference on the Engineering of Computer-Based Systems (ECBS2010)*. Los Alamitos, CA, USA: IEEE Computer Society, March 2010, pp. 183–192.

[8] A. Knöpfel, B. Gröne, and P. Tabeling, *Fundamental Modeling Concepts: Effective Communication of IT Systems*. John Wiley & Sons, März 2006.

[9] P. J. Denning and J. P. Buzen, "The Operational Analysis of Queueing Network Models," *ACM Computing Surveys (CSUR)*, vol. 10, no. 3, pp. 225–261, September 1978.

[10] C. A. Petri, "Kommunikation mit Automaten - Communication with automata," Ph.D. dissertation, Institut für instrumentelle Mathematik, Bonn, Germany, 1962.

[11] S. Wendt, "Operationszustand versus Steuerzustand - eine äusserst zweckmässige Unterscheidung - operational state vs. control state - an extremely useful distinction," University of Kaiserslautern, Kaiserslautern, Germany, Tech. Rep., Februar 1998.

[12] J. D. C. Little, "A Proof of the Queueing Formula $L = \lambda * W$," *Operations Research*, vol. 9, no. 3, pp. 383–387, May - June 1961.

[13] R. H. Reussner, S. Becker, J. Happe, R. Heinrich, A. Koziolek, H. Koziolek, M. Kramer, and K. Krogmann, *Modeling and Simulating Software Architectures – The Palladio Approach*. Cambridge, MA: MIT Press, October 2016.

[14] R. Heinrich, D. Werle, H. Klare, R. Reussner, M. Kramer, S. Becker, J. Happe, H. Koziolek, and K. Krogmann, "The palladio-bench for modeling and simulating software architectures," in *Proceedings of the 40th International Conference on Software Engineering: Companion Proceedings*, ser. ICSE '18. New York, NY, USA: ACM, 2018, pp. 37–40.

[15] S. Seifermann, D. Werle, and M. Ebada, "Mapping data flow models to the palladio component model," in *Proceedings of the 10th Symposium on Software Performance (SSP)*, ser. Softwaretechnik Trends, 2019, pp. 41–43.

[16] S. Kluth, "Discussion on the zorn-hypothesis on inter-server control flow and product form queueing networks," in *Proceedings of the 19th IEEE International Conference and Workshop on the Engineering of Computer Based Systems (ECBS2012)*, S. V. Miroslav Popovic, Bernhard Schätz, Ed. Los Alamitos, CA, USA,: IEEE Computer Society, 2012, pp. 126–134.

[17] T. Steckenborn, "A joint exploration of SAP Cloud Platform Workflow," SAP, Tech. Rep., 2019.

[18] U. V. A. Cuomo, M. Rak, "Performance prediction of cloud applications through benchmarking and simulation," *Int. J. of Computational Science and Engineering*, vol. 0, no. 00, 2004.

[19] W. Zorn, "Hierarchical Modeling based on Service Requests," 2007, Hasso-Plattner-Institute, University of Potsdam.

[20] "Specification Business Process Model and Notation(BPMN) Version 2.0.2," Object Management Group, Tech. Rep., Dec. 2013.

[21] "BPMN Poster," BPM Offensive Berlin, Hasso-Plattner-Institut, Humboldt University Berlin, camunda, inubit, signavio, Tech. Rep., 2011.

[22] B. K. John J. Prevost, KranthiManoj Nagothu and M. Jamshidi, "Prediction of Cloud Data Center Networks Loads Using Stochastic and Neural Models," in *Proc. of the 2011 6th International Conference on System of Systems Engineering*, 2011.

Cooperation Strategies in a Time-Stepped Simulation of Foraging Robots

Liam McGuigan, Catherine Saunders, Roy Sterritt, George Wilkie
School of Computing, Faculty of Computing, Engineering and the Built Environment
Ulster University
Jordanstown, N. Ireland
email: mcguigan-l8@ulster.ac.uk, c.saunders@ulster.ac.uk, r.sterritt@ulster.ac.uk, fg.wilkie@ulster.ac.uk

Abstract—**Large robotic swarms may be used to carry out tasks, such as space exploration, mining, search & rescue operations and more. To enable their use in these fields, the individual robots within a swarm will need to be autonomic, capable of making their own decisions and adjusting their behaviour without relying on regular human intervention. This paper demonstrates the potential for autonomic self-adaptation within a swarm of foraging robots by investigating the performance of different cooperation strategies in different scenarios. The results show that the performances of the strategies are affected by operational conditions that can change over the course of a mission, and that the autonomic capability to self-adapt would prove beneficial. Additionally, the time-stepped simulation used here is compared to the performance of a previous approach using real-time simulation, with a view to identifying which approach is more suitable for embedding within a robot as a means of aiding that autonomic process through simulating potential options. The time-stepped simulation is found to be faster and more efficient, and therefore more suited to embedding.**

Keywords- Swarm robotics; Self-adaptation; Autonomic Computing; Simulation.

I. INTRODUCTION

The use of robotic swarms consisting of a large number of robots operating in concert can benefit applications, such as space exploration [1][2], search & rescue [3] and mine clearance [3][4] among others, taking advantage of a robot's ability to operate in conditions where human involvement is too dangerous or difficult.

The individual craft in a robotic swarm will need to be capable of managing themselves without requiring constant supervision. They may be required to make quick decisions to protect themselves or to act on opportunities, and will need to adapt to best suit the conditions of the task being carried out [5]. This can be achieved by making the swarms autonomic.

Autonomic computing concepts will embody the swarm with the properties of self-configuration, self-healing, self-optimization and self-protection, ensuring that the swarm [6] is implemented by including an autonomic component running a Monitor, Analyse, Plan, Execute, with a shared Knowledge (MAPE-K) control loop to monitor and analyse the situation, and plan and execute any changes to behaviour aided by a knowledge base of pre-set or previously acquired information [7]. Autonomic robotics combines the concepts of MAPE-K from autonomic computing, with Intelligent Machine Design (IMD) from robotics [8][9].

Due to the cost and impracticality of using real hardware during the development of large-scale swarm behaviour with real hardware, simulators are often used in the process [10], able to create artificial swarms of hundreds or even thousands of robots engaged in tasks, such as foraging, surveillance and exploration of unknown environments.

The research presented in this paper has two objectives. The first is to investigate the potential for self-adaptation through selection of a cooperation strategy during a foraging task, through analysis of the performance of three different strategies over the course of the task. The second objective is to identify which of two simulation approaches used would be most suitable for deploying on an individual agent within the swarm as a means of using simulation-in-the-loop to help with the decision to switch.

The rest of this paper is organised as follows. Section II discusses related work on self-adaptation in swarm robotics, and the varying use of simulations in development. Section III describes the cooperation strategies developed in a previous study [11], and the implementation of an alternative simulation for exploring them, setting out the test scenarios to be run. Section IV presents these results and the implications, including a comparison of the two simulation approaches used. Section V concludes the paper with a summary and indicates the future research directions.

II. RELATED WORK

The following subsections discuss current research in swarm self-adaptation, and the use of simulations within swarm development.

A. *Swarm Self-Adaptation*

Self-adaptation of a robotic swarm concerns the ability of the swarm to adjust its behaviour in response to external or internal conditions, such as a foraging swarm choosing to abandon a depleted deposit in order to find newer deposits, or a surveillance swarm organizing itself so as to provide maximum coverage of the target area.

Swarm self-adaptation can be considered based on two factors – the approach to adaptation, and the location within the swarm where this is applied. Approaches to swarm adaptation include engineering emergent processes where adaptation arises naturally out of the agent behaviour [12], reasoning and learning approaches where the swarm explicitly reasons about the decision being made [13] and may learn from experience [14], and evolutionary approaches which explore alternatives through genetic algorithms [15].

Regarding location, a lot of the research focuses on applying adaptation to individual agent behaviour [16]–[18]. This low-level adaptation results in a bottom-up approach to swarm behaviour, with the resulting performance of the swarm arising from the aggregate performance of the individual agents. This can allow for more specific adaptation, such as balancing an individual's conflicting objectives [19], which may be difficult to apply at the swarm level. Agent behaviour adaptation can have the most direct impact on the swarm's performance, but it is difficult for an agent to make an individual decision on aspects of collaboration or coordination between multiple agents.

Adaptation through the selection of swarm-level cooperation strategies can be used to address the problem of collaboration. In this approach, agents within the swarm can collectively determine an alternative approach which is swapped with the existing agent behaviour either in part or in whole. This selection may be driven by an autonomic component that assesses the suitability of alternative strategies [11][14], and may be employed with in a subset of the entire swarm [20].

This research is focused on identifying the potential for swarm-level adaptational changes by assessing the performance of a selection of candidate strategies in a set of scenarios. Through noting any effect the scenario has on the performance of a particular strategy, the benefits of the ability to select an alternative strategy will become apparent.

B. *Use of Simulations in Swarm Development*

Simulation has long been employed as a tool for the development of robotic and swarm simulations, providing the means to test and analyse systems in an artificial environment. Simulators range in complexity, from detailed physical simulations of actual robots [10][21], to abstract approaches where robots move within a grid-based environment. The difficulty of producing an accurate simulation of the real world can manifest as the "reality gap" [22], where results obtained in simulation are not replicated in reality. Nonetheless, it is not necessary for the results of a simulation to be precisely reproducible in the real world for the simulation itself to prove useful.

Simulation need not be restricted to the offline development phase. It may be used to assist the decision making process [23][24], trying out "what-if" scenarios in order to assess the effects of potential actions or strategies ahead of time. For this to be effective, a simulation must be detailed enough to provide useful information, while remaining lightweight enough to be able to run on an individual agent within the swarm.

When choosing or designing a simulator for researching robotic swarms, the accuracy of the physical simulation required will depend on the impact specific hardware has on the research being conducted. Developing a robotic controller without a suitably accurate physical simulation can lead to the robots in the simulation carrying out behaviour that is impossible with the actual robots [25], but when researching purely software based systems, abstractions can be used to trade accuracy for a faster execution time [21].

Further gains in execution time may be made by simplifying the world representation. Grid based approaches need not produce markedly different results to continuous space [26], and can be used in cases where the specific motion of agents can be abstracted.

The majority of multi-robot simulators available make use of discrete time when updating their simulations, in which all agents and physical reactions are updated in sequence with a small time step, rather than independent execution in real time, such as assigning a robot its own execution thread. This ensures synchronous execution of robots [21] and simplifies physical interactions.

The research conducted in this paper abstracts physical movement using cell-based movement within a grid, and the performance is contrasted with a real-time, multi-threaded approach used in previous research [11].

III. TIME-STEPPED SIMULATION OF COOPERATION STRATEGIES

This research makes use of a simulation of a heterogeneous swarm of agents engaged in a variant of a foraging task. The 30x30 world is seeded with 100 each of two different types of items, and 200 robots are divided into two equal groups based on which item they can process. Items are processed in-situ, rather than returned to a home base – the process is analogous to applications, such as mine deactivation, analysis of mineral deposits or environmental clean-up. The task is considered complete when all items have been successfully foraged.

The world is represented as a grid of equal sized cells, one unit square, with items and robots each occupying a single cell. During world generation, items are placed so as not to share cells, but there is no restriction on robots sharing a single cell. Figure 1 shows the world at the beginning of a simulation.

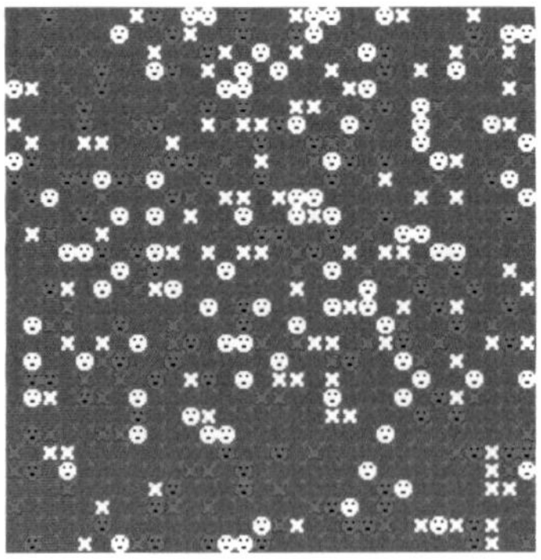

Figure 1. Initial setup of the simulation. The colour of a robot (face) or item (X) indicates its type.

A. *Previous Implementation*

The performance of the time-stepped simulation presented here will be compared with that of the threaded implementation in the previous work [9].

In the threaded implementation, each robot was run on an independent CPU thread, with a reliance on real-time delays when messages required a response, as in the One Responder strategy. Each robot's progress was also artificially delayed in order to allow the task to be viewed within the simulation program. The updating of the individual robots is thus subject to the CPU's thread scheduling, and cannot be predicted.

This reliance on real-time delays is not present in the new time-stepped approach where a unit of time is defined by a single tick of the simulation during which each robot is updated in sequence.

B. *Cooperation Strategies*

Cooperation during the task is determined by the use of one of three strategies, as developed in [11]. When a robot encounters an item that it cannot forage, it broadcasts a help request with a range of 5 units. The behaviour of the robots is then determined by the strategy:

1) Multiple Responders: A receiving robot, if not already engaged in foraging or responding to a previous request, will respond to the request by moving towards the item if it is able to forage it. All receivers, whether they can forage the item or not, will rebroadcast the message. In this way, the message will filter throughout the swarm. The robot initiating the help request plays no further part in the cooperation and returns to exploration.

2) Selective Responders: Behaviour is similar to the Multiple Responders approach, but the message is only rebroadcast if the receiving robot cannot help. This works to reduce the number of robots responding to the request.

3) One Responder: The robot initiating the request waits for offers of help, which are sent by receiving robots that meet the criteria. No rebroadcasting of the message occurs. If no offers are received after a short delay, the requesting robot returns to its previous behaviour, otherwise it assigns the task to the nearest responding robot and resumes exploration. Robots that do not receive assignment after a period of time return to exploration.

Both Multiple and Selective strategies are likely to result in multiple robots moving towards the item. This would provide contingency in the event of robot failure before reaching the target item. Robot failure is not implemented in the current simulation, but will be in a future study.

C. *Robot Behaviour*

The behaviour of each robot is controlled using a finite state machine (FSM). Figure 2 shows a simplified diagram of the transitions between the three states used for the Multiple and Selective Responder strategies.

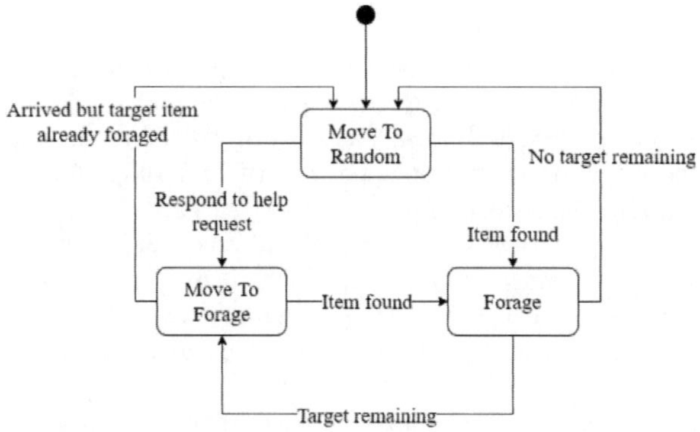

Figure 2. States and transitions used for the Multiple and Selective Responder strategies.

A robot begins in the MoveToRandom state, where it will select a random location in the world and move towards it. Each step, if an item is found, the robot will transition to the Forage state.

In the Forage state, the robot checks if the item is the right type, and forages successfully if so. If not, it will broadcast for help according to the selected strategy. It will then return to its previous state based on whether it is answering a request of its own.

A robot responding to a help request transitions to the MoveToForage state, which is similar to MoveToRandom except the destination is that of the item for which help was requested. To prevent robots from being distracted by new requests, help requests are only processed by a robot in the MoveToRandom state.

When using the One Responder strategy, two additional states are used. A robot broadcasting for help transitions to the WaitForHelpOffers state for two simulation ticks, before selecting the nearest robot. Robots that respond to the initial request transition to the WaitForHelpAssignment state for three ticks before returning to their previous task if not selected.

If no cooperation strategy is used, robots transition between only the MoveToRandom and Forage states.

D. *Simulated Messages*

In a time-stepped simulation, the potential effects of the agent update order need to be managed. For example, during a single update, Agent 2 may broadcast a message that would be received by Agents 1 and 3. If those values also represent their update order, Agent 3 would be able to receive and respond to the message in the same update, while Agent 1 would need to wait until the following update. This is not desirable behaviour.

To avoid this, messages sent by a robot during an update are queued by the simulation and sent out at the end of the update. If an agent that receives a message in turn broadcasts one of its own, this will not be sent out until the next update. In this way, robots are unable to instantaneously receive responses without any time delay.

E. *Experimental Scenarios*

The following scenarios were created in order to test the effects of each cooperation strategy in different situations.

1) Equal Split of Items and Robots: 100 red robots and 100 white robots attempt to locate and forage 100 red items and 100 white items.

2) Robot Type Imbalance: 180 red robots are used and only 20 white robots, while the items are equally distributed, representing a scenario where the swarm configuration deployed is not best suited to the task and must adapt.

3) Item Type Imbalance: 180 red items and 20 white items, with equal robot distribution, representing a scenario where the reality of the mission differs from the expected, and again the swarm must adapt.

Each scenario is tested with two map sizes, 30x30 and 90x90, with the latter used to test performance in less concentrated environments. Each simulation is run 30 times, with the initial placement of items and robots randomised at the start of each run. For the threaded simulation, the Equal and Robot Imbalance scenarios were each run 10 times on the 30x30 map only due to simulation limitations, also with randomisation of item and robot placement.

In assessing the performance of each strategy, the number of simulation ticks until completion of the task is the main metric, as it is a measure of the time taken to forage all items. If the energy cost of actions taken by robots is of interest, then the total number of steps and the number of messages broadcast will also become factors. The simulation does not currently assign an energy cost to individual actions, but the counts may be used as a guide, and for each metric a lower value is considered more efficient.

IV. Results

The following subsections compare the performance of the cooperation strategies in the tested scenarios, followed by a comparison of the two simulation methods employed.

A. *Cooperation Strategies*

Figure 3 shows the ticks to completion, steps taken, and messages sent for each of the test scenarios in a 30x30 grid.

Comparing the results in both the Equal (a) and Item Imbalance (c) strategies, the One Responder strategy is the best performing approach, having the lowest count in each metric. Multiple and Selective Responder strategies can actually perform worse than no cooperation strategy at all, which can be explained by robots that respond to messages halting any exploration while they respond.

In the Robot Imbalance scenario (Figure 3 (b)), however, One Responder does not reliably perform, and is subject to a great deal of variance caused by the initial placement of items and robots, and the subsequent movement of robots within the arena.

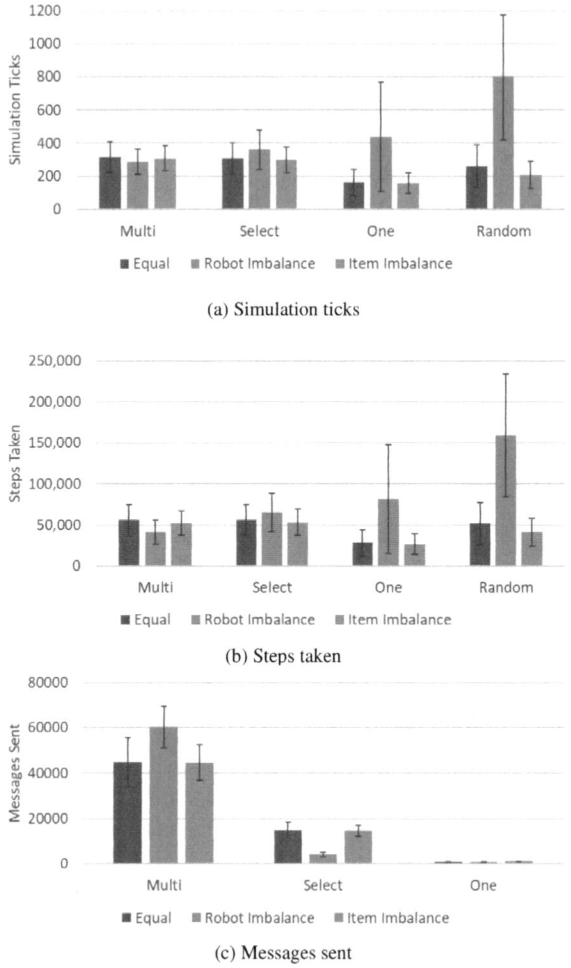

Figure 3. Metrics for each cooperation strategy in a 30x30 map. Error bars represent one standard deviation: (a) simulation ticks, (b) total steps taken, (c) messages sent.

When considering energy costs, Multiple Responders has an extremely high message count setting it apart from Selective Responders, which it otherwise performs very similarly to. A full assessment of the respective efficiency of each would require an assignment of cost to each of the metrics, with the total cost calculated accordingly.

Figure 4 shows the progress of each strategy over time for the three scenarios. In Equal (a) and Item Imbalance (c) scenarios, performance is again similar, however it is notable that using no cooperation strategy at all is the quickest approach until the item count decreases substantially, after which One Responder performs best. This would suggest some system of changing the cooperation strategy used during the test based on the changing situation could lead to stronger overall performance, at least in terms of time taken.

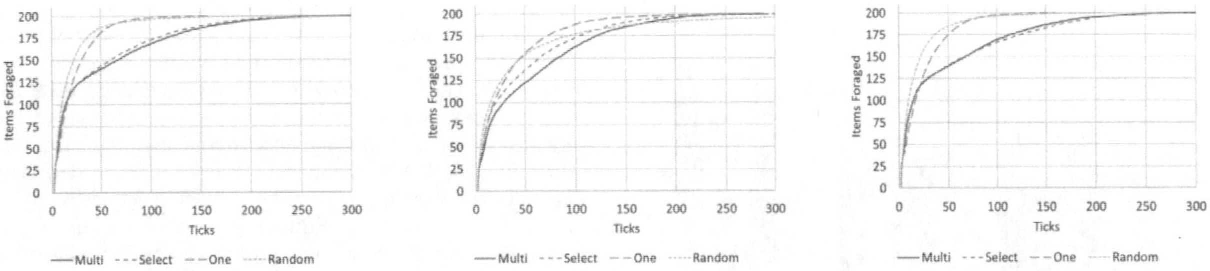

(a) Equal (b) Robot imbalance (c) Item imbalance

Figure 4. Items foraged over simulation ticks for each of the strategies in a 30x30 map: (a) Equal scenario, (b) Robot imbalance scenario, (c) Item imbalance scenario.

In Figure 4 (b), the Robot Imbalance scenario shows only a slight favouring of Random and One Responder scenarios until most items are gathered, but the imbalance of robots then leads to both strategies taking much longer to complete the task than the other approaches. Again, strategy selection during the task could recognise this situation and adopt the strategy most suited.

If individual robot failure is considered, a robot imbalance can occur during the task. A system that can monitor the current swarm composition as well as estimate the progress in the task would therefore be able to adopt a suitable strategy in response to such unpredictable change.

Figure 5 shows the ticks to complete, steps taken, and messages sent for the cooperation strategies in the larger 90x90 grid. Here, it can be seen that the performance of each strategy tends towards that of no cooperation, with large variances in the data and, other than the number of messages sent, similar average values for each metric in each scenario.

It may be expected that the larger map explains the results as messages are not being broadcast far enough in order be received, but a comparison of data in Figure 6 shows that this is not necessarily the case. The proportion of requests receiving a response does not change much between the map sizes for the Multiple and Selective Responders cases, other than when there is a robot imbalance where it can be understood the chances of a robot of the correct type being nearby is significantly lower in a larger area.

The One Responder strategy can be seen to have a much higher percentage of requests receiving a response than the other approaches in a 30x30 map. This is due to the other approaches causing robots who would be able to help to be otherwise engaged in moving to forage an item, and thus unable to respond until they complete that help task. As the One Responder strategy causes only one robot at most to take on a task, other robots remain to be selected. In the 90x90 map, this then drops because of the distance between robots, and more closely matches the other approaches.

The dominant effect in the 90x90 map is the random exploration of the environment, and can be seen in the time taken to complete the task and understood by considering that the number of items remains the same between the two maps. As such, only 2.5% of the cells in a 90x90 map have an item, compared to 22.2% of the cells in the 30x30 map. It is this decreased chance of stumbling upon an item that has the strongest effect on swarm performance.

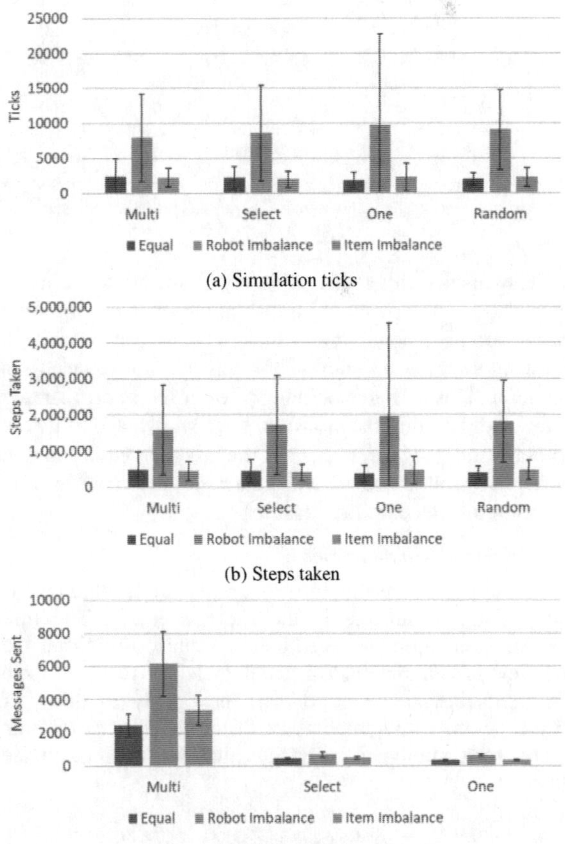

(a) Simulation ticks

(b) Steps taken

(c) Messages sent

Figure 5. Metrics for each cooperation strategy in a 90x90 map. Error bars represent one standard deviation: (a) simulation ticks, (b) total steps taken, (c) messages sent.

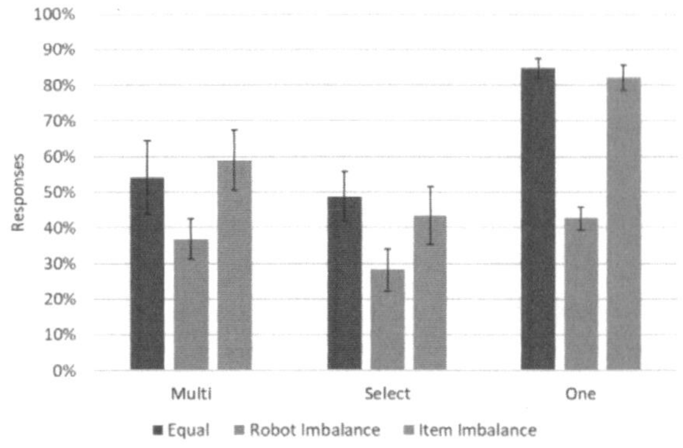

(a) 30x30 map

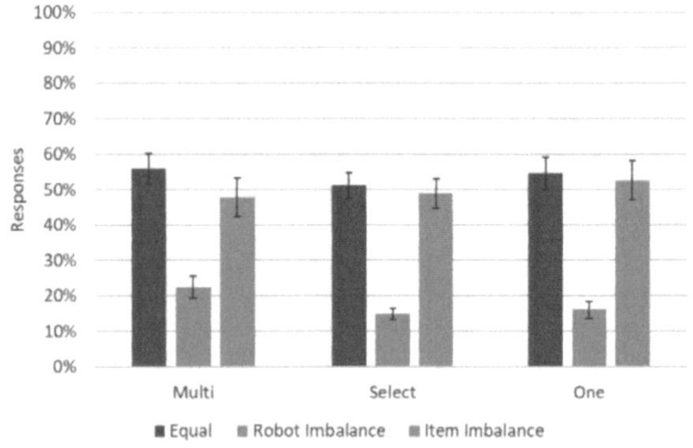

(b) 90x90 map

Figure 6. Percentage of help requests receiving at least one response, for each cooperaton strategy and scenario. Error bars represent one standard deviation: (a) 30x30 map, (b) 90x90 map.

The results show that allowing a swarm to adjust its cooperation strategy during a task, rather than relying on an initial strategy, could prove beneficial to performance by allowing the swarm to adjust its approach in response to the situation. This self-adaptation applied at the swarm strategy level would require the swarm to have knowledge of its own composition, the current state of the task, and environmental factors, as well as the ability to carry out the analysis of the situation in a decentralised fashion.

B. *Simulator Comparisons*

Table I compares the time taken to complete the task for each of the simulators in the Equal scenario. The time-stepped simulation presented here is significantly faster than the previous simulation. This can largely be accounted for by the deliberate delays introduced previously to allow for visualization, with some impact of the reliance on real-time delays for communication, which makes a true comparison difficult.

TABLE I. SIMULATON DURATION (EQUAL SCENARIO)

	Multi time (s)	Select time (s)	One time (s)
Time-Stepped	2.11	0.89	0.17
Threaded	155.14	142.01	130.86

Figure 7 shows that the time-stepped simulation takes a much larger number of steps in the Multiple and Selective Responder strategies, and also shows an increase under One Responder. This unexpected result may be explained by the specific behaviour of the robots in each simulation. In the threaded approach, robots pause frequently, the effect of which is that fewer robots will move in each step. For example, on deciding to respond to a help request a robot pauses for three seconds. Further, if another help request is received during that pause, that too may be processed and the robot may choose to act on that, with a further pause.

The effect of these pauses is to reduce the number of robots moving at any given time. In the time-stepped simulation, a robot will only pause when waiting for help responses or assignments in the One Responder strategy.

It is notable that despite these pauses, robots in the threaded approach take fewer steps overall, rather than taking the same number of steps over a longer period. This suggests there may be a benefit to reducing the number of robots engaged in random exploration, but this will need to be investigated further.

The impact of the two simulations on the host platform was compared and Table II displays the approximate processor and memory usage of the two platforms when running simulations.

Overall, the time-stepped approach will put less strain on the CPU, as despite its higher usage during execution without a display, it will run for a fraction of the time. With a display, the execution is halted between ticks to update the display at a framerate of the user's choosing, and so CPU usage drops. The threaded simulation has no option to disable display updating, but the use of a separate thread for each robot results in a moderate level of CPU usage for a longer period of time.

The lower memory footprint of the time-stepped simulation is most likely due to specific implementation differences. Each robot in the threaded simulation contains a copy of the world map and lists of robots and items, whereas the time-stepped simulation uses a shared resource. While requiring local copies is a factor in any real scenario, it is not required to simulate that unless it is expected that robots will have different local data. If this is a requirement, the memory usage would increase accordingly.

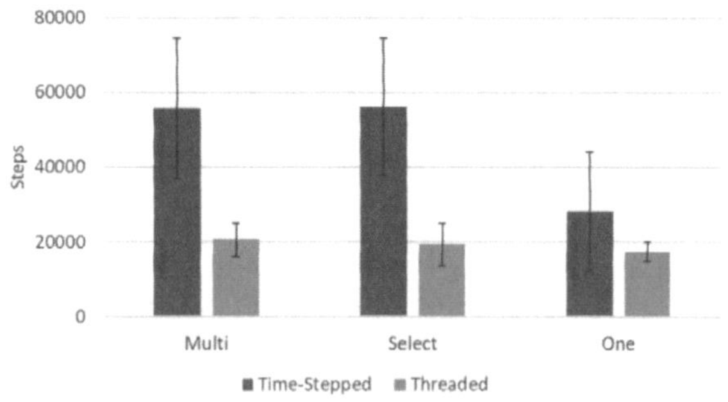

Figure 7. Total steps taken for each simulator using the three strategies in the Equal scenario. Error bars represent one standard deviation.

TABLE II. SIMULATION CPU AND MEMORY USAGE

	CPU (%)	Memory (MB)
Time-Stepped (Live Display)	5-6	30-35
Time-Stepped (No Display)	55-60	30-35
Threaded	35-40	700-750

It can be noted that the stepped approach has the effect of quantizing time, with a tick being the smallest unit possible. This can have the effect of inflating the duration of actions where robots must work in sequence. For example, in the One Responder strategy, it takes 4 ticks to complete the chain of initial broadcast, response, assignment broadcast and eventual robot behaviour change. In this time, another robot could move 4 cells. This has the effect of slowing down that strategy's performance within the simulation. A separate system for dealing with all messages within a single tick may be required to present more accurate results.

The specific implementation details have made comparison of the different strategies between each simulator difficult to achieve, and some of the differences could be removed by re-implementing the previous threaded simulation to adjust the behaviour regarding robots pausing, duplication of data, the requirement for a live display, and the fixed 30x30 map size. This would allow for further comparisons to be made to determine the most suitable approach.

However, as things stand, the quicker execution time and lower impact on the CPU suggests the time-stepped approach is a more favourable system for use as a simulation in the loop for assisting in any adaptation process.

V. CONCLUSION AND FUTURE WORK

The presented research used a time-stepped simulation to investigate the effects of different cooperation strategies for a swarm carrying out a foraging task. It was shown that different situations favour different strategies, with the One Responder strategy proving most effective in a 30x30 map with an equal number of robots, but other strategies providing more reliable performance when faced with an imbalance in the swarm.

Further, different stages of the task will favour different strategies. During the initial phase where large numbers of items remain to be discovered, random exploration with no cooperation strategy produces the best results. Only when a small proportion of the items remain does the adoption of a cooperation strategy start to benefit the performance of a swarm.

Together, these results suggest that giving a swarm the ability to display autonomic adaptive behaviour, adjusting the strategy on the fly based on the current situation, would allow for faster completion of the task.

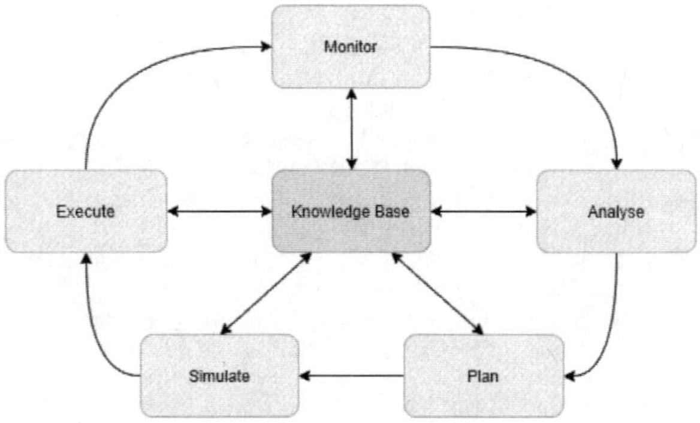

Figure 8. MAPSE-K loop. Simulation is used to test the plans before executing the best performing plan.

The time-stepped simulation was compared against previous work that employed a real-time threaded approach, and was found to have faster execution and reduced load on the host computer. This would make the time-stepped simulation more suitable for use as part of the MAPE-K loop for a foraging swarm, forming MAPSE-K (Figure 8) [1]. This could be achieved by embedding the simulator within one or multiple robots within the swarm, in order to analyse and select strategies without risking reduced performance caused by the trialling of unsuitable candidates in reality.

The expected limited processing capabilities of the host robot mean managing the overhead that simulation entails will become a major factor. A time-stepped approach is thus more suited to this task.

Future work will explore methods of giving the swarm the autonomic ability to adjust its behaviour based on the situation, including the use of simulation-in-the-loop as described. This will include investigating the means by which simulation can be employed in the distributed swarm, allowing for the possibility of incomplete knowledge or local factors influencing the decision as robots in different locations in the field are expected to have different perspectives and experiences. Additional strategies will also be developed that may improve overall performance in this foraging task.

Other factors that may affect performance will need to be considered in future, such as the effects of robot loss during a mission, which will be explored by introducing random failure, including energy costs for actions and message broadcasts that needs to be managed by each robot, or the possibility of unreliable communications that may affect the accuracy of the data in use.

REFERENCES

[1] R. Sterritt et al., 'Inspiration for Space 2.0 from Autonomic-ANTS (Autonomous NanoTechnology Swarms) concept missions', in Proceedings of the 17th BIS Reinventing Space Conference, British Interplanetary Society, Nov 2019

[2] A. Farahani, G. Cabri, and E. Nazemi, 'Self-* properties in collective adaptive systems', in Proceedings of the 2016 ACM International Joint Conference on Pervasive and Ubiquitous Computing: Adjunct, Heidelberg, Germany, Sep. 2016, pp. 1309–1314.

[3] L. Bayindir, 'A review of swarm robotics tasks', *Neurocomputing*, vol. 172, pp. 292–321, Jan. 2016.

[4] I. Navarro and F. Matía, 'An introduction to swarm robotics', ISRN Robot., vol. 2013, pp. 1–10, 2013.

[5] G. Beni, 'From swarm intelligence to swarm robotics', in Swarm Robotics, Berlin, Heidelberg, 2005, pp. 1–9.

[6] IBM, 'An architectural blueprint for autonomic computing, 4th ed.' IBM White Paper, 2006.

[7] J. O. Kephart and D. M. Chess, 'The vision of autonomic computing', *Computer*, vol. 36, no. 1, pp. 41–50, Jan. 2003.

[8] R. Sterritt, G. Wilkie, G. Brady, C. Saunders, and M. Doran, 'Autonomic robotics for future space missions', 13th Symposium on Advanced Space Technologies in Robotics and Autonmation (ASTRA 2015) – ESA/ESTEC, Noordwijk, Netherlands, May 2015, European Space Agency, unpublished.

[9] M. Doran, R. Sterritt, and G. Wilkie, 'Autonomic architecture for fault handling in mobile robots', *Innov. Syst. Softw. Eng.*, Apr. 2020, doi:10.1007/s11334-020-00361-8.

[10] M. Torres-Torriti, T. Arredondo, and P. Castillo-Pizarro, 'Survey and comparative study of free simulation software for mobile robots', *Robotica*, vol. 34, no. 4, pp. 791–822, Apr. 2016.

[11] C. Saunders, R. Sterritt, and G. Wilkie, 'Collective communication strategies for space exploration', *J. Br. Interplanet. Soc.*, vol. 72, no. 12, p. 416-430, 2019.

[12] J. Prasetyo, G. De Masi, and E. Ferrante, 'Collective decision making in dynamic environments', *Swarm Intell.*, vol. 13, no. 3, pp. 217–243, Dec. 2019.

[13] J. Zelenka, T. Kasanický, and I. Budinská, 'A self-adapting method for 3D environment exploration inspired by swarm behaviour', in *Advances in Service and Industrial Robotics*, Cham, 2018, pp. 493–502.

[14] N. Capodieci, E. Hart, and G. Cabri, 'An artificial immunology inspired approach to achieving self-expression in collective adaptive systems', *ACM Trans. Auton. Adapt. Syst. TAAS*, vol. 11, no. 2, pp. 6:1–6:25, Jun. 2016.

[15] N. Bredeche, E. Haasdijk, and A. Prieto, 'Embodied evolution in collective robotics: A review', *Front. Robot. AI*, vol. 5, p. 12, 2018.

[16] K. S. Kappel, T. M. Cabreira, J. L. Marins, L. B. de Brisolara, and P. R. Ferreira, 'Strategies for patrolling missions with multiple UAVs', J. Intell. Robot. Syst., vol. 99, pp. 499-515, Sep. 2019.

[17] G. Leu and J. Tang, 'Survivable networks via UAV swarms guided by decentralized real-time evolutionary computation', in *2019 IEEE Congress on Evolutionary Computation (CEC)*, Jun. 2019, pp. 1945–1952.

[18] M. Frasheri, B. Cürüklü, M. Esktröm, and A. V. Papadopoulos, 'Adaptive autonomy in a search and rescue scenario', in *2018 IEEE 12th International Conference on Self-Adaptive and Self-Organizing Systems (SASO)*, Sep. 2018, pp. 150–155.

[19] F. Yan, K. Di, J. Jiang, Y. Jiang, and H. Fan, 'Efficient decision-making for multiagent target searching and occupancy in an unknown environment', *Robot. Auton. Syst.*, vol. 114, pp. 41–56, Apr. 2019.

[20] M. Puviani, G. Cabri, and L. Leonardi, 'Enabling self-expression: The use of roles to dynamically change adaptation patterns', in *2014 IEEE Eighth International Conference on Self-Adaptive and Self-Organizing Systems Workshops*, Imperial College, London, United Kingdom, Sep. 2014, pp. 14–19.

[21] C. Pinciroli *et al.*, 'ARGoS: A modular, parallel, multi-engine simulator for multi-robot systems', *Swarm Intell*, vol. 6, no. 4, pp. 271-295, Dec. 2012.

[22] N. Jakobi, P. Husbands, and I. Harvey, 'Noise and the reality gap: The use of simulation in evolutionary robotics', in *Advances in Artificial Life*, vol. 929, F. Morán, A. Moreno, J. J. Merelo, and P. Chacón, Eds. Berlin, Heidelberg: Springer Berlin Heidelberg, 1995, pp. 704–720.

[23] F. Kamrani and R. Ayani, 'Using on-line simulation for adaptive path planning of UAVs', in *11th IEEE International Symposium on Distributed Simulation and Real-Time Applications (DS-RT'07)*, Oct. 2007, pp. 167–174.

[24] N. Keivan and G. Sibley, 'Realtime simulation-in-the-loop control for agile ground vehicles', *Lect. Notes Comput. Sci. Subser. Lect. Notes Artif. Intell. Lect. Notes Bioinforma.*, vol. 8069 LNAI, pp. 276–287, 2014.

[25] C. Pepper, S. Balakirsky, and C. Scrapper, 'Robot simulation physics validation', in *Proceedings of the 2007 Workshop on Performance Metrics for Intelligent Systems*, Washington, D.C., Aug. 2007, pp. 97–104.

[26] C. J. E. Castle, N. P. Waterson, E. Pellissier, and S. Le Bail, 'A comparison of grid-based and continuous space pedestrian modelling software: analysis of two UK train stations', in *Pedestrian and Evacuation Dynamics*, Boston, MA,.2011, pp. 433–446.